Bible Student's Commentary

Leviticus

Bible Student's Commentary

Leviticus

Translated by Raymond Togtman

A. Noordtzij

ZONDERVAN
PUBLISHING HOUSE
OF THE ZONDERVAN CORPORATION
GRAND RAPIDS, MICHIGAN 49506

THE BIBLE STUDENT'S COMMENTARY
Originally published in Dutch under the title *Korte Verklaring der Heilige Schrift*, by J. H. Kok, B. V. Kampen, The Netherlands.

Library of Congress Cataloging in Publication Data

Noordtzij, A.
The book of Leviticus.

(Bible student's commentary)
Translation of: Het boek Levitikus.
Includes New International Version
English text of Leviticus.

Includes bibliographical references.
1. Bible. O.T. Leviticus—Commentaries. I. Bible. O.T. Leviticus. English. New International. 1982. II. Title. III. Series: Korte verklaring der Heilige Schrift, met nieuwe vertaling. English.
BS1255.3.N5713   1982   222'.13077   82-11000
ISBN 0-310-45090-X

Designed and edited by Edward Viening

Printed in the United States of America

82   83   84   85   86   87   88 — 10   9   8   7   6   5   4   3   2   1.

Contents

Publisher's Note

Dr. Noordtzij's commentary on Leviticus should prove to be a useful tool in the hands of the diligent Bible student. Its scholarly approach is obvious; its exegetical skill beyond doubt.

If however the publisher calls attention to a few features in the book that require critical comment, a word of explanation appears to be in order. It is not the purpose of this note to raise questions about details of exegesis of individual texts. Its concern is with more fundamental matters. These deal (1) with Noordtzij's view of the authorship of Leviticus, or certain parts of it, and (2) with his approach to the question of how Israel's religious thought world relates to that of the cultural environment of which it was a part, and how God's revelation through Moses relates to both.

These questions are raised in the interest of the general integrity of this series of commentaries, a series that has rightly been commended by many evangelical scholars.

I. *Authorship of the Book*

Dr. Noordtzij's view of the authorship of Leviticus differs somewhat from that of other conservative scholars. The author allows for the Mosaic origin of those laws that are expressly declared to date from Moses (pp. 11–12). But he also posits the existence of various materials in the book datable to a time much later than Moses (see e.g., p. 12, and cf. p. 189). Other commentators, writing in more recent times, do not share Noordtzij's opinion in this regard. W. H. Gispen, a fellow contributor to this series, states in his major commentary on Leviticus, published in 1950, that "there is nothing in the laws as promulgated that cannot have been given in the time of Moses" (*Leviticus, Commentaar op het Oude Testament,* Kampen [1950], p. 11). Gispen also calls attention to the repeated formula used to introduce the individual laws: "and the LORD said to Moses." He would wish to take this formula as "the communication of an historical fact" *(idem)*. Noordtzij, on the other hand, relegates certain laws, introduced with this formula, to a time much later than Moses (see, e.g., p. 189).

For yet another scholarly opinion of recent date, different from that of Noordtzij, cf. also R. K. Harrison, *Leviticus, An Introduction and Commentary,* IVP (1980). After surveying the pertinent data Harrison concludes that "the most logical conclusion concerning authorship and date would be . . . to regard [Leviticus] as a genuine second-millennium B.C. literary product compiled by Moses, with the probable assistance of priestly scribes" (p. 23).

For a further discussion of the composition and authorship, not only of Leviticus but also of the entire Pentateuch, the reader is referred to Volume I of G. Ch. Aalders' commentary on Genesis in this commentary series.

A matter related to authorship is that of Noordtzij's use of the word "lawgiver" throughout his commentary. Obviously the author does not imply that the Book of Leviticus does not bear the imprint of divine revelation and inspiration. At more than one point he calls attention to the divine activity in Israel's legislation. Still, by using "lawgiver" instead of "Lawgiver" Noordtzij puts the human factor in the process of revelation foremost. This human factor does indeed deserve due attention. Yet Noordtzij's exclusive use of that one term could make the reader overlook the divine factor, all the more so since Noordtzij's approach to some facets of Israel's legislation calls for some further critical comment.

II. *Israel's "Religious Thought World."*

The manner in which Noordtzij treats the question of the relationship between Israel's thought world, the thought world of the ancient Near East, and the relation of God's revelation to both, also calls for some further comment.

On the one hand, Noordtzij gives due recognition to the fact that God's revelation to Israel often serves to correct or to overcome erroneous notions that Israel may have held in common with its pagan neighbors (see e.g., pp. 18f., 22, 48, 49, 66f., 177f., 202f.). This is a helpful insight. God's revelation to His people always involves an element of condescension and of accommodation. And in the case of Israel it also involved an element of correction and purification of notions previously held.

Human beings, by virtue or their creaturehood, are inevitably religious beings, but their religion has been deformed and falsified (see Rom. 1:18ff.). When God's special revelation is imparted, these deformations are being rectified. To the extent that Israel held certain erroneous notions in common with its pagan neighbors, it too needed such rectification. (See also the discussion of Geerhardus Vos of the word "holy" in his *Biblical Theology,* where it is rightly recognized that there is a certain holiness notion that is commonly held throughout the ancient Near East, only to receive its true and proper meaning as it is used in connection with the one and only God, the God of special revelation and of Scripture.)

But there are also several points in Noordtzij's commentary where the emphasis lies not so much on correction and rectification, as on accommodation. Noordtzij assumes that there was a common thought pattern that Israel shared with the other nations. He refers to this pattern as being "dynamistic" in nature (see pp. 16f.) The word "dynamistic" is derived from the Greek word *dunamis* (power, force). Dynamistic thinking sees the universe as dominated by forces, or powers, more or less conceived impersonally, controllable by clever manipulation, and sometimes by magic. Such thought patterns can still be found on some of the islands of the South Pacific and elsewhere. Modern code words often used to describe these forces are *mana* and *taboo.*

Dynamistic thought is hardly compatible with the notion of a personal God of which the Bible speaks. To suggest, as Noordtzij does at several places, that the "lawgiver" (who was also the Lawgiver!) accommodated Himself to such a thought pattern in the framing of a specific law pushes the idea of accommodation, legitimate in itself, beyond its proper bounds. Instances of this type of terminology may be found on pp. 86, 99f., 111, 112f., 126, 154, and 215.

By way of illustration, on p. 154 Noordtzij suggests that one of the reasons for the specific legislation discussed at that place is that war among Israel and in the Near East world of that time was viewed as a conflict "between two divine powers." But the question must be faced: Is there, upon the biblical view, room for any "divine power" next to that of God, the God who gives this law to Moses? How then can the law accommodate itself to that other mode of thought in which two divine powers are thought to be in combat?

Related to the above are also Noordtzij's frequent references to the presence of alleged demonic influences whose presence must somehow be counteracted by a law that was given (see pp. 141, 145, 152f., 168, and 170). Noordtzij's failure to make the proper distinctions leads him to suggest at a certain point that a law given by God to Israel through Moses was meant "to prevent the person from inhaling through his mouth and nose further demonic influences" (p. 141). Here again the suggestion of accommodation in the process of revelation leads to rather illegitimate results when the nature of the spirit world is taken into account.

Noordtzij is correct in asserting that the revelation that God imparted to Israel did not immediately give God's people a completely new outlook on life (p. 162). But in his application of this insight he at times fails to observe the proper lines of demarcation between a correct and an incorrect notion of accommodation.

A final point, related to the above, is Noordtzij's treatment of the words "holy," "clean and unclean." In "dynamistic" thought these notions are often understood in a material sense. Noordtzij likewise treats them in this fashion (see e.g., pp. 76, 96).

It is important to make careful distinctions, here as well as elsewhere. Undue simplification can easily occur within the scope of a succinct note of this kind. Noordtzij's concern to point to a certain uniqueness inherent in the notions of the holy, the clean and the unclean, should be appreciated. The Old Testament idea of the holy often associates itself with extreme danger and with the need for proper caution in the handling of the holy things. Holiness moreover attaches itself to material objects. Touching these can even result in some sort of transference, or else in severe punishment such as sudden death.

But the fact that holiness attaches itself to things does not make this notion as such a material one. In this respect there is definite discontinuity between the holiness concept prevalent in the ancient Near East and that which prevails within the pale of special revelation. The fundamental aspect of the biblical idea of the holy is laid down in passages such as Leviticus 11:44, 45; 19:2; 20:7, 26. Israel is to be holy because its God, who redeemed it from the bondage of slavery and sin in Egypt, is holy. Just as there is a discontinuity between that God and the gods of the other nations, so is there a discontinuity in the holiness notion found in Israel's religion, normed as it is by revelation, and the other religions where this norm is not to be found.

Other commentators on the Book of Leviticus, such as W. H. Gispen, have stated the matter more clearly than is done by Noordtzij. Commenting on the laws of the clean and unclean animals, Gispen calls attention to the fact that these laws "do not present us with the precipitate of what at that time was present in Israel's religious consciousness, but rather with divine revelation given through the ministry of Moses and Aaron, cf. 11:1; 12:1; 13:1; 14:1, 33; 15:1" (*Leviticus,* p. 174).

To be sure, Gispen recognizes as much as Noordtzij that God, in giving His laws to Israel, reckoned with the mode of thought that was prevalent in Israel at that time. But Gispen then adds an important qualification: "Though there may have been elements in Israel's thought world which it had in common with the surrounding nations, yet the viewpoint from which the Lord sees the distinction between 'clean' and 'unclean' is totally different.'' To support this contention Gispen appeals to passages such as Leviticus 11:44, 45; 19:2; 20:7, 26, cited above, as well as to Exodus 19:6; 1 Thessalonians 4:7; 1 Peter 1:15, 16. And he concludes by saying: ''Israel is to conduct itself as a holy people, that is, as a people of the Holy One.''

Part of the purpose of this note is to alert readers to the fact that although at certain points Noordtzij is indeed conscious of the ''totally different'' viewpoint of which Gispen speaks, at other points he is not, at least not sufficiently.

Introduction

I. *The Name*

By extending the meaning of passages such as Deuteronomy 1:5; 4:8, 44; 17:18–20; and 33:4, the Jewish synagogue gave the name *Torah* ("instruction, law") to the first book of the Hebrew Bible. Since A.D. 160, this book has been designated by the Greek term *Pentateuch* (the "five-sectioned" [viz., book]), and for the sake of convenience, the Jews followed the example of the Greek translation in subdividing the Torah into five books, which they then called the "five books of the Torah." In accordance with a general Semitic custom, each of these five subdivisions was most often referred to by means of its opening word. The Greek translators, however, attempted to give to each section a name that as far as possible gave an impression of its contents. With the exception of the fourth section, whose Greek name *Arithmoi* was translated into Latin as *Numeri* (Numbers), the names that thus arose have passed into the western European translations by way of the Vulgate. The third subdivision, which the Jewish synagogue designated *Wayyiqrā'* after its opening word, was named *Levitikon* by the Greek translators, and it is known to us as Leviticus, actually a shortened form of (Lat.) *Leviticus liber,* "the Levitical book." The word "Levitical" is here used in the same sense that appears in the Epistle to the Hebrews where the writer speaks of "the Levitical priesthood" (7:11). In view of this, the name corresponds closely to *tôraṯ kōhᵃnîm,* "law of the priests," a designation that is found in rabbinic Judaism. With the exception of the historical material in Leviticus 10:1–7 and 24:10–16, this third subdivision of the Torah is devoted exclusively to the cult, the superintendence of which was the special task of that portion of the tribe of Levi constituted by Aaron and his sons, and to this degree the name *Leviticus* does justice to its contents. The section of the

Pentateuch traditionally called Leviticus thus bears a completely different character from that which is designated Deuteronomy ("second law"), a book that is directed toward the people at large and merely presupposes an extensive sacrificial technique without explaining it.

II. *The Content of Leviticus*

The first seven chapters as a group deal exclusively with the offerings that are to be brought by Israel and indicate how communion with God can be established by these means. It appears from the introductory and closing formulas (Lev. 1:1; 3:17) that chapters 1–3 and 4:1–6:7 (MT [Masoretic text] 5:26) are to be regarded as separate units. Both passages are intended to inform the people at large concerning the circumstances and the manner in which the various offerings spoken of here are to be presented (1:2; 4:2). In contrast, the third subunit (6:8 [MT 6:1]–7:38) is directed to the priests and seeks to impress on them what they are to do in specific situations, or what in the various offerings is to be their portion. The section as a whole terminates with a pair of closing formulas (7:35–38), the first of which (vv. 35–36) relates only to the content of the third subdivision, while the second (vv. 37–38) forms the conclusion to this group of seven chapters in its entirety.

The section begins with the burnt offering (*'ōlâ[h]*), in which the entire animal was burned (ch. 1). This is followed by the grain offering (*minḥâ [h]*), a purely vegetable offering consisting of flour and oil (ch. 2). The cultic procedures that were required both of the priest and of the person presenting the offering are presented in great detail. A fuller explanation of the religious significance of these offerings is not given, however, indicating that this was presupposed as a matter of common knowledge. The same applies to the fellowship offering (*šelāmîm*), although the Hebrew name could be interpreted here to mean thankfulness, either for benefits already received or for blessings obtained by means of prayer (ch. 3).[1]

Leviticus 4:1–6:7 (MT 5:26) speaks of offerings presented for the purpose of obtaining forgiveness for a transgression committed either by an individual or by the entire community. One of these is called the sin offering (*ḥaṭṭā't*), and the other the guilt offering (*'āšām*). In contrast to the offerings spoken of in chapters 1–3, the lawgiver presents a closer description of the meaning and purpose of these offerings, and this indicates that we are here confronted with specifically Israelitic sacrifices that were a special fruit of the revelatory work of God.

---

[1] The author translates the Hebrew *zebaḥ šelāmîm* as "thank offering" (Dutch, dankoffer), while the NIV has "fellowship offering" (KJV and RSV, "peace offering").

There follow in 6:8 (MT 6:1)–7:38 further instructions with regard to the types of offerings that have already been discussed in chapters 1:1–6:7. These are directed to the priests and describe what they are to do in the bringing of the various offerings.

Leviticus 3:17 and 7:22–27 differ in character from the rest of the material presented in these first seven chapters. These verses are not concerned with the bringing of offerings, but rather present the people with certain regulations regarding the consumption of fat and blood, and we should thus have expected them to appear among the laws dealing with food rather than here (cf. also 17:10–14).

A new section is formed by chapters 8:1–10:20, which deals with the circumstances and the manner in which Aaron and his sons are installed in the priestly office. Since the institution of the Aaronic priesthood would appear to be of the utmost importance for the further development of Israel's life, this is presented in great detail. The section begins with a description of the manner in which the regulations of Exodus 29 concerning the tabernacle and its furnishings were carried out. Chapter 9 follows with a description of the priests' assumption of their office and of the offerings that were brought on this occasion. Chapter 10 then concludes this section by relating first (vv. 1–7) the sad story of the death of Aaron's eldest sons, Nadab and Abihu, and then the command that Aaron and his other two sons, Eleazar and Ithamar, are to refrain from any external sign of mourning. This is followed in verses 8–20 by further instructions given to the priests.

Leviticus 11:1–15:33 comprises a new section that deals at length with the necessity of remaining free from any form of cultic impurity. The section begins (ch. 11) with a list of clean and unclean animals and a statement of the two marks by which an animal may be recognized as clean. There then follow regulations regarding cultic uncleanness resulting from childbirth (ch. 12), from skin diseases and similar phenomena appearing in houses and clothing (chs. 13–14), and from the occurrence of more or less unhealthy phenomena relating to sexual life (ch. 15).

In chapter 16, which goes back over the intervening chapters to what had been reported in chapter 10, the ritual of the Day of Atonement is established in which the people and sanctuary are once again made fit for undisturbed communion with the Lord. Chapter 17 then speaks of the Israelites' obligation to bring their offerings exclusively to the tabernacle (vv. 3–9) and to refrain from the eating of blood and carrion (vv. 10–16).

Chapters 18–20 speak of family life and subject sexual activity to definite rules. It is remarkable in this section that the prohibitions are given in chapter 18, while the penalties that follow on the breaking of these and other commandments do not appear until chapter 20. Between these two chapters, which are so closely related in content, appears chapter 19, and despite the lack of methodical order, this is perhaps the most striking chapter in the entire Book of Leviticus. It begins with the well-known demand, ''Be holy because I, the LORD your God, am holy,'' and continues with a series of commandments of which some pertain specifically to the cult (vv. 5–8), while the remainder have far-reaching implications for everyday life. Some of these are like an echo from the Decalogue (vv. 3–4, 11–12, 29–30), while others speak of love for one's neighbor, which is also a duty with respect to aliens (vv. 17–18, 33–34). Along with this are regulations directing the Israelites to have regard for the deaf, the blind, and the aged (vv. 14, 32), to be honest and true in their daily life (vv. 11, 13, 16–18), in the administration of justice (v. 15), and in business (vv. 35–36), and to exercise mercy during the harvest (vv. 9–10, 23–25). And finally, there are additional requirements concerning forbidden sexual relationships (vv. 20–22) and other unlawful practices (vv. 19, 26–28, 31).

Chapters 21–25 bring us once again within the sphere of cultic life. The first matter of concern in this section is the holiness of the priests. Chapter 21 subjects them to strict regulations with regard to marriage, mourning rites, and the necessity for soundness of body, and chapter 22 commands that they treat with respect the Israelites' sacred offerings, which are to remain within the sphere of the holy. Chapter 23 then turns to Israel's holy days and annual feasts, with a precise determination of the date, duration, and ritual being given for each of these. This theme is continued in chapter 25, where the sabbatical year and the Year of Jubilee are dealt with. Between these two chapters stands chapter 24, which begins by supplementing the instructions given in Exodus 25:31–40 and 37:17–24 concerning the golden lampstand (vv. 1–4) and those of Exodus 25:23–30 (cf. also 37:10–16) concerning the bread of the Presence (vv. 5–9). The chapter then prescribes the penalty for the sin of blasphemy by giving us an example, and this is followed by the establishment of the principle of strict equality in retributive justice (vv. 10–23).

Chapter 26 concludes by presenting a moving portrayal of the rewards or punishments that Israel could expect as a consequence of its response to the Lord's decrees and commandments. The chapter as a whole has the form of an address made by the Lord to His people, and its final verse (v. 46) is clearly intended as the conclusion of chapters 25–26 taken together.

Chapter 27, which undoubtedly forms an appendix, speaks of the redemption of persons, animals, or land that had been dedicated to the Lord by vow. The closing formula (v. 34) is essentially a repetition of 26:46.

III. *Conclusions Drawn From the Content*

As appears from the outline given above, the portion of the Pentateuch that is known as Leviticus does not in all respects constitute a systematically organized whole. Chapter 8 is most closely related to Exodus 29, while chapter 16 refers back to chapter 10. The historical material in 24:10–23 is connected neither with what precedes nor with what follows it, and 24:1–9 forms a supplement to Exodus 25:23–40. In addition, the appearance of chapter 27 after the conclusion given in chapter 26 is completely unexpected.

Some have attempted to explain this lack of substantive order by the hypothesis that Moses, the author, recorded the various segments of the book in chronological order, but it appears to me that this theory does not do justice to the facts. To begin with, it is clear that the various sections of Leviticus cannot all date from the same period, for although Israel's sojourn in the desert forms the historical background to the majority of these, there are others that can be explained only in terms of the period after Israel had assumed control of Canaan.[2] Leviticus 16:29; 17:15; 18:26; 19:34; 23:42; 24:16, 22 thus distinguish between the "native-born" in Israel and the "alien," i.e., someone of foreign origin who dwells among the Israelites and conforms to their manner of life. In addition, 5:15; 27:3, 25 speak of the "sanctuary shekel," indicating that there was also another shekel in circulation. As long as Israel lived in the desert, there would have been no need for this kind of differentiation. Once it had assumed a place among the Canaanite nations with their broad social distinctions and their trade and commerce, however, monetary differentiation would have arisen almost of its own accord. Further evidence is formed by the fact that 25:32–34 speaks of the Levitical towns in a manner that clearly indicates that the reference is not to some future state of affairs, but rather to an already established situation. This is indeed also the case with the other regulations pertaining to the redemption of land and houses that appear in chapter 25. The instructions given in 5:7–13; 12:8; 14:21–32 presuppose a great degree of social disparity among the Israelites, and 25:35 speaks of the Israelite who "becomes poor and is unable to support himself among you." Such passages could not apply to a nation wandering about in the desert, for they are explicable only in terms of the societal relationships present in a socially ordered body politic. The possibility of substituting a sum of money for an obligatory sacrificial animal points in this same direction, for a nomad has more cattle than money, whereas the reverse is the case among many citizens in settled, organized societies. This concept

---

[2]See Publisher's Note.

or idea applies to 27:1-9, which speaks of the redemption of persons by the payment of a sum of money. In conclusion, it may be noted that it would not have been possible to keep the altar fire burning day and night while wandering in the wilderness (6:9, 12-13), nor could the fellowship offering have been presented with the regularity directed in 6:12 before Israel had settled in Canaan.

There is also another line of evidence for the fact that the entire content of Leviticus does not date from the same period. Various sections can be found in the book that undoubtedly form later additions to previously existing laws, a development that was apparently made necessary by altered circumstances. It is therefore completely clear that 13:47-59, which speaks of the possible contamination of fabrics or leather with mildew, is such a later insertion. This is evident from the fact that these verses break the connection between 13:46 and 14:1, and in addition, the closing formula in verse 59 indicates that this is a separate law dealing exclusively with the contamination of fabrics and leather. The same consideration applies to 14:21-31, the law concerning the procedure by which a poor person who had been pronounced clean after suffering from an infectious skin disease could again assume a place within the cultic community. The closing formula also forms clear evidence here, and the material in 14:33-53 pertaining to the appearance of mildew in houses belongs to this same category.

It is also clear that the law concerning the Day of Atonement as this is presented in Leviticus 16 could not have been spelled out all at once. Leviticus 16:11-28 is not a continuation of the verses that immediately precede them, but rather elaborate in greater detail on the ritual elements appearing in verses 5-10. In addition, verse 34b refers back over 29-34a to verse 28, and perhaps even to verse 10. Whereas in the earlier part of the chapter Aaron is repeatedly mentioned by name, in verses 11-28 he is merely tacitly assumed as the person carrying out the ritual. Leviticus 25:20-22 also dates from a later period, for the objection to the institution of the sabbatical year that is rejected here arose when the beginning of the year was moved from autumn to spring (perhaps during the time of Solomon), a circumstance that also gave rise to other difficulties.

There are yet more sections than those spoken of above that may well be of more recent origin than the book as a whole. It is thus noteworthy that whereas Leviticus 1:2 speaks exclusively of animals from the herd or the flock as subjects for the burnt offering, 1:14-17 opens the possibility of also sacrificing doves or pigeons. In view of the fact that pigeons are of such great importance as food among the poor in Palestine, it is natural to assume on the basis of what has been said above concerning the social disparities in Israel that these verses originated after the time of Moses. The same consideration applies to 5:7-13, where the poor are allowed to present as their sin offering two doves or pigeons in place of the goat required in 4:28 (cf. also 12:6, 8, the offering of doves or pigeons after childbirth; and 15:14-15, 29-30, the same offering after uncleanness resulting from a bodily discharge).

The following observations point in the same direction. Chapter 7:8-10 has no connection with what is discussed in its context. These verses deal partly with the burnt offering and partly with the grain offering, whereas the preceding verses are concerned with the guilt offering, and they are thus a later insertion. This is also the case with 11:24-40, for whereas verses 1-23 and 41-45 are concerned exclusively with whether or not certain animals are to be eaten, verses 24-40 speak merely of the importance of avoiding contact with carcasses. Further proof for this appears in the fact that, in continuing the discussion of creeping animals, verse 41 would most naturally follow verse 23.[3] With regard to 18:25-29, it is to be noted that what still lay in the future during Moses' time, when the Canaanites were in control of the land, is here depicted as having already occurred. In addition, the above-mentioned distinction between "native-born" and "alien" appears in verse 26, and this could have applied only after the entry into Canaan. All of this indicates that 18:25-29 are more recent and could not have originated before the time of Solomon, when the Canaanites had been assimilated into Israel.[4] Leviticus 24:17-22 is also a later addition, for whereas the preceding verses and verse 23 speak of an incident of blasphemy, this passage is concerned with murder and the inflicting of injury.

IV. *The "Holiness Code"*

Ever since August Klostermann in 1877 in the *Zeitschrift für Lutherische Theologie* (pp. 401ff., especially p. 416; reproduced in his book *Der Pentateuch* [1893], pp. 368f.) used this name to characterize the second half of Leviticus, and particularly chapters 17-26, this portion of the book has been known as the Holiness Code. In his *Die Composition des Hexateuchs* (1889, pp. 152ff.), Wellhausen attempted to demonstrate that within the Priestly Codex as a whole—which he dates during the last years of the Exile—these chapters occupy a singular position. Since that time, the adherents of this school have regarded it as established that Leviticus 17-26 comprises a collection of laws that forms more or less a

---

[3]*Šereṣ*, the term used in both of these verses, means either "teeming" or "creeping animals" (cf. KJV, NEB). The NIV has merely "creatures" in both instances, whereas the author has "creeping animals that move about."

[4]See my book, *Gods Woord,* pp. 390ff.

literary unit, and that it has its own vocabulary, contains points of contact with the Book of the Covenant (Exod. 20–23) and Deuteronomy as well as with Ezekiel, manifests no specifically Mosaic character, and dates from the time of the Exile.

There can be no doubting the fact that more than one of these chapters is quite unique in character. Here more than elsewhere, all emphasis is placed on the Lord's holiness and on the fact that Israel is thereby called to likewise manifest itself as holy. The exhortation to "be holy because I, the LORD your God, am holy" speaks of this (19:2; 20:7, 26; 21:6, 8), as does also the declaration that "I am the LORD who makes him [or they, or you] holy" (21:15, 23; 22:9, 16, 32). The same message comes out in the reminder that "I am the LORD your God" (18:4, 30; 19:3–4, 10, 25, 31, 34; 20:7; 23:22, 43; 24:22; 25:17, 55; 26:1) or simply "I am the LORD" (18:5–6, 21; 19:14, 16, 18, 28, 30, 32, 37; 21:12; 22:2–3, 8, 30–31, 33; 26:2), and to this is sometimes added "who brought you out of Egypt" (19:36; 25:38; 26:13) or "who has set you apart from the nations" (20:24). Along with this, we repeatedly encounter the admonition to "obey my laws and be careful to follow my decrees" (18:4–5, 26; 20:22; 25:18) or some alternative form of this such as "keep my commands and follow them" (20:8; 22:31), and there is also the specific admonition to "observe my Sabbaths" (19:3, 30; 26:2). The admonitory sections in 18:24–30 and 20:22–26 are typical of this part of Leviticus, and almost the whole of chapter 26 consists of admonitions.

It remains a question, however, whether observations such as these form sufficient ground for the conclusion that these chapters constitute a volume of laws that has been inserted within the framework of Leviticus. On first consideration, one is struck by the absence in the text of 17:1 of even the slightest indication that we are here confronted with a new beginning, and related to this is the fact that, although 26:46 does form a closing formula, the section to which it refers extends no further back than 25:1. And yet, if chapters 17–26 indeed formed a separate collection, we should have expected that this would be evident from the text. In support of this, it may be noted that Exodus 24:1, which reads "Then he [the LORD] said to Moses, 'Come up to the LORD, you and Aaron,'" clearly refers back to the words of 19:24: "The LORD replied, 'Go down and bring Aaron up with you.'" The intervening chapters, which on the basis of Exodus 24:3–7 have rightly been named the Book of the Covenant, are thereby marked as an independent whole which the author of the Pentateuch here inserted into his historical narrative. Similarly, Deuteronomy 12:1, "These are the decrees and laws you must be careful to follow in the land that the LORD, the God of your fathers, has given you to possess," clearly forms the beginning of a collection of "decrees and laws" that is not brought to a conclusion until the retrospective words of 26:16: "The LORD your God commands you this day to follow these decrees and laws." It is thus apparent that this section is what is referred to in the phrases "this law" and "this Book of the Law," which occur so often in Deuteronomy (1:5; 4:8, 44; 27:3, 8, 26; 28:58, 61; 29:21, 29; 30:10; 31:9, 11–13, 24, 26; 32:46). The fact that Leviticus 17–26 contains neither an introductory formula nor a conclusion that has reference to all ten chapters is thus unfavorable to the view that regards these chapters as a separate volume that has been inserted within a larger whole.

There is also a second line of evidence against this conception. If these chapters indeed constitute an independent volume, we should expect that they would form a more or less systematically organized whole. This, however, is not the case, as we clearly see. The school of Wellhausen in fact acknowledges this, for Baentsch (commentary, p. 387) and Bertholet (commentary, p. x) claim to have found several (the latter speaks of as many as twelve) to some extent parallel groups of laws that allegedly at first existed independently of one another. The respective authors of these groups of laws were supposedly each concerned with only a part of cultic life and did not take the whole into account, and this, moreover, resulted in the omission of important subjects such as the bringing of offerings, the determination of the portions due to the priests, and the distinction between clean and unclean. How such disparate material could nevertheless be assembled into a scheme that would direct the reorganization of the temple worship in Jerusalem—the alleged intention of the "redactor"—is not clear.

It thus appears to me that, regardless of the question as to when these chapters originated, the notion that Leviticus 17–26 at any time constituted an independent whole does not do justice to the facts.[5] The position that A. Jirku takes in his book *Das weltliche Recht im Alten Testament* (1927) is thus completely understandable, for although he retains the conception of Leviticus 17–26 as an independent unit, he also acknowledges that these chapters do not contain a logical arrangement of laws and thus prefers to style them a "book of law" consisting in a mere compilation of diverse legal requirements.

V. *Dating the Content of Leviticus*

As long as the scholarly consensus remained convinced by the assertion of the rabbis that the entirety of the Pentateuch in the form in which we

---

[5]Cf., e.g., B. D. Eerdmans, *Das Buch Leviticus* (*Alttestamentliche Studien* IV, 1912); S. Küchler, *Das Heiligkeitsgesetz* (1929).

now possess it comes from the hand of Moses—with the sole qualification that the account of Moses' death in Deuteronomy 34 may perhaps have been added later—the question as to the time of origin of the various components within it could naturally not have arisen. This situation changed toward the middle of the seventeenth century, however, and after that time Mosaic authorship became the subject of increasing doubt. In the second half of the nineteenth century, this development culminated in the conception of the Wellhausen school that the Pentateuch is the product of a literary labor that extended over centuries. The successive stages of this allegedly include the Yahwist (ninth century B.C.), Elohist (eighth century B.C.), Deuteronomist (seventh century), and the Priestly Codex (fifth century), and all of these materials were then supposedly brought together by the man (perhaps Ezra?) who, with the exception of a few still later additions, put forward the Pentateuch in its present form around the middle of the fifth century B.C.

As I have explained in "The Old Testament Problem,"[6] there is no doubt in my mind that the conception that the Wellhausen school has presented concerning the process by which the Pentateuch came into being will more and more be revealed as incorrect. Although it is completely true that several writings stand behind the Pentateuch in its present form and that its composition required much more time than the lifetime of a single person, the Wellhausen school has done justice to the clearly ascertainable facts neither in its organization of these writings nor in its determination of their dates. It was prevented from doing this because, on the one hand, it was too much under the spell of the evolutionary theory in its then influential Hegelian form, and on the other hand, it had too little insight into the cultural and religious structure of the ancient Near Eastern world.[7]

An exposition of my thoughts concerning the coming into being of the Pentateuch would of course be beyond the scope of this Introduction, and I must therefore limit myself here to the dating of that portion that is designated Leviticus. As a first consideration, it may be noted that in Leviticus 4:12, 21; 8:17; 9:11; 10:4–5; 13:46; 14:3, 8; 16:26–28; 17:3; 24:10, 14, 23, the people of Israel are dwelling in "the camp" and that outside of this lies "the desert" (16:21–28). In addition, 14:34; 18:3, 24; 19:23; 23:10; 25:2 indicate that the Israelites are en route to Canaan, and there are also a large number of passages that make mention of the "Tent of Meeting," where Israel is to present its offerings and celebrate its feasts. It is of course

---

[6]A. Noordtzij, tr. Miner B. Stearns (Dallas: Dallas Theological Seminary, reprinted from *Bibliotheca Sacra,* 1941).

[7]See my book, *De Oud Testamentische Godsopenbaring en het oud-Oosterse leven* (Utrecht, 1912).

true that not all of these latter verses are of equal relevance in this connection, for this tent remained the Lord's ''dwelling place'' until the downfall of Shiloh during the time of Eli, but it is nevertheless quite clear that in some of them the reference is to the Mosaic period. This is the case in chapter 17, for the law given here assumes that the Tent of Meeting is accessible to every Israelite for every cultic procedure, and the same situation is present in chapter 12, where women are directed to bring an offering at the tent after their period of purification following childbirth. Similarly, in chapters 13–14 it appears that the priest is immediately at hand in order to ascertain whether or not a person, article of clothing, or house has been rendered unclean by the occurrence of an infectious skin disease or other contamination. An infected person must live ''outside the camp'' (13:46), and on the day that he is pronounced clean he is able to present the prescribed offerings. Chapter 15, which deals with more or less unhealthy phenomena pertaining to sexual life and directs that an offering be brought after the seven days of ceremonial cleansing, also belongs in this category.

I am well aware that the school of Wellhausen regards all of this merely as ''verbal dress,'' but to me this is nothing more than a euphemism for ''deliberate deceit.'' Apart from all other considerations, such a viewpoint neglects the fact that no lawgiver would use such ''verbal dress'' if this made the practical observance of the law impossible during the time for which it was written.

I am also conscious of the fact that the adherents of this school have attempted to extricate themselves from this difficulty by acknowledging that a number of the laws of Leviticus contain a large amount of older material. The problem cannot be disposed of so easily, however, for the presumed lawgivers were certainly no archeologists. They wrote for their own time and wished to see their laws obeyed by their contemporaries, so how could they have presented regulations that during their day would have been altogether impossible of execution? It would be possible for me to accept the thought—although I do not believe that this is in fact correct—that during the exilic period there may have existed men who passed off their works under the name of Moses in order to thereby promote the acceptance of their personal opinions and wishes among the people. That in doing this they should have chosen a form that rendered the practical execution of these laws completely impossible, however, is in conflict with what experience teaches concerning the psychological insights of a legislator. Insofar as the school of Wellhausen acknowledges that Moses was not only the leader, but also the lawgiver of Israel—and all attempts that have been made from this side to expose Moses as a fiction have come to nothing—and that some of Israel's cultic regulations and

11

laws go back to him, there can be no basis for denying the Mosaic origin of a law that not only is expressly declared to date from him, but also can be best understood precisely in terms of his time. And the case against this becomes even stronger when the transference of such a law to a much later period (e.g., in or after the Exile) meets with insurmountable difficulties. It is of course true that tradition is not gospel, but its incorrectness must be *proved* rather than simply *asserted,* and the proofs must be based on its own content rather than on mere presuppositions. The roles cannot be reversed here, for the burden of proof lies on those who deny the correctness of the tradition, not on those who continue to accept it after serious, objective investigation.

There is thus no doubt in my mind that the content of Leviticus can be explained without the least difficulty in terms of the circumstances that prevailed during the Mosaic period. In the establishment of the covenant at Mount Sinai, a goal had been set that was to direct the manner in which Israel governed its life, and if in the course of the centuries Israel was indeed to attain this goal, it was necessary that a great variety of laws and regulations be enacted that would eliminate from the people's life whatever was in conflict with it. And since the intention of the covenant was to sanctify the people in order to render them fit for the service of the Lord, it was only natural that regulations be given that would subject cultic life (this being understood in its broadest sense) to this aim. This involved the setting of strict rules for the prescribed offerings, the outlining of detailed conditions that had to be met by the sanctuary and its servants, and the elimination from the communal life of the people of whatever was in conflict with this aim of the covenant.

It is at the same time clear to me that after Israel had settled in Canaan, the need arose more than once to adapt some of the regulations from the Mosaic period to the new circumstances that had then arisen. In this connection, it should be borne in mind that although the main lines of Israel's laws were unalterably fixed, this did not apply to all the various particularities within them. This latter assertion is clearly placed beyond doubt by the following facts:

1. The centralization of the cult is one of the fundamental ideas in the Mosaic legislation, but Samuel nevertheless made use of the local worship at the high places in order to hold the people to the worship of the Lord after the downfall of Shiloh (Mizpah, 1 Sam. 7:9, 12; 10:17; Gilgal, 11:15; Bethlehem, 16:5; Nob, 1 Sam. 21).

2. The right of serving at the altar was reserved exclusively for the house of Aaron, but after many families that were not of priestly blood had been admitted to the service of the altar and thus assimilated into the tribe

of Levi, David sought to put an end to this process of corruption by respecting acquired rights and legitimatizing them in his reorganization.[8]

3. Leviticus 1:5–6 states that it is the task of the person presenting the burnt offering to slaughter the animal, and also to skin it, remove its inner parts, etc., but during the time of the kings it became customary for the priests to do this. In the sacrificial ceremony of Hezekiah, circumstances compelled the Levites to take the role of helpers (2 Chron. 29:34), and it appears in 2 Chronicles 30:17 and 35:5–11 that, in spite of the directions given in Exodus 12:6, they also aided in slaughtering the Passover lambs. This task later came to be regarded as an established right of the Levites.[9]

4. According to Numbers 9:6–7, someone who was not in a state of holiness was to be excluded from the celebration of the Passover, but Hezekiah nevertheless did not hesitate to authorize those who were ceremonially unclean to partake, after he had spoken a prayer requesting that the Lord not cause them to bear the penalty for doing this (cf. Lev. 15:31; 22:3).

All of this proves that the devout in Israel did not at all regard the body of Mosaic laws and regulations as something unchangeable and therefore inviolable.

There is thus no difficulty in accounting for the fact that, as long as the content of the Pentateuch had not yet been closed off—and it seems to me that this could not have happened before the time of the kings—later regulations were here and there added to those that originated during Moses' time (see above).[10] This would naturally have been done by the priesthood, for to it had been entrusted not only the superintendence of the Lord's ceremonial service, but also the preservation of the knowledge of the law (Deut. 33:10). Practices that arose under the pressure of altered circumstances, insofar as they were consistent with the Mosaic legislation, thus inevitably came to be defined more precisely and incorporated into the law, and this was naturally done in a form that corresponded to that of the other laws. In other words, they assumed a place within the framework of the Mosaic laws.

This naturally makes it exceedingly difficult for a modern-day investigator to distinguish the more recent regulations with a sufficient degree of certainty. For this reason, in answering the question as to what in Leviticus is to be regarded as more recent in origin, I have confined myself to those sections where it is completely clear that this is the case.

---

[8]See my *I Kronieken,* pp. 64, 120, 187.

[9]Cf. Ezekiel 44:11; also my book *II Kronieken,* p. 328.

[10]See Publisher's Note.

VI. *The Relationship of the Content of Leviticus to the Thought Patterns of the Syro-Palestinian World*

The problem that lies hidden in the above words was, until a few decades ago, largely unknown. Before that time, the prevalent view had been that at Sinai God gave to His covenant people Israel a form of life that was altogether new by providing them with laws that had been known neither in earlier times nor in other places. This conception on the one hand stood under the influence of the Jewish endeavor to give to the Mosaic laws a character that was exceptional in all respects and to establish the impression that they had no parallels elsewhere, and on the other hand, it was too much oriented to the purely mechanistic manner of viewing the course of history, which had controlled the thought of the western European world for centuries.

Deeper insight into human psychology and into the organic character of history has changed this, however, and whoever takes into account in his studies what has been revealed both in the sweeping discoveries of the history of religions, and in the disclosure of the ancient Near Eastern world, will realize with full clarity that Israel neither was nor could have been divorced from the milieu within which its life arose. Israel was thus no more provided with new forms of life and worship than it was possible for Christendom to disengage converted peoples from their own past and to instill in them a completely new way of thinking.

The sacrificial tariff from Marseilles, which was found in 1845 and dates from approximately the third century B.C., and also the tariff from this same period found in Carthage, had already made clear that the Phoenicians, like the Israelites, had bloody whole offerings, expiatory offerings, and communion offerings, and that of these—as in Israel—the priest kept the breast and the thigh, while the remainder was given to the person bringing the offering. Further similarities with Israel appeared in the fact that the Phoenicians also knew of the grain offering of vegetable matter, that they brought some of the same animals to the altar (the bull and bull-calf, ram, lamb, and male goat), and that they likewise observed the sacrificial meal.

This became even more apparent when archeological treasures began to appear both in the plain of the Tigris and Euphrates rivers and in the Nile valley, and the evidence from Asia Minor and Arabia as well as from the Syro-Palestinian lands joined in making clear to all who took note of it that the Israelite nation, both in thought and practice, remained inextricably bound in countless ways to the ancient Near Eastern world within which it came into being. I have already pointed this out in my *De Oud Testamentische Godsopenbaring en het oud-Oosterse leven* (Utrecht, 1912), and since that time the evidence at our disposal has continually increased. The most recent addition to this comes from the excavations at Ras Shamra under the direction of C. F. A. Schaeffer, the curator of the *Musée des antiquités nationales*. Beginning in 1929, this work has delivered an unsuspected wealth of material that casts an exceptionally clear light on the cultic life of the Syro-Palestinian peoples and should also appear to be of great value for our knowledge of Israel's forms of thought and practice.[11]

In giving one of his writings the title *Origines cananéennes du sacrifice israélite* (Paris, 1921), René Dussaud has asserted more than he can prove and has given the impression that Israel's sacrificial ritual originated after the time of its entry into Canaan. This idea, which is also insupportable for other reasons, has been refuted in an unmistakable way by the discoveries at Ras Shamra, and Dussaud himself acknowledges this in his *Les découvertes des Ras Shamra (Ugarit) et l'Ancien Testament* (Paris, 1937), p. 113. The Ras Shamra texts, all of which date from before the destruction of Ugarit (perhaps by the Assyrians under Tiglath-Pileser I) in the twelfth century B.C., contain many more similarities with the Old Testament ritual than were present in the later Phoenician cultic practices. Since this would not be the place to demonstrate this at length, I will here confine myself to the following observations.

One of the texts of Ras Shamra contains the words *khum,* which corresponds to the *kōhᵃnîm* ("priests") of Israel, and also *qdšm,* which can be nothing other than the *qᵉdēšîm* ("male prostitutes") against whom the Israelites received a dire warning. Another text speaks of a *mtn tm (mattan tam)* or "offering without defect," and the Israelites were likewise ordered to present animals that were *tāmîm* (from the same stem as *tm*), "without defect," in their offerings. Still another text mentions *šlmm,* which were accompanied by sacrificial meals, and this also happened in the *šlmm (šᵉlāmîm,* "fellowship offerings") of Israel. Words appearing elsewhere include *kll,* which like *kālîl* is used as a name for the burnt offering, and *dbh,* which parallels *zebah* in designating an offering that is slaughtered. The texts also speak of the offering of firstfruits, and a narrative appearing in them mentions a feast that in more than one respect is reminiscent of Israel's feast of unleavened bread.

---

[11]Ras Shamra, the ancient Ugarit which had already been known from the Amarna Letters, lies on the western coast of Syria, *ca.* seven miles north of Latakia (the ancient Laodicea ad Mare) and approximately straight east of Salamis on Cyprus. There are five superimposed cultural strata here, of which the most ancient seems to go back to *ca.* 4000 B.C. The French journal *Syria* has published everything that the excavations have uncovered at the site up to now, and still further information can be found in, e.g., J. W. Jack, *The Ras Shamra Tablets* (Edinburgh, 1935); René Dussaud, *Les découvertes de Ras Shamra (Ugarit) et l'Ancien Testament* (Paris, 1937).

These examples, to which more could easily be added, demonstrate that both the names of a number of cultic procedures in Israel and the patterns of thought that accompanied them were no different from what appeared elsewhere in the Syro-Palestinian world. At the same time, the light shed by the new information that the excavations at Ras Shamra have placed at our disposal compels us to reexamine more closely the question of what constituted the distinctive nature of Israel's cultic life.

VII. *The Purpose of These Cultic Laws*

The divine revelation of the Old Testament in its entirety is the product of the Holy Spirit of God, for it was His vital working that directed not only its actual writing, but also the choice of the component sources that were used in it. The question thus inevitably arises as to why God saw fit to assign a place in the Bible to numerous cultic laws, more than one portion of which, as is now gradually becoming clear, was not the exclusive property of Israel. In order to give an answer that sheds at least some light, it is necessary that we first of all correctly discern the place that the cult assumed in Israel's life and the patterns of thinking that governed these cultic activities.

As a first observation, the cult can be defined as the visible form of the religious life. It is thus in a certain sense secondary, for it serves as the more or less appropriate form that the religious life needs in order to unfold its inner content, while the religious life itself is unmediated and independent of any external form. In addition, the cult, in being bound to holy places, times, and actions, is an affair of the community, while the religious life is in nature and essence individual. These statements are of course intended only to distinguish, not to separate the two. The cult is not merely an external concomitant to the religious life, but is rather its vital expression, since the structure of the human personality makes it necessary that the religious consciousness find an appropriate form in which it can both recognize itself and make itself known to others. The value of the cult thus depends on the degree to which it is an expression of genuine spiritual life.

For the ancient person the cult had even greater importance than this, however. By virtue of the dynamistic thinking[12] that was characteristic of the ancient world, the cult was regarded not merely in our sense as the external manifestation of the inner life, but also as the creative source and the vehicle of religious powers. This is related to the fact that the self-concept of the ancient person differed from ours. For modern thought,

---

[12] See Publisher's Note.

which has been strongly influenced by Neoplatonic philosophy, the human being consists of soul *and* body, and the result of this is that we place our bodily nature on a different plane from our mental or spiritual nature and hold these two apart as much as possible in our thinking. The person of antiquity, in contrast—and this applies also to Israel[13]—is convinced of the fact that the human being is a unity. In this conception, the human being does not *have* a soul, but rather *is* a soul (*nepeš*), and this has two sides: bodily and spiritual, or visible and invisible. The physical and the psychical here do not form a duality, as in the modern understanding, for the human being is rather regarded as physico-psychic or psycho-physical in nature. The result of this is that people in the ancient world lived in the conviction that the invisible world exerted its influence on them not only by way of their conscious awareness and their spiritual disposition, but also through their bodies, i.e., through eating and drinking, diseases and ailments, and through everything connected with sexual life.

This concept had two different consequences. In the first place, the religious life embraced a much larger sphere than, to the modern mind, is consistent with the nature of religion. Ancient people regarded also the physical side of human existence in a religious light, and this inevitably meant that their understanding of the concept *sin* had a correspondingly broader reference. Because of this, what we designate an unhealthy aberration or consider to be a normal expression of sexual life was regarded by them as a manifestation of sin, and furthermore, the eating or even merely coming into contact with certain animals could exclude one from the cultic community. It is in this light that the regulations of Leviticus 11–15 should be considered.

The second consequence of the concept discussed above was that cult and religion formed much more of a unity for the consciousness of the ancient person, and thus also for the Israelite, than they do for us. To the ancient Near Eastern mind, word and deed were capable of mutually supporting one another, for the word was regarded as an act made audible and the act as a word made visible. For this reason, the cult, in which word and deed were brought together and framed in terms of one another, was the source of a creative power that was capable of actually realizing that which the religious consciousness aspired after. This explains why the religious act of sacrifice assumed such a prominent place in the cultic life of the ancient Semitic peoples—here again Israel was no exception—which inevitably meant that the priest played a very large role.

It was only natural that cultic life be subjected to strict requirements

---

[13]See Publisher's Note.

throughout the ancient world. The determination of time and place was of great importance, as was also the specification both of the persons who would play the leading roles and of the actions that would be required of the participants. Some amount of preparation was necessary. This included the performance of some actions (e.g., washings) and the abstention from others (e.g., the consumption of certain foods and drinks). Fasts were also sometimes required in order to avoid impeding the efficacy of the holy.

Various of these practices were also known in Israel. Here as elsewhere, the triad composed of offering, priest, and sanctuary assumed the prominent position in cultic life, but all three of these took a form that was characteristic for the Israelites as fruit of the self-revelation of the "Holy One of Israel." The *sanctuary* therefore had no place for any type of image, and it was furnished not only with a continuously burning lamp (1 Sam. 3:3), but above all with the ark, where the Lord would speak to Israel from between the cherubim (Exod. 25:22). Israel's God desired that this sanctuary be a single one, as a reflection of His oneness (Deut. 6:4), and it was here that the reality of the divine revelation was as it were concretized, for from its "location" or "dwelling place" here it led Israel as a "royal priesthood" (1 Peter 2:9), all of whom were prophets of the Lord (Num. 11:29), toward the fullness of time in which it would reach "every tribe and language and people and nation" (Rev. 5:9; cf. Mic. 4:1–5).

In this sanctuary the *priest* carried out his duties. Unlike elsewhere, however, the priest in Israel was not a man possessing special powers, like, e.g., the priest of Diana by Lake Nemi, nor was he someone with visionary ability, like the Arabic *kahin* (the same word as Heb. *kōhēn,* "priest"). Least of all was he some type of sorcerer or medicine man, or someone capable of explaining all types of omens and dreams or of cleansing persons or things from a material contamination with sin. There was no place for any of this in Israel. Here the priest rather became the indispensable mediator between God and man. In the sacrificial service he represented the congregation before God, and in granting the blessing and serving as the vehicle of the divine legal decision he was the representative of God before Israel. The priest was no longer, as formerly, merely an arbitrary family head (Gen. 12:7–8; 13:18; etc.) or one of Israel's young men (Exod. 24:5), for he now had to belong to the line of Aaron, which the Lord Himself had designated for this task (Exod. 28:1–4). He also, unlike elsewhere, did not possess some secret magical or mystagogical priestly knowledge. The priest was not even first of all the bringer of offerings. His assistance was originally not needed in presenting sacrifices (Exod. 20:24–26; 1 Sam. 6:15), and for this reason, the slaughtering of the animal was carried out by the person who brought the offering (Lev. 1:5–6; 1 Sam. 2:13–15) until late in the monarchical period. In Israel, the priest was in the first place the dispenser of the divine oracle by way of the Urim and Thummim, which were carried in the high priestly ephod. These, however, were not a source of secret oracular knowledge, since as means of divine decision they could also be used by non-priests (1 Sam. 23:8; 30:7). The Israelite priest also had to enforce the faithful obedience of the ritual and social-ethical regulations that were designed to teach Israel how it was to order its life as the people of the Lord (cf., e.g., the laws pertaining to marriage and ceremonial purity). He was thus Israel's adviser with regard to the various requirements involved in the worship of the Lord and also with regard to the means for reconciliation and regaining the Lord's favor once His wrath had arisen at the violation of His holiness that resulted from transgressing the law. Over against this second portion of the priestly task, the first portion receded more and more into the background, and after 1 Samuel 28:6 we no longer hear of the dispensing of the oracle. The third element in the task of the priest consisted in presenting Israel's sacrifices (Deut. 33:8–11). Here, also, however, the unique character of the Israelite cult comes to light, for Leviticus makes no mention of a complicated sacrificial service subject to priestly monopolies.

The sacrifice. Until rather recently, it was thought that the patterns of thought that lay behind this cultic practice could be precisely known, and the influence of the views that arose as a result of this presumption still makes itself felt at times. Some regarded the sacrifice as nothing more than an attempt to procure the deity's favor by means of a gift, thus, as a type of barter or exchange that was also carried out with men in high places in order to assure oneself of their aid (Spencer). Others were of the opinion that it was an endeavor to engage in communion with the deity, who was thought to share in the sacrificial meal and partake of the same food and drink (Smend). Still others viewed the offering as related partly to sorcery, and partly to the presenting of food as a gift as this occurs most universally in the veneration of the dead (Loisy). Another concept claimed that it was nothing other than an attempt to master the vital forces by adding life to life (Dussaud). And one last group conceived of the offering as a means of establishing a connection with the holy: the sacrificial animal was regarded as the seat of divine power, and in the offering the greatest part of this would go to the deity, while the remainder could be used for some specific purpose such as prayer or consecration (Hubert and Mauss). The one thing that appears clearly through all these diverse conceptions is the influence of the evolutionary theory. At the same time, they all manifest the desire to open several doors with one key.

It is undeniable that the concept of the offering as "food of God" had been present in Israel. Leviticus 3:11 speaks of burning animals "on the altar as food, an offering made to the LORD by fire." Leviticus 21:8 speaks of the "food of your God" (cf. also v. 17; 22:25), and in Numbers 28:2 the Lord refers to "the food for my offerings made by fire." Indeed, this is made unmistakably clear by the fact that offerings of meat and fine flour were made more palatable by the addition of salt and oil, respectively, that bread and wine also were added to the offerings of meat, that loaves of bread were set before the Lord (the bread of the Presence), and that the offering is called "an aroma pleasing to the LORD" (literally, "aroma of appeasement," Lev. 1:9; etc.).

The question remains, however, whether this line of thinking was still present in Israel, and to this the answer is decidedly in the negative. This is proved by the fact that the ancient terminology could be used in much later times, even though the patterns of thought that had given rise to it had disappeared. Ezekiel has no objection to speaking of the offering as the Lord's food (Ezek. 44:7), nor Malachi to calling the altar the Lord's table (Mal. 1:7), and Ezekiel makes mention of the "pleasing aroma" more than once (Ezek. 6:13; 16:19; 20:28, 41; RSV, "pleasing odor"; NIV, "fragrant incense"). In addition to this, there was no place among the Israelites for the thought that the Lord, who existed before Israel, could be a dependent being in any respect whatsoever. The examples discussed above can thus be seen as nothing other than an indication of the tenacity of cultic terminology, which persists in making use of expressions reminiscent of a distant past when the thoughts to which they give utterance did in fact prevail. Since that time, however, Israel had learned by the light of divine revelation that only a small portion of the Lord's glory (*kāḇôḏ*, literally, "weight") could be beheld (Exod. 33:19–23; cf. Gen. 32:29–31), and that the Creator of heaven and earth has no need of the gift of any man. For Israel, the sacrifice is based on the gracious will of God by which He has entered into a covenant relationship with His people, and the Lord therefore says concerning the blood of the offering in Leviticus 17:11: "I have given it to you . . . on the altar." In contrast to the position taken by Köhler,[14] the sacrifice here then cannot be seen as the result of a human attempt to ascend to the "unknown God," for in it God rather descends to humankind in order to lead it back to Himself. At the same time, it is made clear in the sacrifice that this reestablishment of life in communion with God can proceed only by way of death. The sacrifice is thus given by the

---

[14]Ludwig Köhler, *Old Testament Theology,* tr. A. S. Todd (Philadelphia: Westminster Press, 1936), pp. 181ff.

grace of God as a means of atonement, although the operation of God's grace is not limited by the offering (Exod. 32:30–32). Where there is conscious opposition between man's will and God's, no offering can avail. For this reason, in contrast to the view of the ancient Near Eastern world, there was to the Israelite mind absolutely no atoning power present in the act of sacrifice itself. The offering was not a magical rite that controlled the will of the deity. The value of the offering depended on the degree to which the spiritual disposition of the person presenting it conformed with what was thereby symbolized (1 Sam. 15:22). Deuteronomy 10:16 thus exhorts the Israelites to "circumcise therefore the foreskin of your heart," implying that the material offering would soon be subordinated to the "offering of the lips" (Ps. 141:2). There is therefore a variety of evidence that shows that the concept of the offering as "food of God," although it continually made its influence felt as a survival from the time of the "forefathers" who lived "beyond the River" (Josh. 24:2), was foreign to Israel's legitimate cult.

The concept of the offering as a gift was also present in Israel. This is indicated by the fact that the most general Hebrew term used for offering is *minḥâ(h)*, a word that can also refer to gifts given to kings, domestic or foreign (1 Sam. 10:27; 1 Kings 10:25; etc.), to gifts used to procure the favor of a powerful person (Gen. 32:13 [MT 14], 18–21, [MT 19–22]; 33:10; 43:11), and to compulsory tribute (Judg. 3:15; 1 Kings 4:21; 2 Kings 17:3). It must not be forgotten, however, that such a *minḥâ(h)* could express any of a whole series of motives: both the feeling of unconditional self-surrender and that of mistrust, both supplication proceeding from childlike faith and calculating self-interest. There is therefore no ground whatever for always assuming the presence of the meanest motivation when the word *minḥâ(h)* is used. If, as Heiler has brought to light in his book *Prayer,* [15] such cannot even be proved with respect to so-called primitives, it would be even less the case with Israel. It is true that an offering given in fulfillment of a vow may be regarded as an expression of great caution with respect to the Deity. It is clear already in Hannah's vow, however, that this may also be a manifestation of childlike trust in which the person is properly motivated by the correct knowledge that God's gracious gifts oblige us to respond not only in words, but also in deeds, and that the demonstration of one's willingness to perform a deed cannot be displeasing to the Lord (cf. also the comment on Lev. 7:16). This same consideration applies also to the presentation of freewill offerings and votive gifts.

---

[15] Friedrich Heiler, *Prayer,* tr. and ed. Samuel McComb and J. Edgar Park (London: Oxford University Press, 1932), pp. 23ff.

Israel understood the sacrifice not merely as a gift of the people, however, for it was also a gift presented by God, who in the offering had communion with them. It was precisely through this communion that Israel's offering became a sacrament. The offering here was no longer, as elsewhere, the product of a human desire to engage in communion with the Deity by the aid of some power supposedly lying in the sacrificial animal. As is shown in the covenantal meal on Mount Sinai (Exod. 24:9–11; the communal meal that accompanied the establishment of the covenant between Jacob and Laban can be compared with this, Gen. 31:44–54), the sacrifice in Israel activated the vital bond that united God and His people. The form of God's presence here was not sensuous or magical, for what occurred was rather a personal-ethical communion with Him whose will governed the relationships that were determinative of His people's life. Although elsewhere the sacrificial meal was intended to establish a relationship of blood brotherhood, this idea was excluded from Israel as an absolute impossibility by the all-consuming holiness of the Lord's nature. There was also no place here for a participation in the divine nature such as the Greek mystery religions aimed at, nor for a beneficent power proceeding *ex opere operato* from the rite of sacrifice as such. The actualization of communion with God depended exclusively on the Lord's willingness to enter into a special relationship with His people and to allow them to share in His life. In this manner, Israel's offering became a sacrament.

To conclude our discussion of the sacrifice, the following observation may be made. Whereas elsewhere in the ancient Near Eastern world the right of presenting offerings to the deity was reserved exclusively for the king, because he was regarded as "son of the deity," or for the priesthood, because they alone possessed the secret knowledge necessary for disclosing the way to the deity, the situation in Israel was completely different. Here the king was nothing more than a man of the people, taken by the Lord Himself "from the pasture and from following the flock to be ruler over my people Israel" (2 Sam. 7:8), and like all of his subjects, he too was subject to the law of the Lord. Here the priest was nothing more than a member of the family group which the Lord had called to serve as mediator between Himself and His people and to "minister in the Holy Place" (Exod. 28:43). He was not in possession of a secret ritual, nor was he, as elsewhere, a sorcerer or a healer, for he was called solely "to stand before the Lord to minister and to pronounce blessings in his name" (Deut. 10:8). The sacrifices in Israel were brought by the people themselves, the "holy people" who knew the Lord's decrees and laws, since the latter were directed not to a separate caste, but to the people themselves (Lev. 1:1–2; 4:2; 11:2, etc.). The people thus took an active role in the presentation of offerings rather than being mere observers. He who brought the offering laid his hand on its head, slaughtered it, skinned it, and cut it into pieces (Lev. 1:3–6; etc.).

A proper understanding of the above discussion will enable us to answer the question that was asked in the opening paragraph of this section. All of these cultic decrees and laws, whose authority is based solely on the fact that they are given by the Lord, are not to be regarded from the standpoint of modern hygiene, for their purpose is nothing less than to deal earnestly and concretely with what it means to be the "holy people" of the Lord by placing God in the all-controlling center point of Israel's life and making Him the ultimate goal of every action. As such, they are collected in the Book of Leviticus and given their necessary place within the whole of the divine revelation of the Old Testament for the following reasons:

1. In order that every member of the holy people might know that Israel's cult, rather than being a mere product of priestly knowledge, was based on divine authority, and that it was therefore imperative that the people conduct themselves in accordance with the decrees and laws to which this cult was subjected. It was thereby thoroughly impressed on Israel that it had to reveal itself in its cult as the holy people of the Lord and to make use of the means, placed at its disposal by its covenant God, that would enable it to manifest and maintain this holiness in its own life, i.e., to deal earnestly and concretely with what it meant to live as the holy people of the Lord.

2. In order that every Israelite, knowing that Israel's cult did not have the individual, but the people, as its object (for this reason, the high points of Israel's cultic life concerned the *people* as a whole, the priestly blessing was pronounced on the *people,* and what was unclean was eradicated from the *people*), might become more and more aware that Israel had no place for private tribal or family cults, and also that the individual bore the responsibility for the people, inasmuch as the people granted to him in the ritual the means for saving not only himself, but also his people.

3. In order that every Israelite might be conscious of the fact that, when his people experienced the bitterness of the Lord's wrath, this was not because the Lord was in any respect similar to the other gods, whose anger was an expression of pure arbitrariness, but because Israel in its conduct had violated the Lord's holiness and failed to observe His decrees and laws.

4. In order that later generations, living after the time in which the fullness of the stream of salvation flowed out to "every tribe and language and people and nation" (Rev. 5:9), might be able to survey Israel's national life with its wealth of dramatic incidents in the light of these decrees

and laws and thus be led to the confession of the Lord's right to deal similarly with His people today. This knowledge will then also lead us to acknowledge with Paul that "Israel, who pursued a law of righteousness, has not attained it. . . . Because they pursued it not by faith but as it were by works" (Rom. 9:31–32).

Nevertheless, however important all of this may be in and of itself—and it is my conviction that we do not do justice to the total picture if we do not pay sufficient attention to the above matters—it does not contain the main reason that led to the inclusion of the cultic laws of Leviticus in the Old Testament revelation. Although Judaism may have thought differently, Israel was only the means, and not the ultimate goal, of the divine revelation. From the beginning, the time had been foreseen when the means would have to disappear and the people would reach its end point: the fullness of time, personified in the Christ of God. It is He who was the "end of the law" (Rom. 10:4), but this made it necessary that Israel be able to recognize Him as such. He had to be foreshadowed in the law if He was to be accepted as the consummator of the law.

I am of course aware of the fact that within the Christian church, a large number of sections of the law are regarded as "shadows" or prefigurations of Christ, and I am also not at all blind to the dangers that are attendant on an overly liberal usage of allegory and typology in one's interpretation of the Old Testament.[16] Nevertheless, misuse is no basis for disuse, and the Old Testament scholar errs who in his exegesis fails to deal in a sober and proper way with the matter of typological significance. In so doing, he loses sight not only of the unity of the Old and New Testaments, but above all of Jesus as the Christ of God. In addition, it is only a correct understanding of typology that raises the cultic legislation of Leviticus far beyond the level of a mere religious-historical antiquarian concern. The perspective that this legislation opens on the coming Christ alone makes clear why the Holy Spirit saw to its inclusion in the Old Testament canon, for it is only in this light that the Levitical laws are given their appropriate place and can be understood in their true value for believers of the New Testament period. At Israel's altar is prefigured the cross of Golgotha with its joyful proclamation of the gospel: "the blood of Jesus, his [God's] Son, purifies us from every sin" (1 John 1:7; 2:2). Both from Israel's altar and from Golgotha's cross, the message goes forth that to descend into death is to find true life.

---

[16]See, e.g., Wilhelm Vischer, *The Witness of the Old Testament to Christ,* tr. A. B. Crabtree, vol. 1 (London: Lutterworth Press, 1949).

Leviticus
Commentary

Part One

The Offerings Required by the God of the Covenant
(1:1-7:38)

These first seven chapters constitute a single whole insofar as they all deal with the offerings Israel was to bring to the Lord as His covenant people, but within this there are several clearly distinguishable sections. The first of these is comprised of chapters 1-3, where three types of offering that can be brought voluntarily are discussed in succession. Chapter 1 deals with the burnt offering, chapter 2 with the grain offering, and chapter 3 with the fellowship offering. The chapters are provided with an introductory formula (1:1-2a), but there is no closing formula. What is usually taken for the latter (3:16b-17) is actually nothing more than the accentuation of a thought that is prominent in chapter 3.

The next section, chapters 4-5, is separated from the first by another introductory formula (4:1-2a). The offerings discussed here—the sin offering in 4:1-5:13, and the guilt offering in 5:14-6:7—are specifically concerned with the procuring of atonement. As in the first section, there is no closing formula here, and both of these sections are directed to the Israelites as a group (1:1; 4:1).

The situation is different in the third section, comprised of 6:8-7:21. The regulations given here are directed to Aaron and his sons (6:9), and as appears from the repetition of "the LORD said to Moses" in 6:8 and 6:19, they can be divided into two subsections. Both of these are marked by the repeated formula "these are the regulations for . . ." (6:8, 24; 7:1, 11), which is interrupted only in 6:20 by the statement "this is the offering Aaron and his sons are to bring. . . ." The offerings that are discussed in succession here include the burnt, grain, ordination, sin, guilt, and fellowship offerings. With the exception of the ordination offering, these are the same as were discussed in the first two sections, although the order in which they appear differs.

The fourth section (7:22–34), lastly, is again directed to the Israelites, and it deals first of all with the prohibition against the eating of fat and blood (vv. 22–27; cf. 3:16–17), and secondly with the portion of the fellowship offering that is allotted to the priests (vv. 28–34).

At the end of chapter 7 appear two closing formulas, 35–36 and 37–38. The first of these has reference to the portion of the offerings made by fire that belongs to the priests. The standard concept of this as the conclusion of 6:8–7:34 can in no way be correct, for it at most belongs with 7:28–34, which speaks only of the priestly share in that portion of the offerings made by fire constituted by the fellowship offering. The second concluding statement (vv. 37–38) forms the close of the "regulations for the burnt offering, the grain offering, the sin offering, the guilt offering, the ordination offering, and the fellowship offering," and it is thus intended to serve as a characterization of the contents of chapters 1–7 as a whole.

The First Group of Offerings
(1:1–3:17)

1. *The Burnt Offering* (1:1–17)

1:1 *The Lord called to Moses and spoke to him from the Tent of Meeting.*

Exodus 35–39 gives a broad description of the manner in which the regulations of Exodus 25–31 pertaining to the construction and furnishing of the tabernacle were carried out by Moses and the Israelites. In this, the human actors naturally occupy the prominent position, although there is at the same time the constant reminder that all of this was done in conformity with the declared will of the Lord (Exod. 35:2, 4, 29–35; 36:1, 5; 39:1, 7, 26, 29, 31, 32, 43). It is only in Exodus 40 that the Lord Himself again steps into the foreground, for the book now turns to the manner in which the Tent of Meeting was to be made ready so that the Lord could take residence there. The chapter thus opens with the words: "The Lord called to Moses."

This tent, however, also formed the place where the Israelites presented their offerings in the service of the Lord, and it must now be stated how these were to be performed if they were indeed to accomplish the purpose that the Lord had in mind, viz., the procuring of atonement and the demonstration of self-surrender. For this reason, the Lord spoke to Moses once again, this time from the Tent of Meeting, which was filled with the Lord's glory (*kāḇôḏ,* literally "weight," a word that gives expression to the majesty of His divine nature that is continually translated into deeds) to such a degree that there was no room in it even for Moses. The latter did stand close to the tent, but he remained outside, even when the Lord addressed him from the tent.

Leviticus 1:1 begins by stating that "the LORD called to Moses." This is the third time that we hear of the Lord calling to Moses in this way, for He had done so also at the burning bush (Exod. 3:4) and on Mount Sinai (Exod. 19:3). It was "the LORD" who called. Strictly speaking, this translation is not correct, for the Hebrew text contains the proper name *Yhwh,* which is most likely pronounced "Yahweh" (meaning "He is").[1] The Jews, who took warning from the story presented in Leviticus 24:10–16 and thus sought to render the transgression of the commandment in Exodus 20:7 impossible by avoiding the pronouncement of this name, replaced *Yhwh* with the generic name, *'ăḏōnāy,* "LORD," when the proper name *Yhwh* is used (which happens more than 1000 times in the Old Testament).

It appears from the Talmud and Midrash that the Jews speculated much concerning the meaning of the proper name *Yhwh,* which is undoubtedly related to the verb stem *hwh* ("to be"). In doing so they have proposed no fewer than seven explanations of this: He who has created the world out of nothing, the God of truth, the God of love, the God of faithfulness, the God of eternity, the God of deliverance, and the God of revelation. One of these is found in the French translations of the Bible, which always use the expression *L'Eternel.* It is my view that "He is" rather characterizes God as He who is unchanging and can therefore be depended on by His covenant people.

The Lord spoke to Moses "from the Tent of Meeting." This name first appears in Exodus 27:21, and the same object is also referred to as the "dwelling place" in Leviticus 15:31; 26:11; etc. The term "tabernacle," which has become the standard name for this, is based on the word used in the Vulgate, and it is a felicitous choice in that the Latin term *tabernaculum* can mean not only "tent," but also "wooden hut," and this latter sense is indeed appropriate to the Tent of Meeting. The word "Meeting" is a translation of *mô'ēḏ,* a term derived from the verbal stem *yā'aḏ,* which in the *Niphal* can have the meaning "gather, come together" (Josh. 11:5; Neh. 6:2), sometimes with hostile intentions (Num. 14:35; 16:11; 27:3). In Exodus 29:42–43 and 30:36, the Tent of Meeting is further described as

---

[1] For a Jewish viewpoint concerning this, see D. Hoffman, *Das Buch Leviticus,* I (1905, pp. 95–106.

the place where the Lord would *yā'ad* with Moses and the Israelites, and in Exodus 25:22; 30:6; Numbers 17:4 the ark is spoken of in the same way. It is customary to translate *yā'ad* as "reveal" whenever the term is applied to the Lord, and on this basis some have proposed that this tabernacle be styled the "tent of revelation." The fact that the mythological divine mountain, which the Semitic peoples regarded as the habitation of the gods (perhaps located at the North Pole), is spoken of in Isaiah 14:13 as the "mount of *mô'ēd*," however, and that this can here mean nothing other than "mount of meeting" (NIV, "mount of assembly"), indicates that the Israelites understood *mô'ēd* more in the sense of "meeting, coming together." As the Lord's abode (it is thus called His "dwelling place," Lev. 15:31; 26:11; 2 Sam. 7:6), this tent formed the place where He and the people who drew near to it met with one another, so that the Lord could make known to them His holy will (it is thus also referred to as the "Tent of the Testimony," Num. 9:15; 17:7–8; 18:2) and they could express their desires and present their offerings. Luther translated the Hebrew term into German as "Stiftshütte," which he then described as a "church or religious center (Stift) where the people assembled in order to hear God's word," but this is of course not completely correct.

The attempt to construe this tent as an "oracular tent"[2] does not do justice to the word *mô'ēd* and is nothing more than a product of the desire to debase Israel's religious notions as much as possible. We also need not allow ourselves to be sidetracked by the position, advanced by the Wellhausen school, which regards the tabernacle as nothing other than a replica of the postexilic central sanctuary, for this is too much in conflict with the facts.[3]

1:2 *He said, "Speak to the Israelites and say to them: 'When any of you brings an offering to the* Lord, *bring as your offering an animal from either the herd or the flock.'"*

"Speak to the Israelites and say to them." In the regulations pertaining to offerings presented in chapters 1–7, there are two clearly distinguishable groups; the first of these is directed to the people (1:1–6:7), and the second to the priesthood (6:8–7:21). Both of these groups, however, are framed in terms of one another and are mutually supplementary.

"When any of you brings an offering to the Lord." This is the standard legal form, which in the Hebrew reads: "anyone [literally, 'a man,' or 'a person'], when he. . . ." The same form is used throughout Leviticus and

---

[2]See, e.g., Stade, *Biblische Theologie des Alten Testaments,* p. 44.
[3]See, e.g., Eerdmans, *Das Buch Leviticus,* pp. 42f.

Numbers (e.g., Lev. 2:1; 4:2; 5:1, 15; 12:2; 13:2, 29; Num. 5:6, 12; 6:2; 15:2; 27:8; 30:3). In such expressions, a general case is introduced by *kî* ("when, if"), and an individual case by *'im* ("if," e.g., Lev. 1:3, 10, 14; 3:1; etc.). This "anyone" may not be construed separately from the Hebrew phrase which is translated "of you" or "among you" (as is done by Hertz in his comment on this verse), which would mean that the lawgiver could also be speaking of non-Israelites here.

The word *qorbān,* translated as "offering," is the general term throughout Leviticus and Numbers, and it appears also in Ezekiel 20:28; 40:43; and Mark 7:11. It is applied to both bloody and bloodless offerings, is related to the verbal stem *qārab* ("to draw near, approach"), and the *Hiphil* form of this verb is often used for the bringing of something to God, whether this be an offering or a gift made in behalf of the service of the Lord (cf. Num. 7:3, 10; 31:50; Neh. 10:35). A *qorbān* is thus something that one brings near to God (*hiqrîb,* "to cause to draw near") in order to enable himself to draw near (*qārab*) to God and thus enjoy God's nearness (*qirbâ[h],* cf. Ps. 73:28). The reference here is thus not to an obligatory offering, but rather to one that proceeds from the impulse of one's own heart.

There was no need for the lawgiver to explain what such a *qorbān* consisted of, for in the Semitic world that gave birth to Israel, the custom of bringing offerings assumed such an important place in religious life that everyone knew what a *qorbān* was. The lawgiver naturally proceeded in terms of the world of thought that was also present in Israel, and to this extent he had nothing new to add. What *was* new lies in his mention of the Lord. It was only to Him that Israel could present its offerings, for in the person of its lawful representatives, it had attended the sacrificial meal on Mount Sinai, and after hearing the reading of the Book of the Covenant, it had declared itself willing to live in accordance with its content (Exod. 24). For Israel, the demons and satyrs (literally, goats) of the forest and desert (Deut. 32:17; 2 Chron. 11:15; Ps. 106:37; Isa. 13:21; 34:14) were completely done away with; at least, this is what the lawgiver presupposed (cf. Lev. 17:1–7), just as Paul took his point of departure in the holiness of the Lord's people (Rom. 1:17; 1 Cor. 1:2; 6:1).

Not every animal could serve as an offering, however, for this verse directed that they be taken only from the herd or the flock.[4] This naturally excluded all animals living in the wild, for since these were the property of

---

[4]The donkey (see Exod. 13:13) and camel were not allowed, for these belonged neither to the herd nor the flock. The only birds suitable for offering were doves and pigeons. Among the peoples of the Tigris-Euphrates plain, there is mention of bulls, rams, and pigs, and also fish and wildlife. The animals spoken of in the sacrificial tariff of Marseilles included deer and also birds in general.

no one, they did not meet the requirement that was placed on offerings in Israel, viz., that they be taken from one's own possession. In a sense, it was necessary that one be made poorer by what he brought near *(hiqrîḇ)* to the Lord, and Exodus 13:12 therefore states that the firstborn males of the people's own livestock belonged to the Lord. Offerings could thus not be made of the gazelle or deer, which assumed a place in the cult of the Babylonians, and unclean animals were of course also excluded, even though these might belong to the herd or flock (Lev. 11:26–27; Deut. 14:7–8). The latter were even excluded from everyday use.

The animals that could be used in offerings—all of these being domesticated animals in Israel—were divided into two groups: those belonging to the herd and those belonging to the flock. The Jewish tradition added two further qualifications to this. An offering could not consist of an animal that was worshiped as an idol or that was destined for use as an idol offering, nor could an animal that had killed a man be used *(Temurah* 28b). The more detailed conditions that sacrificial animals had to meet are stated when the lawgiver discusses the various types of offering in which these animals are brought to the Lord. Careful distinction was therein continually made between animals belonging to the herd and the flock, for each of these required a different procedure (cf. Lev. 1:3–9, 10–13, 14–17; 3:1–5, 6–17). At the same time, it was then made clear that in some cases the offering of pigeons and doves was also permitted (Lev. 1:14; 5:7; 12:6, 8; 14:22, 30; 15:14, 29).

A. *Burnt offerings from the herd* (1:3–9)

1:3 *"'If the offering is a burnt offering from the herd, he is to offer a male without defect. He must present it at the entrance to the Tent of Meeting so that it will be acceptable to the LORD.'"*

The burnt offering is the first to be discussed, and this is readily explained by the fact that the thought that it embodies forms the foundation of the entire sacrificial ritual of Israel, the purpose of which was to render the people fit for the service of the Lord by way of self-surrender. For this reason, Israel as a people was commanded to present lamb as a burnt offering every morning and evening "at the entrance to the Tent of Meeting" before the Lord (Exod. 29:38–42, the so-called continual or regular offering, *tāmîḏ*).

The burnt offering dates from very early times. It was already present in pre-Mosaic times (Noah, Gen. 8:20; Abraham, Gen. 22:3, 6, 13), and it appears with Moses both in Egypt (Exod. 10:25) and in the confirmation of the covenant at Mount Sinai (Exod. 24:5). Bloody offerings of this type were also made among the peoples of the Tigris-Euphrates plain.

The Hebrew term for the burnt offering is *'ōlâ(h),* which expresses the fact that this offering "rises" or "ascends," i.e., the portions of the animal that were used in it were completely consumed on the altar fire. First Samuel 7:9 thus speaks of a *'ōlâ(h) kālîl* ("whole burnt offering"), and *kālîl* is used as a synonym of *'ōlâ(h)* in Deuteronomy 33:10 and Psalm 51:19. The total annihilation of the sacrificial animal signifies the complete self-surrender and total subjection to the Lord of the person who brings it.

The conditions that had to be satisfied by an animal from the herd if it was to be suitable as a burnt offering are given first of all. In order to be accepted on behalf of the person bringing it, the animal had to be a male without defect, and it appears from verse 5 that it also had to be young (cf. Lev. 22:20–22). These demands were made of *every* sacrificial animal, and the lawgiver continually placed great emphasis on this (Exod. 12:5; 29:1; Lev. 4:3, 23; 5:18; 6:6; etc.; see especially Lev. 22:19–22). Only in certain specific cases could female animals be offered, but they could never be used in the burnt offering (Lev. 3:1, 6; 4:28, 32; 5:6). The demand that the animal be without defect admitted of no exceptions, however, and this was equally the case in the Babylonian sacrificial texts. In spite of the clear statement of this in Leviticus 22:20–22 and Deuteronomy 15:21, it appears from Malachi 1:8, 14 that the Israelites nevertheless often fell far short of meeting this requirement. The Greek translation renders the Hebrew for "without defect" as *ămōmos,* and in the New Testament books of Hebrews and 1 Peter this same term is applied to the Lord Jesus. Hebrews 9:14 thus declares that He "offered himself unblemished to God," and in 1 Peter 1:19 He is called a "lamb without blemish or defect." Christ is thereby clearly marked as the perfect offering who completely satisfied the Lord's demand. The requirement that the animal be male was on the one hand related to the fact that these were of greater value than females, as was of course also the case in breeding. On the other hand, it was also based on the thought that, being physically stronger, they had more power.[5]

The person bringing an offering was to present his animal "at the entrance to the Tent of Meeting"—i.e., directly by the altar of burnt offering (Exod. 40:6; it later stood in front of the temple, 2 Kings 16:14)—and he thereby gave expression to his desire to dedicate it to the Lord. The animal thus became "acceptable to the Lord" (v. 2),[6] for it was then regarded by

---

[5] See Publisher's Note.

[6] Or, the animal thus made the person presenting it acceptable or pleasing to the Lord. The author translates verse 2 similar to the marginal note in NIV: ". . . so that he will be acceptable to the LORD" (cf., RSV, NEB).

31

Him as truly being an offering which, in meeting with His acceptance, could achieve the desired fruit for the person bringing it (Jer. 14:12; Ezek. 20:40), viz., the Lord's favor as this was manifested in condescending love and gracious mercy. The Lord's favor—which forms the opposite of His anger and wrath (Ps. 30:5; Isa. 60:10)—did not appear unless offerings were brought to His altar, which is called the table (Ezek. 44:16; Mal. 1:7, 12) upon which His food was placed (Lev. 21:6; Num. 28:2).

1:4 *"'He is to lay his hand on the head of the burnt offering, and it will be accepted on his behalf to make atonement for him.'"*

While standing with the animal by the Lord's "table," the person presenting the offering was required to perform a deed that has become known as the "laying on of hands" *(s^{e}mîkâ[h])*. Strictly speaking, this translation is not correct. The Hebrew verb *sāmak* means more than a mere "laying on," for it expresses a certain exertion of pressure as in leaning on or bracing oneself on, and thus as it were, entrusting oneself to. This *sāmak* therefore involved close contact, and through it the person presenting the offering gave expression to the fact that he could not do without the animal. In Leviticus 16:21, the laying on of hands was accompanied by a confession of guilt, a practice that became mandatory in later Judaism. The *sāmak* played a constitutive role throughout the sacrificial ritual: in the burnt offering (Exod. 29:15; Lev. 8:18; Num. 8:12), the fellowship offering (Lev. 3:2), the sin offering (Lev. 4:4; 8:14), the priestly ordination offering (Exod. 29:19; Lev. 8:22), and thus, in individual offerings in general.

There is a question as to whether this *sāmak* was done with one hand or with two. The Mishnah tractate *Menahoth* 93a (see also *Zebahim* 39a) says two hands were required, and Leviticus 16:21 expressly speaks of both hands. In all places, the Hebrew for "hand" is merely *ydw*. The Masoretic text invariably vocalizes this as singular *(yāḏô)*, but it is equally possible that the dual form *(yāḏāw)* is intended, for both of these words were written the same in the ancient, unvocalized text. If the word is regarded as plural, the sense of supporting one's entire being on and thereby entrusting oneself to something, which is a proper translation of *sāmak*, comes to clearer expression. According to D. Schötz[7] the person presenting the offering would lay one hand on the head of the animal and slaughter it with the other, but there is no evidence of this. Such an interpretation deprives the *s^{e}mîkâ(h)* of all meaning, and it leads one to ask why the lawgiver, who deals with everything as briefly as possible, even makes mention of this,

---

[7]*Schuld—und Sündopfer im Alten Testament* (1930), p. 58.

and why he moreover did not rather use the Hebrew verb *śûm* (cf. Gen. 48:18).[8]

It appears from Numbers 8:10, 12; 27:18, 23 and Deuteronomy 34:9 that the purpose of the laying on of hands was nothing other than to transfer the spiritual qualities of the performer to the recipient of the act. In the assumption of office, the successor thereby was given what had constituted the official being of his predecessor. Through this act, therefore, the sacrificial animal received that which had induced the person to present it as an offering, viz., his impurity and sin. The laying on of hands in a sense made the animal into the successor of the person who presented it. It came to stand in his place, so that when the life or ''soul'' of the sacrificial animal was poured out with its flowing blood and sank into death, it was just as if the soul of the person who brought it departed from him and likewise died away. The idea that comes to expression in the laying on of hands is thus that of substitution (see Lev. 16:21–22; 24:14 and the comments on these verses).[9] Since the sacrificial animal was burdened with that which had aroused the Lord's anger (i.e., the resistance of His holy nature to everything that was contrary to it) and thus led the Israelite to present it as a burnt offering, the relationship of this individual to the God of the covenant was transformed. The Lord's anger made way for His favor, along with everything that accompanied this, and the presenting of this animal to which the person's sinful spiritual qualities had been transferred thus made atonement for him.

The Hebrew verb *kipper,* which I have translated as ''make atonement'' in accordance with the example of the Greek translation, actually means something different from what is expressed by the word atonement. If I understand it correctly, *kipper* contains the idea of cleansing by means of sweeping away.[10] Sin is regarded as a material contamination[11] that becomes attached to a person and must be removed either by wiping away *(kipper),* by washing *(kibbēs*—to clean clothes by means of wringing, Ps. 51:2), or by rubbing *(māḥâ[h]).* The ''wiping away'' was enacted by God, and at least in the Torah it proceeded through the mediation of the priest, who with the aid of the life-giving blood removed the sinful deed from

---

[8]The fact that this *sᵉmîḵâ(h)* is not present in the offering of doves or pigeons (Lev. 1:14–17; 5:7–10) is due to the nature of these animals. Its absence in the guilt offering (7:1–10) is readily explained by the fact that this offering was first of all understood as a penalty.

[9]This idea of substitution is also found among the peoples of the Tigris-Euphrates plain. See P. Dhorme, *La religion assyro-babylonienne* (1910), pp. 272f.

[10]See also J. Herrmann, *Die Idee der Sühne im Alten Testament* (1905).

[11]See Publisher's Note.

before the Lord's eyes. In the Psalms and Prophets, however, the priest receded completely into the background and the Lord granted atonement without priestly intercession (Pss. 65:3; 78:38; 79:9; Jer. 18:23; Ezek. 16:63). As a result of this, the Lord no longer saw the sinful deed, for it had ceased to exist for Him. To use the words that the Heidelberg Catechism (Lord's Day 23) uses in view of the perfect offering of Christ, God looks on the sinner "as if [he] had never had nor committed any sin."[12]

1:5 *"'He is to slaughter the young bull before the Lord, and then Aaron's sons the priests shall bring the blood and sprinkle it against the altar on all sides at the entrance to the Tent of Meeting.'"*

Once the sacrificial animal had assumed the place of the offerer by way of the laying on of hands, it could then be slaughtered (the *šᵉḥîṭâ[h]* of the Jews was a later development). This likewise was done "before the Lord," i.e., directly by the altar of burnt offering (cf. Exod. 29:11; Lev. 4:4). The verse does not state on which side of the altar this was, but in all likelihood it was the north side (see v. 11). Here it is first said that the animal was to be young, and the Hebrew expression that is used here, *ben-bāqār,* is the same as appears in Genesis 18:7–8; Leviticus 9:2; Numbers 29:2, 8; and Deuteronomy 21:3. Genesis 15:9 seems to indicate that only three-year-old animals, which were thus in their full strength, could be presented, but Leviticus 22:27 states that an animal as young as eight days was acceptable as an offering.

The slaughtering was carried out by the person bringing the offering, as is indicated in so many words in Leviticus 4:15. It lay in the nature of the case, however, that the offerer in this offering availed himself of the necessary help of the Levites or priests. There can nevertheless be no doubt that it became the prevailing tendency to turn the slaughtering of the sacrificial animals into a specific task of those who served at the temple. This appears not only in 1 Chronicles 23:31, but also in 2 Chronicles 29:34, where it is expressly stated that in the days of King Hezekiah, the skinning of the animals was performed by the priests who, since they were too few in number, received the help of the Levites. In addition, 2 Chronicles 30:17 says that under Hezekiah, the Levites had to kill the Passover lambs "for all those who were not ceremonially clean," and 35:6 states that in the days of Josiah, *all* Passover lambs were slaughtered by the Levites. Ezekiel 44:11 further extends this development by directing that

---

[12]Another possible interpretation of *kipper,* which takes its cue from the meaning of the Arabic verb *kfr,* understands the term in the sense of "cover" and then ascribes to it the secondary meaning of "protect."

the Levites "slaughter the burnt offerings and sacrifices for the people."

The following consideration points in this same direction. Whereas the Tent of Meeting had only one courtyard, which as the site of the altar of burnt offering was accessible to every Israelite who wished to present a sacrifice (Exod. 27:9–18), the temple of Solomon, at least in the latter part of the period of the kings, had two courts (2 Kings 21:5; 23:12, the reign of Manasseh). The one in which the altar of burnt offering stood was called the "inner courtyard" (1 Kings 6:36; 7:12; Ezek. 8:16; 10:3; 40:28), and in Jeremiah 19:14; 26:2 (cf. also Ezek. 8:7) it is referred to simply as the "court" or "courtyard" of the Lord's temple. The second courtyard, which enclosed both temple and palace, is designated the "great courtyard" in 1 Kings 7:9, 12 (2 Chron. 4:9, "large court"; cf. 1 Kings 7:8 in RSV, the "other court"), while in Ezekiel 10:5; 40:17, 31 it is called the "outer court," in Ezekiel 40:18 the "lower pavement," and in 2 Chronicles 20:5 the "new courtyard." The temple courtyard is referred to in 2 Chronicles 4:9 as the "courtyard of the priests," and it appears in Ezekiel 44:17–27 that the holy place was considered to begin with this inner courtyard. Only the priests were allowed to enter, and in going to the outer courtyard they went out to the people. This arrangement inevitably necessitated a complete change in the role of the Israelites in presenting their offerings, with both the slaughtering and skinning of the animal being added to the task of those who served at the temple. It is thus not surprising that the Greek translators and in some places also the Samaritan text changed the singular pronoun of the Masoretic text to the plural form (e.g., vv. 6, 9, 11, 13), for they understood these verses to be speaking of the priests.

When the animal was slaughtered, the priests were directed to "bring" the blood, and the Hebrew term used here *(hiqrîḇ)* is the same as used in verses 2 and 3 applying to the offering as a whole, indicating that the blood formed part of the offering. According to Leviticus 17:11, this blood belonged "on the altar," for it was the blood that contained the soul, or life, of the animal, and in the offering, soul was substituted for soul, or life for life.

Concerning this blood ritual in the burnt offering, it is to be noted that the priests were directed to "sprinkle *(zāraq)* it against the altar on all sides," and this indicates that a fair quantity was involved. This same expression appears in Leviticus 1:11; 3:2, 8, 13; 9:18 in connection with the burnt offering and fellowship offering, and in 7:2 in connection with the guilt offering. The procedure here differs from the sprinkling *(hizzâ[h])* with the finger spoken of in the sin offering (4:6, 17), which was usually followed by putting *(nāṯan)* some of the blood on the horns of the altar.

35

The latter practice involved only a minimal amount of blood, this being related to the character of the sin offering. The sprinkling in the burnt and fellowship offerings was done with a sprinkling bowl *(mizrāq),* which the priest swung back and forth in such a manner that a small portion of the blood spilled out at every turn.[13]

1:6 *"'He is to skin the burnt offering and cut it into pieces.'"*

In the skinning of the animal, which forms the next part of the ritual, the person bringing the offering once again was to become active. The skin, which naturally was not eaten by the people, could for that reason also not be offered to the Deity, and according to Leviticus 7:8 it belonged to the portion of the priest. The animal was thereupon cut into pieces, and in this it clearly appears that the idea of a meal presented to God continued to play a role. It is not sufficient that the animal was merely to be placed on the altar for burning, for it was first to be arranged in pieces there (see also v. 8), just as it was served at a family meal. According to Jewish tradition, ten pieces were prescribed. In connection with Genesis 15:10–20, Hertz interprets this as a symbolic procedure in which the flame passed between the pieces as in the establishment of the covenant with Abraham, but I have to disagree with this interpretation.

1:7 *"'The sons of Aaron the priest are to put fire on the altar and arrange wood on the fire.'"*

The priests now again assumed the leading role, for they were here directed to put fire on the altar and arrange wood on it. What this means is not completely clear, for according to Leviticus 6:9 the altar fire was to be kept up and never allowed to go out, but the intention may well be that the flames were to be stirred up so that the offering would be consumed quickly. This altar fire became a serious concern of the Jewish tradition.[14] Beyond this, I shall only note that the fire hearth measured 36 square meters, and this meant that there could be more than one pile of wood if necessary. First Kings 8:64 even states that, when this hearth was not sufficient for the offerings, an auxiliary fire could be made in the courtyard.

1:8 *"'Then Aaron's sons the priests shall arrange the pieces, including the head and the fat, on the burning wood that is on the altar.'"*

---

[13]Concerning this sprinkling *(z^{e}rîqâ[h]),* see H. W. Wiener, *The Altars,* p. 4.
[14]See D. Hoffmann, *Das Buch Leviticus,* vol. I, pp. 53f.

Once everything had been made ready in this manner, "the pieces, including the head and the fat," were to be arranged on the altar. The Masoretic text has here "the pieces, [viz.] the head and the fat," as if these latter two were equivalent to "the pieces." This cannot be, however, for verse 9 speaks also of the "inner parts and the legs," and what was to be burned on the fire is then summed up as "all of it." If the Masoretic text of verse 8 were correct, a large portion of the animal would not be placed on the altar, but this would conflict with the idea of the burnt offering (see also v. 12). For this reason, my reading of this verse[15] follows a group of seven Hebrew manuscripts and also the Samaritan text, the Septuagint, and the Peshitta. It is indeed completely understandable that the head and the fat should be mentioned separately. The head was removed immediately in the act of slaughtering, and the fat that is spoken of here (*peḏer,* the same word appears also in v. 12 and 8:20) is in all likelihood the fat that surrounded the inner parts (Exod. 29:13, 22; Lev. 3:3). Since these inner parts were dealt with separately (v. 9), it is only natural that the fat also was set apart before the cutting up of the animal began. The verb "arrange" (*'āraḵ*) in this verse once again calls to mind the idea of a meal (cf. the use of *'āraḵ* in Pss. 23:5; 78:19; Prov. 9:2; Ezek. 23:41).

1:9 *"'He is to wash the inner parts and the legs with water, and the priest is to burn all of it on the altar. It is a burnt offering, an offering made by fire, an aroma pleasing to the Lord.'"*

The task of the person bringing the offering had not yet come to an end, for the inner parts (those of the belly, not the breast—thus the Hebrew term *qereḇ*) and the legs were to be washed. This was necessary because these inner parts were made unclean by the presence of undigested food, and the legs by their constant contact with the ground.[16] The direction that this washing be done in water (cf., Exod. 29:17) indicates that it was to be thorough, for all impurity had to be removed. According to the Masoretic text, this was done by the offerer, but the Samaritan text and the Septuagint use the plural form of the verb and thus had the priests in mind. Flavius Josephus (*Antiquities,* III 9, 1) says the same thing in so many words, but this practice in fact only arose later (see discussion of v. 5).

After the inner parts and the legs had been added to the other parts of the

---

[15]The author's reading is similar to NIV.

[16]Compare with this the command that one's sandals were to be removed when standing on holy ground (Exod. 3:5; Josh. 5:15). When entering a mosque it is still necessary to wear slippers.

animal, the priest was to burn "all of it"[17] in the fire on the altar. It may be noted first of all that this verse speaks solely of "the priest," whereas verses 5 and 7–8 refer to "Aaron's sons the priests." This may be related to the fact that, according to Leviticus 7:8, the hide of the animal was given to the priest who made the offering. In addition, it is significant that the Hebrew verb for "burn" here is *hiqtîr* and not *śārap*, for these two were not identical in meaning. The term *śārap* was used when larger or smaller parts of sacrificial animals were destroyed by fire outside of the camp (Lev. 4:12, 21; 6:23; 8:17; 9:11; 10:16; also Exod. 29:14; Ezek. 43:21), and it was applied to burning on the altar exclusively when the reference was to child sacrifice (Deut. 12:31; 2 Kings 17:31; Jer. 7:31) or the incineration of human bones (2 Kings 23:16; 2 Chron. 34:5). The Hebrew *hiqtîr*, in contrast, refers to a ritual burning in honor of the Lord. It apparently involved a large amount of smoke, as was also the case with incense *(qᵉtōret)*, and this smoke was said to form "an aroma pleasing to the LORD." This translation is not completely correct, for the *nîhô(a)h* (from the stem *nû[a]h*—"to rest") refers more to an appeasement or satisfaction of God's anger. Apart from Leviticus 4:31, the term is not used in connection with the sin offering, for this was brought in the event of an unintentional transgression of the Lord's law and thus could not have the character of something which, in being offered to the Lord, was as such pleasing to Him. The expression also is not used of the guilt offering, for this was presented when one had violated something that was the Lord's property, and it was thus tantamount to the payment of a debt (see Lev. 5:14–19). The word *nîhô(a)h* occurs only in connection with the other offerings. The Greek form of this expression is used in Ephesians 5:2, where Paul applies it to the offering of Christ, and it is also alluded to in Philippians 4:18 and Hebrews 13:16.

The expression contains a strong anthropomorphism, for the idea that God smells an offering (see Gen. 8:21) attributes to Him a type of physical pleasure. The Babylonian flood story implies that this conception prevailed in that nation, for it is said there that the gods approached "like flies" from all sides when they first smelled an offering.[18] The idea of God smelling an offering was also known to David, as can be seen in 1 Samuel 26:19 (the Heb. for NIV "accept an offering" literally means "smell an offering," see NASB margin), and it must thus have had wide acceptance. This is not surprising, however, for Israel was and remained a Semitic people in its thinking.

---

[17]Exactly which pieces were involved in this is discussed in the Mishnah tractate, *Yoma* 2, 3f.

[18]See my book, *Gods Woord,* p. 178.

The translation of this verse speaks of an "offering made by fire," although strictly speaking this is not correct and is retained only because of the lack of a better alternative. The Hebrew term used here *'iššê(h)*, has nothing to do with fire (*'ēš*), but rather marks the offering as a means of reestablishing a right relationship with God.

B. *Burnt offerings from the flock* (1:10–13)

1:10–13 *"'If the offering is a burnt offering from the flock, from either the sheep or the goats, he is to offer a male without defect. He is to slaughter it at the north side of the altar before the LORD, and Aaron's sons the priests shall sprinkle its blood against the altar on all sides. He is to cut it into pieces, and the priest shall arrange them, including the head and the fat, on the burning wood that is on the altar. He is to wash the inner parts and the legs with water, and the priest is to bring all of it and burn it on the altar. It is a burnt offering, an offering made by fire, an aroma pleasing to the LORD.'"*

Only two types of domestic animal from the flock could be used in the burnt offering: sheep or goats. These again could only be male, and they were also subject to the requirement that they be "without defect" (cf. v. 3). It is here stated that the animal was to be slaughtered "at the north side of the altar," and although verse 5 does not expressly say this, this must also have been the case with burnt offerings from the herd. The north side of the altar was also intended as the site of slaughtering certain sin offerings (Lev. 4:24, 29, 33; 6:25), in the guilt offering (7:2), and in the offering performed in the ceremonial cleansing (14:13).[19] To explain this, some have attempted to relate it to the mountain of the gods in the far north[20] or to the aurora borealis and the former northern dwelling place of the earliest peoples.[21] It seems to me much more likely, however, that this is to be understood in connection with the ancient practice of having the tent open toward the east, as was also the case with temples. If an offering was made by the tent, the animal was placed so that its head was to the south and its face was turned to the west, and it thus lay on the north side of the tent. In addition, the fact that the ashes were thrown on the east side of the altar (Lev. 1:16), the wash basin was placed to the west of it (Exod. 30:18), and the ascent to the altar was built on its southern side, was also probably related to this ancient custom.[22]

---

[19]For the fellowship offering, see Leviticus 3:2.
[20]Baentsch, see also Isaiah 14:13.
[21]König, *Geschichte der Alttestamentlichen Religion*[3], p. 449.
[22]See Flavius Josephus, *War* V 5, 6; also the Mishnah tractate, *Middoth* 3, 3 and the Talmud tractate, *Zebahim* 53a, 62b.

For the rest, the procedure was the same as that in burnt offerings from the herd. The person presenting the offering slaughtered the animal, cut it into pieces, and washed the inner parts and the legs. The priests sprinkled the blood and arranged the pieces on the wood on the altar, and then "the priest"—here again the singular is used, for the same reason as in verse 9—burned "all of it" on the altar fire. The laying on of hands is not mentioned in this connection, but this doubtless also took place in burnt offerings from the flock, since the matter of substitution could in no way have depended on the size of the animal. It is also not stated here to whom the hide of the animal belonged. The lawgiver was thus not at all concerned with giving a complete list of the steps in the ritual, for he merely presupposed what was known from customary usage. Strong emphasis is placed on only one element in the procedure: "it is a burnt offering, an offering made by fire," i.e., the sacrificial animal was to be burned in its entirety if it was to form "an aroma pleasing to the LORD." Only in this manner could the intention of the Israelite bringing the offering be brought to light, so that soul was substituted for soul, life for life.

C. *Burnt offerings of birds* (1:14–17)

1:14–17 "*'If the offering to the* LORD *is a burnt offering of birds, he is to offer a dove or a young pigeon. The priest shall bring it to the altar, wring off the head and burn it on the altar; its blood shall be drained out on the side of the altar. He is to remove the crop with its contents and throw it to the east side of the altar, where the ashes are. He shall tear it open by the wings, not severing it completely, and then the priest shall burn it on the wood that is on the fire on the altar. It is a burnt offering, an offering made by fire, an aroma pleasing to the* LORD.*'*"

According to Leviticus 5:7; 12:8; 14:21–22, 30, the possibility of using birds in the offerings was presented as a concession to the poor (see also, however, Lev. 15:14, 29; Num. 6:10), and the Mishnah tractate *Menahoth* 110a correctly states this intention: "It matters not whether one gives much or little, so long as he directs his heart to heaven." Only from those to whom much had been given could much be required. It could be expected, however, that in Israel an offering of birds would constitute an exception, and this is indicated by the fact that this possibility is not mentioned in verse 2. The only birds that could be used in such an offering were the dove and the pigeon. For the Semitic person in general, the offering of doves must have been regarded as an abomination, for this bird was the sacred animal of the fertility goddess, Ishtar-Astarte.

For obvious reasons, no requirement was made here with respect to the gender of the animal. Doves and pigeons were both bred in Palestine (cf.

2 Kings 6:25 in RSV and in NIV margin; Song of Songs 2:12) and they thus satisfied the demand that offerings be made only of domesticated animals. The person presenting the offering receded entirely into the background in this context, however, for only the priest played an active role. The latter took the bird and "wrung off" its head. It appears from Leviticus 5:8 that this was done at the neck, and from that verse we see that the head was not completely severed from the neck; in our text, since the head was to be burned on the altar, we see that the head was severed. The blood of the bird was subsequently to be drained out on the side of the altar, for with a dove or pigeon there could naturally be no thought of sprinkling the blood. The "crop with its contents," which in the bird has the same function as the inner parts in the animals discussed above, was then removed and thrown to the east side of the altar. The translation "with its contents," which is based on the Targum, is not completely certain, for the Hebrew term in question does not appear elsewhere. The Septuagint and Vulgate translate this term as "with its feathers" (cf. this verse in KJV and RSV), thus taking it to be the same word that appears in Job 39:13 and Ezekiel 17:3, 7, but they thereby overlook the fact that the verse would then be speaking exclusively of the crop feathers and that this would present a new difficulty. I have thus opted for the translation "contents," and further support for this lies in the fact that the use of the singular pronoun in verse 16 (*'otâ[h]*, "and throw *it*") indicates that the two parts mentioned constitute a single whole. The crop and its contents were thus thrown to the east side of the altar, "where the ashes are," this being done because it was unclean (see above). In this connection, it is to be noted that the reference here is not to the wood ash from the altar, but rather to the ashes from the fat that were left behind after the burning of the animal (see also Lev. 4:12; 6:10–11).

Only after these steps had been taken could the offering proper be presented. In this context there could naturally be no cutting of the animal into pieces, as is spoken of in verses 6 and 12. The only thing that points in this direction was the tearing open of the bird by its wings, but it is expressly stated that these were not to be severed completely (cf. Gen. 15:10). The bird was then placed in its entirety on the altar, with only the unclean parts having been removed from it. Only by way of this procedure could birds presented as burnt offerings form "an aroma pleasing to the LORD," i.e., only thus could they appease the Lord's anger.

Regardless of what animal was brought, the burnt offering in Israel was centered in two main elements: the pouring out of the blood, and the consumption of the animal in the altar fire. The Israelites naturally understood the close connection that exists between blood and life. The flowing away of one's blood is equivalent to the departure of life and the cessation of existence as a living soul. It is for this reason that Leviticus 17:11 declares that "the life of a creature is in the blood," and this also explains the prohibition of Genesis 9:4 against eating meat "that has its lifeblood still in it" and the statement in Deuteronomy 12:23 that "the blood is the life." Since the laying on of hands symbolized the act of substitution, in pouring out the animal's blood the offerer was presenting his life, or soul, to God.

It must be remembered here that the Israelite concept of the soul did not correspond to our view of this as the spiritual side of a person. In their understanding, the human being does not *have* a soul, but rather *is* a soul, and this soul has two sides: visible and invisible. The latter side is a person's life, whereas the former is the physical body. Because humans stand guilty in the totality of their existence, it is not sufficient that the life-giving blood be poured out, for the physical body must also be given over to death. It was the *entire* person, and thus also the *entire* animal, which like the person is a living soul (see Gen. 1:20–21; 9:10, 12; Lev. 11:10), that was to enter into the offering. Only those parts of the animal that were by nature unclean and for this reason did not belong on the altar were removed.

2. The Grain Offering (2:1–16)

A. Grain offerings of flour[23] (2:1–3)

2:1–3 *" "When someone brings a grain offering to the LORD, his offering is to be of fine flour. He is to pour oil on it, put incense on it and take it to Aaron's sons the priests. The priest shall take a handful of the fine flour and oil, together with all the incense, and burn this as a memorial portion on the altar, an offering made by fire, an aroma pleasing to the LORD. The rest of the grain offering belongs to Aaron and his sons; it is a most holy part of the offerings made to the LORD by fire.'"*

Two types of grain offering *(minḥâ[h])* were presented in Israel: those that were made independently, and those that formed a part of bloody offerings. The latter was the case in the daily offering of the community (Num. 28:3–8), in the offerings on feast days (Lev. 23:12–13; Num. 28:9–10), in the burnt offering presented for atonement in the case of an unintentional transgression committed by the entire community (Num. 15:24), in the offering that concluded one's period of separation as a Nazirite (Num. 6:14–15), in the ordination offering of the priests (Lev. 8:26–28), and also in offerings of thanksgiving (Lev. 7:11–14) and certain burnt offerings and sacrifices (Num. 15:1–16).

---

[23]NIV, "fine flour."

Leviticus 2, however, which has an introductory formula (v. 1) that is approximately the same as those in 4:2 and 5:1 and differs from those in 1:2 and 3:1, speaks exclusively of grain offerings that were made independently. Offerings of this type, which appear also in Leviticus 5:11–12; 6:14–23; and Numbers 5:15, play only a subordinate role in the law, and this is completely understandable, since the procuring of atonement through the shedding of blood occupies the prominent position in the cult. For this reason, the Talmud allowed only a very poor person to replace an animal offering with a grain offering: "Whose custom is it to voluntarily bring an offering of flour? The poor man's. The Holy One—praised be He—declares: 'I account it to him as if he had brought his own soul as an offering'" (*Menahoth* 104b). This latter statement was made because verse 1 here does not read *'āḏām kî* ("a man, when he . . .") as in 1:2, but rather *nepeš kî* ("a soul [living being], when he . . ."), a phrase that appears also in 4:2; 5:1, 4, 15; 6:2 (MT 5:21). The statement is of course not completely correct, for according to Leviticus 5:11, it was only in the sin offering that a very poor person was permitted to replace the sacrificial animal with groats or raw meal from the inner kernel of the grain (*sōleṯ*), which was formerly incorrectly taken to be flour or fine flour and is to be distinguished from *gemah,* the flour that easily passed through the sieve.

A *minḥâ(h)* was a gift that one would give to a person placed above him in order to win his favor. Jacob sent such a *minḥâ(h)* to Esau (Gen. 32:13), foreign kings sent them to Solomon (1 Kings 10:25), and Ben-Hadad sent one to Elisha (2 Kings 8:8). It was thus a present that always contained an acknowledgment of the recipient's superiority. A *minḥâ(h)* could also be presented to a deity as a sacrificial gift, and it could in this case be either bloody or bloodless (Gen. 4:3–4; 1 Sam. 2:17; 26:19; etc.). In the law, however, *minḥâ(h)* was used exclusively in reference to bloodless offerings and thus signified the grain offering, and this meaning then also passed into general usage (e.g., Josh. 22:23; Judg. 13:19–23; 2 Kings 16:13).

The main ingredient of a *minḥâ(h)* consisted of raw meal,[24] this being made from wheat according to Exodus 29:2. To this was added oil, which the Israelites regarded as having a vivifying and sanctifying power (thus the use of anointing oil), and also incense, the aroma of fragrant spices which in the East was also highly valued in domestic life (Exod. 30:34–35). After the Israelite had prepared his *minḥâ(h)* by mixing together the meal and oil and adding to this the incense, he brought it to the priest. The priest then took the incense along with a handful of the meal mixed with oil and threw

---

[24]The author translates *sōleṯ* as "raw meal," whereas the NIV has "fine flour." "Raw meal" will always appear in this commentary where the NIV has "fine flour."

it on the altar fire. This portion of the *minḥâ(h)* was designated the *'az-kārâ(h)*, probably because the name of the Lord was called on when it was offered (cf. Exod. 20:24, where the verb related to this Hebrew term is used). The King James Version translates this term as "memorial," since the related verb *hizqîr* can mean "to cause to be remembered," and because of the lack of something better this word has been retained. It appears in Isaiah 48:1 and Amos 6:10, however, that "cause to be remembered" can in the context of cultic life mean "pronounce the name of the Lord," and in Exodus 23:13 this implies that He is honored and served as the only God. In the Revised Standard Version the superscriptions of Psalms 38 and 70[25] indicate that—perhaps at least in later times—one of these psalms was sung at the bringing of such an *'az-kārâ(h)*, and it thus does not seem impossible to me that *'azkārâ(h)* could express the fact that the sacrificial procedure was to be accompanied by a specific liturgical utterance. According to the Jewish exegetes Rashi and Ibn Ezra, it was called *'azkārâ(h)* because at the ascending of the offering God remembered *(zāḵar)* the person who presented it, but this is pure folk etymology.[26]

The portion of the meal mixed with oil that was not burned was given to the priests as the "most holy part of the offerings made to the LORD by fire." This latter phrase implies that there was a certain gradation of degrees of holiness. There were portions of offerings that could be eaten not only by the priest, but also by members of his family if they were ceremonially clean, and such portions could thus be taken outside of the temple, although the place where they were eaten was naturally also to be clean (Lev. 10:14). These portions were simply called "holy," for they formed part of an offering. Other sacrificial portions were designated "most holy" (literally, "holiness of holiness"), however, and these could not be taken out of the sanctuary. They were to be eaten exclusively by the priests themselves in the courtyard of the tabernacle or temple (Lev. 6:16, 26; 10:12–13). That which was "most holy," which included also the sin offering (Lev. 6:25) and guilt offering (7:1), the bread of the Presence (24:9), and the offering of fragrant incense (Exod. 30:36), had to remain within the small circle of those who, so to speak, stood closest to God.

---

[25]The KJV has, less correctly, "to bring to remembrance," while the NIV has simply "a petition."

[26]The translation "fragrance offering," which König offers in *Lehrgebäude* II, 181 on the supposition that the term is related to the burning of incense, is in any case incorrect, for Leviticus 5:12 and Numbers 5:26 speak of an *'azkārâ(h)* without incense. See also König's *Theologie des Alten Testaments*, p. 296, note 4.

B. *Cooked grain offerings* (2:4–10)

2:4–10 *" 'If you bring a grain offering baked in an oven, it is to consist of fine flour: cakes made without yeast and mixed with oil, or wafers made without yeast and spread with oil. If your grain offering is prepared on a griddle, it is to be made of fine flour mixed with oil, and without yeast. Crumble it and pour oil on it; it is a grain offering. If your grain offering is cooked in a pan, it is to be made of fine flour and oil. Bring the grain offering made of these things to the LORD; present it to the priest, who shall take it to the altar. He shall take out the memorial portion from the grain offering and burn it on the altar as an offering made by fire, an aroma pleasing to the LORD. The rest of the grain offering belongs to Aaron and his sons; it is a most holy part of the offerings made to the LORD by fire.' "*

Verse 4, in which a change is made from the third person of verses 1–3 to the second person singular (in vv. 14–16 the second person plural is used), states that a *minhâ(h)* could also be brought in cooked form. Grain offerings baked in an oven could have the form of either *hallôt,* ring-shaped cakes of bread made from raw meal, which was mixed with oil before being baked, or of *reqîqîm,* a type of thin wafer or pancake that was spread with oil after baking. The baked product of course could contain no yeast, for this would effect a change in the character of its ingredients. Fermentation, which is caused by yeast, would call to mind the process of decomposition or decay.

Four types of cooked grain offering are mentioned in these verses. Verse 4 speaks in the first place of two that were baked in an oven *(tannûr),* a clay cylinder that narrowed toward the top, in which the flat cakes of bread were pressed against the inner wall. Verse 5 speaks of a grain offering prepared on a griddle *(mahăbat),* a utensil that some regard as a pan without a rim, while others think it was a flat pan that rested above the fire on three stones. Last, verse 7 speaks of one cooked in a pan *(marhešet),* which was probably a deep vessel with a lid. In all of these cases, it was required that the grain offering be made of unleavened raw meal that was either mixed or spread with oil. Incense was not spoken of in this connection, but it is apparent from verse 2 that its presence was tacitly assumed. In verse 7 it is directed that the grain offering cooked on a griddle be crumbled into pieces, but why this was required only in this form of the offering is not clear to me. It would be difficult to regard this as a parallel to the cutting apart of the sacrificial animals, for then it would be required that the other cooked offerings also be broken into pieces. The rabbis later specified that these pieces could not be smaller than an olive (*Menahoth* 75b).

After the Israelite had presented his cooked grain offering to the priest, the priest was to bring it to the altar in order to offer a portion of it to the Lord as an *'azkārâ(h)*. According to tradition, this was done on the south side of the altar.

C. *General requirements* (2:11–13)

2:11–13 *"'Every grain offering you bring to the LORD must be made without yeast, for you are not to burn any yeast or honey in an offering made to the LORD by fire. You may bring them to the LORD as an offering of the firstfruits, but they are not to be offered on the altar as a pleasing aroma. Season all your grain offerings with salt. Do not leave the salt of the covenant of your God out of your grain offerings; add salt to all your offerings.'"*

These are regulations that applied to all grain offerings, and in part even to all of the offerings in general. First of all, the use of yeast was strictly forbidden. That which was leavened had no place on the altar (Exod. 23:18), although it is evident from the mockery of Amos (Amos 4:5) that this was later forgotten due to heathen influence. For this reason, the leavened loaves of bread that were to be presented at the Feast of Weeks were given in their entirety to the priest (Lev. 23:17), and the leavened bread that formed a part of the fellowship offering was eaten by the person who presented it (Lev. 7:13). Although honey was revered in the Tigris–Euphrates plain as a food of the gods, this also could not be added to the grain offering—not because Israel had to be delivered from the idea that the offering served as food for the Lord (Maimonides' explanation), but rather because the fruit or date honey intended here could easily cause fermentation, and thus, spoiling. Like yeast, however, honey could form part of the offering of firstfruits (Lev. 23:17; Num. 18:12–13; 2 Chron. 31:5).

Neither yeast nor honey[27] were thus allowed, but offerings could include salt, which besides its preservative powers also made the cooked offering more palatable. In addition to this, salt had a symbolic significance in the Near East. A guest would bring salt with him, for to eat salt together was a demonstration of friendship, and those who had "salt between them" were called to help one another. A "covenant of salt" was thus indissoluble (Num. 18:19). Ezekiel was later to prescribe the use of salt in bloody offerings (Ezek. 43:24), and the rabbis urged the eating of bread dipped in salt at the beginning of a meal by observing that the table had the holiness of the altar.

---

[27] It may be noted in addition to this that the Old Testament nowhere speaks of offerings of milk or of anything prepared from it, even though these would be important foods among a cattle-raising people. This must have been related to the fact that milk turns sour so easily.

D. *Grain offerings of firstfruits* (2:14–16)

2:14–16 *"'If you bring a grain offering of firstfruits to the LORD, offer crushed heads of new grain roasted in the fire. Put oil and incense on it; it is a grain offering. The priest shall burn the memorial portion of the crushed grain and the oil, together with all the incense, as an offering made to the LORD by fire.'"*

A third type of *minḥâ(h)* was the grain offering brought from the first produce of the fruits. Such firstfruits were to be presented to the Lord every year, since He was the owner of the land and the Israelites had only the status of tenants (Lev. 23:9; 25:23; Exod. 22:29; 23:19; 34:26; Deut. 26:1–2).

Here the ears of grain could not be made into meal or baked, but rather had to be brought in the form in which they were eaten, viz., as "crushed [or rubbed, either between the hands or a pair of stones] heads of new grain roasted in the fire" (cf. Lev. 23:14). This offering was naturally also mixed with oil and presented with incense (see discussion on vv. 1–3), and here as well the priest burned a portion of the grain mixed with oil together with all the incense on the altar as an *'azkārâ(h)*. Although this is not mentioned here, the remainder of the offering, because it was an *'azkārâ(h)* and was thus "most holy," was eaten within the sanctuary exclusively by the priest (v. 3).

3. *The Fellowship Offering* (3:1–17)

3:1 *"'If someone's offering is a fellowship offering, and he offers an animal from the herd, whether male or female, he is to present before the LORD an animal without defect.'"*

This chapter, the first verse of which corresponds to 1:3, speaks of the bringing of three types of animal (vv. 1, 6, 12) as *zebaḥ š^elāmîm*, an offering that is also referred to more briefly as *š^elāmîm* (e.g., Num. 15:8; Deut. 27:7), one time as *šelem* (Amos 5:22), and in other places simply as *zebaḥ* (e.g., Deut. 12:27; 18:3, NIV, "sacrifice"). What was distinctive in such a *zebaḥ š^elāmîm* was that it formed part of a sacrificial meal that was thought to be attended not only by the person presenting the offering and his family, but also by the Lord. The Lord served as the host, and when the Israelites presented to Him an animal as their offering, He left to them a portion of it as their meal. The Hebrew name for this offering has been translated in various ways. The Vulgate conceives of it as a "peace offering," as does also the Septuagint in the books of Samuel, Kings, and Proverbs, whereas it elsewhere translates the phrase as "salvation offering." More recent exegetes variously regard it as a pact offering, a payment offering, a deliverance offering, or a thank offering. It seems to me, however, that the *zeḇaḥ šelāmîm* is in actuality a communion or fellowship offering that is based in a special sense on the covenant, and that it is intended to give expression to the continual renewal of the latter. It is thus a sacrificial meal that in more than one respect resembles our sacrament of the Lord's Supper.

In close connection with what René Dussaud[28] has said concerning this, I make the following observations. A *zeḇaḥ* was a sacrificial animal. If it was burned in its entirety, it was referred to as a *zeḇaḥ 'ōlôṯ*, whereas if it was partly burned and partly eaten it was called a *zeḇaḥ šelāmîm*. Such a *zeḇaḥ šelāmîm* culminated in a sacred meal at the "table of the Lord " which served as both a reminder and a renewal of the covenant. Unlike elsewhere in the ancient Eastern world, however, where the deity was thought to be present in a sensuous-magical form, what took place here was a personal-ethical communion with Him whose will was determinative for His people's life. There can also be no thought of a relationship of blood brotherhood here, for this was absolutely ruled out by the all-consuming holiness of the Lord's nature. The idea of a participation in the divine nature, such as the Greek mystery religions speak of, is likewise out of place in this context. To the Israelite mind, the actualization of communion with God in the sacrificial meal depended solely on the Lord's willingness to enter into a special relationship with His people and to allow them to share in His life.

Although the word *šelāmîm* itself remains obscure, it is clear that these offerings gave utterance to the gladness that was evoked in sitting at the same table with the Lord. Alongside the burnt offering, which speaks of complete self-surrender, and the grain offering, which forms, an acknowledgment of absolute dependence, the *šelāmîm* occupies a unique position within the whole of Israel's sacrificial system. It is noteworthy that, in contrast to the burnt offering, female animals could also be presented in this offering (vv. 1, 6, 12). This could well be related to the fact that offering and meal belong together there, and the view that this marks it as a second-rate offering is therefore not necessarily true. In fact, although in freewill offerings exceptions were permitted to the prohibition against animals with defects (Lev. 22:23), this restriction was as binding here (vv. 1, 6) as in the other offerings.

The presenting of such a *zeḇaḥ šelāmîm* appears both on joyful occasions (Gen. 31:54; 1 Sam. 11:15) and during times of distress when the people

---

[28]In *Les découvertes de Ras Shamra (Ugarit) et l'Ancien Testament*, p. 111.

implored the Lord for deliverance (Judg. 20:26; 21:4; 1 Sam. 13:9; 2 Sam. 24:25). For this reason, the proposed translation of *zeḇaḥ šᵉlāmîm* as "thank offering"[29] is not entirely correct. If I understand the term *šᵉlāmîm* correctly in this context, the offering gives expression to either the joyful sharing in or the supplicating aspiration toward the state of being *šālēm*, complete or sound in relation to God and other persons, i.e., toward living in *šālôm* (shalom), which is characterized by harmony and thus also peace (cf. Gen. 34:21; 1 Kings 8:61; 11:4; 15:3, 14 [see KJV]). Further information on the fellowship offering is found in Leviticus 7:11–34. It was one of the most common private offerings, and the rabbis thus also regarded it as the most important, saying that after the Messiah has come and all offerings have been rendered superfluous, the bringing of fellowship offerings would nevertheless continue. When after the destruction of Jerusalem it was no longer possible to present offerings, special prayers of thanksgiving took the place of the fellowship offering.

3:2 *"'He is to lay his hand on the head of his offering and slaughter it at the entrance to the Tent of Meeting. Then Aaron's sons the priests shall sprinkle the blood against the altar on all sides.'"*

After the laying on of hands (as in 1:4) had been performed and the oneness of the Israelite with his offering had thus come to expression (also in vv. 8, 13), the sacrificial animal was slaughtered "at the entrance to the Tent of Meeting," i.e., directly by the altar of burnt offering that stood in the courtyard. The priest was then to sprinkle *(zāraq)* the blood "against the altar on all sides." The use of this blood here corresponds to Moses' action in the establishment of the covenant at Mount Sinai (Exod. 24:6), for blood was the most effective means for producing a oneness of life. It is therefore incorrect to regard this ritual procedure with the blood as a means of atonement that purified the unworthy Israelite so that he could be accepted at the Lord's table. Similar to Exodus 24:6, the blood here rather functions as "blood of the covenant." The object of this *zᵉrîqâ(h)*, the sprinkling of the blood against the altar, was to continually renew the faithful Israelite's awareness of the reality of the close bond by which Israel was joined to the Lord and to cause him to draw his life from this. Although the Wellhausen school has made frequent attempts to ascribe a totemistic character to this covenental sharing of the table, it is clear that the fellowship or thank offering had nothing to do with this. The bond that

---

[29]The author nevertheless does translate this as "thank offering." The NIV has "fellowship offering," a translation that is supported by much of what the author brings to light (see above), and this name has thus been substituted for "thank offering" throughout this commentary.

was established here was not physical, but was rather the product of a free act of grace made by the Lord.

3:3–5 *" "From the fellowship offering he is to bring a sacrifice made to the* LORD *by fire: all the fat that covers the inner parts or is connected to them, both kidneys with the fat around them near the loins, and the covering of the liver, which he will remove with the kidneys. Then Aaron's sons are to burn it on the altar on top of the burnt offering that is on the burning wood, as an offering made by fire, an aroma pleasing to the* LORD.' "*

The divine Host was given the fat and kidneys of the animal. The detailed description given here, which presupposes some amount of anatomical knowledge on the part of the priest, reveals what an important role this particular portion of the animal played in the offerings (both in Israel and among other peoples; cf. also vv. 9–10, 14–15). This is not only because the fat was the tastiest item to the Near Eastern palate, but also because it was of decisive importance for the life of the animal. It protected the vital parts of the body, and insofar as it functioned as an energy reserve, it also maintained the animal's life. For this reason, all the fat from the abdominal cavity *(qereḇ)* was brought to the altar, i.e., the "fat that covers the inner parts or is connected to them." The two kidneys with the fat on them were presented as well, as was also the fat near the loins and, last, the "covering of the liver," which may well mean the fat positioned between the liver and the twelve-fingered intestine. These are thus collectively referred to when mention is made of "all the fat" (3:16; 4:8, 19, 26, 31, 35; 7:3), the "fat portions" (8:26; 9:19, 24; 10:15), or simply "the fat" (3:9; 6:12; 7:33; 9:20; 16:25; 17:6). The placing of the kidneys on the altar is explained by the fact that these were thought to be the seat of one's feelings, thoughts, and conscience. It is for this reason that the kidneys and heart are often spoken of together (Pss. 7:9; 26:2; Jer. 17:10; 20:12; NIV generally translates *kᵉlāyôṯ* ["kidneys"] as "heart" and *lēḇ* ["heart"] as "mind").

After the fat had been painstakingly removed, the priest burned it "on top of the burnt offering that is on the burning wood." This thus implies that the morning burnt offering preceded the fellowship offering and had not yet been completely consumed by fire when the fellowship offering was presented (cf. Lev. 6:5). The burnt offering therefore formed the foundation of the fellowship offering. Regarded in the light of future revelation, this means that it is through Christ's surrender of Himself to death on the cross, which is what *all* of Israel's offerings had in view, that harmony and peace *(šālôm)* blossom between God and humankind and the way is opened toward life in communion with Him. In the biblical understanding it was therefore not the meal that was primary, as was the case with the other nations, for this would place the human participants in the center. What rather came first was the offering of life in self-surrender to God and the reconciliation with God that resulted from this. The human participants here did not ascend to God, for it was He who descended to them and occupied the central and sovereign position. The act of eating and rejoicing in the presence of the Lord (Deut. 12:7, 18; 14:23, 26; 15:20; 27:7) could take place only after atonement had been made through the offering, and it then brought to expression the joy and thanksgiving produced by this newly awakened communion with God.[30]

3:6–11 *" 'If he offers an animal from the flock as a fellowship offering to the Lord, he is to offer a male or female without defect. If he offers a lamb, he is to present it before the Lord. He is to lay his hand on the head of his offering and slaughter it in front of the Tent of Meeting. Then Aaron's sons shall sprinkle its blood against the altar on all sides. From the fellowship offering he is to bring a sacrifice made to the Lord by fire: its fat, the entire fat tail cut off close to the backbone, all the fat that covers the inner parts or is connected to them, both kidneys with the fat around them near the loins, and the covering of the liver, which he will remove with the kidneys. The priest shall burn them on the altar as food, an offering made to the Lord by fire.' "*

The procedure was the same if the fellowship offering consisted of an animal from the flock, i.e., a lamb or a goat. With the first of these, the fat tail was expressly mentioned among the fat portions that were to be brought to the altar. To the Near Eastern person, this tail, which could weigh fifteen pounds or more, was a special delicacy, and it was thus often protected by pushing a small cart beneath it. The fat tail was to be cut off "close to the backbone," i.e., it was to be removed and offered in its entirety.

In verse 11, the fat of the offering is not referred to simply as an offering by fire, for the word *food* is also added (see also v. 16; Num. 28:24). The lawgiver repeatedly affirms the fact that offerings were the Lord's food (Lev. 21; 22:25; Num. 28:2; cf. Ezek. 44:7; Mal. 1:7). The Hebrew term used for "food" in these cases is always *leḥem;* and the fact that in this connection the term always has its original meaning of "meat" rather than its later and more common meaning, "bread," forms a proof of how old this expression is. This concept of the offering as the Lord's food speaks clearly of the fellowship of the Host and His guests around the table (cf. Rev. 3:20).

3:12–16a *" 'If his offering is a goat, he is to present it before the Lord. He is to lay his hand on its head and slaughter it in front of the Tent of Meeting. Then Aaron's*

---

[30]See, e.g., E. König, *Geschichte der Alttestamentlichen Religion*[3], pp. 537f.

sons shall sprinkle its blood against the altar on all sides. From what he offers he is to make this offering to the LORD by fire: all the fat that covers the inner parts or is connected to them, both kidneys with the fat on them near the loins, and the covering of the liver, which he will remove with the kidneys. The priest shall burn them on the altar as food, an offering made by fire, a pleasing aroma.'"

A separate paragraph is devoted to the goat. It is not completely clear to me whether the reference is exclusively to the female goat (*'ēz* sometimes refers only to the she-goat), but this seems likely in view of the fact that, in contrast to verses 1 and 6, the words "male or female" are absent here. For the rest, the procedure was the same as with the previous animals. Birds are naturally not spoken of in this context, for an ample meal cannot be prepared from them.

3:16b–17 *"'All the fat is the Lord's. This is a lasting ordinance for the generations to come, wherever you live: You must not eat any fat or any blood.'"*

In verse 16b, what is of particular importance in the fellowship offering is once again clearly stressed, viz., "all the fat is the LORD's"; and in verse 17b this is expanded on in the commandment: "You must not eat any fat or any blood." For the prohibition against eating fat see also Leviticus 7:23–25; for that against eating blood see Leviticus 7:26–27; 17:10; 19:26, and also Genesis 9:4; Deuteronomy 12:16, 23; 15:23; 1 Samuel 14:32–33; Ezekiel 33:25. The reason for these commandments is clear, for "the life of a creature is in the blood," which has been given for making atonement (Lev. 17:11; more briefly, "the blood is the life," Deut. 12:23), and the fat is what sustains life. The soul and life of a creature are God's gift and His possession, and Israel was ever to be mindful of the fact that human beings have no claim on this. The prohibition therefore did not apply merely to the time when Israel would have a temple at which to present offerings, but also to future generations wherever they would dwell. This was called a "lasting ordinance," literally, "eternal," just as the Lord's covenant (Gen. 17:7) and His dominion (Exod. 15:18). All three of these belong inseparably together, for the sovereign dominion of the transcendent God, which comes to expression in the Torah, is crowned by the fact that its ordinances are elevated above the vicissitudes of time.

It can be noted in passing that the conviction that blood and life are most intimately related is also found elsewhere in the Semitic world, and even beyond its borders. The *Enuma Elish,* the Babylonian creation epic, contains the notion that human beings were created from the blood of the gods.[31]

---

[31] See my book, *Gods Woord*[2], pp. 120f.

Among cannabalistic peoples, this conviction led to the drinking of the blood of defeated foes in order to assimilate their vital powers and thereby achieve contact with the invisible world. See also the comments on Leviticus 7:26 and 17:10–14.

Further information concerning the eating of animal fat can be found in the comments on Leviticus 7:23–25. Insofar as this is necessary, it should be pointed out that the prohibition regarding fat applied only to the fat of sacrificial animals, and in these only to those portions that were expressly mentioned. It did not apply to the fat lying within the muscular tissue.

The Second Group of Offerings
(4:1–6:7 [MT 5:26])

These offerings differ from those of the first group in two respects: (1) whereas in the first group the lawgiver proceeded in terms of the assumption that everyone knew what burnt offerings, grain offerings, and fellowship offerings were, in the second group it was necessary to first give a more detailed description of the meaning and purpose of the offerings; (2) whereas the offerings of the first group could always be brought voluntarily, in those of the second group it was necessary that there be a specific cause that made their presentation mandatory (Lev. 4:1, 13, 22, 27; 5:1, 14; 6:2 [MT 5:21]). To my mind, this indicates that these offerings were specifically Israelitic in character. It is for this reason they do not appear in pre-Mosaic times, and also that Job 1:5 and 42:8 speak of burnt offerings where we would expect sin offerings. The school of Wellhausen has claimed that the two offerings in this group did not come into being until the seventh, or perhaps even the sixth or fifth, century B.C., when they took the place of the monetary penalties of the same name spoken of in 2 Kings 12:16. This is in conflict with what the history of religions teaches, however, for monetary penalties in fact often replaced obligatory payments of natural goods. Indeed, Hosea's accusation, "they [the priests] feed on the sins *(ḥaṭṭā't)* of my people" (Hos. 4:8), is a clear allusion to the regulation of Leviticus 6:25–26, which directs that a portion of the sin offering *(ḥaṭṭā't)* was to be eaten by the priest; and Micah 6:7 also alludes to this. Ezekiel speaks of this offering as having been known since ancient times (Ezek. 40:39; 42:13; 43:19; 44:27, 29; 45:17; 46:20). The fact that in the historical writings the sin offering appears only in the later books of Ezra (6:17; 8:35) and Nehemiah (10:33) does not at all mean that the earlier writers had no knowledge of it, but only that the legal terminology did not directly control ordinary usage in Israel. The offerings in general could be summarily referred to by the two Hebrew terms, *'ōlâ(h)* and *zeḇaḥ,* i.e., burnt offerings and sacrifices (Pss. 40:6; 50:8; Isa. 1:11; Jer. 7:21–22;

Hos. 6:6), and *zebaḥ* and *minḥâ(h)* could be used as collective names for bloody and bloodless offerings, respectively (1 Sam. 2:29; 3:14; Ps. 40:6). This is the reason why 1 Kings 18:29, 36 and 2 Kings 3:20 use the Hebrew term for "grain offering" *(minḥâ[h])* when "burnt offerings" would be expected. Further evidence against the Wellhausen theory lies in the fact that Leviticus 4:22 does not speak of the sin of a king, but of a chief or sheik. This indicates the antiquity of the sin offering, as does also the fact that chapter 4 assumes as a matter of course that the person who presents the offering slaughters the animal himself (vv. 15, 24, 29, 33).

1. *The Sin Offering* (4:1–5:13)

4:1–2 *The Lord said to Moses, "Say to the Israelites: 'When anyone sins unintentionally and does what is forbidden in any of the Lord's commands–'"*

Chapter 4 begins the discussion of the offerings that were more particularly directed toward the procuring of atonement. The regulations that applied to these offerings are found in 4:1–6:7 and 6:24–7:10. Leviticus 4:1–12 speaks of the sin offering of the priest, 4:13–21 of the sin offering of the entire Israelite community, 4:22–26 of that of the tribal leader, and 4:27–5:13 of that of the common individual. The regulations applying to the guilt offering appear in 5:14–6:7 (MT 5:14–26).

The sin offering, which also played a role in the ordination of priests (Exod. 29:10–14; Lev. 8:14–17), is discussed not only in these chapters, but also in Numbers 15:22–31. But whereas in the Numbers passage only two specific cases are distinguished, viz., unintentional sin on the part of either the community as a whole (vv. 22–26) or a single individual (vv. 27–31), Leviticus 4:1–5:13 contains a much more extensive treatment of this offering. No fewer than four possibilities are presented here: the transgression of the high priest (4:1–12), the transgression of the whole Israelite community (4:13–21), that of a tribal chief (4:22–26), and that of an individual member of the community (4:27–35). In the first two cases a young bull was used as a sin offering, and after the rites had been performed with the blood and the fat portions had been offered, the animal was to be burned outside the camp. In contrast, the tribal leader was to offer a male goat and the common Israelite a female goat or lamb, and after the ritual procedures with the blood and fat, these animals were to be eaten by the priests (5:13). Leviticus 5:1–13 adds to this a few more instances of unintentional sin on the part of the individual.

There is a remarkable difference between the laws for the sin offering given in Leviticus and those given in Numbers. Whereas Numbers

15:22–26 directs that, in the case of an unintentional sin on the part of the community, a male goat was to be presented as a sin offering together with a young bull for a burnt offering and the prescribed grain and drink offerings, Leviticus 4:13–21 speaks exclusively of bringing a young bull as a sin offering. And while Numbers 15:27–31 states that a one-year-old female goat was to be brought as a sin offering if such a sin was committed by an individual, Leviticus 4:27–35 allows a choice between a female goat or lamb, with no age requirement being given, and 5:1–13 adds to this still other possibilities.

The rabbis have maintained that Leviticus 4–5 is speaking of sins of commission and Numbers 15 of those of omission. Numbers 15:24 expressly states that something is "done," however, and the contrast that is made here (and is not spoken of elsewhere) between unintentional sinning *(šāḡaḡ)* and that which is done "defiantly" (v. 30, literally, "with a high hand," cf. RSV) indicates that there can be no thought of sins of omission in this context. It is necessary to come to grips once and for all with the fact that Israel's laws and regulations were not absolutely unalterable and that the devout in Israel regarded them with much more latitude than was the case in later Judaism, where the Lord's "instruction" *(tôrâ[h])* was distorted into a mere complex of legal items.[32]

Although in Leviticus 4–5 this contrast between deliberate and unintentional sins is not expressed in the same manner as in Numbers 15, it nevertheless still directs the train of thought here. Emphasis is continually placed on the fact that sin offerings were valid only if the transgression was made unintentionally *(biš°ḡāḡâ[h]*, 4:2, 13, 22, 27), i.e., if the guilty party was "unaware of the matter" (4:13; 5:2–4, literally, "it is hidden from [his, their] eyes," cf. RSV) and was only "made aware of the sin" later (4:14, 23, 28; 5:3–4). It should be added that this lack of awareness or "being hidden" naturally does not mean that the party in question was unconscious of his deed, but only that it did not dawn on him that this deed constituted a sin.[33] For sins committed "defiantly" (Num. 15:30), and thus deliberately, no offering could avail. The guilty person was in this case "cut off from his people," which means not mere banishment from the community, but the death penalty, this being carried out either by the people or by a direct intervention of God.[34]

Not all of the situations in which the sin offering was required are

[32] See my book, *Gods Woord*[2], pp. 326f., and my explanation of 2 Chronicles 29:34; 30:17; 35:5–11; see also the *Introduction,* pp. 17–18.

[33] See also, Dr. N. H. Ridderbos, *"De werkers der ongerechtigheid"* in de individuele *psalmen* (1939), pp. 62f.

[34] See A. Schulz, *Der Sinn des Todes im Alten Testament* (1919), pp. 15–20.

mentioned here, for it was also to be brought in the ceremonies of purification or cleansing after childbirth (12:6, 8), after infectious skin disease (14:10–11, 19), after unclean discharges of both men (15:15) and women (15:30), and after the accidental interruption of the Nazirite vow of separation (Num. 6:11). Lastly, sin offerings also constituted part of the ceremonies on the Day of Atonement (Lev. 16:3, 5, 6, 11, 15, 25, 27; Num. 29:11), the Feast of Weeks (Lev. 23:19), the Passover (Num. 28:22), the day of firstfruits (Num. 28:30), and the Feast of Tabernacles (Num. 29:16, 19). The sin offering was distinguished from all other offerings by the particular procedure that took place with the blood: it was either spread exclusively on the horns of the altar of burnt offering (Lev. 4:25, 30, 34; 8:15; 9:9), or it was sprinkled *(hizzâ[h])* within the sanctuary (4:6, 17; 16:14).

One general observation may yet be made. It is standard practice in modern jurisprudence to distinguish between subjective and objective transgression and to demand that the will to transgress be present if a deed is to constitute a violation. This distinction was not known in ancient times, however, and to the Israelite mind the matter of guilt was not necessarily tied to consciousness and will. It was only the deed as such that was at issue. Sin was thus equivalent to concrete actions that strayed from the goal of life and, as an offense against God, aroused His wrath and therefore demanded atonement. The sole case in which the intent of the offender was weighed in the balance concerned the taking of human life, where a distinction was made between murder and manslaughter (Exod. 21:12–14).

A. *The sin offering of the high priest* (4:3–12)

4:3–12 *" 'If the anointed priest sins, bringing guilt on the people, he must bring to the LORD a young bull without defect as a sin offering for the sin he has committed. He is to present the bull at the entrance to the Tent of Meeting before the LORD. He is to lay his hand on its head and slaughter it before the LORD. Then the anointed priest shall take some of the bull's blood and carry it into the Tent of Meeting. He is to dip his finger into the blood and sprinkle some of it seven times before the LORD, in front of the curtain of the sanctuary. The priest shall then put some of the blood on the horns of the altar of fragrant incense that is before the LORD in the Tent of Meeting. The rest of the bull's blood he shall pour out at the base of the altar of burnt offering at the entrance to the Tent of Meeting. He shall remove all the fat from the bull of the sin offering—the fat that covers the inner parts or is connected to them, both kidneys with the fat on them near the loins, and the covering of the liver, which he will remove with the kidneys—just as the fat is removed from the cow sacrificed as a fellowship offering. Then the priest shall burn them on the altar of* *burnt offering. But the hide of the bull and all its flesh, as well as the head and legs, the inner parts and offal—that is, all the rest of the bull—he must take outside the camp to a place ceremonially clean, where the ashes are thrown, and burn it in a wood fire on the ash heap.' ''*

The first case to be discussed in which the presenting of a sin offering was obligatory relates to the "anointed priest." He is mentioned first because, as the representative of the people before God (Exod. 28:12, 29, 38), he was at all times to manifest the holiness that the Lord required of His people (Lev. 21:10–15). For this reason, his sin carried the greatest weight and brought guilt on the entire community. He is referred to as "the anointed" (vv. 3, 5, 16; 6:22) because he had been consecrated by a full anointing (Exod. 29:7; Lev. 8:12, 30), and he is elsewhere also called the "high priest" (Lev. 21:10; Num. 35:25, 28; Josh. 20:6, literally, "great priest"), and later, the "chief priest" (2 Kings 25:18; 2 Chron. 19:11; 24:11; 26:20; 31:10; Ezra 7:5).

If the high priest sinned by doing "what is forbidden in any of the LORD's commands" (v. 2; cf. Gen. 29:26; 34:7; 2 Sam. 13:12), i.e., if he unintentionally transgressed an express prohibition (cf. Lev. 5:17)—for sins committed "defiantly," and thus deliberately, there was only one penalty, viz., death (Num. 15:30)—he thereby brought guilt on the people. The entire community of Israel shared in his sin, and it appears from Leviticus 10:6 that this applied even to what he did outside the performance of his official duties, for by virtue of his anointing he came to embody all of the powers present in the life of the people.[35]

As his sin offering, he was to present a young bull, the largest of the sacrificial animals (1:3; see also Exod. 29:10, 36; Lev. 8:14–17; 16:11), "at the entrance to the Tent of Meeting before the LORD," who dwelled in the sanctuary. It appears from Leviticus 6:25 that it was the northern entrance that is meant here. This is once again followed by the laying on of hands (1:4), which in this context effects a transference of the sin (cf. 2 Cor. 5:21, "God made him . . . to be sin for us"; also see NIV margin here), and then the slaughtering of the animal. Whereas in the burnt offering the blood was immediately sprinkled "against the altar on all sides" (1:5), in the sin offering the high priest was first to take a portion of the blood into the Holy Place and with his right forefinger (14:16) sprinkle (*hizzâ[h]*, which is to be distinguished from *zāraq*; see under 1:5) it seven times "in front of the curtain of the sanctuary" behind which the ark stood, and which therefore in a very special sense formed the Lord's "dwelling." The blood was sprinkled seven times (v. 6) because to the Semitic mind

---

[35] See R. Dussaud, *Introduction à l'histoire des religions*, pp. 242f.

this was the number of completeness or totality. It may be noted in this connection that as the vehicle of life, the blood was regarded as the preeminent means for endowing this sacred area with the power of life. It was thus in particular used for making the altar with its horns, which formed an expression of God's power, more suitable for the work of atonement (cf. Exod. 29:36–37; Lev. 8:15; 9:9; 16:18; Ezek. 43:18–27).

The high priest was then to turn to the altar of fragrant incense which stood in the Holy Place (Exod. 30:6) and, again with his right forefinger, spread a portion of the blood on its horns, i.e., the pieces that protruded upward at its corners (Exod. 30:2). The blood was placed on the horns, for to the Semitic person these formed a symbol of the Deity, and the breaking of them was thus tantamount to the destruction of the altar (Amos 3:14). The spreading of the blood on the altar of incense not only brought it directly before the Lord, but also served as it were to underscore the plea for atonement, since from this altar ascended the fragrant cloud of incense that formed a symbol of supplication and prayer.

It has long been customary to regard the altar of incense as a subsequent development, and some have maintained that the use of incense was a luxury that arose only later. Such views have been rendered untenable by the facts, however.[36] Concerning the location of this altar, Exodus 30:6 states that it was to be placed "in front of the curtain," i.e., in the Holy Place (see also Exod. 40:5). Some have interpreted Leviticus 16:13 as indicating that the altar stood in the Most Holy Place, but there is no ground for this in the Hebrew text, since the words "before the LORD" belong with "put" *(nāṭan)*. Hebrews 9:2–4 states, however, that the second room of the tabernacle, i.e., the Most Holy Place, contained not only the ark of the covenant, but also the golden altar of incense. It is not clear to me on what basis the author of the Letter to the Hebrews makes this assertion.

When the high priest completed this part of the ritual, he returned to the courtyard, the site of the altar of burnt offering, and poured out all of the remaining blood at the base of the altar (v. 7). This act no longer constituted a part of the ritual of atonement, and it is in no way based on the notion that the blood was thereby given to a subterranean deity or demon. Rather, it was merely a result of the desire to remove the blood that was left over from all human use. This was done only in the sin offering, for it was here in particular that the blood possessed a high degree of holiness (see also 4:18, 25, 30, 34; 8:15; 9:9). Only in the ritual of the Day of Atone-

---

[36]See, e.g., Eerdmans, *Das Buch Leviticus,* pp. 28f. This writer claims, however, that the altar of incense no longer existed after the Exile (pp. 31, 53).

ment is it not stated what was done with the remainder of the blood in the sin offerings.

After the symbolism of the atoning power of the blood had thus been brought to its fullest expression, all the fat from the bull of the sin offering was burned on the altar of burnt offering (vv. 8–10). It was essential that *all* of the fat be burned, just as in the fellowship offering (3:3–5), and for this reason an extensive description of these fat portions is given in verses 8–10. It was solely the fat that was burned here, however, and not the entire animal as in the burnt offering. At the same time, the sin offering was meant to procure forgiveness for the sinner, and not to simultaneously serve as a meal. It was therefore not referred to as the Lord's food (3:11), nor was it followed by any grain or drink offering (see also Num. 15:27–28); and if the sin offering was limited to an offering of meal (Lev. 5:11–13), no oil or incense could be added to it (Num. 5:15).

Lastly, the sacrificial animal was to be destroyed precisely in the form in which it remained after the previous parts of the ritual had been performed (vv. 11–12). The hide was not removed, the inner parts were not washed, and the flesh was not cut into pieces, all of which were done in the burnt offering (1:6–9). The sin offering did not serve as food, neither for the Lord nor for the priest. The sin was as it were materially concentrated on the animal as a physical contamination, and for this reason the bull was to be thrown away and destroyed in its entirety, just as was done with the grain offering of a priest (6:23). It was to be taken away from the sanctuary, which would otherwise be defiled by it, and destroyed by fire. This did not form a part of the ritual act of burning, which is referred to by *hiqṭîr,* "to cause to go up in smoke," for the term used here, *śārap,* is the standard word for the profane process of burning. The burning was done in "a place ceremonially clean," i.e., a place free of ritual impurity, specifically, the ash pile outside of the camp (v. 12). The word *clean* here is no euphemism, as some have contended[37] following P. Haupt (*American-Oriental Society Proceedings,* April 1894, p. 103), for in the ancient Semitic world of thought cleanness and uncleanness were equally dangerous matters.[38] According to Leviticus 6:30, this burning was done only with those sin offerings in which the blood was brought into the sanctuary. Leviticus 6:26, 29 and Numbers 18:9–10 therefore both speak of sin offerings that were eaten by the priests, this taking place within the sanctuary since, like the grain offerings (Lev. 2:3, 10), they were "most holy." The burning was done on a wood fire, which produced the cleanest

---

[37]E.g., J. Herrmann, *Die Idee der Sühne im Alten Testament,* p. 75.
[38]See Publisher's Note.

flame, and according to the emended reading of the text in Ezekiel 43:21,[39] the sacred altar fire was later used in this.

Some have suspected that the sin offering for the atonement of the anointed priest was in practice merged with the offering that according to Exodus 29:10 had to be made once a year (see also Ezek. 45:18–20), but this is unlikely. The type of unintentional transgression that had been committed probably also had some bearing on the performance of the ceremony.

B. *The sin offering of the community as a whole* (4:13–21)

4:13–21 *"'If the whole Israelite community sins unintentionally and does what is forbidden in any of the LORD's commands, even though the community is unaware of the matter, they are guilty. When they become aware of the sin they committed, the assembly must bring a young bull as a sin offering and present it before the Tent of Meeting. The elders of the community are to lay their hands on the bull's head before the LORD, and the bull shall be slaughtered before the LORD. Then the anointed priest is to take some of the bull's blood into the Tent of Meeting. He shall dip his finger into the blood and sprinkle it before the LORD seven times in front of the curtain. He is to put some of the blood on the horns of the altar that is before the LORD in the Tent of Meeting. The rest of the blood he shall pour out at the base of the altar of burnt offering at the entrance to the Tent of Meeting. He shall remove all the fat from it and burn it on the altar, and do with this bull just as he did with the bull for the sin offering. In this way the priest will make atonement for them, and they will be forgiven. Then he shall take the bull outside the camp and burn it as he burned the first bull. This is the sin offering for the community.'"*

Verse 13 speaks of an unintentional sin committed by the whole *'ēḏâ(h)* ("community") of Israel, in which the *qāhāl* ("community") remained unaware of the matter. The words *'ēḏâ(h)* and *qāhāl*, both of which indicate the coming together of a large number of people, refer to the people of Israel as a unity. The two words can be used interchangeably, and at times they even appear in juxtaposition (Exod. 12:6; Num. 14:5). They are perhaps best distinguished by saying that *'ēḏâ(h)* refers to the entire community as both a national and religious unit, whereas *qāhāl* refers to the nucleus of this.[40] In any case, the contention of Jewish tradition (*Horayoth* 4b) that the *'ēḏâ(h)* is the highest court of justice, the

---

[39]See my commentary, *Ezechiël*, p. 444.

[40]In this connection, see B. Luther, "Kahal und Eda," ZAW (1938), Heft 1/2, pp. 44–63; L. Rost, *Die Vorstufen von Kirche und Synagoge im Alten Testament* (1938); A. R. Hulst, "Het woord kahal in Deuteronomium," *Nieuwtestamentische Studien* (May/June 1939), pp. 159–66.

Sanhedrin, is nothing more than the transference of a state of affairs that only existed later to a much earlier period. The NIV makes no real distinction between the two terms, for both are translated as "community" in verse 13, and *qāhāl* is rendered as "assembly" in verse 14 and again as "community" in verse 21.

The people of Israel as a whole had unintentionally committed a sin, but the manner in which this may have happened is unclear, since we know nothing concerning the make-up and authority structure of the *'ēḏâ(h)* and *qāhāl*. A young bull was then to be presented as a sin offering in the manner described in the preceding paragraph, the only difference being that the laying on of hands was here performed by the elders as the representatives of the people (Exod. 12:21; Lev. 9:1). According to the Targum of Jonathan, these elders were the twelve tribal chiefs. Instead of the young bull spoken of here, Numbers 15:24; 28:15, 22, 30; 29:5, 16, 19, 22, 25, etc., require that a male goat be brought as a sin offering and a young bull as a burnt offering. Some have attempted to explain this discrepancy in terms of an alteration in practice in which the identity between the offering of the priest and that of the people (bull) made way for an identity between the offerings of the people and the tribal leader (male goat). It is assumed in this that, in the course of time, the bond between the priest and the people was relaxed, while that between the people and the leader grew stronger. Israel's history indicates that the opposite of this was in actuality the case, however, and the explanation of the discrepancy perhaps lies simply in the fact that Leviticus 4 speaks of the transgression of a prohibition, and Numbers 15 of the transgression of a positive commandment.

The priest who presided over the offering was in this instance the high priest, and the slaughtering of the animal was performed by one of the elders. There is one thing present in the legislation here that does not appear in connection with the sin offering of the high priest, for whereas in the latter case it was simply assumed that the sin offering made atonement and procured forgiveness for the person who presented it, in both this (v. 20) and the following sections (vv. 26, 31, 35; 5:13) this is expressly stated. The reason for this difference is obvious, however, for in the first case the high priest played a double role: he was both the one who presented the offering and the one who performed the rites of atonement, and he thus carried out the atonement in his own behalf. See comment on 1:4.

C. *The sin offerings of the leader and the common Israelite* (4:22–35)

4:22–35 *"'When a leader sins unintentionally and does what is forbidden in any of the commands of the LORD his God, he is guilty. When he is made aware of the sin* *he committed, he must bring as his offering a male goat without defect. He is to lay his hand on the goat's head and slaughter it at the place where the burnt offering is slaughtered before the* LORD. *It is a sin offering. Then the priest shall take some of the blood of the sin offering with his finger and put it on the horns of the altar of burnt offering and pour out the rest of the blood at the base of the altar. He shall burn all the fat on the altar as he burned the fat of the fellowship offering. In this way the priest will make atonement for the man's sin, and he will be forgiven.*

"'If a member of the community sins unintentionally and does what is forbidden in any of the LORD's *commands, he is guilty. When he is made aware of the sin he committed, he must bring as his offering for the sin he committed a female goat without defect. He is to lay his hand on the head of the sin offering and slaughter it at the place of the burnt offering. Then the priest is to take some of the blood with his finger and put it on the horns of the altar of burnt offering and pour out the rest of the blood at the base of the altar. He shall remove all the fat, just as the fat is removed from the fellowship offering, and the priest shall burn it on the altar as an aroma pleasing to the* LORD. *In this way the priest will make atonement for him, and he will be forgiven.*

"'If he brings a lamb as his sin offering, he is to bring a female without defect. He is to lay his hand on its head and slaughter it for a sin offering at the place where the burnt offering is slaughtered. Then the priest shall take some of the blood of the sin offering with his finger and put it on the horns of the altar of burnt offering and pour out the rest of the blood at the base of the altar. He shall remove all the fat, just as the fat is removed from the lamb of the fellowship offering, and the priest shall burn it on the altar on top of the offerings made to the LORD *by fire. In this way the priest will make atonement for him for the sin he has committed, and he will be forgiven.'"*

These two sections can readily be dealt with in combination, since the differences between them are minor. In the event of a transgression committed by a leader (*nāśî'*, not the later term *śar* from the time of Ezra and Nehemiah), who could have been the head either of an entire tribe or of a portion of one, the obligatory sin offering consisted not in a young bull, but in a male goat (v. 23). This was fitting, since the leader stood beneath both the high priest and the community as a whole. For a transgression perpetrated by a common member of the community, a female animal, either goat or lamb, was sufficient (vv. 28, 32; Num. 15:27 specifies that it be a "year-old female goat"). "Of the community" in verse 27 is literally "of the people of the land," an expression that in postexilic times was used to refer to the non-Israelite portion of the inhabitants of Canaan (Ezra 4:4; 10:2, 11; Neh. 10:31, NIV, "peoples around [them, us, you]," "neighboring peoples").

In this offering there was no sprinkling of the blood before the curtain in the sanctuary (vv. 6, 17), nor was it put on the horns of the altar of incense

(vv. 7, 18). The blood was here rather spread only on the horns of the altar of burnt offering, and according to the rabbis this was done with the forefinger and was continued just as long as it took to remove all the blood from the finger (also in vv. 30, 34; cf. Exod. 29:12). Only a small amount of the blood was used in the rite of atonement here, and the remainder was withdrawn from all further use by pouring it out at the base of the altar. It seems that in the temple there was a small conduit through which the blood could flow to the brook Kidron, but however this may have been, the blood from these individual sin offerings was never brought within the sanctuary. This indicates that an unintentional transgression committed by a leader or a common Israelite was considered to be less serious than the cases discussed previously, since the guilt here applied only to the individual.

A second difference in these sin offerings was that the animals were slaughtered on the north side of the altar of burnt offering (vv. 24, 29, 33; see under 1:11), and yet a third lies in the fact that an ordinary priest performed the ritual of atonement (6:26, 29). All of the fat was also burned on the altar here, but we are not told what was done with the rest of the animal. As in the private sin offerings, the meat was eaten by the priests, but this could naturally only be done within the sanctuary (6:26, 29; 7:6; Num. 18:10) by those who were ceremonially clean (Lev. 22:3–7; Num. 18:11; cf. also Ezek. 42:13; 46:20). This therefore constituted a fourth difference from the previous sin offerings.

It is striking that verse 31 calls the fat that was burned in the sin offering of the common Israelite "an aroma pleasing to the LORD," for this is the only time that this expression occurs in connection with the sin offering. With others, I suspect that this has been transposed from the discussion of the fellowship offering and must be understood in connection with Leviticus 3:5, 16, and so it would be proper to put the phrase in parentheses.

D. *Other instances of the sin offering* (5:1–13)

Unlike chapter 4 and 5:17–19, this section is not concerned with the transgression of express prohibitions, but rather with cases in which the Israelite had performed no concrete act and was yet to be regarded as guilty. Verses 1–6 therefore mention three further cases which, although they are related to the preceding verses, apply to sins arising from negligence or thoughtlessness rather than to unintentional transgressions.

5:1 *"'If a person sins because he does not speak up when he hears a public charge to testify regarding something he has seen or learned about, he will be held responsible.'"*

63

The first case concerns a person who heard the pronouncement of an *'ālâ(h)* and became implicated in the sin by his failure to report it. The situation that is presupposed here may be described as follows.[41] An Israelite had committed a serious misdeed against one of his compatriots, but because of a lack of witnesses the case could not be proved. Since the sin had been committed only in the eyes of God, the sole recourse for the victim was to compel the guilty party to appear at the altar, i.e., before the Lord, and in His presence to invoke an *'ālâ(h)* on himself. Following the example of the Greek translators, this word has been translated as "curse" or "swearing" (cf. KJV), but "self-malediction" or "oath of purgation" sometimes comes closer to its meaning. The *'ālâ(h)* was still more than this, however, for it was also a maleficent agent that undermined and debilitated the soul or vital substance of a creature. A woman struck by an *'ālâ(h)* was thus rendered sterile (Num. 5:21, 27); an *'ālâ(h)* pronounced on the earth would deprive it of its fruitfulness (Gen. 3:17–19), its inhabitants would perish (Isa. 24:6–13), and the pastures would wither (Jer. 23:10). A person who, although he was aware of his guilt, would pronounce an *'ālâ(h)* in order to prove his innocence, would thus invoke a curse on himself (see Solomon's prayer in 2 Chron. 6:22–23).

In the present circumstance, however, there was a person who was aware that the one who had pronounced the *'ālâ(h)* in order to prove his innocence was in fact guilty, since he had either seen the misdeed performed or had been told about it. Nevertheless, when the judge solemnly summoned the potential witness, this person failed to appear and present his testimony in the case. He thus gave the guilty party the opportunity to conceal himself behind such an *'ālâ(h),* so that the judge was led to deliver an unjust judgment in the name of God and God would, as it were, be compelled to intervene directly by granting to the maleficent curse of the *'ālâ(h)* its full power and allow it to strike the guilty person with divine retribution. In this case, the negligent person was considered an accomplice to the transgression, for his testimony was obligatory. In saying that "he will be held responsible," verse 1 indicates that he shared the status of the evildoer and, like him, was to bear the consequences of his sin in the form of guilt and punishment. Only if he confessed his improper action and expressed his repentance by presenting a sin offering—which does not, however, release the guilty party from his own punishment—could he be exonerated of his complicity in the deed of the latter.

---

[41]*Note:* this section is based on the author's understanding of *'ālâ(h)* as a self-maledictory oath or curse (cf. KJV). It is thus not altogether appropriate to the NIV reading, which regards the term as a public charge or adjuration to testify in a legal case.

5:2–3 *" 'Or if a person touches anything ceremonially unclean—whether the carcasses of unclean wild animals or of unclean livestock or of unclean creatures that move along the ground—even though he is unaware of it, he has become unclean and is guilty.*

" 'Or if he touches human uncleanness—anything that would make him unclean—even though he is unaware of it, when he learns of it he will be guilty.' "

The second case concerns the various ways in which an Israelite could become defiled, i.e., ceremonially unclean, which would not only subject him to the prohibition against participating in cultic life, but would also place him in danger of communicating this uncleanness (which was conceived of as a material contamination[42]) to others. Leviticus 11–15 deals with this matter of ceremonial purity at great length. Here only a few possibilities are mentioned, these relating to the coming into contact with the carcasses of unclean wild or domestic animals or unclean crawling creatures, or with human uncleanness. The fact that these are intended only to serve as examples, however, is shown by the further statement that the requirement here applies to "anything that would make him unclean" (v. 3). This coming into contact or "touching" is not a deliberate deed, but rather something that the person did unconsciously and of which he only later became aware.

Precisely how it may have come to his awareness is not stated. S. Mowinckel[43] attempts to create the impression that this took place by way of the *nāśā' 'ᵃwōnô* (NIV, "he will be held responsible") of verse 1, a phrase that he interprets as "undergo the deserved punishment," which would consist of a disease or something similar. But he neglects to deal with the question of how a disease could make someone aware of the fact that he has come into contact with something unclean and thus lead him to confess this (v. 5). In addition, N. H. Ridderbos[44] has pointed out that if the phrase *nāśā' 'ᵃwōnô* did mean "undergo the deserved punishment," we should expect that it would not appear only in the first case to be discussed (v. 1). Last, it should also be noted that verse 1 does not state that the sin comes to the awareness of the person *by way of* the *nāśā' 'ᵃwōnô*. Rather, the guilty party becomes conscious of his deed, and the *consequence* of this is his *nāśā' 'ᵃwōnô*. Mowinckel's presumed clue is thus in error. The manner in which the offender becomes aware of his action remains hidden from us, and it was perhaps also unknown to the

---

[42]See Publisher's Note.
[43]*Psalmenstudien* I, pp. 134f.
[44]*De "werkers der ongerechtigheid" in de individuele psalmen*, p. 62.

lawgiver.[45] Only the fact that he does become conscious of it is of interest to the lawgiver, and I therefore retain the standard translation of *nāśā' "wōnô*, "he brings guilt upon himself" (NIV, "he will be held responsible"). Precisely what this guilt consists in is also not stated here, for it is only clear that he has done something that was forbidden to a person ceremonially unclean: e.g., entering the sanctuary or partaking of food that was holy. In any case, his guilt subjects him to the threat of being cut off from the community of Israel (Num. 19:13, 20).

5:4 *"'Or if a person thoughtlessly takes an oath to do anything, whether good or evil—in any matter one might carelessly swear about—even though he is unaware of it, in any case when he learns of it he will be guilty.'"*

The third case concerns a person who "thoughtlessly" (literally, "chattering with the lips"), with his heart not being present in his words, took an oath to do something. Whether this was undertaken with the intention of doing something good or evil did not matter, for the act of swearing without due consideration itself constituted a violation of the sanctity of the oath, in which the Lord Himself was implicated (cf. Exod. 20:7). Here too the person later became aware—how this happened is again not mentioned—that he had spoken idly in his careless words, e.g., in making a vow that he either would or could not keep, thereby bringing guilt on himself (cf. Num. 30:7–9).

5:5–6 *"'When anyone is guilty in any of these ways, he must confess in what way he has sinned and, as a penalty for the sin he has committed, he must bring to the LORD a female lamb or goat from the flock as a sin offering; and the priest shall make atonement for him for his sin.'"*

In all three of these instances, the person was *'āšēm* ("guilty"), for the sinful deed brought an *'āšām* ("guilt") on him, which destroyed his harmony and peace with God (cf. 4:13, 22, 27). The latter was then to be restored, and to this end he first made confession (v. 5), an act that in Israel took the place of the magical and incantatory formulas that were used in the ancient Near Eastern world. This confession most likely did not consist in a personal declaration, however, but rather in a liturgical formula (cf. Deut. 26:1–15). The latter served to make clear that the guilty person was fully conscious of the sinful character of his deed (cf. Pss. 32:5; 38:18), and simultaneously to give God the honor that was due to Him. Only after confession had been made could the sin offering be presented. Insofar as

---

[45]See Publisher's Note.

this was necessary, it should be noted that the confession of sin that preceded the offering made it evident that the ancient Near Eastern conception of the sacrificial act as being in itself the source of atoning power was not at all present in Israel. For Israel, atonement was solely a gift of God's grace,[46] and the presenting of an offering was a personal deed performed by someone who was fully conscious of his sin.

If an animal was used for the sin offering, it was to be a female taken from the flock, either a lamb or a goat. Here there was no laying of the hands *(sᵉmîkâ[h])* on the sacrificial animal as in the previous sin offerings, for the confession of sin had taken the place of this. There was no need in this context to describe the ritual that was to be performed on the animal, for this was rendered superfluous by the discussion of the previous sin offerings. In any case, the prescribed procedures in the sin offering *(ḥaṭṭā'ṯ)* served to exonerate the *'āšēm* ("guilty person") from his *'āšām* ("guilt").

5:7–13 *""If he cannot afford a lamb, he is to bring two doves or two young pigeons to the LORD as a penalty for his sin—one for a sin offering and the other for a burnt offering. He is to bring them to the priest, who shall first offer the one for the sin offering. He is to wring its head from its neck, not severing it completely, and is to sprinkle some of the blood of the sin offering against the side of the altar; the rest of the blood must be drained out at the base of the altar. It is a sin offering. The priest shall then offer the other as a burnt offering in the prescribed way and make atonement for him for the sin he has committed, and he will be forgiven.*

"'If, however, he cannot afford two doves or two young pigeons, he is to bring as an offering for his sin a tenth of an ephah of fine flour for a sin offering. He must not put oil or incense on it, because it is a sin offering. He is to bring it to the priest, who shall take a handful of it as a memorial portion and burn it on the altar on top of the offerings made to the LORD by fire. It is a sin offering. In this way the priest will make atonement for him for any of these sins he has committed, and he will be forgiven. The rest of the offering will belong to the priest, as in the case of the grain offering.'"

These verses are concerned with what was to be done if the guilty person was too poor to present an animal from the flock, and since this goes beyond the directions given in Leviticus 4:27–35, the description given here had to be in greater detail. Two situations are mentioned: the person was still able to afford an offering of birds (vv. 7–10), or he could afford only a tenth of an ephah (i.e., approximately 3½ liters) of raw meal.

In the first case, the person was given a choice between two doves and two young pigeons. The number had to be two, for the characteristic

---

[46]See my book, *Gods Woord*[2], p. 90.

feature of the sin offering was the burning of the fat portions. Since in a dove or pigeon the fat portion is very small, a second bird was added, and this was condemned to the flames in its entirety as a burnt offering. Both birds together constituted the sin offering. With regard to the dove or pigeon for the sin offering, the head was first severed almost completely from the neck (cf. 1:15), and the blood was then dealt with in the same manner as in the sin offering of the common Israelite, i.e., a portion of it was put on the altar of burnt offering, and the remainder was poured out at its base (4:30). What was left of the bird then belonged to the priest (6:26, 29). The second dove or pigeon was then completely burned in the prescribed manner as a burnt offering, and *all* of its blood was drained out against the side of the altar (1:15).

In the severest case of poverty, an offering of a tenth of an ephah of raw meal was sufficient, this being equivalent to the smallest grain offering (see Lev. 6:20; Num. 5:15; 15:4; 28:5). The ritual procedure with the blood was altogether absent in this instance, and this indicates that the proposition "without blood, no atonement" at least did not apply to Israel (see also Num. 16:46–47, where atonement was made through the burning of incense). In order that the character of the sin offering be preserved, however, and its distinction from the grain offering not neglected, the lawgiver directed that neither oil nor incense could be added to the meal. According to *Menahoth* 6b, "it would be improper if his offering were adorned" with incense. For the rest, the ritual procedure with the meal was the same as in the grain offering (2:2), and what remained of it became the portion of the priest.

One final observation may yet be made. Except in the sin offering of the high priest who, in being both the guilty person and the person performing the ritual of atonement, occupied a unique position, the assurance was at all times given that the presenting of the sin offering would be followed by atonement and forgiveness (4:20, 26, 35; 5:6, 13). Whoever confessed his sin and presented an offering in accordance with his means received forgiveness, and no one was excluded from this possibility.

2. *The Guilt Offering* (5:14–6:7 [MT 5:14–26])

Although the guilt offering to some degree corresponded to the sin offering, insofar as both were to be brought following an unintentional and unconscious transgression of one of God's commandments (5:14, 17–18) and both were meant to procure atonement (5:16, 18; 6:7; 19:22; Num. 5:8), there is nevertheless a clear difference between these two types of offerings that makes it necessary that they always be distinguished (Lev. 7:37; Num. 18:9; Ezek. 40:39; 42:13; 44:29; 46:20; see also 2 Kings

12:16). In contrast to the sin offering, the guilt offering was concerned with the unintentional appropriation of what belonged either to the Lord (5:14-19) or to a fellow Israelite (6:1-6 [MT 5:20-26]). It was thus presented following an act of "unfaithfulness," *ma'al,* which literally means a sacrilege committed against God or what belongs to Him, a violation of His holiness (5:15; 6:2).[47] It should be noted that both of the cases mentioned above constituted acts of sacrilege, for in the second instance a false oath was taken that called on God to confirm something that was in conflict with the truth.

This difference between the two offerings also came to expression in the manner of procedure, for in those cases where a guilt offering was required, this had to be accompanied by an act of restitution in which a fifth more was added to the value of what had been unlawfully taken (5:16, 6:5). In the regulations presented in Exodus 22:7-14, which however speak only of the theft of what had been entrusted to a person, a double restitution was to be made, while Numbers 5:5-10 presupposes the law of Leviticus 6:1-7 and thus likewise requires no more than $^6/_5$ of the value of what had been stolen. This act of restitution had to precede the presentation of the guilt offering (cf. Matt. 5:23-24).

A second difference in the manner of procedure lay in the fact that, whereas the sin offering was slaughtered by the person who presented it (4:15, 24, 29, 33) and then destroyed by fire (4:21), the animal in the guilt offering was slaughtered and eaten by the priest (14:12). There was yet a third point of difference, this relating to the sin offering made for the transgression of a common individual (the guilt offering always applied only to the individual). Whereas in this sin offering a female animal was sufficient (4:28, 32), the guilt offering was to consist of a ram (5:18; 6:6), and in addition, restitution was to be made in the amount of $^6/_5$ of the value of what had been taken from the Lord (see also 27:13, 15, 19, 27, 31).

The two offerings had one thing in common, however, for they both presupposed that the sin was committed unwittingly and without premeditation. There was to be no conflict between the Lord's will as set down in His law and the will of the offender, for in this case the latter was to be cut off from the people (Num. 15:30; cf. also 19:13, 20). It is evident from the superscriptions in verses 5:14 and 6:1 that the law for the guilt offering was the result of two distinct legislative acts, which dealt respectively with the appropriation of what was holy to the Lord (5:15-19) and the appropriation of what belonged to one's fellow Israelite (6:1-7 [MT 20-26]).

---

[47] See Ehrlich, *Randglossen* II, p. 18; D. Schötz, *Schuld—und Sündopfer im Alten Testament,* pp. 41f.

69

Leviticus 5:14–19

5:14–19 *The Lord said to Moses: "When a person commits a violation and sins unintentionally in regard to any of the Lord's holy things, he is to bring to the Lord as a penalty a ram from the flock, one without defect and of the proper value in silver, according to the sanctuary shekel. It is a guilt offering. He must make restitution for what he has failed to do in regard to the holy things, add a fifth of the value to that and give it all to the priest, who will make atonement for him with the ram as a guilt offering, and he will be forgiven.*

"If a person sins and does what is forbidden in any of the Lord's commands, even though he does not know it, he is guilty and will be held responsible. He is to bring to the priest as a guilt offering a ram from the flock, one without defect and of the proper value. In this way the priest will make atonement for him for the wrong he has committed unintentionally, and he will be forgiven. It is a guilt offering; he has been guilty of wrongdoing against the Lord."

The individual in question here had perpetrated a sin with respect to "any of the Lord's holy things." It is evident from verse 16 that this related to what was called the "food of his God" in Leviticus 21:22 and was there divided into "most holy" and "holy." The former included the bread of the Presence (Lev. 24:9) and the offering of incense (Exod. 30:36), as well as the sin and guilt offerings (Lev. 6:25, 29; 7:1, 6; 10:17; 14:13; Num. 18:9) and the grain offerings (2:3, 10; 6:7; 10:12). The latter included the fellowship offerings (Exod. 29:27–28; Lev. 7:31–34; 10:14–15; 23:20; Num. 6:20), the first offspring of all clean domestic animals (Num. 18:15), the firstfruits of the land (Num. 18:12–13), the tithes (Lev. 27:30–33; Num. 18:26–29), and everything in Israel that was devoted to the Lord (Num. 18:14). Whatever was declared "most holy" could be eaten only within the temple by the priest, whereas what was "holy" could also be shared in by his family in a place that was ceremonially clean.

When an unauthorized person partook of any of these holy things of the Lord, even though he may have done this inadvertently, he stood guilty before the Lord. He had violated the Lord's property (see also 22:14–16), and both a penalty and a restitution had to be paid. This penalty is identified in verse 15 as a "ram . . . without defect," which was to be presented as a guilt offering. The choice of the particular animal was not given to the guilty person, however, but to the priest, who had to determine "the proper value in silver, according to the sanctuary shekel." In other words, the priest set the value that the required ram had to have (cf. RSV, "valued by you in shekels of silver"), and the quality of the sacrificial animal was thus no longer left to the discretion of the person who brought it. The monetary unit that the priest was to use in this valuation was the sanctuary shekel. In

70

explaining this, we should note that the silver shekels were not coins, which first came into existence during the Chaldean-Persian period, but rather bars or rings of silver whose value depended on their weight. In ancient times, however, weights and measures—these were also applied to money (Jer. 32:9–10)—were often altered in a most arbitrary manner insofar as the person in charge of them regarded this as expedient to his own interests (Hos. 12:7–8; Amos 8:5; Mic. 6:10; cf. Prov. 1:11; 16:11; 20:23), and David therefore attempted to put them under the control of the Levites. For this reason, the sanctuary had its own unit of weight, and this formed the standard in determining the value of the fines that were presented there. Such a silver shekel weighed approximately 11.5 grams ($^2/_5$ ounce).

This valuation of the sacrificial animal did not occur in every guilt offering, however, for no mention is made of it in connection with the offerings presented in the ceremonies of cleansing from infectious skin disease (Lev. 14:13) or from accidental interruption of the Nazirite vow (Num. 6:12). It was thus required only in the event of theft. On the basis of the mention in 2 Kings 12:16 of the "money from the guilt offerings," it has been asserted[48] that in this case a monetary payment could be readily substituted for the ram and that the offender did not have to be present at the bringing of the guilt offering. Two objections may be raised here, however. First of all, the verse referred to speaks also of the "money from the . . . sin offerings," and since the sin offering could assuredly not be converted into money, the meaning of this passage must merely be that the priests derived certain profits from both types of offering. Second, it is completely clear in Leviticus 5:16 that the ram was an indispensable element in the ritual of atonement, and verse 18 states that the offender was to bring this animal to the priest himself. There are also other reasons that make it altogether improbable that the guilt offering could be presented in the absence of the transgressor and that it could be converted into money as a matter of course. What was at issue here, after all, was a direct violation of the property of the Lord, which amounted to nothing less than an act of sacrilege, and this could certainly not have been regarded as a matter of indifference. That the lawgiver could have made this allowance is rendered even less likely by his indication in verse 17 that the deed itself was the source of the guilt, since the offender's lack of awareness of this was of no account.

In contrast to the discussion of the sin offering, the specific ritual that was performed with the ram of the guilt offering is not described. In both

---

[48]E.g., Eerdmans, *Das Buch Leviticus,* p. 12.

verses 5:18 and 6:7, the lawgiver was content to place all emphasis on the atonement that was made by the sacrifice of the ram, and it is not until 7:1–10 that a detailed description is given of what was to be done with the blood and fat in the guilt offering. Why this difference exists is not clear to me. It is evident from the rabbinical tradition that the question often arose among law-abiding Jews—probably when there was uncertainty as to whether or not the firstfruits or tithe of something had been presented—whether in a certain instance a deed had not been committed that could be atoned for only by means of a guilt offering. In this case, a "provisional" or "pending guilt offering" *('ašam tālûy)* was brought, this being also referred to as the "guilt offering of the devout" *('ašam ḥasîdîm).*[49]

6:1–7 *The Lord said to Moses: "If anyone sins and is unfaithful to the Lord by deceiving his neighbor about something entrusted to him or left in his care or stolen, or if he cheats him, or if he finds lost property and lies about it, or if he swears falsely, or if he commits any such sin that people may do—when he thus sins and becomes guilty, he must return what he has stolen or taken by extortion, or what was entrusted to him, or the lost property he found, or whatever it was he swore falsely about. He must make restitution in full, add a fifth of the value to it and give it all to the owner on the day he presents his guilt offering. And as a penalty he must bring to the priest, that is, to the Lord, his guilt offering, a ram from the flock, one without defect and of the proper value. In this way the priest will make atonement for him before the Lord, and he will be forgiven for any of these things he did that made him guilty."*

These verses (MT 5:20–26) no longer deal with the unintentional violation of what belongs to the Lord, but rather with the unlawful appropriation of what one knew to belong to one of his countrymen. I use the word "countryman" instead of "neighbor" here,[50] for "neighbor" can extend far beyond the boundaries of one's own nation. In ancient Near Eastern society, and indeed among all ancient peoples, there was a big difference between the actions that were permitted toward a member of one's own people and those that might be done over against a foreigner, for in the latter case much more latitude was allowed than in the former. This applied also to Israel, although the difference was smaller than elsewhere (see Deut. 15:3; 23:20).

The regulation given here is partly concerned with the theft of goods that had been entrusted to a person (cf. Exod. 22:7–15; Num. 5:5–10). The placing of possessions in the safekeeping of another person must have happened frequently in Israel, particularly in areas where it was necessary

---

[49]See, e.g., Hoffmann, *Das Buch Leviticus* I, p. 211.
[50]*Note:* NIV does have "neighbor."

to roam with the herds for months at a time. When this was done, it was natural to leave various objects, including money, in the care of a trusted person or with those who kept watch over the village. Many must have succumbed to the temptation of theft, especially since an inventory of the goods was not always drawn up. The regulation also deals with the denial that one had received something in pledge from another person and with the appropriation of the property of a fellow Israelite: e.g., his land, by moving the boundary stones (Deut. 19:14; 27:17; Job 24:2; Prov. 22:28; 23:10; Hos. 5:10; cf. Mic. 2:2), his wells (Gen. 21:25), or his cattle. Further concerns were cheating a person or extorting something from him (e.g., from a needy person [Lev. 19:13; Deut. 24:14], a buyer [Hos. 12:7–8], or a widow or orphan [Exod. 22:22; Mal. 3:5]), and finally, the withholding of something that one had found that was known to belong to another (Ezek. 34:4, 16).

These are not the same matters that were spoken of in Exodus 22, for the latter fall within the jurisdiction of the judge. The cases of theft here are rather those that could not be decided and punished by means of legal proceedings, where an oath was taken and it was merely one person's word against another's, and only the prodding of the offender's conscience could bring his guilt to light. By undertaking an oath that he knew to be false, he had also implicated the Lord in his action and thus doubled his guilt, and this too had to be paid for. Full restitution for what he had taken naturally had to be made first—Numbers 5:7 states that a confession of sin preceded this—with 20 percent once more being added to the amount (as in v. 16 and Num. 5:7), and after this a ram without defect had to be brought to the priest as a guilt offering, again at the selection of the priest rather than the person who presented it. The breach of trust that the guilty person had perpetrated constituted an offense not only against his fellow Israelite, but above all against God, since it violated the legal order He had established. The gravity of the misdeed no doubt also played a role in this offering (see Lev. 5:14). The law of Numbers 5:5–10 goes beyond that contained in Leviticus 6:1–7, for it briefly touches on what had to be done in the event that the victim had died. This, as well as the conclusion to this section in verse 7 (MT 5:26; cf. also, 5:17), makes it evident that care was taken to eliminate as much as possible all potential lacunae from the law.

Further Requirements Concerning Various Offerings
(6:8 [MT 6:1] – 7:38)

1. *Burnt Offerings* (6:8–13 [MT 6:1–6])

6:8–13 *The Lord said to Moses: "Give Aaron and his sons this command: 'These are the regulations for the burnt offering: The burnt offering is to remain on the* *altar hearth throughout the night, till morning, and the fire must be kept burning on the altar. The priest shall then put on his linen clothes, with linen undergarments next to his body, and shall remove the ashes of the burnt offering that the fire has consumed on the altar and place them beside the altar. Then he is to take off these clothes and put on others, and carry the ashes outside the camp to a place that is ceremonially clean. The fire on the altar must be kept burning; it must not go out. Every morning the priest is to add firewood and arrange the burnt offering on the fire and burn the fat of the fellowship offerings on it. The fire must be kept burning on the altar continuously; it must not go out.'"*

Whereas the first five chapters of the Book of Leviticus were directed toward the Israelites at large, 6:8–7:10 are addressed to ''Aaron and his sons.'' These verses contain priestly instructions for the presenting of the offerings discussed in them, and for this reason they may in no way be considered a later supplement to chapters 1–5, as the Wellhausen school maintains. The burnt offering spoken of here is not the same as the individual offerings dealt with in chapter 1, but rather the morning and evening offering that had to be brought to the Lord by Israel as a religious whole, and this same consideration applies also to the grain offering mentioned in the following verses.

Although verse 12 speaks exclusively of the morning burnt offering, it is evident from verse 9 that the evening burnt offering (referred to as the ''evening grain offering'' in 2 Kings 16:15 and ''evening sacrifice'' [*minḥâ(h)*] in Ezra 9:4–5; Dan. 9:21) is also under consideration here, for the morning offering could of course not have continued to smolder for twenty-four consecutive hours. These verses thus refer back to the law of Exodus 29:38–46 pertaining to the daily burnt offering, which as the ''regular'' or ''continual'' offering *(tāmîḏ)* constituted the central point of Israel's organized worship. It formed the foundation for all of the offerings presented by the Israelites—the other festival offerings were *mŭsāp*-offerings, i.e., additional offerings—and its attendance was the most important task of the priests. According to Daniel 8:11 and 11:31, the cessation of this daily offering meant that the Lord's covenant with Israel was no longer in force. A second set of regulations pertaining to the daily burnt offerings is given in Numbers 28:1–8, and it appears there that both the morning and the evening sacrifice consisted of a lamb as a burnt offering and a tenth of an ephah of raw meal mixed with a fourth of a hin of oil as a grain offering, together with a drink offering of a fourth of a hin of fermented drink. Ezekiel 46:13–15 speaks solely of the morning regular offering, which is there said to consist of a lamb, a sixth of an ephah of meal together with a third of a hin of oil, and no wine.

All other offerings were brought after the morning burnt offering and placed on top of it. The evening burnt offering was the final sacrifice of the day, and since the fire on the altar was not allowed to go out (vv. 9, 12–13), this had to be left smoldering throughout the entire night. The priest's first task of the day was thus to attend to the altar fire. He began by putting on his official attire: a linen tunic or body skirt that extended to the ankles and had narrow sleeves, plus an undergarment or trousers that was worn about the loins in order to heed the warning of Exodus 20:26. They were also to wear a headband and a sash, although these are not mentioned here (see Exod. 28:40–43). In accordance with the requirement of Exodus 3:5, the priests wore no foot attire in the sanctuary.

Clothed in this official dress, the priest now went to the altar of burnt offering, which stood in the courtyard before the sanctuary, and stirred up the fire by removing the ashes and temporarily depositing them at the foot of the altar (on its east side, cf. 1:16). He then took off his official clothes, for these could not be worn exclusively in the sanctuary (Ezek. 44:19), and put on "others," viz., his normal clothing, so that he could bring the ashes outside the camp to a place ceremonially clean, i.e., free from cultic contamination (cf. 4:12). This last act was probably not done every day, however. According to *Yoma* 24a, it later became customary to leave a handful of ashes at the foot of the altar as a reminder of the self-surrender to God that had been symbolized by the regular burnt offering of the previous day. It is expressly stated in this connection that the altar fire could never go out. This naturally means that a small fire was always to be kept burning on the thirty-six square meter fire hearth, a requirement that was also met with elsewhere. It is incomprehensible to me how the Wellhausen school could have come to the notion that verse 13 is speaking of a later, uncommon practice.

After the priest returned to the sanctuary and again put on his official attire, he added wood to the altar fire in order to bring it to a blaze and then burned the morning burnt offering and the fat portions of the fellowship offerings on it (this, of course, assumes that the latter were presented during the course of the day). In ancient times, these burnt offerings were more often communal than private. This was to be done in both the morning and the evening of every day, and also on the Sabbath.

2. Grain Offerings (6:14–18 [MT 6:7–11])

6:14–18 " *'These are the regulations for the grain offering: Aaron's sons are to bring it before the LORD, in front of the altar. The priest is to take a handful of fine flour and oil, together with all the incense on the grain offering, and burn the memorial portion on the altar as an aroma pleasing to the LORD. Aaron and his sons shall eat the rest of it, but it is to be eaten without yeast in a holy place; they are to* *eat it in the courtyard of the Tent of Meeting. It must not be baked with yeast; I have given it as their share of the offerings made to me by fire. Like the sin offering and the guilt offering, it is most holy. Any male descendant of Aaron may eat it. It is his regular share of the offerings made to the LORD by fire for the generations to come. Whatever touches it will become holy.'"*

The context in which these verses appear, and above all the fact that the offering spoken of here was brought not by a common Israelite (as in ch. 2), but by a priest (v. 14), indicate that the grain offering dealt with here was not that of chapter 2, but rather the daily grain offering that formed a part of the *tāmîd*. This section is thus in no way to be regarded as a repeat of chapter 2.[51]

The priest performing the ritual first had to take a handful of the meal mixed with oil and burn this together with all of the incense (cf. 2:1–2) on the altar as the memorial portion (see pp. 43–44). The remainder of the offering was "most holy" (2:3) and formed the part of the "offerings made to the LORD by fire" that He had allotted to the priests for generations to come. They and they alone could eat this—yeast of course could never be added (2:4, 11)—and this was to be done exclusively within the holy place formed by the courtyard of the Tent of Meeting (see Num. 18:9–10). It was only the male descendants of Aaron who could eat of this grain offering, not the women and daughters, for they took no active role in cultic worship. Only Aaron and his sons could be fed from the Lord's table. This portion of the grain offering had to be handled with great care, however, for whoever and whatever—the Hebrew here expresses both, and both should therefore be brought out in translation (see note to v. 18 in NIV)—came into contact with this "most holy" meal became holy as well. We are here confronted with a concept that was also found outside of Israel: ritual holiness could be communicated as readily as ritual uncleanness; like something tangible or material,[52] both become attached to whoever or whatever touched them (see also Exod. 29:37; 30:29). For this reason, all contact between that which belonged to the sphere of everyday life and that which was used for the work of atonement, and was thus laden with special power, had to be avoided (see also 6:27 [MT 6:20]; 7:6, 15–17; 8:31–32; etc.). What the consequences of such contact may have been is not clear. Some think that a person who had thus become "holy" had to be redeemed (27:1–8), while an object that became "holy" came to belong to the sanctuary. The Jewish exegete D. Hoffmann[53] calls this "nonsensi-

---

[51] As is done, e.g., by Baentsch in his commentary.
[52] See Publisher's Note.
[53] *Das Buch Leviticus.*

cal,'' however, and he is probably correct, since it is difficult to understand how the lawgiver could have failed to further expound a requirement that would have had such important consequences. In any case, it is evident from Haggai 2:12–13 that this matter gave rise to many questions in Israel.

3. *Priestly Grain Offerings* (6:19–23 [MT 6:12–16])

6:19–23 *The LORD also said to Moses, "This is the offering Aaron and his sons are to bring to the LORD on the day he is anointed: a tenth of an ephah of fine flour as a regular grain offering, half of it in the morning and half in the evening. Prepare it with oil on a griddle; bring it well-mixed and present the grain offering broken in pieces as an aroma pleasing to the LORD. The son who is to succeed him as anointed priest shall prepare it. It is the LORD's regular share and is to be burned completely. Every grain offering of a priest shall be burned completely; it must not be eaten."*

In contrast to the daily grain offering of verses 14–18, which was brought for the people as a whole, this section speaks of a particular grain offering that the high priest presented for the priesthood, just as he was also to bring a bull as a sin offering "for himself and his household" on the Day of Atonement (16:6, 11).

There is a question as to what verse 20 means in saying "on the day he is anointed." The reference cannot be to the day of Aaron's anointing, for the verse also states that this was a "regular grain offering." It is possible that the offering was to be presented whenever a new high priest took office. Chapter 8, however, which deals with the ordination of the priests, speaks in verse 26 of "a cake of bread" made without yeast, "and one made with oil, and a wafer," which was to be added to the ram of ordination, but it does not mention this grain offering; and the same is true in the directions for the ordination ceremony given in Exodus 29. Yet another possibility is that the pronominal suffix on the object marker *'ōtô* is here to be understood distributively, so that the translation would not be "on the day he [the high priest] is anointed," but "on the day each [of all the priests] is anointed" (see NIV marginal note to v. 20). This anointing of the priests in general is spoken of in Exodus 28:41; 30:30; 40:15; Leviticus 7:36; 10:7; Numbers 3:3. It appears to me that this is indeed what the lawgiver had in mind here. To what degree this anointing of the priests in general differed from that of the high priest is not known, for the Pentateuch contains no description of the ritual that was followed in the former.

Whereas the daily grain offering consisted of meal mixed with oil together with incense, with only a portion of this being burned on the altar and the remainder left to the priests, the priestly grain offering was cooked and then burned in its entirety. The manner in which it was cooked and presented as an offering is not completely clear. The meal had to be prepared in oil on a griddle (see discussion on 2:5) and be "well-mixed." Rashi understands the Hebrew for this preparation as "sufficiently boiled in boiling water," but in my opinion *murbeket* cannot have this meaning. There follows a Hebrew term, *tupînê,* that appears nowhere else and is understood by König[54] as meaning "baked goods," whereas others regard it as a reference to some sort of grain or meal. I have chosen to retain the solution offered by the Syriac translation, which reads *tptnh* instead of *tpyny* and thus has *tᵉp̄uttennâ(h):* "you shall crumble it in pieces." The offering then was to be presented broken into pieces, just as the grain offering spoken of in 2:6, but whereas only a portion of that grain offering was placed on the altar, this priestly grain offering was burned in its entirety *(kālîl).* Verse 23 states that "it must not be eaten," for the priest could not partake of what he himself offered to the Lord as a sign of the consecration of his life.

4. *Sin Offerings* (6:24–30 [MT 6:17–23])

6:24–30 *The Lord said to Moses, "Say to Aaron and his sons: 'These are the regulations for the sin offering: The sin offering is to be slaughtered before the Lord in the place the burnt offering is slaughtered; it is most holy. The priest who offers it shall eat it; it is to be eaten in a holy place, in the courtyard of the Tent of Meeting. Whatever touches any of the flesh will become holy, and if any of the blood is spattered on a garment, you must wash it in a holy place. The clay pot the meat is cooked in must be broken; but if it is cooked in a bronze pot, the pot is to be scoured and rinsed with water. Any male in a priest's family may eat it; it is most holy. But any sin offering whose blood is brought into the Tent of Meeting to make atonement in the Holy Place must not be eaten; it must be burned.'"*

Whereas the preceding offerings (6:8–23) took place beyond the life of the people at large, 6:24–7:34 speaks of offerings that have already been discussed in chapters 3–5 and were a concern of all the Israelites. The previous discussion of these offerings took place from the point of view of the people, however, and the present chapters now deal with them from the standpoint of the priests (see v. 25) and set forth their particular duties in them. In contrast to chapter 3, the fellowship offerings stand last in order here since, as the most common offerings, they demanded the lengthiest treatment.

With regard to the sin offering, it is first of all specified where the slaughtering was to take place: at the site of the burnt offering (i.e.,

[54]*Lehrgebäude* II, p. 155.

according to 1:11 [see comment] at the north side of the altar of burnt offering [see also 4:24, 29, 33]) and "before the LORD," for the altar was the Lord's table (see p. 18).

The procedure that followed the slaughtering is naturally not dealt with here, for this would be superfluous after the discussion in 4:1–5:13. Emphasis is placed, however, on the character of the meat of the sin offering (vv. 25, 30) and on the consequences that followed from this. This meat was not burned outside of the camp after the fat had been offered, as in the sin offerings for the high priest or the community, but rather became the portion of the priest (see also 7:6–7). It was therefore considered "most holy," just as the altars and the other implements of the sanctuary (Exod. 29:37; 30:29, 36–37), and it thus had to be meticulously guarded against any contact with whatever or whoever did not belong within the sphere of the holy, the consequences of such contact being given in verse 27. This meant first of all that it could be eaten within the holy area exclusively by the ceremonially clean (22:3–7; Num. 18:11) male members of the family of the priest who performed the offering (v. 26; see also 7:7), as was also the case with the bread of the Presence (24:9). Verse 29 and 7:6 seem to be speaking of *all* the priestly families, however. The explanation of this is perhaps that the priest who brought the sin offering was authorized to eat of it first along with his sons, whereas the others only had secondary rights to it. According to Ezekiel 42:13; 44:29, this was to take place in one of the rooms that lay on the north and south sides of the sanctuary (see also our discussion on 7:33). This meal did not form the conclusion of the sacrificial ritual, however, as if the eating of the meat signified the complete obliteration of sin.[55] There is nothing that points in this direction, although 10:17 has been so regarded. A second result of the "most holy" character of the priestly portion of the sin offering is that contact with it communicated its holiness,[56] i.e., caused what touched it to participate in its consecration (see v. 18). If its blood was splattered on an article of clothing, it had to be washed exclusively within the Tent, for under no condition could the "holy" blood be taken outside of the sanctuary (4:7). The clay pot in which the meat was cooked—the reference here is apparently to unglazed pottery in which the "holiness" could penetrate the clay—could no longer be used and had to be destroyed by shattering it (see also 11:33, 35). If the pot was made of bronze, it had to be scoured and thoroughly rinsed with water (cf. 15:12), for its "holiness," or so to speak its ritual "contamination," had to be removed before it could be reused (see Mark 7:4).

---

[55] This position is taken by, e.g., E. Riehm, *Der Begriff der Sühne im Alten Testament* (1877), p. 72.

[56] See Publisher's Note.

Permission to eat the meat of the sin offering did not however apply to those cases where a portion of the blood was brought into the Holy Place of the Tent of Meeting (v. 30), viz., the sin offerings presented by the high priest (5:5–7) or by the community as a whole (4:16–18). These offerings had a higher degree of holiness than was present in the other sin offerings. Ezekiel 43:21 required that the bull for the sin offering whose blood was used in consecrating the altar of burnt offering also be burned.

5. Guilt Offerings (7:1–10)

7:1–7 *" 'These are the regulations for the guilt offering, which is most holy: The guilt offering is to be slaughtered in the place where the burnt offering is slaughtered, and its blood is to be sprinkled against the altar on all sides. All its fat shall be offered: the fat tail and the fat that covers the inner parts, both kidneys with the fat around them near the loins, and the covering of the liver, which is to be removed with the kidneys. The priest shall burn them on the altar as an offering made to the Lord by fire. It is a guilt offering. Any male in a priest's family may eat it, but it must be eaten in a holy place; it is most holy.*

" 'The same law applies to both the sin offering and the guilt offering: They belong to the priest who makes atonement with them.' "

The guilt offering had essentially the same character as the sin offering and it was thus subject to the same rules. Like the sin offering, it was "most holy," and it also had to be slaughtered at the site of the slaughtering of the burnt offering (1:11). Since 5:14–6:7 (MT 5:14–26) contains no information as to the ritual procedure that was to be carried out with the ram of the guilt offering, verses 2–5 here state what was to be done with the blood and the fat of the animal.

In the sin offering of a leader and of the common Israelite a portion of the blood was spread on the horns of the altar of burnt offering and the remainder was then poured out at its base (4:25, 30, 34). This constituted the complete rite of atonement. In the guilt offering, on the other hand, the blood in its entirety was "sprinkled against the altar on all sides," as was also true in the burnt offering (1:5) and the fellowship offering (3:2). As with the fellowship offering (3:3–5, 9–11) and the sin offering (4:8–10), the guilt offering involved the burning of all the fat. In the detailed description that is given of this fat, it is striking that no mention is made of the fat that was connected to the inner parts, even though in all other respects the description here parallels those given in the above-mentioned passages. The Samaritan and Greek texts do speak of this fat here, and for this reason I suspect that the Hebrew phrase in question was omitted accidentally and should thus be inserted in translation.

The present context does not speak of the laying on of hands, and this was indeed also not mentioned in the preceding discussion of the sin offerings (6:25; it is spoken of in ch. 4). In view of the character of the *sᵉmîḵâ(h)* (see pp. 32–34), however, there can be no doubt that it formed a part of the ritual of the guilt offering, and the Jewish tradition in fact also assumed that this was the case.

With regard to the question of who could eat what remained of the animal in the guilt offering, verse 6 makes the same requirement as that which applied to the sin offering (6:26, 29): only the male members of the priestly families could eat of it, and this could be done exclusively within the sanctuary.

A new element is introduced in verse 7, for whereas chapter 6 specifies who could eat of the grain and sin offerings (6:16, 18, 26, 29), it is here stated to whom the remains from the sin and guilt offerings belonged. Whatever was left over became the property of the priest who presented the offering. He was thus allowed to keep the hide for himself, although this item was not specifically mentioned in connection with these offerings. The hide acquired a special significance through the laying on of hands, for by way of the *sᵉmîḵâ(h)*, the guilt of the person who presented the offering was transferred to the animal, and by leaving behind the hide of the animal that had stood in his place, the offerer in fact took leave of his own guilt and departed from the sanctuary in a purified state. As is evidenced by the sacrificial tariff of Marseilles and the cultic tablet of Sippar, this same line of thinking also appeared outside of Israel.[57]

7:8–10 *" 'The priest who offers a burnt offering for anyone may keep its hide for himself. Every grain offering baked in an oven or cooked in a pan or on a griddle belongs to the priest who offers it, and every grain offering, whether mixed with oil or dry, belongs equally to all the sons of Aaron.' "*

There then follow three verses that are in fact unrelated to what is under discussion in this section. They are directed to the priests and are added here because the immediately preceding lines have been speaking of the portion of the priests and tacitly assume the presence of the hide in this (v. 7). These verses are concerned partly with the burnt offering and partly with the grain offering. In the burnt offering, the hide of the animal, which is not mentioned in chapter 1, belonged to the priest who performed the offering (v. 8). A distinction is then made in the grain offering between those that were baked or cooked, and those that were either mixed with oil

---

[57]Reference may not be made to Job 2:4 in this connection, for the Old Testament nowhere uses "skin" or "hide" as a synonym for "person."

or made dry, but were in either case left uncooked. The baked and cooked grain offerings (see 2:4–10) belonged to the priest who offered them, whereas the others were for all the priests (vv. 9–10). The uncooked offerings were the common variety and comprised both mixed (2:1–3, 14–16) and dry offerings, the latter consisting of the sin offering of the poor person (5:11–13) and the grain offering for jealousy (Num. 5:15).

Verse 10 states that these uncooked mixed and dry offerings belonged "equally to all the sons of Aaron." It is evident that it had not always been a simple matter to give to each person his allotted share and that the need would have soon arisen for some type of service roster involving the formation of divisions within the priesthood that took turns at active duty (see 1 Chron. 24; Luke 1:8–9). According to the Talmud, these divisions alternated weekly, with each family within a division doing duty for one day, and *Taanith* 27a declares that Moses instituted eight or ten such divisions. With regard to the priestly portion of the burnt and grain offerings, Jewish tradition states that the high priest received as much as the combined shares of all the priests on duty, for in the section concerning the priestly share of the fellowship offerings, the Hebrew of 7:31 literally reads "to Aaron and to his sons," and the repetition of the preposition here is held to indicate that each received a half. This may be a clever analysis, but there is no basis for it.

6. *Fellowship Offerings* (7:11–21)

7:11–12 *"'These are the regulations for the fellowship offering a person may present to the Lord:*

"'If he offers it as an expression of thankfulness, then along with this sacrifice of thanksgiving he is to offer cakes of bread made without yeast and mixed with oil, wafers made without yeast and spread with oil, and cakes of fine flour well-kneaded and mixed with oil.'"

The ritual of the fellowship offering (with regard to the uncertainty concerning this name, see pp. 48–50) has been discussed in chapter 3, and the present section now details the manner in which the meat of the offering and also the accompanying grain offering were to be eaten by the priests. The requirements that follow, however, concern only those fellowship offerings that become the property of the Lord (vv. 11, 20–21, 29), and they thus have no bearing on the ordinary slaughtering that is frequently involved in such a fellowship offering. It appears here that the name "fellowship offering" is actually a collective designation for three types of offering. The first of these is offered "as an expression of thankfulness" (vv. 12–15) and is therefore referred to as a "sacrifice of thanksgiving" (v. 12), a "fellowship offering of thanksgiving" (vv. 13, 15), or simply a "thank offering" (Amos 4:5). Psalms 56:12–13; 107:22; 116:17 indicate that such offerings were willingly presented after recovery from illness or deliverance from danger (see also *Berakoth* 54b). They were thus a product of the spontaneous desire to perform a public deed expressing one's thankfulness for blessings that had been enjoyed, and they were in all likelihood accompanied by the singing of one of the hymns now found among the Psalms (e.g., Ps. 106). Eerdmans is perhaps correct in surmising that fixed liturgical formulas were spoken in connection with the presenting of this offering (cf. Jer. 17:26; 33:11).[58] These offerings stand foremost among the fellowship offerings, as is evident not only from the fact that they are the first to be mentioned, but also because the meat of the animal (according to ch. 3 it could be taken from either the herd or the flock) had to be eaten before the breaking of the following morning (v. 15). In addition to this animal, a grain offering consisting of two types of bread made of unleavened raw meal—*ḥallôt,* cakes of bread mixed with oil, and *reqîqîm,* wafers dipped in oil—had to be included (v. 12). Cakes made from raw meal that was "well-kneaded and mixed with oil" were also to be added to this, but in what respect these differed from the other types of bread is not clear. Another listing of these grain offerings appears in Exodus 29:2, 23 and Leviticus 8:26, where the ordination offering of Aaron and his sons is dealt with.

7:13 *"'Along with his fellowship offering of thanksgiving he is to present an offering with cakes of bread made with yeast.'"*

Verse 13 speaks of cakes of bread made with yeast that were also presented in connection with this offering. These did not themselves constitute a sacrificial gift, however, for Israel would eat no meat without bread. Like the leavened loaves presented at the Feast of Weeks (23:17), this bread was not placed on the altar (2:11), and there is thus no conflict here with the commandment of Exodus 23:18. Amos 4:5 also presents no difficulty in this connection, for the prophet is here reproaching his contemporaries for bringing their thank offerings in an unlawful manner.

7:14 *"'He is to bring one of each kind as an offering, a contribution to the Lᴏʀᴅ; it belongs to the priest who sprinkles the blood of the fellowship offerings.'"*

Of the offerings of unleavened bread, "one of each kind" was to be brought to the Lord as a "contribution," i.e., one of each of the types of

---

[58]*Das Buch Leviticus,* p. 21.

bread mentioned in verse 12. According to tradition, this included also the cakes of bread made with yeast which verse 13 mentions, and of these, ten were to be brought, since according to Numbers 18:26 the contribution for the priest amounted to a tenth (*Menahoth* 77a, b). Such a contribution (*t'rûmâ[h]*) was a portion which, in being set apart for the Lord, signified that the whole was dedicated to Him (Exod. 25:2–3; 29:28; 30:15; Num. 15:19–21; 18:8–11; Ezek. 44:30). Some prefer to call this a "heave offering" (see KJV; NIV translates *t'rûmâ[h]* as both "contribution" and "offering"), but this does not seem correct, for such a contribution was not brought to the altar. It was rather given to the priest who sprinkled the blood around the altar (see also 3:2, 8).

7:15 *" 'The meat of his fellowship offering of thanksgiving must be eaten on the day it is offered; he must leave none of it till morning.' "*

Verse 15 concludes the discussion of this particular offering by directing that the meat of the fellowship offering of thanksgiving (the fat had been burned as an "offering made by fire," 3:3–5, 9–11, 14–16) had to be eaten by the offerer and his family before the dawning of the following morning, and the joyful sacrificial meals could therefore last until late into the night. The meal of course had to take place within the sanctuary (see also 22:29). The thought behind this regulation must have been that he who sat at table with the Lord could bring nothing home with him, but had to trust that he would always receive the satisfaction of his needs from God's hand (see Exod. 16:23).

The poor were gladly invited to share in such a fellowship offering of thanksgiving (Ps. 22:25–26) on the condition that, like the other participants, they were ritually clean (1 Sam. 20:24–26; 21:5; see also Lev. 11–15). It appears from a few scattered clues in the Old Testament that this offering was accompanied by a number of ceremonial actions that probably proceeded approximately as follows. After having prepared himself (Pss. 15; 18:2–6), the Israelite went with his family to the sanctuary, singing appropriate psalms along the way (Pss. 42:4; 100:4), and he there bowed down before the temple of the Lord's holiness (Pss. 5:7; 95:6). The offerings were then presented and the ritual washings performed, and he then went about the altar singing various songs of praise (Ps. 26:6–7), each followed by the well-known refrain: "for the LORD is good and his love endures forever" (Pss. 100:4–5; 106:1; 107:1; 118:1; 136; Jer. 33:11). Although only one psalm (Ps. 100) has the superscription "psalm for *tôḏâ(h)*" (i.e., "for the thank offering," NIV, "for giving thanks"), there must have been a number of psalms that were specifically composed for this solemn occasion. Such songs could of course also be sung apart from the presentation of thank offerings (Ps. 69:30–31; Hos. 14:2; in the latter verse, the Septuagint and the Syriac Peshitta should be followed in reading "the fruit of our lips" in place of "the bulls of our lips," cf. NIV margin).

7:16–19 *" 'If, however, his offering is the result of a vow or is a freewill offering, the sacrifice shall be eaten on the day he offers it, but anything left over may be eaten on the next day. Any meat of the sacrifice left over till the third day must be burned up. If any meat of the fellowship offering is eaten on the third day, it will not be accepted. It will not be credited to the one who offered it, for it is impure; the person who eats any of it will be held responsible.*

" 'Meat that touches anything ceremonially unclean must not be eaten; it must be burned up. As for other meat, anyone ceremonially clean may eat it.' "

The two other types of fellowship offering are the votive offering and the freewill offering, which are also spoken of together in Leviticus 22:21; Numbers 15:3, and Deuteronomy 12:6, 17. Such a votive offering was made in order to "pay" (RSV) or "fulfill" (NIV, Ps. 61:8; Prov. 7:14) a vow that one had made during a time of need (e.g., Gen. 28:20; Judg. 11:30–31; 1 Sam. 1:11; 2 Sam. 15:8). Among the Israelites, who were conscious that they were like potsherds and had no more self-sufficiency than clay in the hands of the potter (Pss. 2:9; 8:4; 95:3–7; 135:6; Isa. 45:9; cf. Gen. 18:27), the undertaking of a vow was at no time naturally regarded as a religious duty. Leviticus 27 and Numbers 30 speak only of what had to be done *if* a vow had been made, and Deuteronomy 23:21–23 expressly states that it was not a sin of one refrained from making a vow, but only if he undertook one and then failed to fulfill it (cf. Eccl. 5:4–6). Such negligence would place the Lord on the same level as the gods of the heathen, for it was not unusual for the heathen to promise something to their gods and then fail to perform it. Both the making of vows and the failure to fulfill them also occurred frequently in Israel, however, for this is indicated by the laws in Numbers 30 and also by the repeated exhortation to pay one's vows (Deut. 23:21; Job 22:27; Ps. 50:14; Eccl. 5:4–6; Nah. 1:15). In this connection, see also Leviticus 27.

The freewill offering[59] was an expression of thankfulness and thus proceeded from the spontaneous impulse of one's heart (2 Chron. 31:14; 35:8–9; Ps. 54:6). It was in particular willingly presented during a visit to the temple at one of the great feasts (Exod. 23:15; 34:20) as a demonstration of reverent recognition of the Lord's gracious rule. The choice of the

---

[59]The law naturally makes no mention of other voluntary contributions, such as dedicated gifts (2 Sam. 8:11; 1 Kings 7:51; 10:16–17; 14:26; 15:15; 2 Kings 12:18; 16:8).

animal to be offered was here not subjected to the same stringent rules that were binding in the other offerings (see Lev. 22:23). Although Leviticus 7 does not mention this, the law of Numbers 15:3–4 directs that both the votive offering and the freewill offering were to be accompanied by a grain offering. Leviticus 7 speaks exclusively of the meat of the offerings and states that this could also be eaten on the day following the presentation of the sacrifice. It is evident from verse 19 that the lawgiver here tacitly assumed that those who brought votive and freewill offerings could bring the meat home with them. Whatever meat might be left over until the third day had to be burned, this being completely understandable in a Near Eastern climate. The regulation of verse 18 indicates, however, that the attempt to retain the meat this long (perhaps during the winter season) was not unknown. Whoever did this "will be held responsible" (see commentary on 5:1), for the meat was said to be *piggûl*, ("impure"), an expression that is used only in connection with the meat of offerings (Lev. 19:7; Isa. 65:4; Ezek. 4:14) and indicates that it had begun to rot. If the sacrificial meat was taken home, it naturally had to be destroyed if it came into contact with anything unclean (v. 19), for "clean" and "unclean" were states produced by powers that were opposed to one another and were therefore irreconcilable.[60]

7:20–21 *" 'But if anyone who is unclean eats any meat of the fellowship offering belonging to the Lord, that person must be cut off from his people. If anyone touches something unclean—whether human uncleanness or an unclean animal or any unclean, detestable thing—and then eats any of the meat of the fellowship offering belonging to the Lord, that person must be cut off from his people.' "*

Whereas the concern until now has been the meat of the offerings, the last two verses of this section speak of the condition that had to be met by those who would eat of this meat: they were to be ceremonially clean. This has nothing to do with our understanding of cleanness as being free from dirt or filth, for "clean" is a positive, not a negative concept, indicating the state in which communion with God is possible. It is the condition for acquiring the holiness that descends from God, for only those who are clean are able to consecrate themselves (see Exod. 19:10, 14–15, 22; Num. 11:18; Josh. 3:5; 1 Sam. 16:5). All uncleanness therefore had to be avoided, for whoever ate the sacrificial meat belonging to the Lord while in an unclean state (literally, "with his uncleanness upon him," v. 20) forfeited his life. This would be the case if the person had been rendered unclean by a skin disease or by some event pertaining to sexual life, or if he

---

[60]See Publisher's Note.

had come into contact with something unclean (cf. 5:2) and had not purified himself by presenting a sin offering.

Verse 20 declares that if this happened, the person "must be cut off from his people." This same expression occurs repeatedly in the law (Exod. 12:15, 19; 30:33, 38; 31:14; Lev. 7:20–21, 25, 27; 17:4, 9, 14; 18:29; 19:8; 20:18; 23:29; Num. 9:13; 15:30–31; 19:13, 20), and some have regarded it as speaking of execution. It appears to me, however, that the meaning of this is rather that the guilty person was expelled from the tribal association and cultic community and thus abandoned to the wrath of the Lord. Pronouncements such as those appearing in Leviticus 17:10 and 20:2–6, where there is clear reference to divine judgment, point in this direction. A person who had committed an especially grievous transgression would be struck by sudden death.[61]

This regulation concerning the necessity of ceremonial cleanness naturally applied to all of the offerings, and in Leviticus 22:1–8 it was made clear to the priests that they were to exercise great caution with respect to the sacred offerings.

7. The Prohibition of Fat and Blood (7:22–27)

7:22–25 *The Lord said to Moses, "Say to the Israelites: 'Do not eat any of the fat of cattle, sheep or goats. The fat of an animal found dead or torn by wild animals may be used for any other purpose, but you must not eat it. Anyone who eats the fat of an animal from which an offering by fire may be made to the Lord must be cut off from his people.'"*

Whereas the previous content of chapters 6 and 7 was directed to the priests, these verses were addressed to the people at large. They had nevertheless received a position among the directions given to the priests that pertain to the fellowship offerings, for it was only in these offerings that the offerer received a portion of the sacrificial meat (see also 3:16–17).

The prohibition against eating the fat of cattle, sheep, or goats (v. 23) would seem to be absolute, but the further description given in verse 25 makes it evident that only the fat of those animals that were presented as fellowship offerings is intended here. The prohibition therefore pertained only to those fat portions mentioned in Leviticus 3:3–4, 9–10, 14–15, and did not apply to the fat lying within the muscular tissue. These fat portions belonged to the Lord (3:17; see also 1 Sam. 2:15–16), but the Israelites retained the right to partake of the fat of other clean animals.

The situation was different with the fat of clean animals that had either

---

[61] See A. Schulz, *Der Sinn des Todes im Alten Testament*, pp. 16f.

died a natural death or been killed by wild animals, however, for this was never to be eaten (v. 24; see also 11:39–40; 17:5; 22:8). In both of these cases the animal had been made unclean, since the death had come either through disease or from contact with wildlife, which was of course always unclean. The consequent uncleanness was as it were concentrated in the fat, for this was what sustained life. The fat of such an animal could however be used for some other purpose. Whether this was also the case with the fat of animals slaughtered for everyday use is not clear, for the law does not speak of this.

7:26–27 *"'And wherever you live, you must not eat the blood of any bird or animal. If anyone eats blood, that person must be cut off from his people.'"*

With regard to the eating of blood, the Israelites were here confronted with an absolute prohibition (see also 3:17; 17:13–14; Deut. 12:16; 15:23). Under no circumstances could this be partaken of, and the commandment applied equally to persons of foreign origin living in Israel (Lev. 17:12). The blood contained the soul or life of a creature, and for this reason it could be used exclusively within the area of the holy. The covenant was confirmed by the sprinkling of blood on the altar and the people (Exod. 24:4–8); the application of blood served to consecrate the priests (Exod. 29:20) and to cleanse a person who had been healed of an infectious skin disease (Lev. 14:7); and blood was also used to make atonement (Exod. 30:10), both for the people and for the sanctuary (Lev. 16:16–17).

In spite of the strictness of this prohibition, the eating of meat with the blood still in it occurred repeatedly in Israel (1 Sam. 14:32–34; Ezek. 33:25). This was related to the idea, also found elsewhere in the ancient Near Eastern world, that the consumption of blood fortifies life, or leads to ecstasy and communion with the deity.[62] There are still today in Islam local cultic practices that involve the tearing apart and eating of live animals. The prohibition against the consumption of blood (see also Lev. 19:26) was also designed to resist the influence of pagan customs. Whoever succumbed to such practices lost all right to a life among the people of the Lord.

8. The Priestly Portion of the Fellowship Offerings (7:28–34)

7:28–34 *The LORD said to Moses, "Say to the Israelites: 'Anyone who brings a fellowship offering to the LORD is to bring part of it as his sacrifice to the LORD. With*

---

[62] See e.g., Chantepie de la Saussaye, *Lehrbuch der Religionsgeschichte*[4], 1925; I, pp. 37, 50; II, p. 514.

his own hands he is to bring the offering made to the LORD *by fire; he is to bring the fat, together with the breast, and wave the breast before the* LORD *as a wave offering. The priest shall burn the fat on the altar, but the breast belongs to Aaron and his sons. You are to give the right thigh of your fellowship offerings to the priest as a contribution. The son of Aaron who offers the blood and the fat of the fellowship offering shall have the right thigh as his share. From the fellowship offerings of the Israelites, I have taken the breast that is waved and the thigh that is presented and have given them to Aaron the priest and his sons as their regular share from the Israelites.'*"

These verses, which like the preceding section are directed to the people at large, form a supplement to the requirements of verses 11–21 in that they are concerned not so much with the person who presented the offering, but deal rather with the priests and establish what was to be their share of the fellowship offering. With regard to the offerer, it is stated that he was to bring his fellowship offering with his own hands (see 8:27–28; Exod. 29:24–26; Num. 6:19–20) and give a part of this to the Lord (vv. 29–30). He did this with his own hands in order to make clear that the offering was not coerced by the priest, but proceeded from the desire of his own heart. The portion of the animal that was to be presented, viz., the breast and the fat, was determined by the Lord Himself, however. The fat spoken of here was identical to the fat portions of 3:3–4, 9–10, 14–15, all of which was to be burned on the altar. The breast, which in cattle, sheep, and goats is also referred to as the brisket, is one of the tastiest parts of the animal. It was to be waved as a "wave offering," i.e., solemnly moved back and forth in order to portray the dedication of the offering. In this ceremony, the priest placed on the hands of the person who presented it the part of the animal to be offered (Exod. 29:25; Lev. 8:27, 29), and he then put his own hands beneath those of the offerer and moved them first forward, in the direction of the altar, and then back toward himself. The entire motion thus graphically marked the offering as a gift (cf. 9:21; 10:15; 14:12, 24; 23:11, 20). The Hebrew term translated as "wave offering" in verse 30 is *tᵉnûpâ(h),* which literally means "waving," the continual back and forth movement of the hands. Related to this is the *tᵉrûmâ(h),* "lifting" or "raising" (KJV, "heave offering"). Here the motion was no longer in the direction of the sanctuary, but rather—at least according to tradition, although I see no basis for this in the law itself[63]—toward heaven, this of course signifying that the offering was proffered, and thus dedicated, to the Lord. Through the *tᵉnûpâ(h)* and *tᵉrûmâ(h),* which lend force to the *hiqrîḇ* or simple presentation of the

---

[63]See e.g. Dillmann-Ryssel, *Die Bücher Exodus und Leviticus* (1897), p. 496.

offering, God is regarded as having accepted the gift and having granted it to the priest. Jewish tradition (*Menahoth* 61b, 62a) asserts that this waving was done four times in succession, once toward each direction of the compass. Such wave offerings and "heave offerings" (the KJV translation of *t*ᵉ*rûmâ*[*h*], where the NIV has simply ". . . that is presented") are also spoken of in Leviticus 8:27, 29; 9:21; 10:15; 14:12, 24; 23:11–12, 20, and Exodus 29:24, 26–27; 35:22; Numbers 6:20; 8:11.

After this ceremonial act, the fat portions were burned on the altar and the breast was given to the members of the priesthood. The priest performing the ritual received as his share the right thigh, which according to tradition (*Hullin* 134b) was the central part of the three-sectioned hind leg. It appears from 1 Samuel 9:24 that, along with the fat tail (according to the emended reading of this verse; NIV, "what was on it"), this was the best part of the animal and was customarily set before the most honored guest. He received the right thigh because, in the Near Eastern mind, the right side was more highly valued than the left (cf. Gen. 48:14). Verse 34 calls this the thigh of the *t*ᵉ*rûmâ(h)* (KJV, "heave shoulder," NIV, "thigh that is presented"), not because it was subjected to the *t*ᵉ*nûpâ(h)* and *t*ᵉ*rûmâ(h)* like the breast in verse 30, but because it was not left at the free disposal of the person who offered it. It was thus simply a "contribution" (v. 32), and only in the case of Exodus 29:27 did the situation differ from this. The Lord gave this thigh to the priest, and although verse 34 mentions "Aaron . . . and his sons," this does not conflict with verse 32, since the breast (which was given to all the priests) is also being mentioned.

9. *Summary* (7:35–38)

7:35–38 *This is the portion of the offerings made to the LORD by fire that were allotted to Aaron and his sons on the day they were presented to serve the LORD as priests. On the day they were anointed, the LORD commanded that the Israelites give this to them as their regular share for the generations to come.*

These, then, are the regulations for the burnt offering, the grain offering, the sin offering, the guilt offering, the ordination offering and the fellowship offering, which the LORD gave Moses on Mount Sinai on the day he commanded the Israelites to bring their offerings to the LORD, in the Desert of Sinai.

The final verses of Leviticus 7 comprise two closing formulas or subscriptions. The first of these (vv. 35–36) relates to the portion of the offerings that was to be given to the priests. It is called the "portion of anointing" (KJV; *mišḥâ*[*h*], the Hebrew term in v. 35, can mean both "anointing" and "portion"), not because it had anything to do with the ceremony of anointing as such, but because the priests had a right to it by virtue of the fact that this anointing made them the Lord's servants in a special sense. At the time of their anointing, the priests' hands were filled with offerings (Exod. 29:24), and ever since that ceremony, the Hebrew phrase *millē' 'eṭ-yāḏ* (literally, "fill the hand") took on the meaning of "consecrate" or "install as priest" (Exod. 28:41; 29:9; Lev. 8:33; Judg. 17:5, 12; 1 Kings 13:33). The derivative noun, *millu'îm,* therefore also means "ordination" or "installation in the priesthood" (Exod. 29:22, 26–27; Lev. 7:37; 8:28; etc.). Verse 36 emphasizes the unchangeable character of these regulations (see also 6:18). The Lord's servants, whose livelihood was entirely drawn from the ceremonial service at the temple, were not left in a position of dependence on the good will of the people (see Introduction, p. 16).

The second subscription enumerates once again the regulations that have been dealt with in the preceding verses. It is striking that the sequence of the laws here differs from that in which they appear in chapters 6 and 7, for the ordination offering (*millu'îm,* see above) follows the guilt offering rather than the grain offering. The prohibition of fat and blood, which clearly separates 7:28–34 from verses 11–21 and was apparently inserted here later, is passed over without mention in this final section.

The present formulation of these laws dates from the time when the Israelites were already dwelling in Canaan.[64] During their wanderings, it would not have been possible to keep the altar fire burning day and night, as is required in 6:9, 12, and this same consideration applies to the regular presentation of fellowship offerings spoken of in 6:12. The conjunction of the various easily distinguishable sections within chapters 1–7 also led to several changes in the formulation that facilitated the correct understanding of a few requirements. Leviticus 6:30 therefore cannot be understood apart from 4:15–16, and 6:25; 7:2 clearly refer back to 1:11.

---

[64]See Publisher's Note.

Part Two

The Lord's Priesthood
(8:1–10:20)

As was the case with all ancient peoples, religion did not exist in Israel apart from external, cultic forms. Offerings and priests everywhere occupied the central position in religious life. A fundamental difference nevertheless appears in the fact that outside of Israel, the priests, although there were physical or bodily conditions they had to satisfy, were recruited from among the people at large, and a person could thus become priest without having to be entitled to this by birth or by his position within society. In contrast, once the Israelites had become a nation and the covenant of the Lord had taken definite form as the pattern for their life, only members of the tribe of Levi were authorized to function as temple servants, while the right of serving in the Lord's offerings was reserved exclusively to members of the family of Aaron.

There is also a second point of difference. Whereas outside of Israel the priest primarily offered the sacrifices that sought to bring peace between human beings and the mysterious forces by which they imagined themselves to be surrounded, within Israel the tasks of counselor and teacher stood at the center of the priestly functions. The priest's foremost duty was to give direction to the Israelites in the subjection of their life to the ritual and ethical requirements of the service of the Lord. In Moses' blessing of Levi (Deut. 33:8–11), the presentation of offerings is therefore mentioned last, whereas the supervision of the people's compliance with their social-ethical and ritual obligations (v. 10, *mišpāṭîm*, "precepts," *tôrâ[h]*, "law") occupies the primary position. The spiritual factor, which is at once religious and ethical, controls everything here. For this reason, Israel had no secret priestly knowledge, and its cult was not a mystery cult, but rather belonged to everyone. The religion of Israel was prophetic rather than priestly in character.[1]

The Ordination of the Priests
(8:1–36)

This chapter contains a description of the manner in which the directions of Exodus 29 and 40:9–15 pertaining to the ordination of Aaron and his sons as priests of the Lord and the consecration of the tabernacle and its furnishings were carried out (see also Exod. 30:26–30). A date is not given for this ceremony, unless the "eighth day" mentioned in Leviticus 9:1 is placed in the first month of the second year, which Exodus 40:17 speaks of. If this were the case, however, we would expect a fuller account of when the ordination occurred, especially since Leviticus 8:33 speaks of the week of ordination. The description is given in great detail, for the institution of the Aaronic priesthood in place of that presided over by family heads (Gen. 12:7; 46:1) or their firstborn sons (Exod. 24:5) would be of the utmost significance for the further development of Israel's life. It should be noted that Leviticus 8 is not simply a reproduction of the material contained in Exodus 29 and 40:9–15, for as will appear later, it departs from this in several places.

8:1–5 *The LORD said to Moses, "Bring Aaron and his sons, their garments, the anointing oil, the bull for the sin offering, the two rams and the basket containing bread made without yeast, and gather the entire assembly at the entrance to the Tent of Meeting." Moses did as the LORD commanded him, and the assembly gathered at the entrance to the Tent of Meeting.*
Moses said to the assembly, "This is what the LORD has commanded to be done."

Preparation. The "entire assembly," in the person of its lawful representatives—according to Ibn Ezra these were the tribal chieftains—first gathered at Moses' command in front of the Tent of Meeting (Exod. 29 does not mention this), and the other elements of the ceremony (viz., the required ordination offerings, the priestly garments, and the anointing oil) were also made ready. Aaron and his four sons (see Lev. 10:1, 16) then joined the assembly, and Moses began the ceremonial acts by which the future prerogatives of Aaron and his sons would be established in accordance with the Lord's command.

---

[1]See my book, *Gods Woord*[2], pp. 326f., 339f.

1. *Washing, Clothing, and Anointing* (8:6–13)

8:6 *Then Moses brought Aaron and his sons forward and washed them with water.*

Moses then had Aaron and his sons brought forward, and after assuming a position directly before the entrance to the Tent, they were washed with water (according to *Yoma* 30f. this was done behind a linen sheet). This needs no explanation, for washing appears frequently as the means for restoring persons or things to a state of ceremonial cleanness (11:32; 13:58; 14:8–9; 17:15–16; Num. 31:23–24; see also Exod. 29:4). Ibn Ezra claims that only the hands and feet were washed, as was always done before entering the sanctuary (Exod. 30:19–20), but Siphra and Rashi maintain that the washing involved complete immersion. Whatever may have been the case, it was necessary that the entire body be washed, for whoever stood in the service of the pure and holy God had to himself be completely clean (cf. Lev. 16:4). The verse thus specifies that this was to be done *bammāyim,* "with water," as was also directed in Leviticus 14:9; 15:13, 16; 16:4, 24, 26, 28, and Numbers 19:7–8. Later, whenever the priests would enter into the sanctuary, it was only required that they wash their hands and feet (Exod. 30:19–21; 40:30–31). Washing in this context constituted a religious act.

8:7–9 *He put the tunic on Aaron, tied the sash around him, clothed him with the robe and put the ephod on him. He also tied the ephod to him by its skillfully woven waistband; so it was fastened on him. He placed the breastpiece on him and put the Urim and Thummim in the breastpiece. Then he placed the turban on Aaron's head and set the gold plate, the sacred diadem, on the front of it, as the Lord commanded Moses.*

Under the guidance of Moses, Aaron then clothed himself in the official high priestly attire that is described in Exodus 29. The linen undergarments of Exodus 28:42 are not mentioned here, for Aaron and his sons would naturally have put these on immediately after their ritual washing.

The first garment to be donned was the *kuttōnet,* a tunic or undergarment (sometimes less correctly referred to as a shirt) which was usually made of linen. It was worn on the naked body, extended to the knees (thus the requirement of Exod. 20:26; 28:42), had short sleeves, and was held in place by a sash or girdle (this is not mentioned in Exod. 29:5). This was followed by the *meʿîl,* the robe that is described in Exodus 28:31–35. This stately vestment was woven in one piece (cf. John 19:23) and likewise reached to the knees, and its hem was adorned with pomegranates made from three different colors of yarn and also with gold bells. The meaning of these latter (perhaps a symbol of the harmony of the spheres?) still remains unclear at present.[2] The next item was the *'ēp̄ōḏ* (ephod), a shoulder garment that according to the description in Exodus 28:6–14 consisted of a type of vest that covered the breast and back down to the hips and was held in position at the bottom by means of a waistband. Over this were placed two shoulder pieces, which were like collars running from back to front over the shoulders and were fastened to each other and to the front of the vest by means of rings. Two onyx stones, which were mounted in gold settings attached to braided chains of gold, were affixed to these shoulder pieces. The *ḥōšen* or breastpiece, which was made from the same materials as the ephod, was fastened at its four corners to the latter by means of rings and chains of gold and also cords. On this breastpiece were mounted twelve precious stones, each engraved with the name of one of the twelve tribes, which were set in gold and arranged in rows of three, and within it were placed the Urim and the Thummim (*'ûrîm* and *tummîm*, Exod. 28:15–30). Nothing is known concerning the nature and appearance of the latter, but it appears in 1 Samuel 14:41–42 (see NIV margin and RSV) that they were used to consult the Lord by means of lot. Lastly, the *miṣnep̄eṯ*, a tiara or turban, was placed on Aaron's head. Although Exodus 28 gives no further description of this, it must have been higher and more costly than those of the ordinary priests, for to the front of it was attached a gold plate or "sacred diadem" (Lev. 8:9) bearing the inscription "HOLY TO THE LORD," which marked its wearer as a person who had been set apart to the service of the Lord. For a fuller description of these matters, see Gispen's discussion of Exodus 28 in his volume of the *Bible Student's Commentary* (pp. 262–73). It may be noted in passing here that the three sections of the sanctuary were reflected in the high priestly attire: the robe corresponded to the courtyard, the ephod to the Holy Place, and the breastpiece to the Most Holy Place.

8:10–13 *Then Moses took the anointing oil and anointed the tabernacle and everything in it, and so consecrated them. He sprinkled some of the oil on the altar seven times, anointing the altar and all its utensils and the basin with its stand, to consecrate them. He poured some of the anointing oil on Aaron's head and anointed him to consecrate him. Then he brought Aaron's sons forward, put tunics on them, tied sashes around them and put headbands on them, as the LORD commanded Moses.*

Only now could the ceremony proceed to the anointing with the sacred oil, which was actually a kind of soap made from olive oil mixed with

---

[2]See R. Eisler, *Weltenmartel und Himmelszelt* (1910).

several fragrant spices (myrrh, cinnamon, cane, and cassia) and had the advantage of drying up quickly so that it could be wiped away easily (Exod. 30:22–33; Ps. 133:2). The purpose of this anointing, which in its application to persons took place only with priests and kings,[3] was in part to fortify the life of the recipient—a use that also appeared in everyday life (Ps. 23:5; Amos 6:6; Luke 7:46)—but its primary intent was to consecrate him, i.e., to set him apart for the service of the Lord. Whoever received the sacred anointing oil was thereby exalted above all his fellows and marked as a person who possessed special rights because he was controlled and led by the Spirit of the Lord (1 Sam. 16:13). Anointing therefore did not signify that someone was dedicated to the Deity,[4] but rather that he was singled out as having been chosen by the Lord. This same thought is expressed in the fact that the tabernacle could not serve as the Lord's dwelling place until the sacred anointing oil had been applied to it in its entirety, i.e., to both the external structure and the furnishings (Exod. 30:26–29).

The ceremony in Leviticus 8 in fact began with this anointing, for even if everything had been constructed and arranged according to prescription under Moses' direction and the glory of the Lord filled the tabernacle as a sign that He had entered His dwelling there (Exod. 40:34–35), the regular ceremonial service could not yet begin. Indeed, even Moses himself was not permitted to enter the tent. It was only when the priests were on the verge of beginning their work that the sanctuary could be consecrated by anointing (see Exod. 29:36f.), and the latter had to precede the former, since "holy" persons could perform their tasks only in a "holy" place. In this context it is well once again to call attention to the fact that Israel, like the entire ancient Near Eastern world, conceived of holiness as something substantive, almost as something material or physical, which became attached to both persons and things. This same line of thought also determined the nature of the concepts *clean* and *unclean*.

The anointing of the priest followed that of the tabernacle. Although Leviticus 7:36 and 10:7 (also Exod. 28:41; 30:30; 40:15; Num. 3:3) give the impression that the sacred anointing oil was poured not only on the high priest, but also on the ordinary priests, neither Leviticus 8 nor Exodus 29 speak of this. All that is described here is the anointing of Aaron, this being followed by the sprinkling of the anointing oil and blood from the altar on Aaron and his sons and also on their garments. In his comments upon

---

[3]Anointing to the office of prophet appears solely in the case of Elisha, where it was apparently performed in order to designate him as the successor of Elijah.

[4]As is maintained by Kittel, *Die Heilige Schrift des Alten Testaments,* I, p. 422.

Exodus 29:1–9,[5] Böhl attempts to resolve this difficulty by claiming ''that initially only the chief priest was considered worthy of this royal honor, which later came to be demanded by the other priests.'' Over against this, Edelkoort maintains in his remarks on Numbers 3:3[6] that whereas in ancient times all priests were anointed, after the downfall of the monarchy this was reserved exclusively for the high priest. The fact that these two solutions are sought in precisely opposite directions forms a clear indication that there is no concrete evidence. Commenting on Exodus 29:4–9, Gispen[7] accepts the rabbinical position, which asserts on the basis of Leviticus 21:10, 12 that the anointing of the ordinary priests followed a different procedure than that of the high priest; in the latter the oil was poured over the head, while in the former it was smeared on the forehead. The verses referred to do not warrant this conclusion, however.

To my mind, the most likely solution is that whereas every new high priest, like every new king, was anointed when he took office, this was not the case with ordinary priests. They were apparently regarded as having been anointed in the high priest, as sharing in his anointing.[8] Concerning the rite of sprinkling with anointing oil, see the comment on verse 30.

In contrast to the detailed description that is given of the dressing of Aaron in the high priestly garments and of his subsequent anointing, the clothing of the ordinary priests is only touched on briefly in verse 13 (see Exod. 29:5–9). Their official attire consisted merely of a *kuttōneṯ* (''tunic,'' see above) with sash, and a headband.

2. *The Sin Offering* (8:14–17)

8:14–17 *He then presented the bull for the sin offering, and Aaron and his sons laid their hands on its head. Moses slaughtered the bull and took some of the blood, and with his finger he put it on all the horns of the altar to purify the altar. He poured out the rest of the blood at the base of the altar. So he consecrated it to make atonement for it. Moses also took all the fat around the inner parts, the covering of the liver, and both kidneys and their fat, and burned it on the altar. But the bull with its hide and its flesh and its offal he burned up outside the camp, as the* Lord *commanded Moses.*

After the completion of all this, the priests were still not ready to perform their ritual tasks and to serve as intermediaries between the Lord and His covenant people, for the offerings prescribed in Exodus 29:10–25 had

---

[5]*Tekst en Uitleg,* 1928.
[6]*Tekst en Uitleg,* 1930.
[7]*The Bible Student's Commentary,* p. 274.
[8]See also the comments on Leviticus 8:10–13 in De Wilde, *Tekst en Uitleg* (1937).

yet to be performed. The first of these was a sin offering consisting of a bull, this being necessary because the priest himself had to receive atonement before he could intercede for others in this regard by means of his own sacrificial activities. Aaron and his sons thus began by laying their hands on the bull of the sin offering and thereby transferring to it their sin and uncleanness (see discussion on 1:4). The offering itself took place in the manner described in Leviticus 4:3–12 (see also Exod. 29:10–14), with one exception: the blood of the bull was not smeared on the horns of the altar of fragrant incense (4:7), but rather on those of the altar of burnt offering. Like the priest, this altar itself had to bear the sign of the blood of the covenant if it was to be fit for the work of atonement (cf. Exod. 29:12, 36–37, and also Ezek. 43:20, where this rite is expanded). Because of the fact that the altar of burnt offering rather than the altar of incense received the blood mark here, Eerdmans[9] maintains that this section was not put into its final form until after the exile, for in his view the altar of incense no longer existed at that time.[10] Apart from the fact that this altar appears both in the books of the Maccabees and in Luke 1:11, this is not enough ground for Eerdmans' position. In Leviticus 4:3–12, where verse 7 speaks of putting the blood of the offering on the altar of incense, the sin offering performed by the priests *after* their accession is under discussion, while 8:14–17 speaks of the sin offering presented *before* they assumed office. It is only here, then, that the blood was smeared only on the altar of burnt offering (see commentary on 4:7).

3. The Burnt Offering (8:18–21)

8:18–21 *He then presented the ram for the burnt offering, and Aaron and his sons laid their hands on its head. Then Moses slaughtered the ram and sprinkled the blood against the altar on all sides. He cut the ram into pieces and burned the head, the pieces and the fat. He washed the inner parts and the legs with water and burned the whole ram on the altar as a burnt offering, a pleasing aroma, an offering made to the* Lord *by fire, as the* Lord *commanded Moses.*

The priests who had now been absolved of their sin next presented in their own behalf a ram as a burnt offering. This formed a sign of the complete dedication of their lives and was performed in accordance with the directions appearing in Exodus 29:15–18 and Leviticus 1:10–13.

---

[9]*Das Buch Leviticus*, p. 53.
[10]*Das Buch Leviticus*, pp. 31f.

4. *The Ordination Offering* (8:22–32)

8:22–29 *He then presented the other ram, the ram for the ordination, and Aaron
and his sons laid their hands on its head. Moses slaughtered the ram and took some
of its blood and put it on the lobe of Aaron's right ear, on the thumb of his right
hand and on the big toe of his right foot. Moses also brought Aaron's sons forward
and put some of the blood on the lobes of their right ears, on the thumbs of their
right hands and on the big toes of their right feet. Then he sprinkled blood against
the altar on all sides. He took the fat, the fat tail, all the fat around the inner parts,
the covering of the liver, both kidneys and their fat and the right thigh. Then from
the basket of bread made without yeast, which was before the* Lord, *he took a cake
of bread, and one made with oil, and a wafer; he put these on the fat portions and
on the right thigh. He put all these in the hands of Aaron and his sons and waved
them before the* Lord *as a wave offering. Then Moses took them from their hands
and burned them on the altar on top of the burnt offering as an ordination offering,
a pleasing aroma, an offering made to the* Lord *by fire. He also took the breast—
Moses' share of the ordination ram—and waved it before the* Lord *as a wave
offering, as the* Lord *commanded Moses.*

Now the ceremony could proceed to the ordination offering proper,
which installed Aaron and his sons in their priestly office. The offering
consisted of a ram, and after the animal was slaughtered, some of its blood
was put on the right ear lobe, the right thumb, and the right big toe of those
who were being ordained to the priesthood (see also Exod. 29:20). The
symbolism of this is clear. The organs of hearing, doing, and walking were
in this manner consecrated to the service of the Lord; the ear was to hear
His commands, the hand was to perform them, and the foot had to walk in
His ways (see also Lev. 14:14–17).

This same rite was also practiced among other peoples, where it was
performed in order to drive away demonic forces. In Israel, however, its
meaning was different. The ritual procedure with the blood was here
doubtless intended as a reminder of the ceremony of the establishment of
the covenant in Exodus 24:8. It formed a reconfirmation of the covenantal
relationship, this being necessary for the priest since he had to manifest in
his life an exceptional degree of holiness (1 Sam. 22:17–21).

The blood thus placed a special bond between the Lord and His priestly
servants (Mal. 2:4–6), just as it put such a bond between Him and His
people (Exod. 24:6–8). As the vehicle of life, blood was regarded as
capable of expelling all of the death-dealing, unclean forces and powers, a
dynamistic notion that Israel shared with many ancient peoples.[11] The ram
of the ordination offering had a peculiar name. It was literally called the

---

[11] See Publisher's Note.

"ram of filling," for the Hebrew words for "fill" or "fill the hand" can be used to mean "install as priest" (see pp. 90–91). The significance of this name comes out clearly in verses 25–27. Certain sections of the ram (viz., the fat portions and the right thigh, see also 7:30–32) were placed by Moses on three differently made pieces of bread and then put in the hands of Aaron and his sons as a token of their priestly office. Moses then slid his hands beneath theirs and solemnly moved the pieces back and forth in order to symbolize the dedication of the offering. This was the "wave offering" spoken of earlier (pp. 88–90), and it was subsequently burned on the altar as a burnt offering. By way of their gifts, the priests were in this manner offered to God, who then gave them back to Moses so that they could devote themselves to His service. That this was indeed the deeper meaning of this rite becomes evident in the dedication of the Levites, for there the persons themselves were waved as a wave offering (Num. 8:10–14).

The breast of the ordination ram was also treated as a wave offering. This became Moses' share which was given to him for his participation in the ordination ceremony of the priests. The Lord, as it were, returned this to Moses as the portion of the ram he was to eat (see 7:31).

8:30 *Then Moses took some of the anointing oil and some of the blood from the altar and sprinkled them on Aaron and his garments and on his sons and their garments. So he consecrated Aaron and his garments and his sons and their garments.*

There is yet one more action that Moses had to perform in the ceremony. Taking some of the anointing oil and also some of the blood from the altar, he sprinkled this on Aaron and his sons and on the priestly garments in which they were still clothed.

In connection with Exodus 29:21, this presents a couple of difficulties. First of all, in Exodus this act forms a part of the blood ceremony that has already taken place, as discussed in verses 22–24, and it thus occurs before the burning of the fat portions of the ordination ram. Because of this, the blood is there spoken of first and the anointing oil as following. In Leviticus, however, where this rite forms the conclusion of Moses' actions, the sprinkling with the anointing oil is mentioned first and that with the blood second. The explanation of this is perhaps that Leviticus gives the historical order and Exodus the logical order. The second difficulty is completely different in nature. It is not at all surprising that the sprinkling of Aaron's sons with anointing oil should be spoken of here, for there had been no mention of this in the previous verses. It is not clear, however, why they were once again sprinkled with blood after the rite of verse 24. In addition, there seems even less reason why Aaron should be involved in this sprinkling with anointing oil and blood (cf. vv. 12, 23). Jewish tradition has attempted to evade at least this latter difficulty by omitting the conjunction *and* from verse 30 in the two places where it appears between "Aaron" and "his garments." The effect of this is to create the impression that this sprinkling applied solely to Aaron's garments. All of the ancient translations, however, and also a large number of manuscripts as well as the text of Exodus 29:21, indicate that this conjunction was present in the original text. We must thus come to terms with the fact that, according to Leviticus 8, Aaron was not only anointed (v. 12), but also sprinkled with anointing oil (v. 30), and that the spreading of blood on the right ear lobe, thumb, and big toe of both Aaron and his sons was followed by a sprinkling of all of them with blood.

It would of course be easy to account for this by regarding Exodus 29:21 and Leviticus 8:30 as later insertions,[12] but such "later hands" usually strike me as nothing more than inventions of convenience. An analogous situation appears in Leviticus 14:10–20, where offerings of purification are spoken of. There also, blood and oil were first spread on the right ear lobe, thumb, and big toe of the person being cleansed, and the remaining oil was then poured on his head. On the basis of this, it seems to me that the repetition of the ritual was intended to underscore the thought that the anointing oil and the blood were to make the bond between God and the priests as strong and effective as possible. De Wilde is thus correct, on this view, in considering the rite of verse 30 as the culmination of the ordination ceremony. In contrast, Hertz's interpretation of this repetition as pointing to the double function of the priests—viz., the spreading of divine light and the proclamation of atonement—is to my mind more a matter of eisegesis than exegesis.

8:31–32 *Moses then said to Aaron and his sons, "Cook the meat at the entrance to the Tent of Meeting and eat it there with the bread from the basket of ordination offerings, as I commanded, saying, 'Aaron and his sons are to eat it.' Then burn up the rest of the meat and the bread."*

As in the fellowship offerings (7:11–21), the ordination was followed by a meal, but this serves here as a confirmation of the covenant that has been enacted between the Lord and the house of Aaron (cf. Gen. 31:46). The meal was formed by the meat of the ordination ram, which was cooked and eaten together with the bread spoken of in verse 26. Since this meat belonged to the ordination offering, however, it possessed a greater degree

---

[12]See, e.g., P. Heinsch, *Das Buch Leviticus,* 1935, p. 46.

of holiness than the fellowship offering, and the meal thus had to take place within the sanctuary. Whatever was left over of the meat and bread was to be burned, as was also done in the most holy offerings (6:30).

5. *The Ordination Week* (8:33–36)

8:33–36 *"Do not leave the entrance to the Tent of Meeting for seven days, until the days of your ordination are completed, for your ordination will last seven days. What has been done today was commanded by the L*ORD *to make atonement for you. You must stay at the entrance to the Tent of Meeting day and night for seven days and do what the L*ORD *requires, so you will not die; for that is what I have been commanded." So Aaron and his sons did everything the L*ORD *commanded through Moses.*

This meal did not yet form the conclusion of the priestly ordination. In order that they not be exposed to possible defilement, Aaron and his sons had to remain within the area of the sanctuary for seven days (for the significance of this number *seven,* cf. also Lev. 4:8; 8:11; Exod. 12:15; 23:15; 29:37), for Moses told them that "your ordination will last seven days" (literally, "he will fill your hand for seven days"). This once again indicates how important it was that the bond between the Lord and the priests be made as firm as possible (see discussion on v. 30). For this reason also, verse 35 warns that all of the Lord's commands were to be observed with the most scrupulous care, and verse 36 contains the assurance that this was indeed done. Expiatory offerings were to be brought daily, as Exodus 29:37 (in contrast to the formulation in Lev. 8:34) indicates in so many words, and if I understand verse 33b and Exodus 29:35 correctly, the burnt and ordination offerings were likewise to be repeated, no less than the other ceremonial acts: the clothing and anointing of Aaron, and the sprinkling of anointing oil and blood on Aaron and his sons as well as their garments. The priests could thus not begin the performance of their official duties until the eighth day. Any shortcoming in the ordination ceremony would place their lives in peril, for to see or draw near to God in an unprepared state meant certain death. In accordance with the Lord's own decree, the priest who would serve as mediator between Himself and His people had to himself be fully sanctified before he could bring about the sanctification of the people by way of his ceremonial tasks. The Old Testament mediators thus had to receive sanctification, whereas the Mediator of the New Covenant sanctified Himself (John 17:19).

The Commencement of the Priestly Ministry
(9:1–24)

1. *Preparation* (9:1–7)

9:1–7 *On the eighth day Moses summoned Aaron and his sons and the elders of Israel. He said to Aaron, "Take a bull calf for your sin offering and a ram for your burnt offering, both without defect, and present them before the LORD. Then say to the Israelites: 'Take a male goat for a sin offering, a calf and a lamb–both a year old and without defect–for a burnt offering, and a cow and a ram for a fellowship offering to sacrifice before the LORD, together with a grain offering mixed with oil. For today the LORD will appear to you.'"*

They took the things Moses commanded to the front of the Tent of Meeting, and the entire assembly came near and stood before the LORD. Then Moses said, "This is what the LORD has commanded you to do, so that the glory of the LORD may appear to you."

Moses said to Aaron, "Come to the altar and sacrifice your sin offering and your burnt offering and make atonement for yourself and the people; sacrifice the offering that is for the people and make atonement for them, as the LORD has commanded."

After the seven days of ordination had come to an end and Aaron and his sons had been fully consecrated to the mediatorial office they were to perform, they began their ministry by presenting offerings under the direction of Moses and in the presence of both the elders and the entire community. Verse 1 mentions these elders separately, for they served as representatives of the nation of Israel as a whole (4:15). Jewish tradition asserts that this took place on the first day of the month of Nisan, i.e., New Year's Day, but this has no support in the text and furthermore is in conflict with Exodus 40:2, 17.

The sacrifices began with the presentation in the courtyard of the Tent of Meeting of the two animals that were to be used in the sin and burnt offerings for Aaron and his house. The sin offering consisted of a bull and the burnt offering of a ram, just as in the priestly ordination (8:14, 18) and also in the later ceremony on the Day of Atonement (16:3). The age of these animals is not given, but the specification that the bull be a calf *(ben-bāqār,* cf. Gen. 18:7–8) indicates that the animal was to be young. Jewish tradition states that it was two years old, whereas on the Day of Atonement a three-year-old bull was presented (16:3; *Rosh ha-Shanah* 10a, cf. 4:3). Both animals naturally had to be without defect.

Since the Lord Himself would appear in order to confirm Aaron's priesthood, a complete round of sacrifices was presented in behalf of the people: sin, burnt, and fellowship offerings, and also the grain offering that had to accompany the latter two. The required animals here were a male goat in the sin offering (see commentary on 4:14) and a bull calf and a lamb, both no more than a year old (see 22:27), in the burnt offering (cf. Num. 28:11–15; 29:2–5, where, however, the offerings occurred on a feast day). This offering was therefore small in comparison with that presented by Solomon (1 Kings 8:63). After the sacrificial animals had been brought to the sanctuary and the assembled Israelites had taken their position there, Moses declared what had to be done before the Lord could appear to them (v. 4) and His glory could be made manifest (v. 6). This glory (*kābôd*, literally, "weight") was revealed in the momentary resplendence of the awesome majesty of the divine nature, in which the Lord's incomparable greatness and infinite might come to expression. The radiance of this convinces man, bound as he is to the realm of the senses, of the fact that God is present and ready to manifest His divine power, but the Israelites were nevertheless compelled to acknowledge that His presence in this instance was still only a matter of particular, limited revelations in which His glory remained obscured. The prophet Ezekiel gives a lengthy description of this *kābôd*.[13]

2. *The Offerings for the Priests* (9:8–14)

9:8–14 *So Aaron came to the altar and slaughtered the calf as a sin offering for himself. His sons brought the blood to him, and he dipped his finger into the blood and put it on the horns of the altar; the rest of the blood he poured out at the base of the altar. On the altar he burned the fat, the kidneys and the covering of the liver from the sin offering, as the LORD commanded Moses; the flesh and the hide he burned up outside the camp.*

Then he slaughtered the burnt offering. His sons handed him the blood, and he sprinkled it against the altar on all sides. They handed him the burnt offering piece by piece, including the head, and he burned them on the altar. He washed the inner parts and the legs and burned them on top of the burnt offering on the altar.

At Moses' command, Aaron came to the altar of burnt offering carrying the sacrificial animals in order to accept his office. (In view of this command of Moses, Siphra claims that Aaron was at this point filled with fear.) These animals were intended for Aaron and his house. Although the Masoretic text of verse 7 has "for yourself and the people" (as in NIV), this cannot be correct, for the atonement for the people came later. The Septuagint has "for you and your house" here, and I would follow this reading (cf. NEB).

---

[13]See my commentary, *Ezechiël*, pp. 46–55.

This part of the ceremony began with a sin offering of purification that was presented in conformity with the ritual of 8:14–17. Since this was a special offering and was not brought in connection with a particular sin, the procedure differed from that outlined in 4:3–12. Verse 9 expressly states that Aaron's sons assisted him, and it was thus made clear that they also entered into their ministry on this day. The statement in verse 10 that the sin offering was burned on the altar indicates that, in accordance with the requirement of 6:12–13, the fire had not gone out after the seven days of ordination. The flesh and the hide of the animal were disposed of as directed in 4:11–12, for as the objects of the sin offering, the priests could naturally not eat of it themselves.

As a sign of complete self-surrender (see pp. 32–34)—for this reason, the laying on of hands is expressly mentioned here, whereas in the sin offering it is merely presupposed—a burnt offering immediately followed, this being presented in accordance with the ritual of 8:18–21. Aaron's sons cut the animal apart (cf. 1:6) and handed it to him "piece by piece," and after the unclean sections had been washed, everything but the hide was burned on the altar.

3. *The Offerings for the People* (9:15–21)

9:15–21 *Aaron then brought the offering that was for the people. He took the goat for the people's sin offering and slaughtered it and offered it for a sin offering as he did with the first one.*

He brought the burnt offering and offered it in the prescribed way. He also brought the grain offering, took a handful of it and burned it on the altar in addition to the morning's burnt offering.

He slaughtered the cow and the ram as the fellowship offering for the people. His sons handed him the blood, and he sprinkled it against the altar on all sides. But the fat portions of the cow and the ram—the fat tail, the layer of fat, the kidneys and the covering of the liver—these they laid on the breasts, and then Aaron burned the fat on the altar. Aaron waved the breasts and the right thigh before the LORD as a wave offering, as Moses commanded.

Now that the priests had been placed in a right relationship with the Lord, they could begin their task of procuring atonement for the people. This began with the presentation of a sin offering, which Aaron subjected to the same procedure "as he did with the first one" (v. 15; cf. 4:21), i.e., the sin offering for the priests (vv. 8–11). For the same reason as in this previous sin offering, the ritual here differs from that outlined in Leviticus 4 (vv. 13–21). The flesh of the animal was thus not eaten (cf. 10:19), as was otherwise the case (5:13), but was rather burned. A burnt offering consisting of the animals mentioned in verse 3 then followed, this being presented in accordance with the directions given in chapter 1. A grain offering was then also brought, and as was required in 2:2, only a handful of this was burned on the altar. In stating that this was burned "in addition to the morning's burnt offering," verse 17 implies that the *tāmîd* was already being regularly presented at this time. This could not be the case, however, for the offerings discussed in the present chapter preceded the beginning of the regular sacrificial service. For this reason, I am inclined to regard this phrase as a later insertion and would thus place it in parentheses.

Last of all, a fellowship offering was presented on behalf of the people, and the procedure here follows that of chapter 3 in which the blood was sprinkled "against the altar on all sides" and the fat portions were burned on top of the altar. With the breasts and the right thigh, which according to 7:30–34 constituted the priestly portion of all the fellowship offerings, Aaron performed the symbolism of the wave offering (see pp. 88–90). What was done with the rest of the meat from the animals used in the fellowship offering is not stated, but it appears from 23:20 that this also was given to the priests.

9:22 *Then Aaron lifted his hands toward the people and blessed them. And having sacrificed the sin offering, the burnt offering and the fellowship offering, he stepped down.*

After the prescribed offerings had been presented in this manner by Aaron and his sons, Aaron stepped down from the raised platform of the altar. Before doing this, however, he raised his hands toward heaven and pronounced the high priestly blessing on the people (Num. 6:22–27). Aaron was thus the first person to make use of the exclusive priestly prerogative (Deut. 10:8; 27:14; the kings later encroached on this privilege, however[14]) to bless the people, i.e., to speak words charged with the divine potency that now dwelled in him, and in so doing to cause the spiritual power given by God to descend on them.

9:23–24 *Moses and Aaron then went into the Tent of Meeting. When they came out, they blessed the people; and the glory of the LORD appeared to all the people. Fire came out from the presence of the LORD and consumed the burnt offering and the fat portions on the altar. And when all the people saw it, they shouted for joy and fell facedown.*

---

[14]See my commentary, *I Kronieken*.

To conclude the ceremony, Moses and Aaron went within the tabernacle, this being the first time the latter was permitted to do so. This action thus served as a final confirmation to the people of the legitimacy of Aaron's priestly office, and the fact that he was accompanied by Moses lent even greater strength to this. Their departure from the sanctuary demonstrated that Aaron's presentation of the offerings was in accordance with the Lord's will and had received His favor. They then pronounced another blessing on the people who could henceforth live in the assurance that their priests had been ordained by God Himself to the ministry of sacrifice and atonement.

As Moses had promised earlier (vv. 4, 6), the glory of the Lord (see above) now appeared in order to stamp the seal of His approval in an unmistakable manner on what Moses and Aaron had done that day in His sanctuary. The precise visible form this took is not stated, but it is likely that it was the pillar of cloud, spoken of elsewhere (see Exod. 16:10), which came out of the Tent of Meeting (Exod. 40:34–35). Along with this there appeared a flame of fire that ignited the offerings lying on the altar and instantly consumed them (cf. 1 Kings 18:38). This latter phenomenon naturally did not point to the heavenly origin of the altar fire, as De Wilde maintains,[15] for the fire had already been kindled in the previous offerings of chapter 9. As is indicated in verses 4 and 6, it rather gave expression to the Lord's acceptance of the offerings for the priests and the people (cf. Judg. 6:21; 1 Kings 18:38; 1 Chron. 21:26; 2 Chron. 7:1). This was indeed how the people regarded it, for they fell to the ground in joyful adoration, overwhelmed at being the special objects of the Lord's favor and might.

The Death of Nadab and Abihu
(10:1–7)

10:1–2 *Aaron's sons Nadab and Abihu took their censers, put fire in them and added incense; and they offered unauthorized fire before the LORD, contrary to his command. So fire came out from the presence of the LORD and consumed them, and they died before the LORD.*

On the same day they assumed their priestly office (9:9, 12–13, 18), Aaron's two eldest sons, Nadab and Abihu, who along with their father and the seventy elders had accompanied Moses in the confirmation of the covenant on Mount Sinai and there beheld the God of Israel (Exod. 24:1, 9–10), committed a deed that cost them their lives. Each of them placed

---

[15] *Tekst en Uitleg*, p. 92.

incense in a burning censer and brought this "before the LORD." It appears from verse 4 (cf. 9:5) that they did this in the courtyard and were about to carry the burning incense into the Tent of Meeting. What their intention may have been is unclear, for it is only stated that the fire that they placed in their censers was regarded as "unauthorized,"[16] i.e., displeasing to God, when they added incense to it and sought to bring it into the presence of the Lord (see also Num. 3:4). Why it was so regarded is also not expressly stated, and because of this a variety of suggestions have been offered. In view of verses 8–9, some rabbis have proposed that they were under the influence of strong drink, while others have thought that they uttered legal pronouncements from the law in the presence of their teacher Moses. The former suggestion is groundless, however, and the latter forms a clear example of the transference of an idea or thought from the time of the scribes to the Mosaic period. In my opinion, those who maintain that they filled their censers with "unholy fire" (see RSV) that had not been taken from the altar (cf. Lev. 16:12; Num. 16:46) are also in error, for verse 1 would then state that they "put unholy fire in them." Their sin could also not have consisted in the fact that they burned incense that had not been made in the manner prescribed in Exodus 30:34–38, for verse 36 indicates that this requirement was only added later. The final words of Leviticus 10:1 state that Nadab and Abihu committed an arbitrary act that was "contrary to [the LORD's] command." Apparently, they must have attempted to present the daily offering of incense, which according to the regulation of Exodus 30:7–9 was to be kindled on the altar of incense standing directly before the Most Holy Place by no one other than the high priest himself. Because of this, the fire in their censers was at once regarded as "unauthorized," so that the smoke from the incense did not protect them (cf. Lev. 16:12–13). No such arbitrary deed was permitted in the Lord's ceremonial service, least of all by those whom He had called to renounce their own will in the performance of His.

The punishment followed immediately on their sinful act. As had occurred shortly before (9:24), fire came out "from the presence of the LORD," but whereas this had previously been a sign of divine approbation, it now formed an expression of His disfavor and wrath. The fire struck down the two guilty priests before they entered the Tent, and they met their deaths in the courtyard ("before the LORD," see also, Num. 11:1; 16:35; 2 Kings 1:10, 12) where Israel was supposed to find life through the atoning power of its offerings. This day, which could have been the happiest of Aaron's life, thus became the most tragic. Since verse 5 states that

---

[16]The author translates the Hebrew term here as "strange" (cf. KJV).

Nadab and Abihu were still in their tunics when they were carried away, the rabbis have regarded this event as a mysterious phenomenon in which their bodies were not touched by the fire. This goes beyond what is indicated in the text, however.

It may be noted in this connection that the Wellhausen school has made more than one attempt to deny the historicity of this tragic death of Aaron's sons. Some regard the latter as personifications of the northern Israelite priesthood, while others claim that they are the ancestors of priestly lines that were deposed from office. It is unfortunate for this latter position that Numbers 3:4—which Wellhausen himself regards as belonging to the Priestly Code along with Leviticus 10—explicitly states that Nadab and Abihu died without leaving sons (see also 1 Chron. 24:2).

10:3 *Moses then said to Aaron, "This is what the Lord spoke of when he said:*
" 'Among those who approach me
I will show myself holy;
in the sight of all the people
I will be honored.' "
Aaron remained silent.

Moses immediately made clear to Aaron why the Lord had manifested Himself as a consuming fire in this manner. He recalled a statement that the Lord had made previously, although when and where this was spoken is not mentioned, and the saying appears nowhere else. The saying, which is rhythmically constructed, gives the explanation of what had happened. Although its meaning is clear, the translation of it presents difficulties. The first word, *qārôḇ,* refers to someone who approaches or stands near a person or has a close relationship with him. A literal translation would be "my near ones," but this may be expanded to "those who approach me," (as in NIV) or "whom I permit to approach me." The priests are designated by this same term in Ezekiel 42:13; 43:19. Rashi has "my chosen ones" here, but *qārôḇ* nowhere appears with this meaning. The next term, *niqdaš,* here means to manifest oneself as the Holy One through the upholding of the covenantal requirements. The adjective "holy" marks the Lord as one who is separated and set apart, who is thus different from all others and absolutely unique in nature, and who therefore demands recognition of this uniqueness on the part of those who approach Him. It may be added that He could reveal Himself as holy both through the manifestation of His grace (Ezek. 20:41; 28:25; 36:23; 38:16; 39:27) and, as here, through the execution of judgment (also Num. 20:13; Ezek. 28:22). Another Hebrew term that should be discussed here is *nikbaḏ.* A common translation of this is "to glorify oneself" or "to be glorified" (cf. KJV, RSV), but this is not entirely correct. I thus prefer the translation "to manifest one's glory,"[17] i.e., His "weight" *(kābôḏ)*, revealed in His power and might (cf. Exod. 14:4, 17–18; Isa. 26:15; Ezek. 28:22; 39:13).

The meaning of this divine saying that Moses calls to remembrance is clear. Those who by virtue of their office are called to constantly draw near to the Lord and remain in the vicinity of the sanctuary that forms His "dwelling" are placed in a perilous position, for in all that they do or avoid doing they must continually bear in mind that the Lord would never allow His holiness (i.e., the absolute uniqueness of His divine nature) to be taken lightly. Any such deeds of theirs would invariably meet with a manifestation of His glory, which in this situation took the form of an act of annihilation accomplished by His power and might. For those who are called to take part in the Lord's ceremonial service, a higher office involves a greater degree of responsibility, for the danger of falling short and experiencing the Lord's punishment on sin is proportionate to the measure of grace that one has received. This same thought also is expressed in Amos 3:12; Luke 12:48; and 1 Peter 4:17. In the kingdom of God, riches place a person under obligation, and the Talmud thus says with full justice, "With regard to the righteous God is very demanding, even down to a hair's-breadth."

After having heard this explanation of the death of his sons from his brother Moses, Aaron remained silent. The Hebrew term used here is the strongest expression for "being silent": to allow no sound to pass one's lips. To the expressive Near Eastern mind, its use here thus made the most powerful impression imaginable. The same word appears also in Job 29:21; Lamentations 2:10; 3:28; and Amos 5:13. By his silence, Aaron acknowledged God's right to manifest His power in this way (cf. Ps. 39:9).

10:4–5 *Moses summoned Mishael and Elzaphan, sons of Aaron's uncle Uzziel, and said to them, "Come here; carry your cousins outside the camp, away from the front of the sanctuary." So they came and carried them, still in their tunics, outside the camp, as Moses ordered.*

Moses now commanded Mishael and Elzaphan, Aaron's cousins (Exod. 6:18, 20, 22), to remove from the courtyard of the sanctuary the corpses of the two priests who had been struck down by God's judgment. It is noteworthy that this command was given to non-priests rather than to Aaron's other two sons. Although contact with the corpse of a close relative did not in general defile members of the priesthood (Lev. 21:1–2), Eleazar and Ithamar were here not permitted to touch the bodies of their brothers. The reason for this is not so much that they were at the point of beginning their

---

[17]NIV has "I will be honored."

priestly duties, but rather because they would soon eat the sacrificial meal (vv. 12–14), and participation in this was forbidden to those in mourning. Mishael and Elzaphan thus carried the bodies of Nadab and Abihu to their burial outside the camp.

10:6–7 *Then Moses said to Aaron and his sons Eleazar and Ithamar, "Do not let your hair become unkempt, and do not tear your clothes, or you will die and the LORD will be angry with the whole community. But your relatives, all the house of Israel, may mourn for those the LORD has destroyed by fire. Do not leave the entrance to the Tent of Meeting or you will die, because the LORD's anointing oil is on you." So they did as Moses said.*

Aaron and his sons were not present at this burial. They were not permitted to leave the sanctuary, nor could they display any external sign of mourning, although this was in most cases forbidden only to the high priest (21:10). Two such signs are specified here: leaving one's hair hanging loose and unkempt, uncovered by a headcloth (see NIV margin on v. 6; 13:45), and tearing one's clothes.[18] In verse 7, Aaron and his sons are told that they were to remain by the Tent of Meeting "because the LORD's anointing oil is on you." The vivifying power[19] of this anointing oil could not be hindered by the least contact with the realm of death, which comes to expression in the rites of mourning (see also 8:33; 21:10–12). Only the people were permitted to mourn "the burning which the LORD has kindled" (v. 6). This phrase[20] is an allusion to the custom that is also spoken of in 2 Chronicles 16:14 and 21:19. During the burial ceremony, the possessions that had surrounded the deceased person during his lifetime were burned in the belief that he would recover these in the next life and once again make use of them. Excavations have uncovered numerous traces of this practice.

Further Regulations Pertaining to the Priests (10:8–20)

1. The Prohibition of Wine and Fermented Drink for the Priests (10:8–11)

10:8–11 *Then the LORD said to Aaron, "You and your sons are not to drink wine or other fermented drink whenever you go into the Tent of Meeting, or you will die. This is a lasting ordinance for the generations to come. You must distinguish between the holy and the profane, between the unclean and the clean, and you must teach the Israelites all the decrees the LORD has given them through Moses."*

---

[18]Concerning the practice of mourning, see my commentary, *Ezechiël*, pp. 261f.

[19]See Publisher's Note.

[20]The NIV of verse 6 has "mourn for those the LORD has destroyed by fire," whereas the author's translation corresponds to that of the KJV and RSV.

111

There is here no historical connection with the preceding verses that would indicate that Nadab and Abihu committed their sinful deed under the influence of wine or fermented drink (see above). Proverbs 31:6–7 suggests at most that the Israelites perhaps had the custom of giving "stimulating drinks" to those in distress. It is nevertheless completely clear why this prohibition is placed immediately after the ordination of the priests. Wine and fermented drink[21] were often used in the attempt to make contact with the invisible world, and Israel's priests were forbidden to take part in this practice. The Spirit of the Lord, which filled them in the performance of their office, could not be brought into contact with drinks that were of another spirit, and the priests therefore could not partake of intoxicating drinks while they were on duty (see the reproach of Isa. 28:7). Verse 10 states that they were to "distinguish between the holy and the profane." The latter term does not refer to what was common and permissible in everyday life, but rather to all that was not imbued with divine influence (cf. 1 Sam. 21:5–6; Ezek. 22:26; 42:20; 44:23). One could not enter the area of the Holy One unless he was himself holy, and whoever would eat of what was holy (e.g., the meat of offerings) had to remain free of contact with what was profane and thus of an unholy spirit. Only in this manner could distinction also be made between the clean and the unclean, i.e., between who and what could or could not be brought near to the Lord, and also between what could or could not be eaten or touched. The priests were to set good examples in this, for the entire law would otherwise be made a mockery and the holy God, who had given this law to Israel as a rule for its life, would be profaned (see Ezek. 22:26; 44:23). In order to impress on the priesthood how important it was that they fulfill this regulation in their activities, the Lord spoke these words directly to Aaron, without Moses' mediation (see also Num. 18:1, 8, 20).

I must add that when I first consider the sequence "the holy and the profane," "the unclean and the clean" I am surprised. We should expect this to be "the holy and the profane," "the clean and the unclean," and this is the order in which De Wilde arranges these adjectives in his discussion of Leviticus. It must not be forgotten, however, that the idea of taboo had been present in Israel and that the notions of "holy" and "unclean" therefore originally corresponded to one another in more than one respect.[22] Only in

---

[21] "Strong drink," the traditional translation (see KJV, RSV), is not entirely correct, for Israel did not know of the process of distillation. The reference is perhaps to a drink prepared from fruit or honey, possibly with the addition of spices (cf. Isa. 5:22). Some think it was made from dates, and another possibility is beer, for this had been known in Babylon and Egypt centuries before Abraham.

[22] See Publisher's Note.

the light of divine revelation did "holy" and "unclean" come to be distinguished as that which in some way belonged to the Lord and that which was subject to unholy influences, respectively. This idea of taboo continued to make itself felt, however, for the Jews declared the name Yahweh to be taboo and thus refrained from speaking it, and they also forbade the touching of the written characters of the holy text, since this was thought to make a person unclean.

2. The Priestly Portion of the Grain and Fellowship Offerings (10:12–15)

10:12–15 *Moses said to Aaron and his remaining sons, Eleazar and Ithamar, "Take the grain offering left over from the offerings made to the Lᴏʀᴅ by fire and eat it prepared without yeast beside the altar, for it is most holy. Eat it in a holy place, because it is your share and your sons' share of the offerings made to the Lᴏʀᴅ by fire; for so I have been commanded. But you and your sons and your daughters may eat the breast that was waved and the thigh that was presented. Eat them in a ceremonially clean place; they have been given to you and your children as your share of the Israelites' fellowship offerings. The thigh that was presented and the breast that was waved must be brought with the fat portions of the offerings made by fire, to be waved before the Lᴏʀᴅ as a wave offering. This will be the regular share for you and your children, as the Lᴏʀᴅ has commanded."*

These verses do not contain additional general requirements pertaining to the eating of the daily grain offering (6:18) or of the breast and right thigh of the fellowship offering (7:30–34). It appears from verse 12 that, in connection with the death of Nadab and Abihu, they are rather concerned with the offerings that Aaron had presented in behalf of the people after his ordination (9:4, 17–21). It must now be specified who was permitted to eat of the priestly portion of these offerings and where this was to take place. There is no evidence for the notion that Aaron and his sons were now considered unworthy to eat of these offerings, for verse 12 directs that they were to do this in the courtyard beside the altar. A distinction is made in this section between a "holy place" and a "ceremonially clean place." The area occupied by the sanctuary was holy, and the "most holy" portion of the grain offering (i.e., the share given to the priests) was thus to be eaten in the courtyard, this being done exclusively by the male members of the priestly families (2:3, 10). In contrast, the entire Israelite camp was ceremonially clean, and for this reason persons with infectious skin diseases had to remain outside its boundaries (ch. 14). Jewish tradition states that in later times the entire city of Jerusalem was regarded as clean (*Zebahim* 55a). The fellowship offering thus had to be eaten within the camp, and since this was not considered most holy, the entire priestly family, women included, were allowed to participate in the meal.

3. The Misunderstanding Concerning the Goat of the Sin Offering (10:16–20)

10:16–20 *When Moses inquired about the goat of the sin offering and found that it had been burned up, he was angry with Eleazar and Ithamar, Aaron's remaining sons, and asked, "Why didn't you eat the sin offering in the sanctuary area? It is most holy; it was given to you to take away the guilt of the community by making atonement for them before the LORD. Since its blood was not taken into the Holy Place, you should have eaten the goat in the sanctuary area, as I commanded."*

Aaron replied to Moses, "Today they sacrificed their sin offering and their burnt offering before the LORD, but such things as this have happened to me. Would the LORD have been pleased if I had eaten the sin offering today?" When Moses heard this, he was satisfied.

The presentation of legal requirements is here interrupted by an historical episode, although a legal decision is nevertheless implicit in this. When Moses sought to ascertain whether the goat of the sin offering had been dealt with in the manner prescribed in 6:24–30 (MT 6:17–23), it appeared that Eleazar and Ithamar had burned the animal when it should have been eaten. What was at issue was not the meat of the animal that Aaron had presented as a sin offering for himself and his house (9:8–11), for this was not to be eaten by the priests, but rather that of the sin offering which was brought for the people (9:15). Moses' inquiry led to the discovery that, although the blood of the animal had not been taken into the sanctuary (v. 18), its flesh had nevertheless been burned up (v. 16). The verb form used here, *śōrap̄,* naturally does not indicate that this was a deliberate, conscious deed.[23] As was also done elsewhere, the Masoretes here vocalized this term as a *Pual,* for the *Qal* passive had by then become obsolete. Eerdmans[24] maintains that, by not taking the blood into the sanctuary, Aaron had violated the requirement of 4:16–18, but he loses sight of two things. First of all, chapter 4 is concerned solely with instances of inadvertent sin, where the guilty party only became conscious of the nature of his deed later and then brought the required sin offering on his own initiative. This is not the case in the sin offering spoken of in 9:15, however. Second, Moses' anger was not prompted by the fact that the blood was not brought into the sanctuary, for in accordance with 6:25, 30 (MT 6:18, 23), this was

---

[23] As De Wilde maintains, *Tekst en Uitleg,* p. 95.
[24] *Das Buch Leviticus,* p. 58.

not supposed to be done in this offering. He rather rebuked Aaron's sons because they did not eat the sin offering when they knew that its blood had not been taken into the sanctuary and the meat therefore should have been eaten in a holy place. It is evident from verse 19 that this was indeed how Aaron understood Moses' words. He acknowledged the error committed by his sons; the meat of this sin offering should have been eaten rather than burned, for it had been given to the priests "to take away the guilt of the community" (v. 17). This was of course not accomplished by eating the meat of the offering (see discussion of 6:24–30), for the statement means rather that, in being given the animal and performing the ritual of atonement on it, they were responsible for Israel's unrighteousness. Aaron, however, excused their deed by reminding Moses of the confusion that had arisen on this festive day of the priestly ordination due to the divine judgment that had fallen on Nadab and Abihu. In his grief he failed to mention their names, but he appealed to the fact that "such things as this have happened to me" and notes that an error of this sort could easily be made under such circumstances. In addition, he inquired whether Moses was completely sure that he and his two sons were indeed permitted to eat the meat of the sin offering for the people on a day in which the Lord's burning wrath had been revealed in such a dreadful manner.

Moses apparently was unable to give an immediate answer to this question, for he would otherwise have commanded that the regulations of chapter 4 be followed. Instead of this, he withdrew his reproach and then remained silent. Moses' failure to respond is thus similar to Jeremiah's action at a later date (Jer. 28:11). The Lord's true servants speak only when they have first heard from the Lord.

Part Three

Regulations Concerning Clean and Unclean
(11:1–15:33)

The first seven chapters of Leviticus have presented the means by which Israel was enabled to enter into communion with the Lord, and chapters 8–10 have related how the priests whom He appointed were ordained to their mediatorial office, along with the awesome revelation of His holiness that accompanied this. The next main section of the book, chapters 11–15, now turns its attention to all that could lead to an interruption of this communion, whether the duration be brief or lengthy, and also to the means by which communion could once again be restored. Whereas the first two sections focused on the sanctuary, we are now brought within the sphere of Israel's everyday life, with all its possibilities of defilement. It is thereby made clear that, in Israel, everything was placed in a religious light, and that the Lord's instruction, with all of its regulations pertaining to what could not be handled, tasted, or touched (Col. 2:21), had no other aim than the sanctification of the life of every member of the chosen people.

Before beginning the discussion of chapters 11–15 proper, I shall first make a few general observations. Israel shared the concepts "clean" and "unclean" with other nations. These notions are not primarily concerned with the realm of the physical or even that of the ethical, but they belong rather within the sphere of the cult and ritual. Uncleanness shut off the possibility of participating in the ceremonial service of the Lord, and because it was contagious, it at the same time excluded an infected person from dealings with his compatriots.

116

Although in Israel the concepts of "clean" and "unclean" were not identical to those of "holy" and "unholy," there was nevertheless, as in other nations, a close connection between these two pairs. The language of the Israelites itself serves notice of this. Whoever would be holy (i.e., consecrate himself) had to bring himself into a condition of cultic cleanness by means of washing, fasting, and sexual abstinence (Exod. 19:10, 14–15; see also Num. 11:18; Josh. 3:5; 1 Sam. 16:5; etc.), or he had to help to remove devoted (i.e., accursed) persons or things from among the people (Josh. 7:13). In some cases, even the priests had to consecrate themselves in this manner (Exod. 19:22).

The difference between the two concepts may be described as follows. The holiness of a person, object, or place was the expression of the positive force that resided within it if it had some form of contact with the holy God. The word "holy" is thus opposed to "profane," which applied to all that was excluded from the cult (cf. Lev. 21:5–6, 15; 22:9–10), and it designates a unique sphere that was set apart from everything beyond it. The Latin word *sanctus*, "holy," expresses the same thing, for the verb *sancire* from which it is derived means "to circumscribe, set off." The ground around the burning bush from which the Lord spoke to Moses was called "holy" (Exod. 3:5), the sanctuary was holy because the Lord dwelled within it (Exod. 29:31–32; Lev. 6:16, 26–27; 7:6; 10:13; etc.), and the priests who performed the Lord's ceremonial service were therefore also holy (Lev. 21:7–8). It should be noted here that, in Israel, the dreadful and impersonal character of holiness receded into the background, while attention was focused on the fact that it was supernatural and beyond comparison with the earthly realm (Isa. 8:12–13). Because of this, holiness could not be manipulated as if it were something magical or material. Furthermore, this also means that qualification as holy did not reflect on the religious-ethical worthiness of the individual or community, but rather expressed nothing more than the fact that the individual or community belonged to the Lord and was therefore subject to His will and bound by a specific demand on his or its life.

The concept of clean lies on a completely different plane. It is concerned, not with the holy as such, but rather with the condition that had to be satisfied by any person or thing that came into contact with the area of divine holiness. The relationship between the two may be stated thus: no holiness without cleanness. To the Israelite mind, the concepts of clean and unclean were not mutually exclusive, for the carcass of the red heifer that was used in preparing the water of cleansing itself had the power to make clean, but the handling of it nevertheless rendered the priest and his helper unclean (Num. 19:2–8). The Israelites also regarded uncleanness and sin

117

as being closely related. Because of this, the ritual of cleansing is referred to in Numbers 8:21; 19:12–13, 20; 31:19–20, 23 as "purification from sin" (see RSV, NEB; the verb form used in these verses is the *Hithpael* of *ḥāṭa'*, "to sin"; cf. also Num. 19:9), and in certain cases the bringing of burnt and sin offerings formed part of the ritual of cleansing (Lev. 12:6–7; 14:10–20; 15:15).

A person was rendered unclean first of all if he had had any form of contact with the worship of foreign gods (Jer. 2:7, 23; 3:2; 7:30; Hos. 6:10; etc.) and also through everything connected with this: turning to mediums and prophesying spirits (Lev. 20:6), making use of mourning rites borrowed from such worship (Lev. 19:27–28; Deut. 14:1), or engaging in religious prostitution (Lev. 19:29). Since the Lord is "the living One," a person was also made unclean by coming into contact with anything related to death and decomposition: a corpse (Lev. 21:1–4, 11; Num. 6:6–7; 19:11–16), a carcass (Lev. 11:8, 11, 24–40), a grave (Num. 19:16), and also infectious skin diseases and mildew (Lev. 13–14). Other sources of uncleanness were various phenomena or functions of sexual life: bodily discharges, menstruation, copulation (Lev. 15); also the eating of meat from certain animals (Lev. 11; Deut. 14:4–21). Whoever was in such a state of uncleanness could not participate in cultic life, was excluded from every sacrificial meal, and was forbidden to touch any consecrated object (Exod. 19:10–15; 1 Sam. 20:24–26; 21:4–5; Ezek. 44:26–27). Such a person first had to wash himself and change his clothes, for uncleanness was something material[1] that became attached to one's body and clothing.

In the discussion of the respective requirements, I shall have ample opportunity to treat various of these matters in greater detail and to shed further light on their meaning within the framework of Israel's religious life. It has been remarked that these regulations pertaining to ritual cleanness promoted the externalization of Israel's religious life. There is, to be sure, an element of truth in this, for all cultic activities, even prayer, can have this effect. One must not forget, however, that if divine revelation was not to remain foreign to the life of the people but was rather to penetrate it to an increasing degree and elevate it to a higher spiritual level, it was compelled to make use of the existing state of affairs. In this regard there could be no creation *de novo*. The question was rather whether there was an element operative in Israel's national life that had *re*-creative power, and that directed this life along new paths, and the entire Old Testament forms prove that this was indeed the case.[2] The fact that this

---

[1] See Publisher's Note.
[2] See my book, *Gods Woord*[2], pp. 326f.

observation applies also to their concepts of cleanness is demonstrated by Israel's passage from a purely cultic to an ethical-religious point of view. This is evident from such passages as Genesis 4:11–12; Numbers 35:33–34; Deuteronomy 21:8–9; and especially Ezekiel 18:5–13, which demands both cultic purity and a life in accordance with the demands of divine righteousness. Even more significant in this regard are Psalms 15 and 24:4, where the demand for cleanness of heart and hand as the *sole* condition for participation in the worship of the Lord sheds the clearest light on the relative worthlessness of the requirements pertaining to ritual cleanness. The connection between cleanness and morality was both related to and a product of the fact that, in Israel, the concept of sin increasingly lost its cultic content and came to be regarded as applying to the ethical quality of a deed.[3]

The structure of these chapters is clear. Chapter 11 begins by giving a detailed enumeration of clean and unclean animals, i.e., those that in no way endangered one's participation in the ceremonial worship at the tabernacle and thus could be freely used as food, and those which, if eaten, excluded one for a shorter or longer period of time from the possibility of sharing in the cultic life of the people. The next chapter discusses what was to be done by a woman who had given birth in order that she could resume her position within the cultic life of Israel. Chapters 13 and 14 then deal at length with the manner in which various eruptions on the skin were to be diagnosed, the consequences that these had for the infected person, and the means by which the latter could be cleansed and reinstated into the social and cultic life of the people. Various eruptions on houses and clothing are also discussed in this context. Last, chapter 15 treats phenomena pertaining to sexual life that resulted in a disturbance of the communion with God that normally occurred in the cult.

Clean and Unclean Animals
(11:1–47)

The Pentateuch contains two lists of clean and unclean animals: Leviticus 11 and Deuteronomy 14:3–20. Although the prevailing view within the Wellhausen school regards the list of Deuteronomy 14 as more ancient, it appears to me that the opposite is true. This is indicated by the following differences between the two lists: (1) Whereas Leviticus 11 merely specifies the marks by which quadrupeds could be identified as clean (vv. 2–3), Deuteronomy 14:4–6 explicitly names ten clean animals. (2) Whereas Leviticus 11:20–23 enumerates four types of flying insects

---

[3]*Gods Woord,* pp. 91f.

with legs that could be eaten, Deuteronomy 14:20 merely makes the general statement: "any winged creature that is clean you may eat." The latter thus clearly assumes that the relevant law was already known, and it neglected to give an explicit enumeration since the eating of insects would have been of less importance to the Israelites once they had left the wilderness and settled in Palestine. (3) Whereas Leviticus 11:4–6 constantly repeats the reason why the respective animals could not be eaten, this is not the case in Deuteronomy 14:7. (4) Whereas Leviticus 11 speaks solely of the Israelite, Deuteronomy 14:21 also mentions the alien *(gēr)* dwelling among them and states that a carcass could be given or sold to such a person. The former thus clearly applies to a wandering nation, while the latter requirement is completely understandable in terms of the conditions that prevailed when they had assumed control of Canaan. It may be noted further that Leviticus 11:39–40 does not forbid the Israelites from eating the carcasses of clean animals, but merely requires that they cleanse themselves after having done so, whereas Deuteronomy 14:21 absolutely forbids the eating of anything found dead. Since the latter requirement is more stringent, it must have been made later. Whether Deuteronomy 14 is based on Leviticus 11 or whether both of these derive from a more ancient writing is a question that naturally can no longer be answered.

It is readily apparent that a list of clean and unclean animals such as that given in Leviticus 11 could not have arisen all at once. The notion that a lawgiver could have individually drawn up such a list goes against all common sense. If a list of this nature was to have the authority of law, it had to form a part of a people's life rather than being merely imposed on them, i.e., it must have assumed its appropriate place within the communal life of the people from generation to generation before it could have been explicitly formulated in this manner. This thus means that its origins lay in Israel's distant past. That the author of 4 Maccabees, who in 5:25–26 writes: ". . . we know that the Creator of the world sympathizes with our nature in the framing of his laws. And those things which will suit our nature he has permitted us to eat; but the meats which would prove the contrary, he has forbidden us to use,"[4] was himself unaware of this fact naturally forms no argument against it. The contention of the rabbis that considerations of health were the primary concern in these regulations also forms no contrary proof. If it is indeed demonstrable, as Hertz[5] maintains, that the life expectancy of the Jews was higher than that of any other race,

---

[4]Henry Cotton, *The Five Books of Maccabees in English* (Oxford: The University Press, 1832), p. 236.

[5]Joseph Herman Hertz, *The Pentateuch and Haftorahs, Leviticus* (London: Oxford University Press, 1936), p. 94.

this still would in no way support the rabbinical position, if for no other reason than that the observance of these food laws came to be either largly or entirely neglected. If the food laws were in fact based on sanitary considerations and their observance did promote health, it would be inconceivable why it had to be explained to Peter that they had lost all force of law within the Christian church (Acts 10:12–15).

The fact that this list—either as a whole or only in part, for this can of course no longer be determined—goes back to a time that already lay in the distant past during the Mosaic period makes it altogether impossible to explain why some animals were considered clean and others unclean. The only thing that can be asserted with at least some measure of probability in this regard is that it must have been primarily religious considerations that were decisive in these regulations. Whatever was unclean was therefore not only forbidden as an offering (Gen. 8:20), but also could not be presented to the Lord among the firstborn animals (Lev. 27:27; Num. 18:15) or tithes (Lev. 27:32). Further evidence for this view is formed by the fact that several of the animals designated as unclean here assumed an important place within the cultic life of one or more Semitic peoples. It is thus clear from Isaiah 65:4; 66:3, 17 that the flesh of pigs was eaten in illegitimate pagan meals; and it is certain that the pig was the domestic sacrificial animal among the ancient Canaanites, for this is indicated by, e.g., the discovery of bones from this animal at Gezer. It was also regarded as a sacred animal in Syria, and as late as the Christian era the pagan inhabitants of Haran sacrificed a pig once a year. The Egyptians believed that there was contact between the pig and both gods of the underworld and demons, and they related how the evil god Seth in the form of a black pig wounded Horus.[6] In Babylonia, the pig was the sacred animal of the god Tammuz and was sacrificed in order to drive away the demon Labartu, and pig teeth were much in demand as amulets. The pig was also widely regarded as a demonic animal. It is known that camel flesh formed the main component of sacrificial meals among the ancient Arabs and that they also held certain camels as sacred. The Egyptians believed camels to be demonic. The dog was regarded in Egypt, Iran, and northern Syria as a sacred animal and in Babylonia as demonic, and the Hittites had gods who stood on dogs. Isaiah 66:17 speaks of the rat as a sacrificial animal, and in Haran field mice were offered in sacrifice. The unclean animals described in verse 27 naturally included the cat, and this was a sacred animal among the ancient Egyptians. The head and paw of the hare are still today used as amulets by the Arabs, and owls are revered in Arabia as the incarnation of dead persons.

---

[6]Erman, *Die ägyptische Religion,* p. 337.

According to a rabbinic legend, the hoopoe (v. 19) was thought to be in possession of a magic herb, and the chameleon (v. 30) was also regarded as having magical powers. Fish without scales (v. 10) bore somewhat of a resemblance to snakes, and the snake was the foremost demonic animal among Near Eastern peoples. This reptile often became an object of worship, and as the relief of the serpent goddess found in 1928 at Tell Beit Mirsim indicates, this also occurred among the Canaanites.[7] Over against this, fish having fins and scales (v. 9) were regarded as clean and could therefore be eaten.

In presenting the above information, I do not at all wish to create the impression that each of the animals mentioned in chapter 11 was labeled as clean or unclean merely because it did or did not have some place in the cultic life of one of the Semitic nations. A puzzle such as that presented by Leviticus 11 cannot be solved by means of a single clue, and other considerations doubtless also played a role here. It is nevertheless absolutely clear that the prohibition against eating was still made for religious reasons when it applied to animals that fed on carrion. This is the case with the birds listed in verses 13–19, and in Job 39:30 the same is explicitly stated of the eagle: "His young ones feast on blood, and where the slain are, there is he." It is beyond doubt that the Old Testament's judgment of carrion as unclean is religiously motivated, just as is the prohibition against eating blood and bloody flesh.

A religious background cannot always be discovered for the classification of other animals as unclean, however. In these cases, the natural aversion that people felt toward certain animals no doubt played a role, but it remains open to question whether this was the only factor. The small winged creatures spoken of in verse 20 were considered repugnant, and included the great number of insects that multiplied with such disconcerting rapidity and formed such a plague to human life in the East; the same was true of various crawling animals that sought their food in the ground. These matters will be discussed further in the comments on the respective verses that follow.[8]

Last, it should be noted that the foods that are forbidden here were not merely "not clean," but that uncleanness was rather a positive quality that made something "detestable" (v. 12). Whoever ate of such a thing therefore excluded himself from Israel's cultic community, and in stepping

---

[7]See Albright, ZAW (1929), pp. 6f.

[8]See also J. Döller, *Die Reinheits- und Speisegesetze des Alten Testaments in religionsgeschichtlicher Beleuchtung* (1917), where a large amount of comparative material has been assembled. Cf. in particular, pp. 231f.: the purpose of the laws concerning cleanness and food.

outside of the covenant he ceased to serve the Lord. In contrast, whoever abstained from such unclean foods consecrated himself and was holy (v. 44), thus satisfying the demand that was made in the covenant (cf. also 20:25–26; Deut. 14:21).

1. *Clean and Unclean Quadrupeds* (11:1–8)

11:1–8 *The LORD said to Moses and Aaron, "Say to the Israelites: 'Of all the animals that live on land, these are the ones you may eat: You may eat any animal that has a split hoof completely divided and that chews the cud.*

" 'There are some that only chew the cud or only have a split hoof, but you must not eat them. The camel, though it chews the cud, does not have a split hoof; it is ceremonially unclean for you. The coney, though it chews the cud, does not have a split hoof; it is unclean for you. The rabbit, though it chews the cud, does not have a split hoof; it is unclean for you. And the pig, though it has a split hoof completely divided, does not chew the cud; it is unclean for you. You must not eat their meat or touch their carcasses; they are unclean for you.' "

The hoof form and rumination are here given as the marks by which clean and unclean quadrupedal animals were to be distinguished. With regard to the form of the hoof, it is explicitly stated that this had to be split and completely divided if the animal was to qualify as clean. All quadrupeds that had this characteristic and also chewed the cud were clean. These included not only the ox, sheep, and goat, which were domestic animals, but also the seven wild animals listed in Deuteronomy 14:5. Any animal that exhibited only one of these two features was unclean, and the camel, coney, rabbit, and pig were mentioned as such in verses 4–7. Although it is true that neither the coney (also spoken of in Ps. 104:18; Prov. 30:26) nor the rabbit actually chews the cud, as verses 5–6 assert, both of these nevertheless make the mouth movements characteristic of ruminating animals. It is therefore obvious that this classification of animals as nonruminants and those that chew the cud was based on popular conviction rather than scientific investigation, an observation that has also been made by the ancients. For this reason also, the camel was included here, although because of its thick elastic sole it does not have a completely divided hoof. With regard to the camel and pig, see above. It is not known why the coney and the rabbit had to be considered unclean in Israel ("for you," vv. 7–8). In the case of the rabbit, it is suspected that this was because this animal sleeps with its eyes open. One-hoofed animals such as the horse and donkey (cf. Exod. 13:13) were forbidden to the Israelites, and it appears from verse 27 that this was also the case with plantigrades such as the cat, dog, and bear. The Talmud tractate *Hullin* 59a asserts that the clean ruminants lack incisors in their upper jaw and claims that this is the feature that was determinative in the classification.

2. *Clean and Unclean Aquatic Creatures* (11:9–12)

11:9–12 *"'Of all the creatures living in the water of the seas and the streams, you may eat any that have fins and scales. But all creatures in the seas or streams that do not have fins and scales—whether among all the swarming things or among all the other living creatures in the water—you are to detest. And since you are to detest them, you must not eat their meat and you must detest their carcasses. Anything living in the water that does not have fins and scales is to be detestable to you.'"*

The distinguishing mark here is whether or not the animal has fins and scales. Whatever lacks the latter, e.g., the eel, the crayfish, and the salamander, was unclean. The aversion felt toward these animals was even greater than in the case of the unclean quadrupeds. They were summarily forbidden to the Israelites as unclean and were characterized as "detestable" (v. 12; cf. Deut. 14:13), and it appears from Isaiah 66:17 and Ezekiel 8:10 that this latter expression was used in reference to things connected with the worship of foreign gods.

3. *Clean and Unclean Flying Creatures* (11:13–19)

11:13–19 *"'These are the birds you are to detest and not eat because they are detestable: the eagle, the vulture, the black vulture, the red kite, any kind of black kite, any kind of raven, the horned owl, the screech owl, the gull, any kind of hawk, the little owl, the cormorant, the great owl, the white owl, the desert owl, the osprey, the stork, any kind of heron, the hoopoe and the bat.'"*

Since not all of the animals spoken of in this section can be identified, the translation of these verses is extremely uncertain.[9] In contrast to the preceding verses, it is here first of all stated that these creatures as a group were detestable. All of the animals mentioned are birds of prey that feed on carrion and a variety of refuse and prefer to nest in ruins and desert areas, both of which terrified the Israelites with their sinister creatures (Isa. 13:21–22; Zeph. 2:13–15). The screech owl, great owl, and raven appear also in Isaiah 34:11, the desert owl in Psalm 102:6, and the bat in Isaiah 2:20.

---

[9]See NIV marginal note to verse 19. There are for this reason several differences between the author's translation of chapter 11 and that of the NIV, as will be indicated in the footnotes that follow.

4. *Small Flying Creatures* (11:20–23)

11:20–23 *" 'All flying insects that walk on all fours are to be detestable to you. There are, however, some winged creatures that walk on all fours that you may eat: those that have jointed legs for hopping on the ground. Of these you may eat any kind of locust, katydid, cricket or grasshopper. But all other winged creatures that have four legs you are to detest.' "*

In these verses, all insects, which were so plentiful in the East and formed such a noxious pestilence to human life, were for obvious reasons declared unclean. Only four exceptions were made to this general rule, and these were characteristic for a nation wandering in the desert, since they all concerned the locust. The correct modern equivalents for the four Hebrew terms used here are not known, and I have thus chosen to leave them untranslated.[10] It is uncertain whether *all* locusts were thereby declared clean. The rabbis likewise had difficulties in this regard, and they therefore made a summary prohibition against the eating of every kind of locust (*Hullin* 59a).

It should once again be noted that the distinguishing features specified here have no anatomical value, for there are in fact no flying animals having four legs. The lawgiver could of course do nothing more than reproduce the conceptions of his own day in such matters. The fact that he nevertheless took pains to enable the reader to distinguish between the clean and unclean animals of this group appears most clearly in verse 21.

5. *Defilement Through Contact With Carcasses* (11:24–40)

11:24–40 *" 'You will make yourselves unclean by these; whoever touches their carcasses will be unclean till evening. Whoever picks up one of their carcasses must wash his clothes, and he will be unclean till evening.*

" 'Every animal that has a split hoof not completely divided or that does not chew the cud is unclean for you; whoever touches the carcass of any of them will be unclean. Of all the animals that walk on all fours, those that walk on their paws are unclean for you; whoever touches their carcasses will be unclean till evening. Anyone who picks up their carcasses must wash his clothes, and he will be unclean till evening. They are unclean for you.

" 'Of the animals that move about on the ground, these are unclean for you: the weasel, the rat, any kind of great lizard, the gecko, the monitor lizard, the wall lizard, the skink and the chameleon. Of all those that move along the ground, these

---

[10]The terms are *'arbeh, sol'ām, ḥargōl,* and *ḥāḡāḇ*. The NIV respectively translates these as "locust," "katydid," "cricket," and "grasshopper." Like the author, the NEB regards them all as locusts: "great locust," "long-headed locust," "green locust," and "desert locust."

are unclean for you. Whoever touches them when they are dead will be unclean till evening. When one of them dies and falls on something, that article, whatever its use, will be unclean, whether it is made of wood, cloth, hide or sackcloth. Put it in water; it will be unclean till evening, and then it will be clean. If one of them falls into a clay pot, everything in it will be unclean, and you must break the pot. Any food that could be eaten but has water on it from such a pot is unclean, and any liquid that could be drunk from it is unclean. Anything that one of their carcasses falls on becomes unclean; an oven or cooking pot must be broken up. They are unclean, and you are to regard them as unclean. A spring, however, or a cistern for collecting water remains clean, but anyone who touches one of these carcasses is unclean. If a carcass falls on any seeds that are to be planted, they remain clean. But if water has been put on the seed and a carcass falls on it, it is unclean for you.

"'If an animal that you are allowed to eat dies, anyone who touches the carcass will be unclean till evening. Anyone who eats some of the carcass must wash his clothes, and he will be unclean till evening. Anyone who picks up the carcass must wash his clothes, and he will be unclean till evening.'"

Verse 41 continues the discussion of "creeping animals" (*šereṣ*, the term used in both v. 23 and v. 41[11]) that was left off in verse 23, and I therefore join others in regarding verses 24–40 as a later insertion. This position is also borne out by the content of these verses, for whereas verses 1–23 and 41–45 are concerned exclusively with whether or not certain animals were to be eaten, verses 24–40 speak merely of coming into contact with carcasses. In addition, the present section gives a precise specification of how long the resultant uncleanness was to last and what was to be done in order to remove it, while in verses 1–23 the lawgiver is content to merely declare the respective animals unclean. The closing formula in verses 46–47 also indicates that at one time verses 24–40 did not form a part of the law of Leviticus 11. Why these verses were inserted in precisely this place is a question that is of course difficult to answer, but I suspect that the content of verses 43–45 made them an unlikely sequel to this. When they were inserted is also impossible to determine.

I should here note that I have chosen not to translate the verb *nāḡaʻ*, which occurs repeatedly in these verses, as "touch," since this indicates a deliberate act. It is evident from chapter 4 that an unconscious transgression of God's law also made a person guilty, and for this reason I prefer the neutral translation, "come into contact with."[12]

---

[11]The author translates *šereṣ* as "creeping animals" in both of these verses (cf. KJV). His argument is not as obvious in terms of the NIV, which merely has "creatures" in both cases. Another possible translation is "swarming things" (v. 41 in RSV), and the NEB has "teeming creatures" in the two verses.

[12]The NIV does translate *nāḡaʻ* as "touch."

Implicit in these verses is the notion that uncleanness was something contagious. Whoever came into contact with what was unclean was himself made unclean and was thereby excluded from the cultic community for a shorter or longer period of time. This idea, which derived from a dynamistic mode of thought and was shared by Israel with the entire ancient world,[13] can be found throughout the Pentateuch (see e.g., Num. 5:1–4; 19:11–13; 31:20). A distinction is made in this section between coming into contact with a carcass and picking one up. In the former case, the person remained unclean until evening and removed the uncleanness by washing his body (v. 24), whereas in the latter case the clothing also had to be washed (v. 25).

Three causes of uncleanness are discussed in succession: coming into contact with the carcasses of unclean quadrupeds (vv. 26–28), with the carcasses of unclean animals that "move about on the ground" (vv. 29–38), and with the carcasses of clean animals (vv. 39–40). The latter refers only to those animals that had not been slaughtered in the prescribed manner, i.e., that had either died a natural death or been killed by other animals. Uncleanness resulted from contact with the carcasses of animals that did not exhibit the two features specified in verse 3 (v. 26; see above). In verse 27, this category is expanded by the addition of those animals that "walk on their paws," e.g., the dog, cat, and bear. Verses 29–31 form a supplement to verses 20–23 and include among the "creeping animals"[14] the weasel, rat, and other creatures. Although we would not classify these animals in the same manner, this was probably done because of their digging and their short legs. The translation of these animal names is here again uncertain.

Verse 32 introduces a new element that has not been mentioned up to this point: any object of daily use that came into contact with the carcass of one of these animals was made unclean. Although this statement is here limited to the animals listed in verses 29–30, this does not imply that things stood differently with the carcasses of other animals. The lawgiver naturally restricted himself to the possibilities of everyday life and remained within the domestic sphere, and he therefore spoke only of those "creeping animals" that lived in the vicinity of humans and whose carcasses could therefore easily come into contact with such things as pottery and clothing. Articles made of wood, cloth, hide, or sackcloth were to be washed, whereas clay pottery, which was easily replaceable, had to be shattered (v. 33; cf. 6:28).

---

[13] See Publisher's Note.

[14] "[Animals] that move along the ground" in verses 29 and 31 of NIV is their translation of šereṣ, while the author again has "creeping animals" in both cases. See footnote on p. 126.

Verse 34 deals with the possibility that food was present in a pot when such a carcass fell into it. If the food was dry, it remained clean, but food prepared with water became contaminated. This distinction is related to the fact that the latter adheres to a pot or utensil and that water forms a fertile medium for the proliferation of unclean matter (it should be kept in mind that clay pottery was not glazed). For the same reason, any drink in such a pot was also considered unclean. The same distinction applied to any seed for planting on which a carcass had fallen: if the seed was wet, it was defiled by the carcass, whereas dry seed remained clean (vv. 37–38). An oven or cookstove that had been contaminated by a carcass was also to be broken (v. 35). For a description of the type of oven spoken of here, see the comment on Leviticus 2:4. The term *kîr,* which I have translated as "cookstove" for lack of a better word,[15] refers to a small fireplace made in the ground on which two pots could be set (*Shabbath* 38b). Such ovens and cookstoves could easily be replaced by new ones. Water had to be treated with greater care, however, since it was sometimes quite scarce in Israel, and it is in this light that the reading of verse 36 must be regarded. Here it is stated that a spring or cistern, both of which naturally stood open and were thus easily exposed to defilement, was not made unclean through contact with a carcass. The lawgiver, who in the final analysis was compelled to take into account the limits of what was feasible for the Israelites, apparently made this allowance in view of the fact that both springs and cisterns were constantly replenished and freshened by the addition of new water. He nevertheless added that whoever removed a carcass from such a drinking place was made unclean by it. Water standing in jars was not spoken of in this context, for these were generally made in a shape that excluded all possibility of defilement.

Verses 39–40 speak of clean animals that had not been slaughtered, but instead had either died a natural death or been killed by other animals. In this case, the remains were considered to be a carcass and thus unclean, for the blood was still in the body. A person who came into contact with such a carcass was made unclean, and whoever ate of it or picked it up had to wash his clothes, and he remained unclean until evening. Leviticus 17:15 is more stringent in this regard, for it is there required that a person who ate of a carcass also had to bathe with water (see comment on this verse). The rabbis attempted to evade the conclusion to which these verses point, viz., that such animals were to be destroyed, by direction that, although their flesh caused defilement, the hide, bones, and horns were exempt from this and could therefore be put to use. This can only be regarded as a clear

---

[15]The NIV translates it as "cooking pot."

example of the type of thinking that Jesus reproached His contemporaries for in Matthew 15:3–6. Leviticus 7:24 makes such an exception only with respect to the fat, stating that this was not to be eaten, but "may be used for any other purpose." The rabbis have on the other hand interpreted these verses as meaning that the flesh of animals that had not been ritually slaughtered was unclean, but this is not at all what the lawgiver had in mind.

6. *Prohibition Against Eating Small Creeping Animals* (11:41–45)

11:41–45 *"'Every creature that moves about on the ground is detestable; it is not to be eaten. You are not to eat any creature that moves about on the ground, whether it moves on its belly or walks on all fours or on many feet; it is detestable. Do not defile yourselves by any of these creatures. Do not make yourselves unclean by means of them or be made unclean by them. I am the LORD your God; consecrate yourselves and be holy, because I am holy. Do not make yourselves unclean by any creature that moves about on the ground. I am the LORD who brought you up out of Egypt to be your God; therefore be holy, because I am holy.'"*

As has already been noted, these verses form a continuation of verses 20–23. Whereas the latter verses were speaking of creeping animals with wings[16] (i.e., insects), *however,* the present passage deals with creeping animals in general and distinguishes between those that move on their belly and those that have four or more feet (v. 42). The Hebrew term translated as "belly" here, *gāḥôn,* appears elsewhere only in Genesis 3:4. The rabbis directed that the third letter of this (*wāw*) was here to be written doubly large in manuscripts (and today also in print), for it stands at the exact center of the Pentateuch (*Kiddushin 30a).*

The degree of repulsion that the Israelites felt toward these "creeping animals" is indicated not only by the fact that they were called "detestable" (vv. 41–42) and that whoever ate of one became defiled[17] (v. 43), but also in that the Israelites were in this connection twice reminded of the Lord's holiness (vv. 44–45) and of what He had done for them (v. 45). These statements must have been made precisely here because such animals formed a particular danger.

I should here call attention to the fact that the exhortation of verse 44, "consecrate yourselves and be holy, because I am holy," is repeated more than once in chapters 19–21 and can also be found in Exodus 19:6; Numbers 15:40; and Deuteronomy 23:14. This forms the core of the entire Old

---

[16]Once again, the NIV translates *šereṣ* in verses 20–23 as "creatures" or "insects" (v. 20), while the author has "creeping animals." See footnote on p. 126

[17]The author uses the stronger term, "abominable," here (see KJV and RSV).

Testament revelation, which never ceases to place all emphasis on the Lord's holiness (i.e., the uniqueness of His nature over against all other gods) and on this basis to demand of Israel that it manifest in its own life a reflection of this uniqueness. Whereas the lawgiver here sets forth a variety of external activities that bring to light this uniqueness, in the prophets this demand on the life of Israel is internalized. Their writings exhort the people to cleanse their hearts instead of their hands, but Judaism unfortunately later lost sight of this once again.[18]

7. *Closing Formula* (11:46–47)

11:46–47 *"'These are the regulations concerning animals, birds, every living thing that moves in the water and every creature that moves about on the ground. You must distinguish between the unclean and the clean, between living creatures that may be eaten and those that may not be eaten.'"*

The content of these verses indicates that they date from the time when verses 24–40 did not yet form part of this chapter and the regulations here were concerned exclusively with whether or not certain animals could be eaten.

Purification Following Childbirth (12:1–8)

12:1–8 *The LORD said to Moses, "Say to the Israelites: 'A woman who becomes pregnant and gives birth to a son will be ceremonially unclean for seven days, just as she is unclean during her monthly period. On the eighth day the boy is to be circumcised. Then the woman must wait thirty-three days to be purified from her bleeding. She must not touch anything sacred or go to the sanctuary until the days of her purification are over. If she gives birth to a daughter, for two weeks the woman will be unclean, as in her period. Then she must wait sixty-six days to be purified from her bleeding.*

"'When the days of her purification for a son or daughter are over, she is to bring to the priest at the entrance to the Tent of Meeting a year-old lamb for a burnt offering and a young pigeon or a dove for a sin offering. He shall offer them before the LORD to make atonement for her, and then she will be ceremonially clean from her flow of blood. These are the regulations for the woman who gives birth to a boy or a girl.

"'If she cannot afford a lamb, she is to bring two doves or two young pigeons, one for a burnt offering and the other for a sin offering. In this way the priest will make atonement for her, and she will be clean.'"

---

[18]See, M. Friedländer, *Die Jüdische Religion* (1922), pp. 363f.

The remarks that were made in the introduction to the preceding section on chapter 11 naturally apply likewise to chapter 12, and the background to the law that is formulated here also began long before the time of Moses. In order to rightly understand these regulations, it is necessary to bear in mind that, because of her menstruation and the miraculous and secret formation of a human being within her womb, woman was always regarded in ancient times as a more or less mysterious being, and that her motherhood in particular was thought to be an indication that she possessed supernatural powers. For this reason it was almost universally believed that the blood of menstruation had special, magical properties. Ideas of this sort can be found in, e.g., Flavius Josephus (*War* IV 8, 4).[19] The ancient person generally considered sickness and death to be the work of demons,[20] and since it was not uncommon for a woman to die in childbirth, it was inevitable that she should be regarded especially during the days of her pregnancy and delivery as a favorite object for a variety of demonic attacks that sought her death. Because of this, many peoples would quarantine menstruating and childbearing women.[21]

Women were also quarantined in both of these cases in Israel. Chapter 12 is concerned exclusively with women who had given birth, and the isolation of menstruating women will be discussed further in connection with Leviticus 15:19–30. In becoming a mother, a woman was made unclean. This of course does not mean that the bearing of children in and of itself produced the uncleanness, for the possession of numerous offspring was regarded in Israel as a special blessing of God (Gen. 24:60; 30:1; 1 Sam. 1:5–6). The cause of the uncleanness rather lay in everything that accompanies childbirth, e.g., the afterbirth, blood loss, and the physical indisposition that results from this. For this reason, the uncleanness that follows childbirth was of the same degree, and thus also duration, as that produced by a woman's monthly period: seven days (cf. 15:19). In both cases the uncleanness was something positive, i.e., it had a contaminating power that made the woman as such a danger to her environment. This positive uncleanness lasted seven days if birth had been given to a son, but if the offspring was a daughter, the duration of the uncleanness was twice as long. The reason for this was not so much that a lesser value was placed on females, but rather the belief that Israel shared with other nations that the bearing of a girl was accompanied by greater difficulties and dangers for the mother. The number seven, which represented completeness or

---

[19]See also *Archiv für Religionswissenschaft* (1914), pp. 405f.; Ploss, *Das Weib* II, pp. 376f.

[20]See Publisher's Note.

[21]See J. Döller, *Die Reinheits- und Speisegesetze des Alten Testament,* pp. 18f.

perfection, was altogether appropriate in this context (see also 4:6).

Although the woman's positive uncleanness was relatively brief, the cessation of it did not end her period of isolation, for she still could not leave her house and participate in the cultic life of her family and people. The process of her purification continued beyond this, and she remained excluded from all association and contact with the realm of the holy. This requirement is readily understandable in view of the reverence that was demanded of a person when entering into communion with the holy God. A similar gradation in the process of purification is found in the case of a woman who had recovered from an abnormal bodily discharge (15:25–30) and of a person who had been cured of an infectious skin disease (14:1–32). The second period of separation following childbirth lasted for 33 days if the child was a boy, and for 66 days, i.e., twice as long, if it was a girl. This therefore meant that with a baby boy, the total duration of the woman's isolation was $7 + 33 = 40$ days, and with a baby girl it was $14 + 66 = 80$ days. The appearance of these numbers here is not accidental. The number 40, at least, was also significant in Egypt and Greece. The Jews have therefore asked why these periods were precisely 40 and 80 days. In the Book of Jubilees (3:8), it is asserted that this was a consequence of the fact that Adam and Eve were placed in Paradise on the fortieth and eightieth days, respectively. This, of course, is no explanation at all, and indicates only that the author no longer knew the real reason. The explanation is perhaps rather that this regulation was related to the thought appearing in the Mishnah that the male and female embryos were respectively formed in 41 and 81 days.[22]

In the birth of a son, the eighth day was of particularly great significance to both the parents and the child, for it was then that the operation of circumcision was carried out (in ancient times this was performed with a flint knife, Exod. 4:25; Josh. 5:2–3). Unlike elsewhere, the purpose of this was not to indicate puberty or to satisfy hygienic requirements, and even less did it serve to dedicate the male genitals. Circumcision rather signified the inclusion of the child in the covenant that the Lord had enacted with Israel. The rite thus served to bind the child to God and to His people. Through this act of his parents, he was dedicated to the Lord and marked as one who belonged to the Lord's people and was thus obligated to make the Lord's commandments into the rule for his own life. According to verse 3, the circumcision was to be performed on the eighth day. The rabbis have interpreted this literally as meaning that the rite had to be performed during

---

[22]For other explanations, see J. Döller, *Die Reinheits- und Speisegesetze des Alten Testament,* pp. 12f.

the daytime, even if the eighth day was the Sabbath (cf. John 7:22).[23]

In subjecting the newly born son to the rite of circumcision, the difference between Israel and the other nations with respect to the uncleanness of the mother was clearly underscored. The old patterns of thought had been broken through, for there was here no longer any connection with demons, but rather a covenant with the Lord. This same consideration applies also to the offerings that the mother brought in order to put an end to her uncleanness and time of isolation. Both a burnt offering and a sin offering had to be presented, each of these being larger than the corresponding offering made following menstruation (cf. 15:29–30). The burnt offering expressed a renewed dedication of life, and the sin offering, which was made for unconscious sins and uncleanness (ch. 4), brought about purification. Only in the event of poverty were the offerings of Leviticus 15:29–30 sufficient. The offerings were presented, not to demons, but to the God of the covenant, and both mother and child were thereby dedicated to Him.

The fulfillment of these requirements presented no difficulties whatsoever during the time when Israel was wandering in the desert, and problems arose only after the people had assumed control of Canaan. Although 1 Samuel 1 indicates that many families made the prescribed yearly visit to the sanctuary and Luke 2 states that Joseph and Mary went to Jerusalem in order to present the offering of the poor, it is nevertheless questionable whether all new mothers, especially the less devout, did this as well. It should be remembered in this connection that there was no central sanctuary prior to the time of the kings, and that even under the monarchy this did not assume its intended predominating position in cultic life. In the days of Ezra and Nehemiah, the province of Judah was so small that there could have been no objection to going to Jerusalem. This again ceased to be the case later, however, and the Mishnah therefore does not speak of such a custom. What Joseph and Mary did (Luke 2:21–24) must therefore have been the exception. In Judaism, it became the rule that the mother was to go to the synagogue, which was accessible to everyone, in order to give thanks for her recovery by means of the prescribed prayers and to make petition for her child.[24]

Abnormal Growths on Persons and Objects
(13:1–59)

The various pathological phenomena spoken of in Leviticus 13 and 14 are referred to in the Hebrew text by the term *ṣāra'aṯ* (''stroke''; the term

---

[23]Concerning these matters, see also J. van Nes, *Het Jodendom* (1933), pp. 89f.

[24]Cf., M. Friedländer, *Die Jüdische Religion,* pp. 381f.

is derived from a root that contains the idea of being struck), and a person who was thereby afflicted was called *ṣārûa'* ("struck [by God]," or among the Arabs, "fought against by God"). The Greek translators rendered *ṣāra'aṭ* as *lépra,* a term that was carried over in the Vulgate, and they translated *ṣārûa'* as *leprós.* Because of this, it has become standard in Western translations to regard the Hebrew terms as a reference to leprosy,[25] but the Septuagint is probably not speaking of this particular disease. The term leprosy has thus been the occasion for misunderstanding. It is usually thought that these chapters were concerned with what *we* think of as leprosy, a dreadful, repulsive, and as yet incurable disease caused by bacteria that were evidently closely related to those responsible for tuberculosis. The description of the various cases appearing in chapter 13, however, indicates that recovery could occur in more than one of these, and *ṣāra'aṭ* could therefore only be a collective name that embraces diseases that must be more loosely classified as cutaneous eruptions. The Mishnah (*Negaim* I 4) thus asserts that there were no fewer than 16, 36, or even 72 types of *ṣāra'aṭ,* and this could never be the case if the term referred solely to leprosy. The latter disease, in fact, had only two varieties: one that attacked the skin, producing tubercles that continually burst open, and consisted of a process of necrosis (tubercular leprosy), and another that infected the nerves and caused ulcerating blisters especially on the extremities, which degenerated into repulsive sores and led to the rotting away of fingers and toes (anesthetic leprosy, which results in a complete loss of feeling). Modern dermatologists think that leprosy is either only slightly contagious or entirely noncontagious. They also maintain that, under conditions of extreme cleanliness of body, clothing, and environment, the disease can be cured if it is diagnosed early, and that it can only survive in lands where hygiene is disastrously neglected. It is nevertheless understandable that during a time when medicine was still in its infancy and more faith was placed in magical practices than in appropriate curative measures, anything that resembled a skin eruption was classified as *ṣāra'aṭ.* In the ancient Near Eastern world, where the hideous character of leprosy and the suffering it produced were well known, this disease more than any other was ascribed in the influence of demonic powers, and it was feared as much as death itself (see 2 Sam. 3:29). The Israelites referred to it as *hanneǧa'* ("the stroke," or "the plague").[26]

---

[25]The NIV uses the general expression, "infectious skin disease" (see the marginal note to 13:2), but cf. KJV and RSV.

[26]The Old Testament speaks five times of cases of *ṣāra'aṭ* (Num. 12:10; 2 Kings 5:1, 27; 7:3; 15:5), while in the New Testament it appears three times (Matt. 8:2–3; 26:6; Luke 17:12). With regard to the question of what ailment *ṣāra'aṭ* refers to, see J. Döller, *Die Reinheits- und Speisegesetze des Alten Testament,* pp. 86f.

The inclusion of these regulations within the framework of the Mosaic law was naturally not prompted first of all by sanitary considerations, and their purpose must not be regarded as an attempt to prescribe a method of healing. Because it was considered a result of demonic influences,[27] disease made a person unclean, i.e., rendered him unfit for participation in cultic life and thus excluded him from the sanctuary. Since, especially at this early date, it was exceedingly difficult to ascertain whether a particular minor skin ailment represented the initial stages of the dreaded disease of leprosy, it is strongly emphasized that every suspicious eruption on the skin had to be shown to the priest—the medical expert of those days—in order that he might determine whether it was a cause of uncleanness and necessitated that the infected person be quarantined from the cult (see also Deut. 24:8). Whether fear of contagion was also a factor in this and the isolation of the patient was thus also motivated by social concerns can of course no longer be ascertained. The lawgiver himself had no other purpose than to safeguard the congregation of the Lord against any source of cultic contamination, for an individual who had been smitten by "the plague" could make the entire community unclean. The lawgiver was therefore concerned only with the religious side of leprosy, for this disease conflicted with the ritual purity that was demanded of every member of the Lord's congregation.

Such considerations led to the establishment of an exceedingly meticulous diagnostic procedure and the postponement of decision if there was any cause for doubt. It is readily understandable that the diagnosis carried out by the priest should be confined to those symptoms that were present in the initial stages of this skin disease: the whitening of the hairs in the infected area, the hypertrophy of raw flesh, and the subcutaneous spreading of the infection. Obviously, an extended period of observation (e.g., vv. 5, 21) would often be an urgent necessity in such a diagnosis.

Some features of the clinical picture presented in this chapter have led to the suspicion that the dreaded disease was in fact the elephantiasis that appeared among the Arabs, but it seems to me that more than one type of skin ailment is being described here. It should lastly be noted that the lawgiver was in this context concerned exclusively with the circumstances that existed during Israel's sojourn in the desert, when the priest on duty at the tabernacle was readily at hand for diagnosing all the cases of skin disease that might arise. There is no evidence as to how this law was adapted to later circumstances, and Deuteronomy 24:8 gives no indication in this regard (see also discussion on 14:1–9, 33–53).

---

[27]See Publisher's Note.

1. The Initial Symptoms (13:1–8)

13:1–8 *The Lᴏʀᴅ said to Moses and Aaron, "When anyone has a swelling or a rash or a bright spot on his skin that may become an infectious skin disease, he must be brought to Aaron the priest or to one of his sons who is a priest. The priest is to examine the sore on his skin, and if the hair in the sore has turned white and the sore appears to be more than skin deep, it is an infectious skin disease. When the priest examines him, he shall pronounce him ceremonially unclean. If the spot on his skin is white but does not appear to be more than skin deep and the hair in it has not turned white, the priest is to put the infected person in isolation for seven days. On the seventh day the priest is to examine him, and if he sees that the sore is unchanged and has not spread in the skin, he is to keep him in isolation another seven days. On the seventh day the priest is to examine him again, and if the sore has faded and has not spread in the skin, the priest shall pronounce him clean; it is only a rash. The man must wash his clothes, and he will be clean. But if the rash does spread in his skin after he has shown himself to the priest to be pronounced clean, he must appear before the priest again. The priest is to examine him, and if the rash has spread in the skin, he shall pronounce him unclean; it is an infectious disease."*

These verses speak of a skin eruption that gave rise to the suspicion that the affected person had the initial symptoms of "the stroke." The Hebrew of verse 2 literally speaks of an abnormality on "the skin of his flesh" (cf. ᴋᴊᴠ), and it is thus likely that what is referred to here is the outer layer of skin or epidermis. Such an eruption could take the form of a "swelling," which probably means a tubercle or tumor, a "rash" (or scab or scale), or a "bright spot." The latter was a white skin blemish that sometimes turned reddish, and this played an important role in the investigation as to the true nature of the skin ailment (see vv. 2, 4, 19, 23–28, 38–39; 14:56–57). Any person who developed one of these three symptoms had to appear before the priest for a diagnosis. If the latter determined that the eruption was subcutaneous and had caused the normally black hair growing on it to turn white—the typical mark of so-called white leprosy—he declared that this was a case of the disease (*ṣāra'aṭ*, see above) that made a person ceremonially unclean, i.e., removed his right to participate in cultic life and enter the sanctuary.

If however the case was subject to doubt, the patient had to be put into "isolation" for a week, this apparently being an intermediate state between clean and unclean, and he then had to present himself for a further examination. If there was then no indication that the eruption had spread, the period of isolation was extended for another week, and if after the completion of this the priest determined that the sore still remained unchanged, the person was pronounced clean and readmitted to cultic life. The repeated examination had thus disclosed that the eruption was entirely harmless, and as a demonstration of this, the person was to wash his clothes in order to make known to all that he had been wrongly suspected of having *ṣāraʿat*.

If it appeared after the first week of isolation that the skin eruption had spread, however, the person had to present himself to the priest once again for another examination. In the event that this confirmed the suspicion of infection, the patient was pronounced unclean and excluded from the cultic community, for the eruption was then indeed an instance of *ṣāraʿat*.

2. *Diagnosis of Later Stages* (13:9–17)

13:9–17 *"When anyone has an infectious skin disease, he must be brought to the priest. The priest is to examine him, and if there is a white swelling in the skin that has turned the hair white and if there is raw flesh in the swelling, it is a chronic skin disease and the priest shall pronounce him unclean. He is not to put him in isolation, because he is already unclean.*

"If the disease breaks out all over his skin and, so far as the priest can see, it covers all the skin of the infected person from head to foot, the priest is to examine him, and if the disease has covered his whole body, he shall pronounce that person clean. Since it has all turned white, he is clean. But whenever raw flesh appears on him, he will be unclean. When the priest sees the raw flesh, he shall pronounce him unclean. The raw flesh is unclean; he has an infectious disease. Should the raw flesh change and turn white, he must go to the priest. The priest is to examine him, and if the sores have turned white, the priest shall pronounce the infected person clean; then he will be clean."

When a person developed symptoms that caused him to fear that he had been struck by "the plague," he was to immediately present himself to the priest for examination. If in the infected region the latter found white hairs (see above) on the suspected swelling and also the growth of raw flesh, the patient had indisputably been struck *(ṣāruaʿ)* by white leprosy (the elephantiasis of the Arabs). The priest was evidently here confronted with an open lesion. The patient had disregarded the initial symptoms of the disease and allowed it to progress, and the swelling had developed into an open sore. When this happened it was naturally no longer necessary to put the person in isolation, for he immediately was to be pronounced unclean.

There is also the possibility, however, that the symptoms of disease broke out over the entire body at once and the person turned white from head to foot. He became completely covered with white scales, and after these gradually fell away the disease had run its course. In this case the priest was not confronted with elephantiasis, i.e., the so-called leprosy of the Arabs, but rather with leukoderma (white skin, vitiligo), a consequence of the loss of the natural skin pigmentation. This condition in itself was not dangerous, and a person who suffered from it was therefore not considered unclean. Uncleanness was pronounced only when raw flesh appeared in addition to this, for then the presence of elephantiasis had to be suspected. If the raw flesh diminished and turned white, however, the priest pronounced the patient clean. The washing of the person's clothing was not necessary in this instance, for he had not been put in isolation.

3. *Two Particular Cases* (13:18–28)

13:18–28 *"When someone has a boil on his skin and it heals, and in the place where the boil was, a white swelling or reddish-white spot appears, he must present himself to the priest. The priest is to examine it, and if it appears to be more than skin deep and the hair in it has turned white, the priest shall pronounce him unclean. It is an infectious skin disease that has broken out where the boil was. But if, when the priest examines it, there is no white hair in it and it is not more than skin deep and has faded, then the priest is to put him in isolation for seven days. If it is spreading in the skin, the priest shall pronounce him unclean; it is infectious. But if the spot is unchanged and has not spread, it is only a scar from the boil, and the priest shall pronounce him clean.*

"When someone has a burn on his skin and a reddish-white or white spot appears in the raw flesh of the burn, the priest is to examine the spot, and if the hair in it has turned white, and it appears to be more than skin deep, it is an infectious disease that has broken out in the burn. The priest shall pronounce him unclean; it is an infectious skin disease. But if the priest examines it and there is no white hair in the spot and if it is not more than skin deep and has faded, then the priest is to put him in isolation for seven days. On the seventh day the priest is to examine him, and if it is spreading in the skin, the priest shall pronounce him unclean; it is an infectious skin disease. If, however, the spot is unchanged and has not spread in the skin but has faded, it is a swelling from the burn, and the priest shall pronounce him clean; it is only a scar from the burn."

Verses 18–23 speak of a situation in which the scab of a boil that was thought to be healed acquired a suspicious white or reddish-white color. This once again indicated the possible presence of "the plague," and the affected person therefore immediately had to go to the priest for further examination. If the latter determined that the infection was subcutaneous and that the hair in it had turned white (cf. v. 3), the suspicion of leprosy was confirmed and the person had to be pronounced unclean at once. If there was reason for doubt, however, as in the case where the diseased area had faded (see v. 2), the patient was put into isolation for a week. A spreading of the disease during this period indicated that the person was unclean, but in the event that the affected area had remained unchanged, the priest pronounced him clean, for it was then clear that the color of the scab was misleading.

A similar phenomenon could occur in connection with a burn on the skin (vv. 24–28), and the same procedure was naturally followed in this diagnosis. The descriptions of these matters, to be sure, are very long-winded. This was necessary, however, not only because of the difficulty that was involved in making a correct diagnosis at that early date, but above all because nothing less than the purity of the congregation of the Lord was at stake.

4. Abnormal Growths on the Head or Chin (13:29–37)

13:29–37 *"If a man or woman has a sore on the head or on the chin, the priest is to examine the sore, and if it appears to be more than skin deep and the hair in it is yellow and thin, the priest shall pronounce that person unclean; it is an itch, an infectious disease of the head or chin. But if, when the priest examines this kind of sore, it does not seem to be more than skin deep and there is no black hair in it, then the priest is to put the infected person in isolation for seven days. On the seventh day the priest is to examine the sore, and if the itch has not spread and there is no yellow hair in it and it does not appear to be more than skin deep, he must be shaved except for the diseased area, and the priest is to keep him in isolation another seven days. On the seventh day the priest is to examine the itch and if it has not spread in the skin and appears to be no more than skin deep, the priest shall pronounce him clean. He must wash his clothes, and he will be clean. But if the itch does spread in the skin after he is pronounced clean, the priest is to examine him, and if the itch has spread in the skin, the priest does not need to look for yellow hair; the person is unclean. If, however, in his judgment it is unchanged and black hair has grown in it, the itch is healed. He is clean, and the priest shall pronounce him clean."*

These verses deal no longer with *ṣāra'at*, but rather with *neteq*, which in verse 30 is called a *ṣāra'at* of the head or chin. *Neteq* designates an ailment that induces scratching (*nātaq*, which can mean "to scratch away"; cf. "scabies," from the Latin verb *scabere*, "to scratch"), and it is thus the same thing that we refer to as "itch" or "scabies." The signs of disease in this case were a subcutaneous infection and hair that was thin and yellow rather than its normal black. If the priest ascertained the presence of these symptoms, the patient had to be pronounced unclean immediately, but if they were absent, he had to be put into isolation for seven days and then subjected to a further examination. If there were then still no disturbing signs, the person had to be shaved except for the diseased area and isolated for another seven days. In the event that the ailment had not spread during this period and it appeared that there was no subcutaneous infection, the priest pronounced the patient clean and he then washed his clothes as a token of his cleanness (see v. 6). If the disease had spread, however, the person was immediately pronounced unclean regardless of the color of the hair.

5. *Two More Particular Cases* (13:38–44)

13:38–44 *"When a man or woman has white spots on the skin, the priest is to examine them, and if the spots are dull white, it is a harmless rash that has broken out on the skin; that person is clean.*

"When a man has lost his hair and is bald, he is clean. If he has lost his hair from the front of his scalp and has a bald forehead, he is clean. But if he has a reddish-white sore on his bald head or forehead, it is an infectious disease breaking out on his head or forehead. The priest is to examine him and, if the swollen sore on his head or forehead is reddish-white like an infectious skin disease, the man is diseased and is unclean. The priest shall pronounce him unclean because of the sore on his head."

Verses 38–39 deal with a harmless rash designated by the term *bōhaq* (*bāhaq* = "to shine"). The symptoms in this case were dull, white spots appearing on the skin. The priest here again made an examination, but if this revealed no further signs of disease, the eruption was declared harmless and there was no need for further attention. Such a *bōhaq* could last for one or two months, but it neither caused pain nor was it contagious.

Verses 40–44 speak of the loss of head hair, and a distinction is made here between baldness of the forehead and baldness of the hind part of the head. Such baldness could of course be completely harmless, but if there were secondary symptoms and the priest discerned the presence of a reddish-white sore (cf. v. 19), the occurrence of *ṣāra'at* was to be feared and the person had to be immediately pronounced unclean.

6. *The Clothing and Demeanor of an Infected Person* (13:45–46)

13:45–46 *"The person with such an infectious disease must wear torn clothes, let his hair be unkempt, cover the lower part of his face and cry out, 'Unclean! Unclean!' As long as he has the infection he remains unclean. He must live alone; he must live outside the camp."*

The clothing and hair of someone with an infectious skin disease were to serve as signs of mourning (see 10:6), for such a person had been touched by death or "death's firstborn" (Job 18:13). He could for this reason no longer take part in the life of Israel (see also Num. 12:12). Leaving one's hair hanging loose and unkempt by not putting on a headcloth (cf. Ezek. 24:17), a practice that was also required of the Nazirite (Num. 6:5), formed a sign of mourning and was thus forbidden to the high priest in Leviticus 21:10. Verse 45 states that an infected person also had to cover his *śāpām*. In 2 Samuel 19:24 this term designates the mustache, whereas in the present context as well as in Ezekiel 24:17, 22 and Micah 3:7 it refers to the entire lower part of the face. This had to be covered as another sign of mourning. The purpose of this was perhaps to prevent the person from inhaling through his mouth and nose further demonic influences,[28] or alternatively, to restrain him from communicating these to others by exhaling. Last, the person had to cry out "unclean! unclean!" whenever someone approached him, so that the other person could be warned to stay at a distance (cf. Lam. 4:15). The same consideration led the Jews to whitewash their graves so that everyone would be able to see and avoid such unclean places in the dark. It later even became customary for a person with an infectious skin disease to wear a bell, this serving the same purpose as the "leper's clapper" of medieval times. Such a person was naturally not permitted within the camp, and he was thus compelled to live alone outside its boundaries (see also Num. 5:2; 2 Kings 7:3-4; 15:5).

7. *Contamination of Fabrics and Leather* (13:47-59)

13:47-59 *"If any clothing is contaminated with mildew—any woolen or linen clothing, any woven or knitted material of linen or wool, any leather or anything made of leather—and if the contamination in the clothing, or leather, or woven or knitted material, or any leather article, is greenish or reddish, it is a spreading mildew and must be shown to the priest. The priest is to examine the mildew and isolate the affected article for seven days. On the seventh day he is to examine it, and if the mildew has spread in the clothing, or the woven or knitted material, or the leather, whatever its use, it is a destructive mildew; the article is unclean. He must burn up the clothing, or the woven or knitted material of wool or linen, or any leather article that has the contamination in it, because the mildew is destructive; the article must be burned up.*

"But if, when the priest examines it, the mildew has not spread in the clothing, or the woven or knitted material, or the leather article, he shall order that the contaminated article be washed. Then he is to isolate it for another seven days. After the affected article has been washed, the priest is to examine it, and if the mildew has not changed its appearance, even though it has not spread, it is unclean. Burn it with fire, whether the mildew has affected one side or the other. If, when the priest examines it, the mildew has faded after the article has been washed, he is to tear the contaminated part out of the clothing, or the leather, or the woven

---

[28]See Publisher's Note.

or knitted material. But if it reappears in the clothing, or in the woven or knitted material, or in the leather article, it is spreading, and whatever has the mildew must be burned with fire. The clothing, or the woven or knitted material, or any leather article that has been washed and is rid of the mildew, must be washed again, and it will be clean."

These are the regulations concerning contamination by mildew in woolen or linen clothing, woven or knitted material, or any leather article, for pronouncing them clean or unclean.

The extent to which the Israelites feared the occurrence of infectious skin disease is indicated by the addition of this long section to the law concerning such ailments. These verses were in fact added later, for they break the connection between verse 46 and 14:1. They are concerned with some type of contamination, the precise nature of which remains unclear (perhaps deterioration resulting from dampness,[29]), which could appear on clothing, woolen and linen fabrics, and leather goods. Just as with people, such contaminated articles were to be subjected to a detailed examination by the priest and isolated for seven days, and if it then appeared that the suspect area had spread, the affected article was to be burned. If there was no spreading, however, the article was to be washed and then set apart for another seven days. In the event that the contaminated area still remained unchanged after this time, the article was to be burned, but if it appeared that the spot had faded, the contaminated part was to be torn away. If the contamination then reappeared in the article, it was still to be destroyed by fire.

In the translation of these verses, it is customary to follow the Septuagint interpretation of *šᵉtî* and *'ereb* as referring to the "warp" and the "woof" of the fabric,[30] but it is not at all certain that this is correct. The context rather seems to indicate that the reference is to materials that had not yet been fashioned into clothing, but what particular materials these may have been is not known.[31]

Cleansing From Infectious Skin Diseases
(14:1–32)

1. *The Ceremony of Cleansing* (14:1–9)

14:1–9 *The LORD said to Moses, "These are the regulations for the diseased person at the time of his ceremonial cleansing, when he is brought to the priest: The priest is to go outside the camp and examine him. If the person has been healed of*

---

[29]The NIV interprets this as mildew.

[30]Cf. KJV and RSV.

[31]The NIV translates *šᵉtî* and *'ereb* as "woven" and "knitted material."

his infectious skin disesase, the priest shall order that two live clean birds and some cedar wood, scarlet yarn and hyssop be brought for the one to be cleansed. Then the priest shall order that one of the birds be killed over fresh water in a clay pot. He is then to take the live bird and dip it, together with the cedar wood, the scarlet yarn and the hyssop, into the blood of the bird that was killed over the fresh water. Seven times he shall sprinkle the one to be cleansed of the infectious disease and pronounce him clean. Then he is to release the live bird in the open fields.

"The person to be cleansed must wash his clothes, shave off all his hair and bathe with water; then he will be ceremonially clean. After this he may come into the camp, but he must stay outside his tent for seven days. On the seventh day he must shave off all his hair; he must shave his head, his beard, his eyebrows and the rest of his hair. He must wash his clothes and bathe himself with water, and he will be clean."

These regulations naturally applied only to those who were once unclean and were now declared to be healed,[32] and they were of no concern to persons affected by harmless skin conditions. The situation presupposed here is obviously that of Israel during its wanderings in the desert, for when it was time for the recovered person to observe the ritual of cleansing, the priest found him outside the camp. The law presented here is therefore very ancient in both form and content. It has been contended that the writer of Numbers 12 was unacquainted with the regulations of Leviticus 14,[33] but the fact that the Lord Himself gave special instructions regarding Miriam's leprosy indicates that the former chapter deals with an exceptional situation that was beyond the purview of the ordinary law. There is a question as to whether it was possible to observe these regulations after the Israelites had taken possession of Canaan. In this connection, a clear distinction must be made between the pronouncing of a person clean or unclean and the ceremony of cleansing following recovery from a disease. In the former case a visit to the sanctuary was not necessary, for all that was required was an examination by a priest, and these dwelt throughout the entire land. The ceremony of cleansing could take place only in a sanctuary, however, for it involved the presenting of prescribed offerings. With regard to this, it must be remembered that Israel did not have a central sanctuary before or during the monarchy (see p. 133) The Jerusalem temple never assumed the position that David and Solomon had intended for it, and it was only after the

---

[32]I have used the phrase "declared to be healed" rather than merely "healed" here in order to take a position against Mowinckel (*Psalmenstudien* IV [1923], p 23) and Lods (*Les idées des Israélites sur la maladie, ses causes et ses remèdes*, BZAW 41, pp. 190f.), both of whom maintain that the rites of Leviticus 14 were originally intended as curative measures. This view is also opposed by N. H. Ridderbos, *De "werkers der ongerechtigheid in de individuele psalmen."*

[33]E.g., Edelkoort, *Numeri*, p. 128 *(Tekst en Uitleg)*.

Exile that circumstances permitted the command: "go, show yourself to the priest and offer the gift Moses commanded" (Matt. 8:4; Mark 1:44; Luke 5:14; 17:14).

Since the affliction with *ṣāraʻaṯ* was considered a living death (Num. 12:12) in which the person was disgraced by God (Num. 12:14) and placed under His wrath (as Job was regarded by his friends), the priest, who alone was qualified to judge such matters, first had to establish that the person was truly healed before he could be readmitted into the life of the community. For this same reason, the rites of cleansing were clearly designed to express the thought that the recovered person had been brought back to life. This had a twofold meaning, viz., a return to the life of the national community and also to life in communion with God, but it should be noted that both of these were bound up together, since Israel was not simply a nation, but rather the totality of those who served the Lord. The ceremony of cleansing thus involved the use of living birds (the birds were to be clean and therefore could not be any of those listed in 11:13–19; according to the rabbis and also the Vulgate, they were sparrows) and "living" or "fresh" water,[34] i.e., water from a spring. These elements naturally could not be provided by the person being cleansed, for the new life had yet to be imparted to him. The birds, which could not be doves or pigeons, were not regarded as sacrificial animals; they were not placed on the altar, nor was any of their blood sprinkled against the side of the altar. To these must be added two items that were thought to have curative powers: cedar wood, which was highly valued in Israel (also in Babylonia and Egypt), and hyssop, a plant that mysteriously sprouted from walls and was used in cleansing (Exod. 12:22; Num. 19:6, 18; Ps. 51:7). The cedar wood and hyssop were tied together with scarlet yarn, a woolen thread that was dipped in crimson, the brilliant red dye extracted from the eggs and body of the kermes insect. Red is the color of blood, the carrier of life (Gen. 9:4; Lev. 17:11, 14; Deut. 12:23) which as such protected against sickness and death, and it therefore served as a symbol for one who had returned from deathly illness to the fullness of life. Cedar wood, hyssop, and scarlet thread also appear together in Numbers 19.

One of the two birds was slaughtered above a clay pot filled with fresh or living water, and the blood thus became mingled with the water. The priest then used the hyssop bundle, which served as a brush, to sprinkle the patient, and this was done seven times as a sign of completion (cf. 4:6).

---

[34]The Hebrew expression in verses 5 and 6 is *mayim ḥayyîm,* which literally means "living water" (cf. ASV marginal note), and is so translated by the author. This is generally taken to mean "running" or "fresh water," the respective translations of the RSV and NIV, but cf. Jer. 2:13; 17:13; Zech. 14:8, where the NIV translates the same expression as "living water."

The bird that remained alive, which had been immersed in the bloody water along with the hyssop and cedar wood, was then set free.

The release of the living bird is usually regarded as having the same significance as the sending away of the scapegoat in the ceremony of the Day of Atonement (16:21). The bird was thus thought to carry away the person's uncleanness, and the water with which the latter was sprinkled would then serve the same purpose as the water of cleansing in Numbers 8:7 and 19:1-10. Such an interpretation, however, loses sight of the fact that the bird was not brought into contact with the person who had been healed and was now to be pronounced clean. The latter was sprinkled with fresh or living water which, by virtue of the ingredients that had been mingled with it, was regarded as especially effective in bringing life and health. The bird was dipped in this same "living" water and then released. In this ritual, the bird thus formed a symbol of the person being cleansed, for just as the former was restored to the fullness of life, the latter was delivered from his deathly disease and readmitted to his place among the people. The same ritual appears later in the purification of a house that had been contaminated (14:49-53). Only at this point was the healed person made clean. He had escaped from death and begun a new life. The custom of releasing a living bird was present also in Arabia, where at the end of her year of mourning a widow would allow a bird to fly away bearing the uncleanness of her mourning. In the Tigris-Euphrates plain, a sick person would pray that his illness might fly away like a bird, and similar notions were also known in Europe.[35]

The person now had to wash his clothes and bathe with water in order to rid himself still more of the uncleanness that clung to him and thus to further defend against the disease-producing demonic forces that uncleanness often harbors.[36] In addition to this, he was directed to shave off *all* his hair, a requirement that appears also in Numbers 6:18; 8:7; and Deuteronomy 21:12-13. This action is based on the notion, also appearing outside of Israel, that the forces operative in a person's body reside in his hair and nails (which continue to play an important role in superstition) as well as his saliva and perspiration. Only on completion of these cleansing activities could the healed person return to the camp. He was still not permitted to participate in the life of his family, however, for he remained in an intermediate state (cf. Exod. 19:15; 1 Sam. 21:5-6). After seven days, the complete process of cleansing formed by washing, shaving, and bathing had to be repeated, and only at this point were all rights restored to

---

[35] See J. Döller, *Die Reinheits- und Speisegesetze des Alten Testament,* pp. 96, 124.
[36] See Publisher's Note.

the person so that he could resume his position within the cultic life of the people.

2. *The Offerings of Cleansing* (14:10–20)

14:10–11 *"On the eighth day he must bring two male lambs and one ewe lamb a year old, each without defect, along with three-tenths of an ephah of fine flour mixed with oil for the grain offering, and one log of oil. The priest who pronounces him clean shall present both the one to be cleansed and his offerings before the* LORD *at the entrance to the Tent of Meeting."*

In order to demonstrate this renewed status, a series of offerings composed of a guilt offering with its accompanying grain offering, a sin offering, and a burnt offering was now to be presented "before the LORD" (v. 11). The offerings consisted of two male lambs, one year-old ewe lamb, three-tenths of an ephah (i.e., *ca.* 11.1 liters) of raw meal[37] mixed with oil, and a log (i.e., *ca.* ½ liter) of oil. The person being cleansed brought these elements to the entrance of the sanctuary, as was also to be done by a woman being cleansed following childbirth (12:6). It became customary in postexilic times to present the patient at the Nicanor gate, situated between the men's court and the women's court, the latter of which was not considered to belong to the sanctuary proper (*Sotah* 8a).

14:12–18 *"Then the priest is to take one of the male lambs and offer it as a guilt offering, along with the log of oil; he shall wave them before the* LORD *as a wave offering. He is to slaughter the lamb in the holy place where the sin offering and the burnt offering are slaughtered. Like the sin offering, the guilt offering belongs to the priest; it is most holy. The priest is to take some of the blood of the guilt offering and put it on the lobe of the right ear of the one to be cleansed, on the thumb of his right hand and on the big toe of his right foot. The priest shall then take some of the log of oil, pour it in the palm of his own left hand, dip his right forefinger into the oil in his palm, and with his finger sprinkle some of it before the* LORD *seven times. The priest is to put some of the oil remaining in his palm on the lobe of the right ear of the one to be cleansed, on the thumb of his right hand and on the big toe of his right foot, on top of the blood of the guilt offering. The rest of the oil in his palm the priest shall put on the head of the one to be cleansed and make atonement for him before the* LORD*."*

The guilt offering was presented first of all. The view that this was brought in order to make satisfaction for the patient's long absence from

---

[37]The large quantity was necessary because of the many activities of the priest in this ceremony; cf. Numbers 15:4.

the sacrificial service in consequence of his illness[38] is incorrect, for the same would then have been required after any lengthy illness (cf. Luke 8:43). The guilt offering was rather brought because infectious skin disease, like illness in general, was regarded as a consequence of some guilt that the person had brought on himself, and thus, as a specific punishment of God (Num. 12:10–11; 2 Chron. 26:19–20). The offering thus served as a renewed consecration of life. The ritual followed here differs from that which was standard in the guilt offering in that the lamb and the log of oil are treated as a wave offering (*tᵉnŭpā* [*h*]) in order to symbolize the offerer's self-surrender to God (see discussion on 7:30, also Num. 8:11). In addition, a male lamb sufficed for this offering, whereas a ram was otherwise required (5:15). The animal was slaughtered in the prescribed place (v. 13), viz., on the north side of the altar, and as in the ordination offering of Aaron and his sons, some of its blood was then smeared on the patient's right ear lobe, right thumb, and right big toe (cf. 8:22–24). The same was done with the oil after some of it had first been sprinkled seven times "before the Lord," i.e., in the direction of the Holy Place, and what oil remained was then put (not poured, as in 8:12) on the head of the healed person.

It may be noted here that this ceremony was doubtless originally intended to expel the demonic forces that were manifested in infectious skin disease, and it was therefore negatively conceived. In Israel, however, the ritual was given a positive direction. The guilt offering was no longer an act of exorcism, for the putting of blood and oil on the right ear lobe, thumb, and big toe of the person indicated that it rather formed a renewed consecration of life (see commentary on 8:22–24).

14:19–20 *"Then the priest is to sacrifice the sin offering and make atonement for the one to be cleansed from his uncleanness. After that, the priest shall slaughter the burnt offering and offer it on the altar, together with the grain offering, and make atonement for him, and he will be clean."*

The most important part of the ritual of cleansing has now been completed, but further offerings still had to be presented. The sin offering formed by the female lamb here had the character of a purification or purging of uncleanness, and the male lamb that served as the burnt offering signified the patient's renewed surrender of himself to the service of the Lord. The grain offering, which consisted of the 11 liters of raw meal mixed with oil—the remaining oil formed a drink offering—gave expression to the thankfulness that the healed person had for being reinstated into

---

[38]See, e.g., Von Orelli in RE³ II, p. 298.

the cultic community. The ritual of cleansing, which corresponded in many ways to the priestly ordination (cf. 8), was therefore composed of three main elements: (1) the smearing of blood and oil on the healed person (vv. 10–18), (2) the sin offering (v. 19), (3) the burnt and grain offerings (v. 20).

3. *The Offerings of the Poor* (14:21–32)

14:21–32 *"If, however, he is poor and cannot afford these, he must take one male lamb as a guilt offering to be waved to make atonement for him, together with a tenth of an ephah of fine flour mixed with oil for a grain offering, a log of oil, and two doves or two young pigeons, which he can afford, one for a sin offering and the other for a burnt offering.*

"On the eighth day he must bring them for his cleansing to the priest at the entrance to the Tent of Meeting, before the LORD. The priest is to take the lamb for the guilt offering, together with the log of oil, and wave them before the LORD as a wave offering. He shall slaughter the lamb for the guilt offering and take some of its blood and put it on the lobe of the right ear of the one to be cleansed, on the thumb of his right hand and on the big toe of his right foot. The priest is to pour some of the oil into the palm of his own left hand, and with his right forefinger sprinkle some of the oil from his palm seven times before the LORD. Some of the oil in his palm he is to put on the same places he put the blood of the guilt offering—on the lobe of the right ear of the one to be cleansed, on the thumb of his right hand and on the big toe of his right foot. The rest of the oil in his palm the priest shall put on the head of the one to be cleansed, to make atonement for him before the LORD. Then he shall sacrifice the doves or the young pigeons, which the person can afford, one as a sin offering and the other as a burnt offering, together with the grain offering. In this way the priest will make atonement before the LORD on behalf of the one to be cleansed." These are the regulations for anyone who has an infectious skin disease and who cannot afford the regular offerings for his cleansing.

As in the purification of a woman who had recovered from giving birth, special concessions were here made for those who were unable to afford the standard offerings of cleansing. This relaxation of the requirements naturally did not apply to the guilt offering (see above), but only to the sin and burnt offerings. In each of these, it was sufficient for a poor person to present a dove or a young pigeon, and the required grain offering was reduced to one-tenth of an ephah of raw meal. Although the size of the offerings was therefore reduced, the three elements of the ritual were still retained (see discussion on vv. 19–20). The closing formula in verse 32 underscores the fact that these concessions applied exclusively to the poor. It may also be noted that this formula clearly indicates that these verses constituted a separate law that had been inserted within the overall framework of the requirements pertaining to various types of skin disease.

Mildew on Houses
(14:33–57)

14:33–53 *The LORD said to Moses and Aaron, ''When you enter the land of Canaan, which I am giving you as your possession, and I put a spreading mildew in a house in that land, the owner of the house must go and tell the priest, 'I have seen something that looks like mildew in my house.' The priest is to order the house to be emptied before he goes in to examine the mildew, so that nothing in the house will be pronounced unclean. After this the priest is to go in and inspect the house. He is to examine the mildew on the walls, and if it has greenish or reddish depressions that appear to be deeper than the surface of the wall, the priest shall go out of the house and at the entrance close up the house for seven days. On the seventh day the priest shall return to inspect the house. If the mildew has spread on the walls, he is to order that the contaminated stones be torn out and thrown into an unclean place outside the town. He must have all the inside walls of the house scraped and the material that is scraped off dumped into an unclean place outside the town. Then they are to take other stones to replace these and take new clay and plaster the house.*

''If the mildew reappears in the house after the stones have been torn out and the house scraped and plastered, the priest is to go and examine it and if the mildew has spread in the house, it is a destructive mildew; the house is unclean. It must be torn down—its stones, timbers and all the plaster—and taken out of the town to an unclean place.

''Anyone who goes into the house while it is closed up will be unclean till evening. Anyone who sleeps or eats in the house must wash his clothes.

''But if the priest comes to examine it and the mildew has not spread after the house has been plastered, he shall pronounce the house clean, because the mildew is gone. To purify the house he is to take two birds and some cedar wood, scarlet yarn and hyssop. He shall kill one of the birds over fresh water in a clay pot. Then he is to take the cedar wood, the hyssop, the scarlet yarn and the live bird, dip them into the blood of the dead bird and the fresh water, and sprinkle the house seven times. He shall purify the house with the bird's blood, the fresh water, the live bird, the cedar wood, the hyssop and the scarlet yarn. Then he is to release the live bird in the open fields outside the town. In this way he will make atonement for the house, and it will be clean.''

This law, which applied to circumstances that arose only after the Israelites had established themselves in Canaan, is concerned with the appearance of greenish or reddish ''depressions'' in the walls of houses, a phenomenon that remains unclear to us.[39] Such an ''eruption,'' which

---

[39]The NIV interprets this as mildew, whereas the author has ''the plague of leprosy'' (cf. KJV; RSV, ''leprous disease''). ''Spreading mildew'' in Leviticus 14:34 of NIV translates the same Hebrew phrase, *neḡaʿ ṣāraʿat,* as ''infectious skin disease'' in 13:2–3.

appeared only on the inner wall, could sometimes be "destructive" (v. 44), just like certain growths on fabrics (13:51–52). Similarly to instances of *ṣāraʿat* on human beings (13:3, 20, 25, 30), it gave the impression of lying deeper than the surface of the wall (v. 37). Perhaps what is being spoken of here is parasitic growths, some of which were in fact designated *lepraria* because of their resemblance to *lepra*. One possibility is a type of lichen that appeared on eroded stones and on walls undergoing moisture deterioration. It is clear, however, that such houses had not been contaminated by the presence of lepers within them. Whatever the case may have been, the Canaanite and Israelite houses in which these phenomena occurred usually contained very little wood, were made of clay tiles that were further plastered with clay on the inner side, and rested on a foundation of two or three layers of stones that were either quarried or gathered in the fields.

As soon as suspicious phenomena appeared in a house, the priest had to be notified so that he could subject it to an examination. As a precautionary measure, the priest first had the house evacuated so that he would not later have to pronounce its entire contents unclean. It should be noted here that persons and objects became unclean only after the priest had made a formal declaration to this effect. The procedure that was followed was then the same as with fabrics. Just as the contaminated portion had to be torn out of a piece of material (13:56), the contaminated stones had to be removed from a house and replaced with new ones. In order to avoid any further possibility of contamination, the rejected stones were thrown into an unclean place outside the town. The inner walls of the house then had to be meticulously scraped and replastered. It was nevertheless possible for the eruption to recur after all of this had been done (vv. 43–44), and in this case the entire house had to be torn down and thrown outside the town. Here again it was naturally taken to an unclean place (v. 45), just as a person with an infectious skin disease had to remain outside the camp in the realm of uncleanness.

The house remained closed as long as the examination was in process (v. 38), and whoever entered it for any reason (e.g., eating, sleeping) was made unclean and then had to be cleansed in the prescribed manner (in this case, by washing his clothes, v. 47). If the eruption did not return and the house did not need to be torn down, it was subjected to the same ceremony of cleansing as was performed in the case of a human being (see pp. 142–46). It is fitting that the Hebrew term used in verses 49 and 52 is *ḥiṭṭēʾ* (the *Piel* of *ḥāṭaʾ*, "to sin"), which literally means "to purify from sin" (NIV, "purify"; see pp. 117–18). The same term was used when the altar of burnt offering was consecrated to its work of atonement (8:15; cf. Exod.

29:36), and Ezekiel later also applied it to this altar (Ezek. 43:20, 22–23) as well as to the sanctuary (45:18). Uncleanness was equivalent to sin, for whoever or whatever was contaminated by it was prevented from attaining the goal that the Lord had set.

14:54–57 *These are the regulations for any infectious skin disease, for an itch, for mildew in clothing or in a house, and for a swelling, a rash or a bright spot, to determine when something is clean or unclean.*
These are the regulations for infectious skin diseases and mildew.

These verses contain two closing formulas. The longer of these (vv. 54–57a) reenumerates the topics discussed in chapters 13–14, while the shorter one is more general and merely speaks of *ṣāraʿat*.[40] The longer one also briefly describes the task of the priests: to give *tôrâ(h)*, i.e., instruction (cf. KJV), concerning various types of growths and to determine what was clean or unclean. The longer formula strikes me as a later insertion that was added when the regulations concerning fabrics and houses were incorporated into the law.

Bodily Discharges of Men and Women
(15:1–33)

Like the preceding chapters, this section presupposes the circumstances that prevailed during Israel's sojourn in the desert, when the sanctuary was nearby and the priest was accessible at all times (cf. vv. 14, 28, which speak of appearing at the Tent on the eighth day). The regulations given here pertain to the extremely delicate subject of sexual life, with its normal and abnormal bodily phenomena. The various matters spoken of are not all equally clear. On the one hand, it is evident that the Israelites regarded the satisfaction of the normal impulses of sexual intercourse between man and woman as in conformity with the Lord's creation ordinances, and that everything connected with sexual life was therefore brought within the sphere of the holy. On the other hand, it cannot be denied that they were conscious of a certain incompatibility between the satisfaction of sexual needs, even if this was done within the limits set by God, and the possibility of entering the sanctuary. The distorting effect of sin in human life, and especially in the human mind, is clearly apparent here. This distortion brings about a natural shame toward everything connected with sex, since the egocentric thinking characteristic of human nature introduces into sexual life an element that was originally foreign to it and which makes its

---

[40]In accordance with its interpretations of the phenomena spoken of in chapters 13 and 14, the NIV here translates this single term as "infectious skin diseases and mildew."

effects felt in normal sexual intercourse. It is for this reason that chapter 15 even contains regulations pertaining to sexual intercourse within marriage (see below).

1. *Male discharges* (15:1–18)

15:1–12 *The LORD said to Moses and Aaron, "Speak to the Israelites and say to them: 'When any man has a bodily discharge, the discharge is unclean. Whether it continues flowing from his body or is blocked, it will make him unclean. This is how his discharge will bring about uncleanness:*

"'Any bed the man with a discharge lies on will be unclean, and anything he sits on will be unclean. Anyone who touches his bed must wash his clothes and bathe with water, and he will be unclean till evening. Whoever sits on anything that the man with a discharge sat on must wash his clothes and bathe with water, and he will be unclean till evening.

"'Whoever touches the man who has a discharge must wash his clothes and bathe with water, and he will be unclean till evening.

"'If the man with the discharge spits on someone who is clean, that person must wash his clothes and bathe with water, and he will be unclean till evening.

"'Everything the man sits on when riding will be unclean, and whoever touches any of the things that were under him will be unclean till evening; whoever picks up those things must wash his clothes and bathe with water, and he will be unclean till evening.

"'Anyone the man with a discharge touches without rinsing his hands with water must wash his clothes and bathe with water, and he will be unclean till evening.

"'A clay pot that the man touches must be broken, and any wooden article is to be rinsed with water.'"

The chapter deals first of all with unhealthy aberrations that can occur in the sexual life of males. The precise nature of these phenomena is unclear. Some have proposed hemorrhoids or the excretions from syphilitic ulcerations. The Septuagint and Vulgate follow the Jewish tradition in regarding these phenomena as instances of spermatorrhea, the involuntary release of droplets of sperm resulting from a weakening of the sexual organs. This is unlikely, however, for the Hebrew term for "sperm" *(zera')* does not appear in this connection. More probable is a discharge of mucus resulting from a catarrhal inflamation of the urinary tract. Verse 2 speaks of a "discharge from his *bāśār,"* a term that usually means "flesh" or "body" but here (also in v. 19; cf. KJV and RSV) refers specifically to the sexual organ. The disorder can have two alternate forms: the mucus discharge flows out of the body, or it is blocked within (v. 3).

These unhealthy phenomena naturally made a person unclean, for as has been observed earlier (see discussion on ch. 12), the Israelites, like the entire ancient Near Eastern world, understood them as an expression of demonic forces operative within the body.[41] Since uncleanness was contagious, every person or thing that the infected person came into contact with was also rendered unclean. Verses 4–12 make clear how scrupulously this rule was to be observed. Spitting in someone's face, spoken of in verse 8, was of course a sign of contempt (Num. 12:14; Deut. 25:9). It is only in this context (v. 11) that touching a person with the hand is expressly stated to transmit uncleanness. The commandment to *rāḥaṣ bammayim,* which appears six times in verses 4–12, does not refer specifically to the taking of a bath,[42] but rather means "to wash oneself thoroughly with water." The same expression is used also for the washing of the pieces of the burnt offering (1:9, 13; 8:21) and the washing of Aaron and his sons (8:6). Verse 13 speaks of washing the *bāśār* with fresh water, but I suspect that the reference here is to the entire body (see RSV), not to the sexual organ as in verse 2. This is more clear in verse 16, where the Hebrew expressly speaks of "the whole *bāśār.*" The stringency of the requirements (see v. 12) indicates that the uncleanness resulting from this disorder was regarded as very strong.

15:13–15 *"'When a man is cleansed from his discharge, he is to count off seven days for his ceremonial cleansing; he must wash his clothes and bathe himself with fresh water, and he will be clean. On the eighth day he must take two doves and two young pigeons and come before the LORD to the entrance to the Tent of Meeting and give them to the priest. The priest is to sacrifice them, the one for a sin offering and the other for a burnt offering. In this way he will make atonement before the LORD for the man because of his discharge.'"*

When a man has recovered from this disorder, he remains unclean for seven days, just as a person who has had an infectious skin disease (14:10) or a woman who has had a discharge (15:28). After this, he must wash his body and his clothing, and he may then present the offering of cleansing on the eighth day. The fact that the guilt offering presented after recovery from an infectious skin disease (14:12) is not required here indicates that this sexual abnormality, because it was curable and less serious in its consequences, was considered less significant than the former ailment. The same thing is evident from the fact that the smallest possible presentations are here sufficient for both the sin offering (5:7) and the burnt offering (1:14), a dove or a young pigeon being all that was required in either case (cf. 12:8; 14:30). The measure prescribed for a bodily discharge in Num-

---

[41] See Publisher's Note.
[42] This is the reading in the NIV.

bers 5:2 is more severe, for it is there stated that, like a person who suffered from an infectious skin disease or was defiled by contact with a dead body, anyone having this sexual abnormality was to be expelled from the camp. Since the Lord dwelled at its center, the entire encampment would be contaminated by the presence of such persons.

15:16–18 *" 'When a man has an emission of semen, he must bathe his whole body with water, and he will be unclean till evening. Any clothing or leather that has semen on it must be washed with water, and it will be unclean till evening. When a man lies with a woman and there is an emission of semen, both must bathe with water, and they will be unclean till evening.' "*

Two other possibilities of defilement are mentioned in addition to the above disorder, although neither of these requires the bringing of an offering. The first concerns what is referred to in Deuteronomy 23:10 as a "nocturnal emission" (RSV, "what chances to him by night"), an involuntary discharge of semen that can occur during the night and that in no way need be caused by an abnormality in the sexual organs. The uncleanness resulting from this lasted until evening, and the entire body had to be washed along with any piece of clothing or leather (e.g., forming part of the bed) that had been contaminated by the semen. Deuteronomy 23:9–11 adds to this that one who had such a nocturnal emission during a military campaign had to remain outside the camp during the time of his uncleanness. In this connection, it must be kept in mind that to the ancient Near Eastern person a war was in essence a holy event, since the adversaries were not merely two nations, but two divine powers.[43] The sacredness of battle is evident in such passages as 1 Samuel 21:5; 2 Samuel 11:11; Isaiah 13:3; Jeremiah 6:4; Joel 3:9; and Micah 3:5 (see NEB), and a priest therefore always accompanied warriors (Deut. 20:2).

The second possibility of defilement, which could occur even within marriage, relates to sexual intercourse. That verse 18 is indeed speaking of this is evident from the fact that Leviticus 19:20 and Numbers 5:13 use the same Hebrew expression.[44] To the Israelite mind, and also for many other ancient peoples, copulation made both the man and the woman unclean and necessitated that both wash their entire bodies and withdraw from the cultic community (see also Exod. 19:15). This would seem to be in conflict with the high valuation that the Old Testament places on marriage (see above), and for this reason many exegetes formerly sought to evade the clear

---

[43]See Publisher's Note.
[44]Some have argued that it refers to the mere lying next to a man who has a nocturnal emission (v. 16).

meaning of the text by contending that the verse is here still speaking of the above-mentioned nocturnal emission. It must not be forgotten, however, that Israel was in this respect a child of its age and that divine revelation worked in an organic rather than a mechanical manner.

Jewish tradition maintains that these requirements applied exclusively to the priests. They were allegedly not permitted to enter the camp—according to the rabbis this included the sanctuary and the Levitical encampment adjoining it—in order to eat the priestly portions of the offerings until they had performed the prescribed washings. The rabbis even went so far as to reject out of hand as unacceptable a directive ascribed to Ezra that made these verses also binding for lay persons who read the law. The present requirements do not admit of such a restricted application, however (see discussion on verses 31–33).[45]

2. *Female Discharges* (15:19–30)

15:19–30 *" "When a woman has her regular flow of blood, the impurity of her monthly period will last seven days, and anyone who touches her will be unclean till evening.*

" "Anything she lies on during her period will be unclean, and anything she sits on will be unclean. Whoever touches her bed must wash his clothes and bathe with water, and he will be unclean till evening. Whoever touches anything she sits on must wash his clothes and bathe with water, and he will be unclean till evening. Whether it is the bed or anything she was sitting on, when anyone touches it, he will be unclean till evening.

" "If a man lies with her and her monthly flow touches him, he will be unclean for seven days; any bed he lies on will be unclean.

" "When a woman has a discharge of blood for many days at a time other than her monthly period or has a discharge that continues beyond her period, she will be unclean as long as she has the discharge, just as in the days of her period. Any bed she lies on while her discharge continues will be unclean, as is her bed during her monthly period, and anything she sits on will be unclean, as during her period. Whoever touches them will be unclean; he must wash his clothes and bathe with water, and he will be unclean till evening.

" "When she is cleansed from her discharge, she must count off seven days, and after that she will be ceremonially clean. On the eighth day she must take two doves or two young pigeons and bring them to the priest at the entrance to the Tent of Meeting. The priest is to sacrifice one for a sin offering and the other for a burnt offering. In this way he will make atonement for her before the LORD for the uncleanness of her discharge.' "

This section deals first of all (vv. 19–24) with what the Israelites re-

---

[45] See also Hertz, *Pentateuch and Haftorahs*, p. 146.

ferred to as the *niddâ(h)* of a woman. The Greek translators rendered this term as "uncleanness," but this is a description rather than an actual translation, since it merely indicates the consequences of *niddâ(h)*. *Niddâ(h)* designates that which is excreted, and it is thus a reference to the monthly period of a woman. The notion that this is a cause of cultic uncleanness was present throughout the ancient world, where the sexual life of a woman with its regularly recurrent loss of blood was regarded as altogether mysterious and as a sign of physical indisposition (see discussion on ch. 12). The uncleanness of a menstruating woman appears also in Genesis 31:35, and the mysterious character of menstruation can be seen in the fact that the verb that is used for it *(zûb)* is also applied in such passages as Psalms 78:20; 105:41, and Isaiah 48:21 to the miraculous gushing forth of water from the rock. Although the *niddâ(h)* as a rule lasted for only four days, the period of uncleanness is here as in 12:2 set at seven days (see also 15:13). During these seven days, the woman was to remain isolated. Any man who violated her separation period, even if he did not have sexual relations with her—the consequence of this would be death for both of them (18:19; 20:18)—also became unclean for seven days. It is thus not surprising that whoever and whatever came into contact with a menstruating woman likewise became unclean and that anyone who was thereby defiled had to wash his clothes and body.

Verses 25–27 speak of a phenomenon that is also considered unhealthy today and that could last for years at a time (cf. Matt. 9:20; Luke 8:43–44). This disorder was present whenever a discharge extended beyond the seven days of normal menstruation (v. 19), and it could also occur along with the latter. The resulting uncleanness was equivalent to that produced by menstruation, another indication that the latter was regarded as a symptom of disease. Whoever was contaminated by this uncleanness was to take the same measures spoken of above.

What was to be done by a woman after the cessation of her menstruation or other abnormal discharge is discussed in verses 28–30. After remaining separated from others for another week, she was to present two doves or young pigeons, one as a sin offering and one as a burnt offering. It is surprising that although those who had been defiled by a menstruating woman had to wash their clothes and bodies (vv. 21–22), the same was not prescribed for the woman herself. Apparently, the lawgiver considered this as self-evident after what had already been said (cf. Ezek. 16:9).

Regarding the woman in Matthew 9:20–22 and Luke 8:43–48 who suffered blood loss, it may be noted in passing that in terms of this law, her contact with Jesus made Him unclean. By not telling the woman to present the prescribed offerings after she had been healed, the Lord demonstrated that He was greater than Moses.

3. *Admonitions to the Priests* (15:31–33)

15:31–33 *" 'You must keep the Israelites separate from things that make them unclean, so they will not die in their uncleanness for defiling my dwelling place, which is among them.' "*

These are the regulations for a man with a discharge, for anyone made unclean by an emission of semen, for a woman in her monthly period, for a man or a woman with a discharge, and for a man who lies with a woman who is ceremonially unclean.

The regulations close with an admonition directed to the priests. The fact that such a statement appears nowhere else indicates that the types of defilement dealt with here, which not only were intimately related to sexual life, but also could have serious consequences for the community and thus for cultic life as well, were of particular importance to the lawgiver. The priests were to warn the Israelites that they had to separate themselves from these specific sources of uncleanness. This warning acquired an even deeper significance against the background of the regulations in chapter 18 that pertained to the possibilities of corruption that could arise in the Israelites' sexual life, and it is thus understandable that precisely in this context a warning was issued against defiling the Lord's "dwelling place" (cf. Num. 19:13). This mention of the Lord's "dwelling" or tabernacle has given the rabbis the opportunity to argue that the regulations presented in this chapter applied solely to those who entered the sanctuary or served in sacred activities. Even the proponents of this notion must have been aware of its altogether arbitrary nature, however. The only thing that could have induced such an interpretation must have been the fact that, in view of the sexual practices that prevailed during their time, there would have been no other way to maintain the legal force of these regulations (see discussion of vv. 16–18).

The chapter concludes with a closing formula similar to that appended to the law concerning infectious skin diseases (14:54–57). The opening portion of verse 32 is more ancient, whereas what follows is a description that was inserted later.[46]

---

[46]Jewish causistry has dealt at length with the matter of menstruation. The Babylonian Talmud devotes an entire tractate *(Niddah)* containing ten subdivisions to this, while the relevant sections of the Palestinian Talmud and the *Shulhan 'Arukh* contain four and eighteen divisions, respectively. See J. Döller, *Die Reinheits- und Speisegesetze des Alten Testaments in religionsgeschichtlicher Beleuchtung,* pp. 46f.

Part Four

The Day of Atonement
(16:1–34)

16:1–2 *The LORD spoke to Moses after the death of the two sons of Aaron who died when they approached the LORD. The LORD said to Moses: "Tell your brother Aaron not to come whenever he chooses into the Most Holy Place behind the curtain in front of the atonement cover on the ark, or else he will die, because I appear in the cloud over the atonement cover."*

Through the sudden death of his sons, the tragedy of which was greatly increased by the circumstances under which it occurred (10:1–2), Aaron had been given an overwhelming impression of the Lord's holiness. The question of how the priest could be safeguarded against the outbreaking of this holiness was thus most urgent, for he could not be left in the dark as to whether the possibility of entering the sanctuary proper, i.e., the place where God dwelt, was subject to certain restrictions, and if so, what these could have been. The answer to this question is given in Leviticus 16.

Aaron could not go behind the curtain into the Most Holy Place "whenever he chooses." The Hebrew here (v. 2) literally reads "Holy Place" (*qōḏeš,* cf. KJV, RSV), but it is clear that the Most Holy Place is being spoken of (see Exod. 26:33), and the same is referred to as the "sanctuary area" in verse 3. Although this was not the case among the other nations of the ancient Near Eastern world, in Israel the priest never entered this section of the sanctuary at his own discretion. Permission to do so was granted exclusively by its "Resident," who appeared "in the cloud over the atonement cover." This was not the cloud of smoke from the incense spoken of in verse 13, but rather the pillar of cloud (Exod. 13:21; 14:19; etc.) that concealed the Lord's glory to such a degree that the Israelites were able to look on it. In resting on the atonement cover, which was the most important part of the ark, the portable sanctuary of the invisible God, this cloud formed a sign that the Lord dwelled there (Exod. 19:9; 40:36–38; etc.). In the cloud the Lord "appeared," or literally, allowed Himself to be seen, a thought that appears nowhere outside of Israel.[1]

Although verse 2 directs that Aaron could not enter the Most Holy Place at all times, it is not immediately stated when he was allowed to do so. According to verse 34 and also Exodus 30:10, this could take place only once a year, and verse 29 specifies that it be done on the tenth day of the seventh month. The same date is mentioned in Leviticus 23:26–32 and 25:9, and this day is there given the name "Day of Atonement." Jewish tradition refers to it in brief as "the Day" (*Yoma*), Josephus (*Antiquities* XIV 4, 3) speaks of "the fast day," Philo of "the feast of the fast," and the rabbis designate it "the great fast." The Day of Atonement is not mentioned elsewhere in the Old Testament. Ezekiel 45:18–20 does speak of a day of purification, but this was held the first day of the seventh month, and in my opinion, Zechariah 3:9 does not allude to this day either. Hebrews 9:7 contains a reference to the Day of Atonement, however, and in Ecclesiasticus 50, Jesus son of Sirach eulogizes the high priest Simon and his performance of the ritual of this day. The Day of Atonement apparently did not have the same prominence in national life, at least during the time before the Exile, as the three great feasts of Passover, Weeks, and Tabernacles, this being no doubt partly due to the priestly and ceremonial character of this day.

16:3 *"This is how Aaron is to enter the sanctuary area: with a young bull for a sin offering and a ram for a burnt offering."*

Before Aaron was permitted to enter the Most Holy Place, he had to undertake a variety of preparatory measures. In order to make atonement for his own sins and those of his "household" (v. 6), i.e., the entire priesthood, he first had to present two offerings: a young bull as a sin offering (cf. 4:3; 8:14–17) and a ram as a burnt offering (cf. 8:18). These offerings were necessary because if one was to serve as mediator, his own sins first had to be removed. Jewish tradition subjected the high priest to further requirements. For seven days he had to reside in a section of the temple that had been especially set apart for this purpose, and during this

---

[1] See my book, *Gods Woord*[2], pp. 75f.

period the elders read and expounded to him the ritual of the Day of Atonement. He was to remain awake the entire final night, reading portions of the Books of Job, Ezra, Chronicles, and Daniel, and if sleep threatened to overcome him, boys kept him awake by snapping their fingers (*Yoma* 19b).

16:4 *"He is to put on the sacred linen tunic, with linen undergarments next to his body; he is to tie the linen sash around him and put on the linen turban. These are sacred garments; so he must bathe himself with water before he puts them on."*

When he appeared in his mediatorial role, the high priest was not permitted to put on the shoulder pieces, breastpiece, robe, or diadem (cf. Exod. 28:4), and he was thus not clothed in his full official attire. He rather wore only the normal priestly garments—undergarments, tunic, sash, and turban, all made of white linen—and he was then distinguished from the ordinary priests only by the turban. Before dressing himself in these, he naturally first had to wash or bathe his body with water. The white linen symbolized humility and purity (Ezek. 9:2; 10:2–7; Dan. 10:5), but it was at the same time festal attire. The rabbis observe that it was put on in confidence that "all who turn to their Maker in a penitent spirit will receive from His hands not judgment, but grace."[2]

16:5–10 *"From the Israelite community he is to take two male goats for a sin offering and a ram for a burnt offering.*

"Aaron is to offer the bull for his own sin offering to make atonement for himself and his household. Then he is to take the two goats and present them before the LORD at the entrance to the Tent of Meeting. He is to cast lots for the two goats—one lot for the LORD and the other for the scapegoat. Aaron shall bring the goat whose lot falls to the LORD and sacrifice it for a sin offering. But the goat chosen by lot as the scapegoat shall be presented alive before the LORD to be used for making atonement by sending it into the desert as a scapegoat."

Only now could the high priest proceed to the rites of atonement for the people, who are here intentionally referred to as the "community" (KJV and RSV, "congregation"; *'ēḏâ* [h]). This included all of the Israelite families with all their members, both old and young, male and female, for all of them, women included,[3] had a place in the religious life of Israel and all had been called to participate in and maintain the purity of the Lord's ceremonial worship. The community brought two male goats as a sin

---

[2]See Hertz, *Pentateuch and Haftorahs,* p. 152.
[3]With regard to the women, see M. Löhr, *Die Stellung des Weibes zu Jahvereligion und Kult* (1908).

offering and a ram as a burnt offering. Both goats were concerned with atonement, one with the fact of atonement in and of itself and the other with the effect of this in removing sin. The latter goat was to be presented alive (vv. 10, 20), while the life of the former was to be sacrificed in making atonement. The name used here for these goats is not *'attûd,* the standard Hebrew term, but rather *śe'îr 'izzîm,* the expression that is always used in connection with the sin offering (4:23–24, 28; 5:6; 9:3; 23:19; etc).

The two goats were placed at the entrance of the Tent of Meeting "before the LORD," and the latter phrase is naturally used here in its most literal sense, for the Lord was to see what took place (cf. Gen. 11:5). Two lots were then made ready, one of these having inscribed on it *leyahweh,* and the other, *la'azā'zēl.* The latter inscription has given rise to a host of questions. The Greek translators did not regard *'azā'zēl* as a proper name, but rather connected it with *'āzal,* a verb whose derived form *'azalzēl* allegedly changed to *'azā'zēl.* The verb *'āzal* does not appear in the Old Testament, but it supposedly means "go away," and in the *pilpel,* "send away." The phrase *la'azā'zēl* would therefore have the meaning "in order to send away." The same understanding of this appears in the Latin translation, which has *capro emissario.* Such an interpretation leads to a contorted and forced translation, however. Verse 10b would read "in order to send it into the desert *la'azā' zēl* [i.e., in order to send away]," and verse 26a would be "the man who releases the goat *la'azā'zēl* [i.e., in order to send away]." Since such readings are of course not possible, the translation is simply altered to "in order to send the goat 'for carrying away' into the desert" in 10b, and to "the one who releases the goat 'for carrying away'" in 26a.[4] In this manner, the phrase *la'azā'zēl,* which was originally understood as a statement of purpose, is made into something like a proper name, and "send" is at the same time changed to "carry."[5] It seems to me that in so doing, this interpretation exceeds the limits of what is permissible. Following the view of some rabbis, others have regarded the expression as a reference to the place where the goat was dispatched. The meaning is then taken to be "rugged cliff," for because the desert lay far from Jerusalem, it later became custom to cast the animal from a steep cliff which lay nearer by (*Yoma* 66a).[6]

In spite of the obscurity of the Hebrew phrase, one thing is certain. Since there can be no doubting the fact that the inscription *leyhwh* on the first lot

---

[4] See De Wilde, *Leviticus.*

[5] The NIV (also KJV) adopts a similar interpretation and translates *la'azā' zēl* as "scapegoat" or "goat of removal" (see marginal note to v. 8). The author's reading follows that of the ASV and RSV.

[6] See NEB in verses 8, 10, 26: "for the Precipice."

must be translated as "(intended) for Yahweh," there is every reason to translate *la'ᵃzā'zēl* on the second lot as "(intended) for Azazel,"[7] regardless of how this name must then be understood. It is also clear that this translation alone allows verses 10 and 26 to read smoothly. If *l'yhwh* refers to a personal being, this must also be the case with *la'ᵃzā'zēl*. It is thus evident that Azazel must be regarded as a desert demon that was capable of feeding on an animal laden with the sins of the entire nation of Israel. This naturally does not imply that he was the chief of the fallen angels who taught the human race to live in iniquity (Enoch 6:7; 8:1; etc.), and there is just as little ground for identifying him with Satan.[8] Such notions are pure speculation that does not find the least support in the Old Testament, for no further information is given there concerning Azazel.

There can be no doubt that the Israelites believed in the existence of demons that inhabited the desert. Deuteronomy 32:17 and Psalm 106:37 speak of such beings, referring to them as *šēḏîm* (NIV, "demons"),[9] and in Leviticus 17:7; 2 Chronicles 11:15, and Isaiah 13:21; 34:14, they are designated *śᵉ'îrîm* (literally, "hairy ones"; NIV, "goat idols" and "wild goats," RSV, "satyrs"). Other desert demons include Lilith (*lîlît,* NIV, "night creatures," RSV, "the night hag"), spoken of in Isaiah 34:14, and the *'ᵃlûqâ(h)* (following the Targum, NIV and RSV translate this as "leech") of Proverbs 30:15. In the New Testament, such creatures are called "evil [or unclean, RSV] spirits" and are said to wander in "arid places" (Matt. 12:43; Luke 11:24) and to dwell in the ruins of the fallen city of Babylon (Rev. 18:2). We read in Mark 5:13 that they were capable of causing a herd of pigs to rush into the sea. It is about as easy to state how the Israelites pictured such beings as it would be for a modern Western person to describe kobolds, gnomes, goblins, and other such repulsive creatures. We must always bear in mind that when the Lord formed Israel as His own people, He did not provide it with a world of thought that was in all respects new and absolutely unique. The light of divine revelation rather of necessity had to radiate through the prism of Israel's existing consciousness and to draw its forms and manners of conceiving things from within this.[10]

In opposition to this understanding of *la'ᵃzā'zēl,* some have argued that Leviticus 17:7 expressly forbids the offering of sacrifices to demons.[11] This

---

[7]See ASV and RSV in verses 8, 10, 26.

[8]As is done by, e.g., Ernst Wilhelm Hengstenberg, *Egypt and the Book of Moses,* tr. R. D. C. Robbins (Edinburgh: T. and T. Clark, 1845), pp. 160ff.

[9]It is possible that the consonants *šdm* in Genesis 14:3, 8, 10 should also be vocalized as *šēḏîm* rather than *śiddîm,* the reading that was understandably chosen by the Masoretes.

[10]See my book, *De Oud Testamentische Godsopenbaring en het oud-Oosterse leven,* pp. 15f.

[11]See, e.g., W. J. de Wilde, *Leviticus,* 1937, p. 110.

however overlooks the fact that 16:21–22 is not speaking of an offering made to Azazel, for the goat bearing Israel's sins was sent *alive* into the desert. The belief in demons has here lost its religious force, for Azazel had come to represent the realm of uncleanness that lay outside the theocracy, similar to the north country after the return from exile (Zech. 6:5–8).

Attempts have naturally also been made to determine the actual meaning of the name Azazel. Some regard it as a compound of *'āzaz* ("to be strong") and *'ēl* ("god"), so that it would mean "the strong god," while others prefer to derive it from *'az* ("strong") and *'āzal* ("to go away") and thus arrive at the meaning "the strong one that departs." A third interpretation says that the name means "the small hairy one." All such views, however, assume without question that the term must be of Hebrew origin and thus overlook the fact that such a name could only have stemmed from the distant past.

As a final observation, it should be noted that there is no mention at all of any worship or even fear of Azazel. The ceremony rather forms a strong expression of contempt, for Moses' contemporaries, who were accustomed to presenting offerings to the desert demons (see discussion on 17:1–9), must have been greatly struck by the fact that it was here Israel's sins were fed to Azazel.

Whereas the high priest presented the goat on which the lot designated "for the LORD" had fallen as a sin offering, this naturally being done in the manner described in 4:13–21, the goat "for Azazel" is left standing "before the LORD" (v. 10a). The purpose of this is described in verse 10b as follows: "to make atonement over it, that it may be sent away into the wilderness to Azazel" (RSV).[12] Two distinct actions are thus spoken of in conjunction here, the second of which could only follow after the first had been completed. Whether the translation reads "make atonement on it" (as in Exod. 30:10) or "over it," it is in either case clear that the rites of atonement had to be performed on the second goat before it could be sent to Azazel. What these rites were is described in verse 21.

16:11–17 *"Aaron shall bring the bull for his own sin offering to make atonement for himself and his household, and he is to slaughter the bull for his own sin offering. He is to take a censer full of burning coals from the altar before the LORD and two handfuls of finely ground fragrant incense and take them behind the curtain. He is to put the incense on the fire before the LORD, and the smoke of the incense will conceal the atonement cover above the Testimony, so that he will not die. He is to take some of the bull's blood and with his finger sprinkle it on the front*

---

[12]The author's translation of this verse corresponds to the RSV reading given here. The NIV reads: "to be used for making atonement by sending it into the desert as a scapegoat."

of the atonement cover; then he shall sprinkle some of it with his finger seven times before the atonement cover.

"He shall then slaughter the goat for the sin offering for the people and take its blood behind the curtain and do with it as he did with the bull's blood: He shall sprinkle it on the atonement cover and in front of it. In this way he will make atonement for the Most Holy Place because of the uncleanness and rebellion of the Israelites, whatever their sins have been. He is to do the same for the Tent of Meeting, which is among them in the midst of their uncleanness. No one is to be in the Tent of Meeting from the time Aaron goes in to make atonement in the Most Holy Place until he comes out, having made atonement for himself, his household and the whole community of Israel."

Verses 11–28 do not form a continuation of the verses that immediately precede them. Although verse 6 has stated that Aaron was to present the bull as a sin offering for himself and his household, this is repeated in verse 11. Verse 15 also mentions the goat of the sin offering for the people, which was spoken of in verse 9.

Some have attempted to explain this repetition by claiming that these verses, which further elaborate on the elements of the ritual presented in verses 5–10, date from much later than the earlier part of the chapter, perhaps even as late as the postexilic period. This is altogether impossible, however, unless we wish to suppose that the lawgiver would venture to prescribe rites of atonement that were to be carried out on the atonement cover and the ark during a time when neither of these existed any longer; and the case against this is strengthened even more by the fact that the rites performed on and for the atonement cover were of such great importance in the purification of the sanctuary from sin (vv. 14–15). It seems to me that the most that can be said with regard to chapter 16 is that it was not put together in its present form all at once. Evidence for this appears not only in verses 11–28, which further elucidate the first ten verses, but also in verses 29–34. This will be made clear in the further comments on these verses. It is worth noting in this connection that, for those whose main endeavor is to uncover two or more "layers" within a single chapter, each of which would then naturally date from a different time, Leviticus 16 is a most difficult chapter. The distinction between older and more recent sections never gets beyond subjective hunches, and every attempt to do this has produced different results.[13]

When Aaron had slaughtered the bull and was ready to present it as his own sin offering, he placed sacred fire from the altar in a censer along with two handfuls of "finely ground fragrant incense" (the preparation of this is

---

[13] See Bertholet, pp. 51–53; Heinisch, *Leviticus,* pp. 77–80; Eerdmans, *Das Buch,* pp. 73f.

described in Exod. 30:34–38) and brought this into the Most Holy Place.

Jewish tradition maintains that "household" in verse 6 (but not in v. 11) refers exclusively to the high priest's wife and therefore denies to a widower the right to perform the ritual of the Day of Atonement, but it added further requirements. It was commanded that the high priest make the following confession of sin: "O Yahweh, I have sinned, I have committed iniquity, I have transgressed against You [the three words appearing in 16:21; see KJV and RSV], I and my family. I beseech You by Your Name, grant atonement for the sins and iniquities and transgressions with which I have sinned and committed iniquity and transgressed against You, I and my family." The sacred covenant Name could be spoken by the high priest only on the Day of Atonement. Because of the incident related in Leviticus 24:10–16, this name was otherwise never taken upon the lips, but was always—even in the reading of the sacred books in the synagogue—replaced by either "God" *('elhîm)* or "Lord" *('adōnāy)*. After the pronouncement of this name, the priests as well as the people assembled in the courtyard would throw themselves to the ground and call out: "Blessed be His Name, whose glorious kingdom is eternal and everlasting" (*Yoma* 35b).

The high priest then entered the Most Holy Place carrying the censer filled with burning incense, and the smoke from this served to almost completely obscure his view of the atonement cover with its cherubim and the ark with the "Testimony," i.e., the law of the Ten Commandments (Exod. 25:16). The concealment of these things was extremely important, for in Israel, to look upon God meant certain death (v. 13; Exod. 20:19; 33:20; Judg. 6:22–23; 13:22; Isa. 6:5). Those who are of the opinion that the altar of incense stood within the Most Holy Place (see discussion on 4:7) naturally maintain that this was ignited with fire from the censer and then filled with the fragrant incense. This position finds no support in verse 13, however, and it is furthermore made highly unlikely by the fact that there could then have been a moment when the Most Holy Place was not filled by the smoke from the incense.

The tradition as reported in *Yoma* states that the high priest now walked backward out of the Most Holy Place, which became more filled with the smoke from the incense, and after pronouncing a prayer in the Holy Place, he then went back to the altar of burnt offering in the courtyard. He there took some of the blood from the bull of the sin offering for himself and his household—a priest had continually stirred the blood to prevent coagulation—and returned with this to the Most Holy Place. With his finger he sprinkled a portion of this blood on the atonement cover "on the east side," i.e., the front side, and also seven times on the ground directly in front of this, so that the entire Most Holy Place was brought into contact with the atoning blood. The ritual here therefore went much further than the blood manipulations in the sin offerings presented for the high priest (4:3–12) and the people (4:13–21). Since the ark no longer existed after the Exile, the ceremony naturally could not then have taken the same form. The tradition states that at that time the high priest set the censer with incense on the sacred rock, and this led to the belief that the ark had formerly stood in precisely that place.

The high priest then once again left the Most Holy Place and returned to the courtyard in order to slaughter the goat intended for the sin offering of the people. With a portion of the blood of this animal, he went back into the Most Holy Place and repeated the same procedures with it. The inner chamber of the sanctuary—the precise place where the Lord resided—thus for a second time received the sign of the blood of the covenant, which alone was capable of protecting the sanctuary against contamination by the uncleanness of the Israelites and therefore preserving the possibility of communion with the God of the covenant. The same rite was then performed with the blood in the Holy Place; here also it was sprinkled seven times on the ground before the curtain. The Tent of Meeting was in this manner restored to a state of holiness so that it could once again satisfy the demands that the Lord had set on the place where He met with His people (v. 16). The high priest performed this entire ritual alone, for no one, not even another priest, could enter the sanctuary "until he comes out" after having completed the ceremonial activities (v. 17).

Verses 16 and 21 speak of Israel's "uncleannesses," "transgressions," and "sins," verse 19 of their "uncleannesses," and verse 22 of their "iniquities" (kjv and rsv).[14] In accordance with Israel's understanding of atonement, all of these terms must naturally be regarded as applying exclusively to sins committed unintentionally, otherwise there would have been no need for Israel to go into exile and to experience so many other acts of divine judgment. The rabbis were of course much occupied with the question as to the precise meaning of these words, and it became their conviction that "transgression" designates the entering of the sanctuary by someone who knew he was unclean, and "sin," the same act committed by someone who was unaware of his uncleanness. In conformity to ancient Near Eastern religions in general, they thus relegated all these matters to the cultic sphere, transforming religion into a purely priestly affair and thus depriving it of its true meaning, when actually the intent of divine revela-

---

[14]The author's translation of the Hebrew terms here corresponds to kjv and rsv. niv has "uncleanness," "rebellion," and "sins." See discussion on p. 165.

tion was to elevate Israel from the cultic to the spiritual plane.

After the high priest had brought the Holy Place into contact with the atoning blood, the tradition states that he pronounced the following prayer: "May it please You, O Yahweh our God, that this year be a year of rain. Do not allow us to be without a ruler from the house of Judah. See that your people Israel do not live in poverty, so that no Israelite need beg for his food from another or from foreigners; and hear not the prayer of travelers" (*Yoma* 53b). This last request was of course made because travelers desire fair, dry weather, which would be disastrous for Palestine.

16:18–19 *"Then he shall come out to the altar that is before the* Lord *and make atonement for it. He shall take some of the bull's blood and some of the goat's blood and put it on all the horns of the altar. He shall sprinkle some of the blood on it with his finger seven times to cleanse it and to consecrate it from the uncleanness of the Israelites."*

The ceremony now proceeded to the purification from sin of "the altar that is before the Lord." There is a question as to whether it is the altar of incense or the altar of burnt offering that is referred to here. Both of these are said to stand "before the Lord," the former in 4:7 and the latter in 4:18 (also 1:5). The Jewish and the Christian traditions agree on this point in opting for the altar of incense.[15] It appears to me, however, that verses 20 and 33 must be regarded as decisive in resolving this issue. The successive mention there of atonement for the "Most Holy Place," the "Tent of Meeting," and the "altar" would indicate that the latter was found outside the Tent, and verse 17 already stated that the high priest had come out after purifying the Tent of Meeting from sin. There are also two further lines of argument: (1) Anyone who believes that verse 18 is speaking of atonement for the incense altar is nevertheless compelled to admit that verse 20—even though this is clearly a summary of the progressive acts of atonement—refers to the altar of burnt offering. This would thus mean that a new object of purification is added in verse 20 without mention of how this purification takes place. (2) The altar of incense standing before the curtain forms part of (see discussion of 4:7) what is referred to in the above threefold summary as the "Tent of Meeting," which can only be the Holy Place. There is thus as little reason for the lawgiver to explicitly mention the purification of this altar as there is for him to specify the other objects in the Holy Place, viz., the golden lampstand and the table for the

---

[15] Also Franz Delitzsch in the *Zeitschrift für kirchliche Wissenschaft und Leben* (1880), pp. 117f., and Strack in his comments on this verse.

bread of the Presence. I am thus led to conclude that the altar spoken of in verse 18 is the altar of burnt offering.

The purification of the altar of burnt offering was performed with a mixture of blood from the bull and the goat, some of this first being smeared on the horns and another portion then being sprinkled seven times with the finger over the altar itself. Atonement was thus made for the entire sanctuary and all that it contained, for the declaration of Galatians 3:22 that everything is subject to sin applies also to this.

16:20–22 *"When Aaron has finished making atonement for the Most Holy Place, the Tent of Meeting and the altar, he shall bring forward the live goat. He is to lay both hands on the head of the live goat and confess over it all the wickedness and rebellion of the Israelites–all their sins–and put them on the goat's head. He shall send the goat away into the desert in the care of a man appointed for the task. The goat will carry on itself all their sins to a solitary place; and the man shall release it in the desert."*

The following rite, in which the "live goat" (v. 21) intended for Azazel played its important role, concerned the people of Israel themselves. The high priest naturally began by performing the $s^e m\hat{\imath}\underline{k}\hat{a}(h)$ or laying on of hands (see discussion on 1:4) as a sign of the transfer to the goat of both the priests' and the people's sins, and while doing this he pronounced a confession of sin (see discussion on 5:5). According to the tradition related in the Talmud tractate *Yoma* (66a), this was limited to the following statement: "O God, your people, the house of Israel, have sinned; they have committed iniquity and transgressed against You" (the same three expressions appear in vv. 16 and 21 [KJV and RSV], see discussion on these verses). Since the high priest as it were supported the $s^e m\hat{\imath}\underline{k}\hat{a}(h)$ by speaking these words (it should be borne in mind that for the Israelites a word was not a mere sound, but something having substantial reality; $d\bar{a}\underline{b}\bar{a}r$ is thus alternately translated as both "word" and "thing"), the goat was indeed burdened with the sins of all Israel (cf. Isa. 53:6; John 1:29), which in verse 21 are said to be put on its head. When the goat was released, it carried off the people's sins (v. 22), thus forming another expression of the dynamistic mode of thought peculiar to the Israelites.[16] An arbitrarily chosen person took the goat "into the desert" (v. 21) and "to a solitary place" (v. 22). The latter expression, which appears nowhere else in the Old Testament, naturally refers to an area from which the goat would not be able to return.[17]

---

[16] See Publisher's Note.

[17] Some (e.g., L. Dürr, *Heilandserwartung*, p. 135) have thought to find a parallel to the goat for Azazel in a part of the ritual of the Babylonian New Year's festival. It seems to me

The sanctuary and people were therefore set free from *all* their sins (vv. 16, 21), but this naturally did not include those sins committed "defiantly" (Num. 15:30, literally, "with high hand"), for the perpetrator of such a deed was to be immediately cut off from the people. Rabbinical exegesis maintains that "transgression" refers to rebellion,[18] "sin" to unintentional departures from the law, and "iniquity"[19] to intentional violations, concluding from this that ordinary sin offerings atoned only for such unintentional departures and that intentional sins were dealt with on the Day of Atonement. This interpretation, however, only forms another example of the rabbis' facility for evading the demands of the Mosaic law. It is of course completely correct for rabbi Hertz,[20] in an allusion to Numbers 15:26, to say that repentance can lend to intentional sins the character of "error," i.e., that a sinner's repentance demonstrates that his intentional sins were due *largely* to ignorance and were thus regarded by God as errors. The law does not admit of such qualifications as "largely," however. It was only centuries later that Micah, in light of the continued unfolding of divine revelation, could say: "you will . . . hurl *(tašlîk)* all our iniquities into the depths of the sea" (7:19), a declaration that led the rabbis to institute the New Year's rite of *tašlîk*, which gave expression to the casting away of former sins.

16:23–28 *"Then Aaron is to go into the Tent of Meeting and take off the linen garments he put on before he entered the Most Holy Place, and he is to leave them there. He shall bathe himself with water in a holy place and put on his regular garments. Then he shall come out and sacrifice the burnt offering for himself and the burnt offering for the people, to make atonement for himself and for the people. He shall also burn the fat of the sin offering on the altar.*

"The man who releases the goat as a scapegoat must wash his clothes and bathe himself with water; afterward he may come into the camp. The bull and the goat for the sin offerings, whose blood was brought into the Most Holy Place to make atonement, must be taken outside the camp; their hides, flesh and offal are to be burned up. The man who burns them must wash his clothes and bathe himself with water; afterward he may come into the camp."

---

that this view is mistaken, however. In the ceremony in question, the temple was cleansed with a slain sheep, and the cadaver, having become fouled with the various impurities from the temple, was then thrown into the Euphrates. Since the priests involved in this rite had also been made unclean, they were excluded from the temple for several days. See also D. Schötz, *Schuld–und Sündopfer,* pp. 98ff.

[18]The NIV reflects a similar approach and translates the Hebrew term in question as "rebellion" in verses 16 and 21, whereas the KJV and RSV have "transgression."

[19]The term used in the KJV and RSV of verse 21, where the NIV has "wickedness."

[20]*Pentateuch and Haftorahs,* pp. 162f.

After the procedures for purifying the sanctuary and the people from sin had been completed in the prescribed manner, the high priest entered once more into the Tent of Meeting and took off the white linen attire in which he had performed his duties up to this point. He then had to wash himself thoroughly (or take a bath) "in a holy place," i.e., within the boundaries of the sanctuary (cf. 6:26; see discussion on 8:6). Since after the purification from sin it was once more appropriate for the high priest to appear in the splendor of his office, he put on his regular high priestly garments (8:7–9) in order to perform his further tasks. Burnt offerings were now brought in behalf of both the priesthood (v. 3) and the people (v. 5), for both of these were once again permitted to approach the Lord with their respectful sacrificial gifts (cf. 8:18–21; 9:12–14; 14:19–20; etc.), the atoning power of which was spoken of already in 1:4. Whether these were to be offered before or after the burning of the fat portions of the sin offering (v. 25; see 4:8–10, 19, 35; 8:16; 9:10) is not altogether clear, but in view of the normal sequence of sin offering and burnt offering, the latter is more probable. It is in any case evident that verses 25–28 do not preserve the historical order of the activities discussed here, for before mention is made of what was to be done with the bull and goat for the sin offerings (vv. 27–28), verse 26 states that the man who had returned from bringing the goat for Azazel to "a solitary place" (v. 22) was to thoroughly wash his clothes and body (see discussion on 8:6). This forms another indication of the composite character of this chapter.

It was a natural consequence of the dynamistic thinking[21] of the Israelites that the clothes and body of the man who carried the animal away should have acquired a portion of the latter's uncleanness because of his close contact with it. Because of his uncleanness, he had to cleanse both his clothing and his body before he was permitted to reenter the camp (v. 26). The same applied to the man who brought the hides, flesh, and offal of the two animals used in the sin offerings outside of the camp for burning (vv. 27–28; cf. 4:11–12, 21). The latter was to be done on a wood fire in a ceremonially clean place, as directed in 4:11–12.

16:29–34 *"This is to be a lasting ordinance for you: On the tenth day of the seventh month you must deny yourselves and not do any work—whether native-born or an alien living among you—because on this day atonement will be made for you, to cleanse you. Then, before the LORD, you will be clean from all your sins. It is a sabbath of rest, and you must deny yourselves; it is a lasting ordinance. The priest who is anointed and ordained to succeed his father as high priest is to make atonement. He is to put on the sacred linen garments and make atonement for the*

---

[21]See Publisher's Note.

170

Most Holy Place, for the Tent of Meeting and the altar, and for the priests and all the people of the community.
"This is to be a lasting ordinance for you: Atonement is to be made once a year for all the sins of the Israelites."
And it was done, as the LORD commanded Moses.

Summary. Whereas the previous part of the chapter was directed to Aaron and described his duties as high priest on the Day of Atonement, these verses were addressed to the people and sought to make clear to them what they had to do each year for their participation in the ceremony of atonement on that day.[22] The people were to take an active part in this ceremony, demonstrating by their conduct that they were fully conscious of standing guilty before the Lord and therefore in need of atonement. They were thus directed to *'innâ(h) nep̄eš,* "humble themselves" or "deny themselves." Outside of its use in the regulations pertaining to the Day of Atonement (Lev. 16:29, 31; 23:27, 32; Num. 29:7), this expression appears only in Psalm 35:13, where its meaning is more closely defined by the added words, "with fasting," and in Isaiah 58:3, 5, where it occurs in parallelism with "fast." The latter verses thus indicate that such self-denial or humiliation was accompanied by fasting.[23] The phrase *'innâ(h) nep̄eš* expresses the withholding of all food from one's "soul" (*nep̄eš,* cf. KJV in vv. 29, 31, "afflict your souls"), i.e., the principle of life that constitutes one as a person and enables one to act. Such abstinence, as it were, exerts "pressure" on the soul (*'ānâ [h],* the *Qal* form of *'innâ [h],* means "to be bowed down"), which causes it to suffer in a certain way; this intensifies a person's awareness that he has not acted in accordance with the Lord's demands and that he stands in the need of atonement for having fallen short in his manner of life. For the Near Eastern person, fasting gave expression to perishing and death, and it was thus an essential element in all mourning (1 Sam. 31:13; 2 Sam. 3:35) and also in national ceremonies of repentance (Judg. 20:26; 1 Sam. 7:6; Esth. 4:16). Through their self-denial, the people were to indicate that they were active participants in the ceremony of atonement performed by the high priest.

There was also another element in the Israelites' conduct that expressed this participation, this imparting to the Day of Atonement an altogether unique character. This day, which was Israel's only legally prescribed day of fasting, was to be a *šabbaṯ šabbāṯôn* (NIV, "sabbath of rest," v. 31), an

---

[22]Leviticus 26:29–33 emphasizes the fact that the Day of Atonement was a day of rest and penance, whereas Numbers 29:7–11 draws attention to the offerings that were to be presented.
[23]See NIV marginal note to verses 29 and 31.

expression that is also used for the Day of Atonement in Leviticus 23:32, while in Exodus 31:15; 35:2, and Leviticus 23:3 it is applied to the Sabbath day, and in Leviticus 25:4 to the sabbatical year. The Hebrew phrase speaks of complete rest, i.e., the abstention of all Israelites on the Day of Atonement from any deed that could form an expression of life. The injunction applied to everyone, "whether native-born or an alien living among you" (v. 29), this presenting another clear indication that these verses could have assumed their present form only after the Israelites had established themselves in Canaan. The "native-born" was the indigenous resident, one who was a member of the ruling nation and therefore possessed full rights of citizenship with all of the material and spiritual advantages that accompanied this. In contrast, the "alien" was a person of non-Israelite blood who enjoyed the hospitality of Israel but derived no rights whatever from this. Such a person nevertheless had one advantage over the foreigner: if he married, both he and his family could participate in the tribal life of Israel (Exod. 22:21; 23:9; Deut. 10:18–19; 14:29; 16:11), although their status still remained second-class (cf. Deut. 14:21).

The Israelites were to repeat this ritual from year to year, for they were here given a "lasting ordinance" (vv. 29, 31). Verses 32–33 thus emphasize the fact that the regulations pertaining to the ceremony of atonement were intended not only for Aaron, but also for his successors. In order to once again bring to light the thought that forms the basis of all the rites performed on the Day of Atonement, attention is drawn to the fact that the high priest was not to wear his stately official attire, but rather the "sacred linen garments" that expressed humility (see p. 160). It is also reiterated that no part of the sanctuary could be omitted in the work of atonement. Everything that had in any way come into close contact or proximity with a sinful human being, even if this was the priest in the performance of his official duties, was to be cleansed of the defilement that thereby became attached to it.

The chapter closes with a pair of statements that in their relation to the preceding material once again attest to its composite character. Verse 34b goes back over 29–34a to verse 28, and perhaps even to verse 10, since in the opening part of the chapter Aaron is repeatedly mentioned by name, while in verses 11–28 he is merely tacitly presupposed as the person performing the ceremony.

The Day of Atonement, which the Wellhausen school wrongly regards as an invention of the postexilic writers,[24] played an increasingly large role in the Jewish consciousness during the time after the Exile, and as a result

---

[24]See, e.g., Kugler, *Von Moses bis Paulus* (1922), pp. 125–33.

it outlived the institution of the high priesthood. When Israel's sacrificial service came to an end after the downfall of the city and temple of Jerusalem, the spiritual significance of this day was in a certain sense even heightened, for the meaning of and need for repentance then came to be experienced more deeply. This, at least, is what was expressed by Rabbi Akiba, who actively supported the revolt in A.D. 135 of Bar Cochba, his contemporary, which resulted in the destruction of the last remnants of national Jewish unity in Palestine: "Happy Israel, for whom do you cleanse yourself? And who is it that cleanses you? Your father, who is in heaven, for [Ezek. 36:25] 'I will sprinkle clean water on you, and you will be clean.'" Judaism placed all emphasis on the first of these questions and neglected the second, however. It followed the path of self-purification and in this paid more attention to the second tablet of the law than to the first. In reading the confession of sin used in the synagogue on the Day of Atonement, one is struck at finding almost exclusively transgressions against one's neighbor, and these are more often those committed with the tongue than those of the heart. It is therefore not surprising that in recalling these words of Akiba, Dr. Hertz[25] draws attention to the fact that "the initiative for atonement lies with the sinner. He cleanses himself upon the Day of Atonement by way of unflinching self-examination and honest confession, and he resolves not to repeat the transgressions of the previous year." Judaism is not conscious of being in need of a Mediator; according to Maimonides (d. 1204), the act of repentance atoned for all iniquity. The Jewish Day of Atonement thus has a completely different character from that of the Christian church as this is celebrated on Good Friday, when the "high priest in the order of Melchizedek" entered the inner sanctuary and in rending the curtain brought about an eternal atonement (Heb. 6:19–20). For Judaism, atonement is made through repentance, but according to Scripture, it cannot be obtained without bringing a sacrifice (Rom. 3:25; 5:10; Heb. 9:15; 1 John 2:2; 4:10).

Jewish tradition also asserts that it was on the Day of Atonement that Moses came down from Mount Sinai for the second time with new tablets of the law and announced the Lord's gracious pardon for the sin of the golden calf (Exod. 34:29–32). Further information on the Day of Atonement appears in Leviticus 23:26–32.

---

[25] *Pentateuch and Haftorahs,* p. 162.

Part Five

The Site of Offerings and the Prohibition of Blood
(17:1–16)

This chapter is a combination of four legal ordinances: verses 3–7, 8–9, 10–12, and 13–14. Each of these begins with the juridical formula, "any man of the house of Israel" (v. 13 has "of the people of Israel" [cf. RSV], but in the Syriac Peshitta and the Targum this is likewise "house of Israel"), which the NIV translates simply as "any Israelite." The regulations then follow with a description of the forbidden deed and conclude with a statement of the punishment. To these four regulations a fifth is added concerning the eating of carcasses (vv. 15–16).

17:1–7 *The LORD said to Moses, "Speak to Aaron and his sons and to all the Israelites and say to them: 'This is what the LORD has commanded: Any Israelite who sacrifices a cow, a lamb or a goat in the camp or outside of it instead of bringing it to the entrance to the Tent of Meeting to present it as an offering to the LORD in front of the tabernacle of the LORD—that man shall be considered guilty of bloodshed; he has shed blood and must be cut off from his people. This is so the Israelites will bring to the LORD the sacrifices they are now making in the open fields. They must bring them to the priest, that is, to the LORD, at the entrance to the Tent of Meeting and sacrifice them as fellowship offerings. The priest is to sprinkle the blood against the altar of the LORD at the entrance to the Tent of Meeting and burn the fat as an aroma pleasing to the LORD. They must no longer offer any of their sacrifices to the goat idols to whom they prostitute themselves. This is to be a lasting ordinance for them and for the generations to come.'"*

The Wellhausen school is incorrect in interpreting verses 3–7 to mean that every instance of slaughtering was to be regarded as an act of offering.

Such a position does violence to the content of these verses, and it also fails to take into consideration the fact that it would have been virtually impossible to do away with what is referred to as "profane slaughtering." The regulation rather clearly intends to put an end to the custom of using the sacrifices of cattle, sheep, or goats (also blood libations and offerings of fat) to give honor to the "goat idols" or "demons" (see NIV margin) spoken of in verse 7. During the time of Moses, this practice prevailed both within and outside Israel, and it has already been noted on pages 161–62 that the Israelites believed in the existence of desert demons, these being alternately designated *šēḏîm* ("demons") and *śeʿîrîm* (the term used in v. 7; literally, "hairy ones"[1]). Since it was thought wise to remain on good terms with these beings—Bedouins still take this same attitude toward the *jinns*—many Israelites would eat no meat without allowing the desert demons to share in the meal by granting to them a portion of the blood or fat of the slaughtered animal.

The translation of these verses presents peculiar difficulties in that the verb *šāḥaṭ* can mean both "slaughter" and "sacrifice." This is a consequence of the fact that, to the ancient Near Eastern and thus also the Israelite mind, slaughtering and sacrificing were closely related, albeit not identical, concepts, since no animal was slaughtered without the deity (this being understood in the broadest sense possible as referring to the entire world of spirits) also receiving a portion of it. The fact that slaughtering thereby became an act of offering is evident in verse 5, where the lawgiver uses the Hebrew verb *zāḇaḥ* ("to sacrifice") and its derivative noun *zeḇaḥ* ("a sacrifice") in order to make fully clear the cultic character of this action. The same is expressed by the description of the Israelites' activity in verse 7 as *zānâ(h) ʾaḥarê* ("to whore after," NIV, "prostitute [themselves] to"), a phrase that typifies all the various forms of idolatry that Israel indulged in (e.g., Exod. 34:15–16; Lev. 20:5; Deut. 31:16; Judg. 2:17; 8:33). The image of idolatry as *zānâ(h)* ("to whore, play the harlot"), the submitting of a married woman to another man, is appropriate to Israel's conception of its covenant relationship with God as corresponding to the marriage bond. Israel was in a sense married to the Lord, and for this reason it could have no intercourse whatever with other gods or spiritual powers.

In order to put an end to such practices both within and outside the Israelite camp, it is here commanded that all slaughtering[2]—this naturally pertains only to animals without defect, for no one would venture to pre-

---

[1] In 2 Chronicles 11:15, this term refers to all idols, however they are conceived.

[2] The author translates *šāḥaṭ* in verse 3 and *zāḇaḥ* in verse 5 as "slaughter" (cf. KJV and RSV, "kill," "slay"), while the NIV has "sacrifice" in both instances.

sent an imperfect specimen even to the "hairy ones"—take place at the entrance to the Tent of Meeting and be performed in the manner of an offering (*qorbān*, see 1:2–3; 2:1; 3:1; etc.), i.e, the Lord was to receive His portion of the animal (v. 4). Since this "offering" was to have the character of a fellowship offering (see discussion of 3:1, the blood was sprinkled (*zāraq*, v. 6; cf. 3:2) against the altar of burnt offering and the fat portions were burned on top of it (cf. 3:3–5). Verse 4 explicitly states that anyone who failed to obey this commandment and thus preserve the custom of honoring the desert demons would be considered guilty of bloodshed. Since bloodguilt could be atoned for only by means of blood, such a person had forfeited his life (see discussion on 7:20).

It is evident that this ordinance would have in one sweep done away with a variety of earlier practices that originated during the time of the "forefathers . . . beyond the River" (Josh. 24:2). Although the Wellhausen school wrongly transposes this law to the period of the Exile—this being done for the mere reason that at that time a completely different future was anticipated than what actually came to pass in the days of Ezra and Nehemiah (see e.g., Ezek. 36)—the law in its present form was appropriate solely to the circumstances that prevailed during Israel's sojourn in the desert, when the herds were kept within a limited area. The settlement in Canaan made this formulation of the ordinance obsolete, and Deuteronomy 12:10–27 therefore does away with the prohibition against slaughtering outside of the sanctuary. Nevertheless, the directions given in the latter passage insure that the eating of the flesh did not take on the character of a sacrificial meal (both clean and unclean persons could partake of it, vv. 15, 22), and the consumption of blood, which was to be poured out "on the ground like water" (vv. 16, 24), remained forbidden.[3]

17:8–9 *"Say to them: 'Any Israelite or any alien living among them who offers a burnt offering or sacrifice and does not bring it to the entrance to the Tent of Meeting to sacrifice it to the LORD—that man must be cut off from his people.'"*

A second regulation immediately follows, but the form of this clearly indicates that verse 8 must originally have been preceded by something different. This passage deals with the bloody offerings that the people presented, these being as elsewhere (e.g., Exod. 18:12; Num. 15:3) collectively designated "burnt offerings or sacrifices." The Israelites and also persons of foreign origin who resided among them were permitted to bring

---

[3]The claim made by S. A. Fries in *Die Gesetzesschrift des Königs Josia* (1903), p. 13, that Leviticus 17:1–7 contains a prohibition against presenting offerings to idols has no basis whatsoever.

such offerings exclusively to the Lord, and they could be made only at the entrance to the Tent of Meeting. This ordinance was directed not to the priests, but to the people, who were also the subject of the immediately preceding verse. Two types of offering are mentioned that were the most significant in this regard: "burnt offerings," which were completely consumed in the altar fire (1:7–9), and "sacrifices," in which the Lord was given only the blood and the fat portions, with the meat being eaten by the offerer and his family in a joyous sacrificial meal (ch. 3). This regulation supplements the commandment given in Exodus 22:20 in that aliens are here explicitly included within the terms of the covenant. The life of any Israelite or alien who transgressed against this was forfeited, for among the Lord's people offerings could be presented solely to the God of Israel.

17:10–14 *"'Any Israelite or any alien living among them who eats any blood–I will set my face against that person who eats blood and will cut him off from his people. For the life of a creature is in the blood, and I have given it to you to make atonement for yourselves on the altar; it is the blood that makes atonement for one's life. Therefore I say to the Israelites, "None of you may eat blood, nor may an alien living among you eat blood."*

"'Any Israelite or any alien living among you who hunts any animal or bird that may be eaten must drain out the blood and cover it with earth, because the life of every creature is its blood. That is why I have said to the Israelites, "You must not eat the blood of any creature, because the life of every creature is its blood; anyone who eats it must be cut off.'"

Whereas Leviticus 3:17 and 7:26–27 have already mentioned in passing the prohibition against eating blood and the resultant punishment of extirpation, 17:10–14 return to this matter at greater length. The commandment has two sides. On the one hand, it is based on a positive valuation of blood as the seat of life which, as such, belongs to the Giver of life and must therefore be given back to Him. On the other hand, it has the negative intention of extricating the Israelites from the various idolatrous practices in which blood formed the main element, all of which were a consequence of the desire to achieve contact with the invisible realm of gods and spirits by eating the blood of animals and thereby adding their vital powers to one's own.[4]

Two reasons for this prohibition are given in verse 11. The first of these, "the life of the body [flesh] is in the blood," corresponds to the commandment made in Genesis 9:4. The life of all creatures is the property of God, and human beings therefore have no claim on this (see also Lev.

---

[4]William Robertson Smith, *Lectures on the Religion of the Semites,* 3rd ed. (New York: The MacMillan Company, 1927), pp. 313, 338, 619.

19:26; Deut. 12:23–25; Ezek. 33:25; Zech. 9:7). The second reason, which is more positive in intent, consists in the fact that the Lord preserves for Himself the right to determine the manner in which the blood can and must be employed. This does not imply that the blood was considered to be the Lord's "food." Although animistic religions indeed regarded blood as the favorite food of the deity,[5] this notion is expressly disavowed in such passages as Psalm 50:13[6] and is incompatible with the conception of the Lord's nature present throughout the Old Testament. The directions given in the fourth regulation (vv. 13–14) that the blood of animals unsuitable for offerings (e.g., wild animals) was to be drained out and covered with earth also speaks against such a notion. As the vehicle of life that was used in making atonement, the blood was to be covered up in this fashion lest it cry to heaven for vengeance (Gen. 4:10) and constitute evidence of murder.

The punishment that fell on the transgression in this case was not left in the hands of human authority, for the Lord declared that He would execute judgment Himself and "set my face against that person" (v. 10). The same expression appears in Leviticus 20:3–6; 26:17, and although its meaning remains obscure, it doubtless involves the destruction of the sinner (v. 14). The lawgiver thus sought in these regulations to put an end to all the various idolatrous and superstitious customs in which blood was involved, but the difficulty that confronted this attempt to eradicate the Israelites' inveterate beliefs regarding the consumption of blood is evident from such passages as 1 Samuel 14:32.

17:15–16 *"'Anyone, whether native-born or alien, who eats anything found dead or torn by wild animals must wash his clothes and bathe with water, and he will be unclean till evening; then he will be clean. But if he does not wash his clothes and bathe himself, he will be held responsible.'"*

These final two verses are concerned with the eating of the flesh of animals that met their death other than by human hands (see also Lev. 22:8; Exod. 22:31; Ezek. 4:14; 44:31). The regulation naturally pertains only to clean animals (cf. 11:39), for partaking of the meat of unclean animals, however they may have died, was altogether forbidden. Since the flesh of a dead animal had the blood still in it, this commandment is related to the above prohibition against the eating of blood. Nevertheless, transgression did not meet with the punishment stated in verse 14, for whereas there the consumption of the blood was intentional, in this case the need to prevent

---

[5]R. Smend, *Religionsgeschichte* (1893), p. 127.

[6]Ezekiel 44:7 is purely an anthropomorphism and indicates nothing more than the particular place that blood assumed in the sacrificial ritual.

meat from being wasted was taken into consideration. Eating the meat of an animal found dead of course still made a person guilty, but the uncleanness that resulted from this could be removed by washing one's clothes and bathing with water (11:39–40 does not require bathing). Failure to satisfy this requirement rendered suspect the person's intention in partaking of the flesh, and in this case "he will be held responsible" (v. 16; cf. 5:1; 7:18), i.e., he had incurred guilt that had to be expiated in the manner prescribed by the lawgiver.

Whereas the prohibition was here addressed to the people in general and thus applied to both the native-born and the alien—11:39–40 does not explicitly mention the latter—the transgression of it by a priest, which the lawgiver deals with in 22:8–8, had somewhat different consequences. Eating any flesh that had been found torn by wild animals was of course absolutely forbidden to the priesthood, for it would render impossible the performance of their official duties. The particular demands made on the priests in this regard are spoken of in Ezekiel 4:14 and 44:31 (cf. KJV, RSV) also indicates the strong repugnance that was felt toward the eating of any unclean meat. With regard to the eating of carcasses, Deuteronomy 14:21 states that although this was forbidden to the Israelites, it was of no consequence to aliens and foreigners, and such meat could therefore be given or sold to them. Exodus 22:31 forbids the consumption of meat torn by wild animals and directs that this be thrown to the dogs.

The lawgiver was apparently here confronted with a very complex situation in which the intent of the person who ate the forbidden meat played an important role. The attitude that the New Testament church took toward the eating of the blood and meat of animals appears in Acts 15:20, 29; 21:25. It may lastly be noted that, on the basis of these verses, Judaism required all slaughtering of animals to be done by specially designated persons (*šōḥᵉṭîm*) who saw to it that the blood was drained out as much as possible, with the remainder being washed away and the meat then spread with salt. Whatever was not treated in this manner was considered a carcass and thus subjected to the requirement of verse 15.

Part Six

The Demand for Ethical Purity
(18:1–20:27)

Laws Pertaining to Marriage
(18:1–30)

Chapters 18–20 form somewhat of a unity in that chapter 20 reflects on the content of the two that precede it. The first chapter in this group is concerned with the delicate subject of family and sexual life and the many dangers to which this was exposed, both because of the passionate nature of the Near Eastern person and the corrupting influence of polygamy, and because of the variety of immoral tendencies that resulted from the dominating position of Baalism in western Asian culture. These dangers were magnified by the fact that, in this part of the world, the wife was considered the property of her *ba'al* ("lord, owner, husband")—a married woman was thus called a b^e'*ûlâ(h)*, "controlled one"—and was thus subject to his good pleasure. In Exodus 21:7–10 it is therefore assumed as a matter of course that a female slave was completely at the disposal of her master in a physical sense, and that if the latter so desired, she had to become his concubine.

The light of divine revelation makes it necessary that life be regarded as a unity, however, and for this reason the Lord not only directed how and when Israel was to present its offerings, but also how it was to consecrate the entirety of its life to Him so that this would form a reflection of His own holiness. The fact that sexual life would be an extremely important subject of this demand is readily understandable in terms of the conditions that prevailed in the ancient Near Eastern world, for the latter had no notion whatsoever of the sacredness of marriage, especially since the immoral worship of the fertility goddesses negated all conception of purity by making the abandonment of one's body to various sensual pleasures a religious obligation. Israel therefore had to be made fully conscious of its unique character within the realms of both cultic and family life. It was necessary that it come to know the Lord as Lawgiver also for sexual life, and that whoever overstepped the boundaries that He had drawn not only forfeited his own life, but also exposed the life of the people as a whole to the gravest dangers.

1. *Introduction* (18:1–5)

18:1–5 *The Lord said to Moses, "Speak to the Israelites and say to them: 'I am the Lord your God. You must not do as they do in Egypt, where you used to live, and you must not do as they do in the land of Canaan, where I am bringing you. Do not follow their practices. You must obey my laws and be careful to follow my decrees. I am the Lord your God. Keep my decrees and laws, for the man who obeys them will live by them. I am the Lord.'"*

In order that the regulations that follow be discerned in their proper character and regarded in a religious light, chapter 18 begins with an introduction—the opening words, "The Lord said to Moses," mark this as a new beginning, the corresponding conclusion appearing in 19:37—that has as its sole purpose to place in sharp relief the uniqueness of the nation of Israel. The Israelites were not to allow themselves to be seduced into following the practices of either Egypt, from which they had just departed after having undergone a variety of corrupting influences (Ezek. 23:3; cf. Jer. 18:15; 22:21; Amos 5:26), or Canaan, where they would shortly arrive and be confronted with equally serious dangers.

This is driven home by the repetition at the beginning (v. 2), middle (v. 4), and end (v. 5) of this introduction of the emphatic three-word Hebrew phrase that is generally translated "I am the Lord your God" (as in NIV), although it could perhaps better be rendered as "I, the Lord, am your God." The latter translation expresses more clearly the fact that the Israelites could at no time entertain the thought that Yahweh ("the Lord") was a god *('elōhîm)* like the other gods *('elōhîm)*. The Lord demanded that they devote the entirety of their life to His service and that they abandon altogether the attempt to become "a law for themselves" (Rom. 2:24). They had no rights other than the privilege of doing the Lord's will, and their situation was therefore not one of autonomy (self-law), but theonomy (God-law). The Lord alone gave the "decrees" *(ḥōq)* and "laws" *(mišpāṭ)* by which the Israelites were to order their lives (v. 4), for He was the sole source and standard of all human activity. In declaring that "I, Yahweh, am your God," the Lord was asserting that He would command and the people were to obey. This was the very condition of their life, for in demanding obedience to His decrees and laws, the Lord added that "the man who obeys them will live by them" (v. 5). The thought that following the Lord's decrees and laws meant life to the Israelites appears also in such passages as Leviticus 20:22–24; 26:3–12. The Targums of Onkelos and Jonathan as well as Rashi would restrict this "life" to the coming world, but some commentators correctly understand that life comes only from following God's commands in this world and disregarding the example of pagans and unbelievers (see e.g., Exod. 20:12; Deut. 4:26; 11:21).

The pronouncement, "I, the LORD, am you God," appears in Leviticus 18:2, 4, 30; 19:3–4, 10, 25, 31, 34; 20:7, 24; 23:22, 43; 24:22; 25:17, 38; 26:1, 13, 44, the shorter statement, "I am the LORD," in 18:5–6; 19:12, 14, 16, 18, 30, 32, 37; 21:12; 22:2–3, 8, 30–31, 33; 26:2, while the declaration, "I am the LORD, who makes you [or him, or them] holy," occurs in 20:8; 21:8, 15, 23; 22:9, 16, 32. Various matters relating to this are discussed further in the Introduction.

2. *Forbidden Marriages* (18:6–18)

18:6–18 *"'No one is to approach any close relative to have sexual relations. I am the* LORD.

"'Do not dishonor your father by having sexual relations with your mother. She is your mother; do not have relations with her.

"'Do not have sexual relations with your father's wife; that would dishonor your father.

"'Do not have sexual relations with your sister, either your father's daughter or your mother's daughter, whether she was born in the same home or elsewhere.

"'Do not have sexual relations with your son's daughter or your daughter's daughter; that would dishonor you.

"'Do not have sexual relations with the daughter of your father's wife, born to your father; she is your sister.

"'Do not have sexual relations with your father's sister; she is your father's close relative.

"'Do not have sexual relations with your mother's sister, because she is your mother's close relative.

"'Do not dishonor your father's brother by approaching his wife to have sexual relations; she is your aunt.

"'Do not have sexual relations with your daughter-in-law. She is your son's wife; do not have relations with her.

"'Do not have sexual relations with your brother's wife; that would dishonor your brother.

"'Do not have sexual relations with both a woman and her daughter. Do not have sexual relations with either her son's daughter or her daughter's daughter; they are her close relatives. That is wickedness.
"'Do not take your wife's sister as a rival wife and have sexual relations with her while your wife is living.'"

The present verses are actually not so much concerned with marriage as with sexual intercourse. This is indicated by the fact that the commandment repeatedly made by the lawgiver literally means "expose the nakedness of" (cf. KJV, RSV; the NIV translates this as "have sexual relations with"), a phrase that expresses the presence of impure motives (Ezek. 16:36; 23:18; Hos. 2:9–10) and is therefore used in describing the fate of a woman who has been taken captive (Isa. 47:3; Lam. 1:8; Ezek. 16:37). The commandments thus pertained to relationships that were normatively opposed by a person's innate moral sense and subjected sexual life to the discipline of God's law.

The general rule that governed all of these cases is stated first of all (v. 6): there were to be no sexual relations with a blood relative. The Hebrew for "blood relative" (NIV, "close relative") here literally means "flesh of his body," i.e., anyone who formed a part of his own "body," and it should be remembered in this connection that the word for "body" here *(bāśār)* was used also as a specific reference to the sexual organs (see discussion on 15:2). The expression "flesh of his body" therefore reveals how strongly the family was conceived as a physical unity and indicates that sexual relations with such a close blood relative really constituted nothing more or less than sexual intercourse with oneself.

Sexual intercourse is then successively forbidden with: one's own mother, one of his father's other wives, one's sister or half sister, one's granddaughter or stepgranddaughter, one's stepsister, an aunt that was the sister of one's father or mother, an aunt that was the wife of one's father's brother, and one's mother-in-law, daughter-in-law, or sister-in-law. Having concurrent sexual relations with two women who were sisters is also prohibited. The rabbis further extended the rules given here by adding the category of secondarily forbidden marriages, these being distinguished from the former in that such a marriage was to be annulled by divorce, although the children born of it were not considered illegitimate *(mamzēr)*.

Two things are noteworthy in these regulations. First of all, it is evident that because of the prevailing practice of polygamy, family relationships could become extremely complex. Since both the initiation and the annulment of marriage were quite simple—for a man the initiation required merely the payment of a bride price, and annulment the writing of a certificate of divorce—children could be found within the same family who, although they were born either to the father or the mother, would have no blood relationship in our Western way of thinking. It is not difficult to imagine what dangers could have arisen when such a diversity of individuals lived together in a Near Eastern dwelling. The fact that these regulations were enacted against real and not merely hypothetical abuses is evident not only from the character of ancient Near Eastern legislation, but also from the reproaches that men such as Jeremiah and Ezekiel directed against their male contemporaries (Jer. 5:8; Ezek. 22:10–11). The danger was only increased by the fact that in Israel, as throughout ancient Near Eastern culture, the eldest son assumed *all* the rights of his father after the latter's death, a custom that explains the actions of Reuben (Gen. 35:22) and Absalom (2 Sam. 16:20–22).

In the second place, we are struck by the high regard for the bond of marriage between man and woman that is implied in the formulation of these prohibitions. This is expressed already in verses 7–8, where such great importance is attached to the marriage partners' status as "one flesh" (Gen. 2:24) that the dishonoring of one's mother or another wife of one's father is considered tantamount to dishonoring the father himself (see also 20:11; Deut. 22:30; 27:20). The same thing is also implied in verses 14 and 16.[1] Closely related to this is the strong bond existing between members of the same family that comes to clear expression in these regulations. This is evident in verse 9, which speaks not only of one's full sister, but also of a sister born to one's father or mother either "in the same home or elsewhere," i.e., as the fruit of another relationship, whether legitimate or illegitimate. Verse 11 speaks of the daughter of a wife of one's father other than one's own mother, born before the woman became married to one's father. Since this marriage took both her and her mother into the family of the father, she was to be considered a full sister. It should be noted that things stood differently in this regard during patriarchal times (Sarah was the half sister of Abraham, Gen. 20:12) and that marriage to one's half sister was also considered possible by Tamar (2 Sam. 13:13). Similarly, in contrast to the regulation of verses 12–13, it appears in Exodus 6:20 and Numbers 26:59 that the parents of Moses and Aaron were related as nephew and aunt.

The regard in which close blood relationships were held appears also in verses 17 and 18. Verse 17 forbids one to have sexual relations with both a woman and her daughter or granddaughter, whether concurrently—a

---

[1]The so-called levirate marriage spoken of in Deuteronomy 25:5–6 naturally in no way violates the prohibition of verse 16, for it is here assumed that the brother was still alive.

natural possibility in a polygamous society—or in succession, so long as both were alive. This rule applied even though none of the women were natural blood relatives of the man, and to break it constituted *zimmâ(h)*, incest. Deuteronomy 27:23 thus pronounces a curse on any man who had sexual intercourse with his mother-in-law. In the prohibition of verse 18 against having concurrent sexual relations with two sisters, "sister" must naturally be understood in the extended sense that is given to this relationship in the preceding verses. The marriage of Jacob to both Leah and Rachel indicates that this was not forbidden in patriarchal times, and it indeed also occurred elsewhere in the ancient Near Eastern world.[2]

In comparison to the marriage laws appearing elsewhere in the world of that day, the regulations of Leviticus 18:6–18 are extremely stringent and attest to a very high view of this relationship. In a country such as Egypt, marriages between brother and sister were not at all uncommon, and there were also many other socially acceptable sexual abuses. The Code of Hammurabi[3] does forbid sexual intercourse between father and daughter, mother and son, stepmother and stepson, and father-in-law and daughter-in-law, but the other possibilities discussed in the present regulations are not even mentioned. The legislation of the Hittites was probably the most inferior in this respect; according to it, a man was held blameless if his mother or daughter were regarded as having desired intercourse on their part. In the Code of Hammurabi (§154), it was sufficient to banish a man who had sexually violated his granddaughter, whereas a man who had dealt similarly with his daughter-in-law was merely cast into the water (§155).

One further comment must be added to what has been discussed above. It has been pointed out that verses 6–18 make no mention of the possibility of sexual intercourse between a father and his daughter. Some have sought to account for this by claiming that such an act would have been unthinkable, but in a world were the possibility of sexual relations between mother and son had to at least be reckoned with (v. 7), this explanation can carry no weight (cf. Gen. 19:31–35). I therefore agree with others in suspecting that the words "your daughter, or" were mistakenly omitted in transcription from the beginning of verse 10, immediately before "your son's daughter," and I would thus insert this in translation.[4]

---

[2]English marriage law long understood verse 18 to mean that marrying the sister of a deceased wife was forbidden. It was not until "the deceased wife's sister's marriage act" of 1907 that this prohibition was done away with.

[3]See my book, *Gods Woord*[2], pp. 330f.

[4]Concerning this matter, see also Dr. M. David, *Vorm en wezen van de huwelijkssluiting naar de oud-Oosterse rechtsopvatting* (Leiden, 1934).

3. *Other Instances of Unchastity* (18:19–23)

The lawgiver here discusses other sexual abuses, some of these taking place outside of domestic life and others having a religious background.

18:19 *"'Do not approach a woman to have sexual relations during the uncleanness of her monthly period.'"*

It was already a necessary consequence of the regulation of Leviticus 15:24 that sexual intercourse was not permitted with a woman during the time of her purification (see also 20:18). Such abstinence was even demanded *within* the marriage relationship, for in the light of divine revelation, man and woman were to sanctify the intimacy of their conjugal life to the Lord. Although this does not follow from verse 19, Jewish tradition demanded sexual abstinence not only during the monthly period of the woman *(niddâ[h])*, but also for the seven days that followed *(ṭohʳâ[h])*. Hertz[5] notes that the incidence of cancer of the uterus was much lower among Jewish women than elsewhere and believes this to be related to this regulation.

18:20 *"'Do not have intercourse with your neighbor's wife and defile yourself with her.'"*

This verse once again enjoins against what was already proscribed in the Decalogue (Exod. 20:14, 17): one could not have sexual intercourse with the wife of his neighbor ("neighbor" is naturally here understood as "countryman"; see discussion on 6:2). Whoever did this made himself unclean and thereby excluded himself from the Lord's worship. The severe consequence that the transgression of this regulation had for the two offenders appears in Leviticus 20:10; Deuteronomy 22:22; Ezekiel 16:38, 40; and John 8:4–5. Outside of Israel, the man could often make satisfaction for this sin by the mere payment of a fine; in other cases the death penalty was executed only on the woman, and sometimes full pardon was granted.[6]

18:21 *"'Do not give any of your children to be sacrificed to Molech, for you must not profane the name of your God. I am the Lord.'"*

Verse 21 deals with the dedication of children to *Malik* or *Melek,* the western Semitic god of the devouring sun. In the synagogal tradition, the

---

[5] *Pentateuch and Haftorahs,* pp. 181ff.

[6] See, e.g., the old Assyrian Code, §13, 15*b,* the Hittite Code, II, §83f., and the Code of Hammurabi, §129.

consonants of this name, *mlk,* were always pronounced with the vowels of the Hebrew term *bōšet,* "shame," and from this is derived the English form of the name, *Molech* (the Greek spelling in the Septuagint is *Molóch).* The ritual to which the children were subjected is called in Hebrew *he῾ĕbîr bā᾽ēš,* a phrase that is usually translated as "pass through the fire" (see KJV, RSV, and NIV margin, here and in 2 Kings 23:10), a euphemism for burning that would indicate that the verse was speaking of child sacrifice. In Numbers 27:7–8, however, *he῾ĕbîr* means "to transfer into the possession of another," and in Exodus 13:12 the term clearly takes on the meaning of "dedicate" and thus contains a reference to the deity. This deity could be either the Lord, as in this verse from Exodus ("you are to give over to the LORD the first offspring of every womb"), or a pagan god such as Molech. On this interpretation, it is readily understandable that the verb *he῾ĕbîr* of Leviticus 18:21 should be replaced in 20:2 by *nātan,* "give." In order to remove all possibility of misunderstanding, I would thus substitute the single word "dedicate"[7] for the usual expression, "pass through the fire." The addition of the phrase "in [or through] the fire" (cf. 2 Kings 23:10) clearly marks this as a symbolic action, but what exactly was done can of course no longer be determined. The only thing certain is that the children became the property of the *Melek* (Molech) and were devoted to his service.[8] Although the worship of *Melek* and his "consort" *M᾽eleket* ("the queen," Jer. 7:18; 44:17–19, 25) remains relatively obscure to us, the general character of Palestinian religion guarantees that it had highly immoral tendencies and involved both male and female prostitution (cf. 1 Kings 14:24; 15:12; 22:46; 2 Kings 23:7). It is because of this that the prohibition of dedicating children to *Melek* was given a place among these regulations pertaining to sexual intercourse. To commit this action desecrated the name of the Lord, i.e., deprived it of its holiness and brought it within the sphere of the profane. Such an appeal to the Lord's name expressed the strongest condemnation of this worship of *Melek,* and this is made even more emphatic by the repetition at the close of this verse of the awesome declaration, "I am the LORD," a reminder of His holy nature with its destructive zeal *(qin᾽â[h])* against all that stands opposed to it.

18:22 "*'Do not lie with a man as one lies with a woman; that is detestable.'*"

This verse also brings us into the realm of pagan practices. Sodomy and pederasty had a place within more than one ancient Near Eastern religion,

---

[7]The NIV has "sacrifice."

[8]See my commentary, *II Kronieken,* pp. 310f.

and they were indulged in both within and outside of Canaan (Gen. 19:5; Judg. 19:3–4; see also Rom. 1:27; 1 Cor. 6:9). An Israelite who engaged in such practices was guilty of an "abomination" (KJV; RSV; NIV, "detestable"), i.e., an act that was repugnant to the Lord and therefore resulted in the destruction of its perpetrator (Lev. 20:13; Deut. 23:18). The fact that this sin was not unknown within the circle of Israel is evident from such passages as Judges 19:22 and Hosea 9:9; 10:9. To be sure, such shameful deeds also form a sorry commentary on modern culture.

18:23 " 'Do not have sexual relations with an animal and defile yourself with it. A woman must not present herself to an animal to have sexual relations with it; that is a perversion.' "

The close proximity in which shepherds lived to their herds and the divine honor that was sometimes ascribed to animals led both men and women into a total disregard for human dignity and for the limits that God had set on human conduct. It goes without saying that such "perversion" (*tebel*, literally, confusion of natural boundaries) would be altogether forbidden to the Israelites (see also Lev. 20:15–16; Exod. 22:19; Deut. 27:21). The fact that, e.g., the Hittite Code took a completely different position with regard to such practices is evident from II §73, 85a, 86a.

4. *Severe Warning* (18:24–30)

18:24–30 " 'Do not defile yourselves in any of these ways, because this is how the nations that I am going to drive out before you became defiled. Even the land was defiled; so I punished it for its sin, and the land vomited out its inhabitants. But you must keep my decrees and my laws. The native-born and the aliens living among you must not do any of these detestable things, for all these things were done by the people who lived in the land before you, and the land became defiled. And if you defile the land, it will vomit you out as it vomited out the nations that were before you.
" 'Everyone who does any of these detestable things–such persons must be cut off from their people Keep my requirements and do not follow any of the detestable customs that were practiced before you came and do not defile yourselves with them. I am the LORD your God.' "

Whereas verse 3 reminded the Israelites of their past and warned them about the future, it is here made fully clear to the people as they approached the Promised Land that because of the sexual abuses of the Canaanites, the land could no longer endure their uncleanness and thus "vomited out its inhabitants." The people and land became defiled because, when sexual life was separated from love and marriage, it degenerated into an animal activity that was an affront to human dignity. The holy nature of the Lord, the God of Israel, would not allow Him to leave unpunished such a disruption of the norms that He himself had set. Both Israelites and persons of foreign origin who chose to dwell among them (i.e., aliens, see discussion on 16:29) therefore had to refrain from following the example of the Canaanites, for whoever did so became defiled and was deprived of communion with the Lord as well as a place among His people. If the people as a whole succumbed to this example, they could expect the same fate that befell the Canaanites, for as the Lord's own possession, the land of Canaan could not endure such sinful practices.

As a final observation, it should be noted that verses 25–29 depict what still lay in the future during Moses' day as having already occurred, for at that time the Canaanites were still in control of Palestine. Similarly, the distinction that verse 26 makes between "native-born" and "aliens" was possible only *after* the Israelites had taken possession of Canaan. Both of these things indicate that these verses were a later insertion that must have been written after the time of Solomon, when the Canaanites were finally assimilated into Israel. Verse 30 thus originally followed verse 24.[9]

Sanctification of Life
(19:1–37)

To the Western mind, the content of this chapter seems rather heterogeneous and gives the impression of being a more or less arbitrary assemblage of commandments that deal partly with religious, partly with moral, and partly with civic life. We are disposed to regard life as composed of various realms that, to our way of thinking, have little or no connection with one another. The perspective of the ancient Near Eastern world was more unified, however, for not only were the cultic and moral spheres considered to be two sides of the same concern—this is apparent, e.g., in the noted second tablet of the Babylonian *Šurpu* series—but civic and political life were also controlled by a religious outlook. The whole of life was thus religious in character. The reality of this is determinative for the present chapter and is evident in the repeated reminder of the relationship that existed between the Lord and Israel. This relationship is formulated in two different ways: "I, the LORD, am your God" (or "I am the LORD your God," see discussion on 18:2) appears seven times, in verses 3, 4, 10, 25, 31, 34, and 36, and the shorter statement, "I am the LORD," eight times, in verses 12, 14, 16, 18, 28, 30, 32, and 37 (it may be observed that the Septuagint also have the first formulation in vv. 28, 32,

---

[9]See Publisher's Note.

and 37, and the Syriac Peshitta, in vv. 28 and 32). This grave reminder of the strong bond that tied Israel to the Lord is preceded in verse 2 by the admonition, "be holy because I, the LORD your God, am holy" (see also 20:7, 21:8).

The sum and substance of what chapter 19 demands is nothing less than the sanctification of life, and the manner in which the various elements of this are combined makes clear that, regarded in the light of divine revelation, our distinctions between matters having greater or lesser importance are altogether out of place. The continual reminder of the bond that the covenant had established between the Lord and Israel serves notice to the people that they were at all times to bear in mind both the privileges and the obligations that derived from this special relationship. The common basis of these privileges and obligations lies in Israel's calling to manifest the fullness of life that comes from obeying the Lord's law, which forms an expression of the holiness of His divine nature. The Lord's people were permitted to do what no other nation of the ancient Near Eastern world *could* do. The gods of the latter in no way formed patterns for the sanctification of life, while the Israelites could in contrast be exhorted to live as "imitators of God" (Eph. 5:1) who are "perfect . . . as your heavenly Father is perfect" (Matt. 5:48), thus satisfying the demand made in Leviticus 19:2 to "be holy because I, the LORD your God, am holy."

It is not surprising that chapter 19—J. Hempel[10] appropriately designates this the "fundamental social-ethical law" of Yahwism, the most succinct formulation of which is given in verse 18: "love your neighbor as yourself"—should repeatedly hark back to the law of the Ten Commandments with its concise statement of the basic ideas on these matters. Commandments 1 and 2 thus reappear in verse 4, commandment 3 in verse 12, commandments 4 and 5 in verse 13, commandment 6 in verse 16, commandment 7 in verse 29, commandments 8 and 9 in verses 11–16, and commandment 10 in verse 18. This, however, in no way implies that the chapter can be considered a counterpart or revision of the Decalogue.[11]

19:1–2 *The LORD said to Moses, "Speak to the entire assembly of Israel and say to them: 'Be holy because I, the LORD your God, am holy.'"*

The regulations collected in chapter 19 are directed to "the entire assembly of Israel," a reference to the people as a national and religious unit (see discussion on 4:13), and call on them to "be holy" *(qdš)*. Holiness was an important concern also to those outside of Israel, who remained

---

[10] *Gott und Mensch im Alten Testament*, p. 28, note 1.

[11] Baentsch, e.g., takes this position in his commentary.

untouched by divine revelation, and the word *qdš* for them likewise expressed the idea of separateness or uniqueness. In this case, however, the term had a purely cultic significance. Although it expressed separation for the worship of the gods, the latter were only rarely conceived as unique, and the descriptions that pagan worshipers gave of the actions of such deities in no way conformed to the Old Testament notion of holiness.[12] Women who devoted their bodies to the immoral worship of the fertility goddess were thus designated (Akkadian) *qadištu* or (Heb.) *qᵉḏēšâ(h)* (see Gen. 38:21–22; Deut. 23:18; Hos. 4:14), and the Old Testament refers to their male partners as *qāḏēš* (Deut. 23:18; 1 Kings 14:24; 15:12; 22:46; 2 Kings 23:7). The Ras Shamra texts also speak of such cultic prostitutes—the KJV calls these "harlots" and "sodomites"—and they likewise played an important role in Babylon (Code of Hammurabi 178–82, 187).

To be sure, the Old Testament also uses the word *holy* in a cultic sense to refer to external separation from the profane sphere of everyday life, apart from the inner significance that may have been attached to this. Israel's priestly legislation concerning the matters of cleanness and holiness forms sufficient indication of this. Cultic persons and objects were called "holy" because they were set apart for the ceremonial worship of the Lord in the sanctuary. This holiness had a different background than elsewhere, however, for its source and ground lay in the holiness of the Lord Himself, the uniqueness of whose nature is emphasized throughout the whole of scriptural revelation. It was thus made fully clear that there lay an infinite distance between God, who is altogether righteous, faultless, and pure (Hab. 1:13), and the imperfect, unrighteous, completely defiled and impure, sinful nature of human beings, who as mere "dust and ashes" (Gen. 18:27) can only abase themselves before the divine majesty of their Maker (Isa. 6:5). A person has no share in holiness except insofar as this descends from God and is unfolded in a life dedicated to His service. It is therefore possible for a holy person to become defiled, i.e., to pass from the sphere of holiness to the sphere of uncleanness. Holiness in this understanding embraces the whole of life, and the distinction between cultic and ethical holiness is thus a Western invention. Bertholet misunderstands the Near Eastern mind when he maintains that, in Leviticus, God's holiness means His cultic exclusiveness and not, as in the prophets, His ethical sublimity.[13] The light of divine revelation made it increasingly clear to the Israelites that cultic holiness was only the external manifestation of ethical

---

[12]See my book, *Gods Woord*², pp. 140f., 181.
[13]See his commentary on Leviticus, p. 66.

holiness, and that the exhortation of verse 2 was calling for a manner of life that comprised both cultic and moral factors and thus had implications for the entirety of their existence. When the people endeavored to divorce the cultic sphere from the ethical, the prophets came forward in protest and emphasized the need to regard life as a unity. Their preaching culminated in Ezekiel's vision of the future (chs. 40–48), where the external manifestation of the holiness that lay within was depicted in the images of his own day.[14]

Because all holiness derives ultimately from God, chapter 19 begins its delineation of the way of life that Israel was to follow by reminding the people that the Lord is holy, and this is moreover constantly impressed on them with the recurrent warning "I, the LORD, am your God." Only on this foundation could Israel build its life and properly discern its holy or unique character (cf. Exod. 19:6; 22:31; Lev. 11:44–45; Deut. 7:6; 14:2; 26:19; 28:9). Such a life had to be built up and developed, for the fact that the holy God set Israel apart in order to serve Him was not sufficient in and of itself. His intention in this was to see the unblemished purity of His own nature reflected in a holy people, and the Israelites were therefore to order their life in accordance with the divine example. The holiness required of Israel was not to be manifested in a vague mysticism, for it had a definite content that was to come to concrete expression in everyday life, and the divine power that was operative within it impelled believers toward particular attitudes and actions. As has already been observed in the introductory comments on chapter 11, the dreadful and impersonal character of the holy found elsewhere in the ancient Near Eastern world receded into the background in Israel, while attention was focused on the fact that it was supernatural and beyond comparison with the earthly realm. The concept of holiness was thereby given a more profound meaning; sanctification became a duty (see 20:7–8), and ethical demands were placed on anyone who would have fellowship with the Holy One (cf. Pss. 15 and 24).

19:3 *"'Each of you must respect his mother and father, and you must observe my Sabbaths. I am the LORD your God.'"*

The first regulation is concerned with respect for one's mother and father. This is not a simple repetition of the fifth commandment, however, for whereas the Hebrew verb used there is *kibbēḏ* ("to honor" i.e., to recognize their *kāḇôḏ,* their moral "weight" or significance), in the present context the word is *yārē'* ("to fear"), which indicates awareness of the authority given to them by God for directing the lives of their children.

---

[14]See my commentary, *Ezechiël,* pp. 401–6.

The same response was thus owed to one's parents as to the Lord, who must likewise be an object of *yārē'* or "fear" on the part of human beings (see vv. 14, 32; 25:17). It should be noted here that the difference between "honor" and "fear" does not consist in the fact that the former is positive and the latter negative (the view of Rashi in *Kiddushin* 31b). "To fear" means to acknowledge someone as master and to humbly subject oneself in moral obedience to such a person's will (cf. Josh. 4:14; KJV, "fear"; NIV, "revere").

Whereas the commandment in the Decalogue mentions the father first and then the mother, in the present context the order of these is reversed. Following the *Mekhilta* on Exodus 20, Rashi is of the opinion that this was done "because it is known to Him that the son *fears* his father more than his mother; the father precedes the mother when honor is spoken of (Exod. 20:12), however, since it is known to Him that the son *honors* his mother more than his father, for she wins him over with soft words" (*Kiddushin* 30b). The error of this position is evident from 21:2, however. The reason is rather that in a polygamous society, children generally have a more intimate attachment to their mother than to their father. The fact that the Septuagint, Vulgate, and Peshitta place the father first in verse 3 indicates that this state of affairs subsequently changed. In connection with this matter, see also 20:9.

Verse 3 then turns immediately to the observance of the Sabbath. According to the rabbis, this was because respect for one's parents could not exceed the respect due to God (*Baba Metzia* 32a), but there is actually no comparison between the respective commandments in this context. Exodus 20:8 commands that the Sabbath be "remembered" *(zākar),* whereas the present verse as well as the law of Deuteronomy 5 (also Exod. 31:13–14, 16; Lev. 19:30; 26:2) use the word "observe" *(šāmar).* There is a slight difference between these terms in that *šāmar* is the translation of *zākar* into deeds. "Sanctifying" (KJV) or "keeping holy" (RSV, NIV) the Sabbath day is spoken of also in Nehemiah 13:22 and Jeremiah 17:22, 24, 27. See the discussion of the Sabbath in the comments on Leviticus 23:3.

19:4 *"'Do not turn to idols or make gods of cast metal for yourselves. I am the* LORD *your God.'"*

The regulation in verse 4 prohibited two distinct things: idolatry and the worship of images. The second concern was broader, for it included the possibility of worshiping Yahweh in an image (e.g., the golden calf; see also Deut. 4:15–18). The Hebrew term translated as "idols" here and in 26:1 literally means "nonentities," things that amounted to nothing and thus were of no value. This same word also occurs repeatedly in Isaiah (2:8, 18, 20; 10:10–11; 19:1, 3; 31:7) and elsewhere (1 Chron. 16:26; Pss. 96:5; 97:7; Ezek. 30:13; Hab. 2:18). The Israelites were absolutely forbidden to turn to idols or "gods of cast metal," whether to implore their aid or to attempt to gain an insight into the future—it appears in Deuteronomy 31:20 that this was equivalent to worship, with all that this involved—for the Lord reserved this position exclusively for Himself (see also Lev. 19:31; 20:6; Hos. 3:1).

19:5–8 *"'When you sacrifice a fellowship offering to the LORD, sacrifice it in such a way that it will be accepted on your behalf. It shall be eaten on the day you sacrifice it or on the next day; anything left over until the third day must be burned up. If any of it is eaten on the third day, it is impure and will not be accepted. Whoever eats it will be held responsible because he has desecrated what is holy to the LORD; that person must be cut off from his people.'"*

After all other gods had been excluded, it was made clear to the Israelites that even though the Lord, like these other gods, desired offerings, there was no room for the thought that prevailed elsewhere that the presenting of offerings was mandatory, and that the sacrificial act was sufficient in and of itself. Although an Israelite could be motivated by the desire to bring an offering ("when you sacrifice"), it was nevertheless the Lord's will rather than this human desire that was the central and decisive factor. The offering was to be made in such a way that the person who presented it "receives favor" or "is accepted" (the Hebrew literally means "to your favor" or "acceptance"),[15] so that the Lord could look down with pleasure on the offerer and his sacrifice and grant forgiveness of sins (cf. 2 Sam. 24:23; Jer. 14:10, 12; Ezek. 20:40–41; 43:27; Hos. 8:13). The verses speak exclusively of the bringing of fellowship offerings (see ch. 3; 7:11–21), not only because this was the most common private offering, but also because the sacrificial meal that accompanied it could easily become the occasion for various irregularities. It is therefore readily understandable why the sole concern here should be the manner in which the sacrificial flesh was to be eaten (only the fat of fellowship offerings was burned on the altar, 3:3–5, 9–11, 14–16). There was always a danger that, in this meal, the eating of the meat could become the primary matter and that the concept of it as an offering would be completely lost sight of. This explains the command that whatever remained until the third day had to be burned, since otherwise that which had been holy to the Lord would be transformed

---

[15] The author's translation here corresponds to RSV and NEB, whereas NIV has "that *it* will be accepted on your behalf." See discussion on 1:3.

into its opposite by being drawn into the realm of the profane and treated without proper discernment (1 Cor. 11:29). The sacrificial meat could therefore only be eaten fresh (see also 22:29–30; it may be noted in this connection that Near Eastern persons today still prefer "gamy" or slightly tainted meat), and whoever failed in this would "be held responsible" and be "cut off from his people" in the Lord's anger (in Deut. 13:9; 17:7, 12, etc.; this was equivalent to being put to death).

Because of the danger that could arise here, it is completely understandable that the lawgiver should return to the fellowship offering even after the lengthy discussion in 7:11–21. The repeated assertion that verses 5–8 must be a later addition cannot even be regarded as probable, for no one has ever made clear what could have prompted a "redactor" to insert these verses—which deal with the same subject as 7:11–21, but are not completely identical to that passage—at this point. In 22:29, the lawgiver returns once more to this matter of finding "acceptance" or "favor" in such an offering.

19:9–10 *" 'When you reap the harvest of your land, do not reap to the very edges of your field or gather the gleanings of your harvest. Do not go over your vineyard a second time or pick up the grapes that have fallen. Leave them for the poor and the alien. I am the LORD your God.' "*

The customs spoken of here, viz., not reaping into the corners of a field or gathering the gleanings from a vineyard, and intentionally overlooking a sheaf in the harvest (see also 23:22; Deut. 24:19), were also found in other nations. With them, there was undoubtedly a religious background present here. A portion of the produce was left behind to the spirits that were thought to inhabit the fields in order to gain their favor and on this basis secure the expectation of a rich harvest in the coming year. This did not form an offering, however, for the field spirits were thought to reside in the stalks and fruits.[16] The Israelites' ancestors undoubtedly had been acquainted with this practice (see vv. 23–25), but there was naturally no place for it any longer. Although the customs were allowed to remain, they had to be deprived of their background and henceforth given a place within the people's service of the Lord. The harvest was to be used for the work of mercy that formed a part of the Israelite's obligation to his neighbor, and the poor as well as aliens (with regard to aliens, see discussion on 16:29) were therefore allowed to eat what had previously been intended for the field spirits (see also 23:22; Deut. 23:24–25; 24:19–22; Ruth 2). In this

---

[16]See Beer in ZAW (1911), p. 152; Schür in ZAW (1912), p. 154; and also ZAW (1933), p. 272, where attention is drawn to a parallel notion found in the Nuzi texts.

manner, the practice of mercy was to become one of Israel's virtues (Job 31:16–22). It was entirely consistent with this for the rabbis to say that a person actually was duty bound to thank a beggar, since he had given him the opportunity to show mercy. Ruth 2:19b therefore properly means, "the name of the man whom I have favored is Boaz." This form of mercy is still today held in honor among the Jews in Palestine.[17] Such solicitude for the poor and destitute was also found in ancient Near Eastern culture outside of Israel, as appears in both Babylonian and Egyptian texts as well as those of Ras Shamra.[18]

19:11–12 *" 'Do not steal.*
" 'Do not lie.
" 'Do not deceive one another.
" 'Do not swear falsely by my name and so profane the name of your God. I am the LORD.' "

These verses speak of stealing, lying, deceiving, and the taking of false oaths, all of which have always been found on the dark side of human social life. These actions are all closely related to each other and witness to a single state of mind that is produced by an egocentric attitude. Stealing is the violation of the property of someone else, lying and deceit are the violation of the truth, and to swear falsely (literally, "to falsehood") violates God's holy name, which is taken in oath in order to lend to untruth the semblance of truth. All of these are done solely out of the desire to serve oneself. Relationships in Israel were to be controlled by mutual trust, however, for this alone produced complete cooperation, both among human beings (no stealing, lying, or deceiving) and between the covenant God and His people (no false swearing).

Along with their many casuistic observations, the rabbis have also made some commendable remarks on these prohibitions, one of these being that the truth indeed had to be told, but it was also to be spoken in love. Hertz (p. 195) cites a splendid utterance of the poet William Blake in this connection: "A truth that's told with bad intent, beats all the lies you can invent."

Last, it may be noted that the words "one another" in verse 11 form an approximate translation of a Hebrew phrase that literally means "a man, his countryman" (see also 6:2 [MT 5:21]). We must bear in mind that the Israelites were granted greater latitude in their dealings with members of

---

[17]See Dalman, *Arbeit und Sitte in Palästina,* I (1928), p. 586; III (1933), pp. 60–66.

[18]Concerning the latter, see R. Dussaud, *Les découvertes de Ras Shamra et l'Ancien Testament* (1937), p. 98.

other nations. The regulations in this chapter do not extend beyond the circle of Israel, and it was left to the progressive unfolding of divine revelation to break through these national restrictions.

19:13 *"'Do not defraud your neighbor or rob him.*
"'Do not hold back the wages of a hired man overnight.'"

The next regulation forbids the defrauding of one's neighbor (cf. 6:2; Deut. 24:14–15). The Hebrew verb used here, *'āšaq,* which the RSV and NEB translates as "oppress," refers to an injustice that was perpetrated through the use of force. It applies to any misuse of a person's own position in order to take advantage of a neighbor. In the following verb, *gāzal* ("to rob, take by force"), the use of force is emphasized even more. This misuse of one's own position, which is purposely added to the first instance, could least of all be done with respect to a hired laborer, i.e., a free wageworker who was paid by the hour (Matt. 20) and led a hand-to-mouth existence. Such a person's wages were to be paid immediately, for to do less would be to deprive him of his just deserts and, in view of the inconstancy of the monetary system of that day, to cheat him (cf. Jer. 22:13). This commandment later came to be regarded by some as too stringent, and the Talmud Tractate *Baba Metzia* 110b thus permitted an employer to delay payment of the required wages until the following morning. The Israelites nevertheless had to learn that the Lord Himself took the side of those who were unable to defend themselves (Exod. 22:21–27; Deut. 27:18–19; James 5:4). The rabbis applied this prohibition also to the giving of errant advice to the ignorant, the attempt to seduce a Nazirite into the consumption of forbidden drink, and the selling of lethal weapons to children. They have correctly observed that no one who fears God may take advantage of another person's ignorance or helplessness.

19:14 *"'Do not curse the deaf or put a stumbling block in front of the blind, but fear your God. I am the LORD'"*

It is stated here that cursing a deaf person stands on the same level as causing a blind person to stumble. In this connection, it must be remembered that the Israelites considered it a malediction to possess destructive power that could undermine a person's vital powers if proper action was not taken to oppose this with a word of blessing (see discussion on 5:1). A deaf person was of course not capable of doing this, since he remained unaware of the curse that had been spoken (cf. Ps. 38:13–14). His situation was therefore the same as that of a blind person who could not see an obstacle in his path, for both were absolutely defenseless with respect to such low deeds. The Israelites were always to remember that the Lord took the part of the deaf and the blind and thus to desist from such actions for fear of His vengeance. In Deuteronomy 27:18, a curse is pronounced on those who led the blind astray, and Job 29:15 enunciates the proper ideal of serving as "eyes to the blind."

19:15 *" 'Do not pervert justice; do not show partiality to the poor or favoritism to the great, but judge your neighbor fairly.' "*

Although this verse, like verse 13, prohibits unjust dealings with one's neighbor, the present regulation differs in being concerned with the public administration of justice. Ancient Near Eastern society operated primarily in terms of unwritten law, in which the social position of the respective parties could exert more influence than considerations of justice. The demands of the law could thus often be frustrated by the commission of *ʿāwel* ("injustice, perversion"), whether this arose from feelings of sympathy, from fear of the rich and powerful, or through the influence of other members of society who also had an interest in the case. This was never to happen in Israel, however. The same law applied here to all persons (cf. Exod. 23:2–8; Deut. 16:19–20; Zech. 8:16), for law was no mere human invention, but was rather the codification of God's will (see Exod. 21:1). The justice of the Lord stands behind and supports a nation that exercises justice in its own affairs. In Israelite society, the law was to be administered with total impartiality, and there was therefore no room for any form of class justice.[19]

19:16 *" 'Do not go about spreading slander among your people.*
" 'Do not do anything that endangers your neighbor's life. I am the Lord.' "

Hebrew *rāḵîl*, the term that is translated "spreading slander" here, is related to a verb, *rāḵal*, which describes the work of a traveling merchant. It therefore referred to a person who made it his business to spread scandalous gossip concerning his neighbors in order to gain some form of profit from this (cf. Prov. 11:13; 20:19; Jer. 6:28; 9:3). Rashi, who proposes that *rāḵîl* be read as *rāḡîl*—a term derived from the verb *rāḡal,* which in the *Piel* has the meaning "to spy out"—translates this verse as "you shall not go about as a spy," viz., with the object of spreading word of whatever evil might be discovered. This may be a suggestive interpretation, but the word *rāḡîl* is not present in the Hebrew text. The gathering and passing on of the latest news of course continues to form a profitable business for many merchants.

---

[19]Cf. A. Menes in BZAW (1928), pp. 34f.

Verse 16 places such activity on the same level as endangering a neighbor's life. The latter phrase here refers, not to the committing of murder, but rather to the act of contributing in some way or other toward the pronouncement of a negative judgment in a legal case, since in the severe standards of justice that prevailed at that time this often meant the death penalty. The rabbis have thus stated with full justice that one who could appear as a witness for the defense but neglected to do so was also guilty, and they likewise applied this commandment to a person who remained a passive observer when someone's life was imperiled (*Sanhedrin* 73a).

19:17–18 *" 'Do not hate your brother in your heart. Rebuke your neighbor frankly so you will not share in his guilt.*

" 'Do not seek revenge or bear a grudge against one of your people, but love your neighbor as yourself. I am the LORD.*' "*

These verses enjoin against the harboring of hatred or rancor and thus turn from sins of action to sins committed in thought. At the same time, however, they make clear that it was not sufficient to remain free from such a sinful disposition, since this was also to be transformed into an attitude of love.[20] This attitude was never to lead a person to remain silent in the face of another's shortcomings, for the regulation also called one to "frank rebuke," i.e., to openly tell a neighbor in what respect he had wronged someone, something that the Lord Jesus also commanded (Matt. 18:15–17; cf. Prov. 19:25; Amos 5:10). In no case could evil be returned for evil, for this would cause a person to share in the guilt of another and thus make him liable to punishment (see v. 8; 5:1; 22:9; Num. 18:32).

The negative "do not hate" is therefore here converted into the positive: a person was to frankly rebuke his neighbor in love. The latter is the "royal law" spoken of in James 2:8 (see also Rom. 13:9; Gal. 5:14), which Jesus regards as no less important than love for God, since in this respect there can be no separation between Creator and creature (1 John 4:20). Judaism also never forgot this commandment, although it preferred to give to it the negative formulation—"do not unto others what you would not have done unto you"—which continues to find more adherents than the positive form even within the Christian church. When a pagan asked for a statement of Israel's law in its shortest form, Hillel, the contemporary of Jesus, expressed this as "whatever is hateful to you, do not do this unto your countryman," and he added that "this is the whole law; all else is merely

---

[20]See in this connection L. H. K. Bleeker, *De zonde der gezindheid in het Oude Testament* (1907).

199

interpretation.''[21] There remains an enormous difference between this saying of Hillel and God's demand, however. Furthermore, in Jesus' requirement a person's neighbor is not limited to members of his own people (Luke 10:29–37), and pre-Christian Judaism was never able to ascend to this thought. Ben 'Azzai, a contemporary of Rabbi Akiba (*ca.* A.D. 130), was the first to preach general love for humankind on the basis of Genesis 5:1 (see *Siphra* on this verse, and also *b^erē'šît rabba* c. 24), but despite the attempt of Hertz to prove the contrary,[22] the demands of Judaism did not extend beyond the circle of the children of Israel. The rabbis nevertheless state that if a person saw a friend and a foe in trouble, he was to help his enemy first (see *Siphra* on Deut. 22:1). With regard to this matter, see also verse 34.

19:19 *"'Keep my decrees.*
   "'Do not mate different kinds of animals.
   "'Do not plant your field with two kinds of seed.
   "'Do not wear clothing woven of two kinds of material.'"

Next follows a new series of commandments introduced by the exhortation to "keep my decrees." These were primarily directed against what the Israelites considered to be unnatural associations: the crossbreeding of animals, the cultivation of two different crops in the same field, and the weaving of two different fabrics into a single article of clothing. The second and third of these are spoken of also in Deuteronomy 22:9, 11, where they are separated (v. 10) by a prohibition against yoking an ox and a donkey to the same plow. While this can readily be explained by the consideration that too much would then be demanded of the weaker donkey, the two other prohibitions present greater difficulties. The assertion that the intention here was to uphold the law of nature that forbids the combination of what God desires to keep separate, since He created everything "according to its kind,"[23] cannot be taken seriously, for this would lead to the conclusion that the same prohibitions still apply today. In any case, it is clear that mules were used in Israel since the time of David and that no one took offense at this (2 Sam. 13:29; 18:9; 1 Kings 1:33; 18:5; etc.). In addition, priestly garments were woven from a combination

---

[21]The high moral level that was attained even by some persons outside of Israel is evident from the following utterance of a Babylonian sage: "Do no evil to your adversary; requite with good whoever does evil to you, and deal justly with your enemy" (Gressmann, *Altorient. Texte zum Alten Testament*[2], p. 292).

[22]*Pentateuch and Haftorahs*, pp. 220f.

[23]See, e.g., de Wilde, *Leviticus*, p. 126.

of wool and linen at least during the postexilic period (Josephus, *Antiquities* IV 8, 11, and the tractate *Kilaim* 9, 1).

Maimonides (d. 1204) states in *Morè* III 37 that the prohibition regarding clothing was based on the fact that idol priests attempted to perform sorcery by working fabrics taken from plants and animals into their garments, and his suspicion that there was a religious background to these commandments is in all likelihood correct. The prohibitions against cultivating two products in the same field, crossbreeding animals, and making clothing from two types of material, were probably related to the thought, also met with elsewhere, that every kind of plant and animal had its own "life principle" which, if mingled with another, was exposed to the danger of being enervated and could even cause harm. Sowing two types of seed in the same field placed the harvest in danger and, according to Deuteronomy 22:9, caused it to become defiled (or holy, see RSV, NIV margin), i.e., unsuited for normal use. Hybridization led to the formation of animals that were unable to produce offspring, and the interweaving of two fabrics into a garment—Deuteronomy 22:11 explicitly mentions wool and linen—gave rise to an unsound product that could only have harmful effects for its wearer. All of this naturally did not mean that the background to such customs lived on in Israel. It was rather an inheritance from a distant past, just as our society still has customs that ultimately derive from a similar mode of thought.

19:20–22 *"'If a man sleeps with a woman who is a slave girl promised to another man but who has not been ransomed or given her freedom, there must be due punishment. Yet they are not to be put to death, because she had not been freed. The man, however, must bring a ram to the entrance to the Tent of Meeting for a guilt offering to the LORD. With the ram of the guilt offering the priest is to make atonement for him before the LORD for the sin he has committed, and his sin will be forgiven.'"*

These verses, which interrupt the progression from verses 19–21 to verses 23–25 and would seem to be more at home in chapter 20 than here, deal with the act of sexual intercourse with a slave woman who belonged to another and, in accordance with the prevailing custom, was to be regarded as his concubine (see Exod. 21:7–11). The regulation is therefore not concerned with unnatural association, but rather with what could be considered the inflicting of harm on the property of someone else (similarly to Exod. 22:16). The slave woman in question had evidently already been promised to a free man as his concubine, but she had neither been set free by her present owner nor ransomed by her future master. Since the sexual intercourse had not taken place with a betrothed free woman, the law of

Deuteronomy 22:23–24 with its prescription of the death penalty did not apply here, and a *biqqōreṯ* was sufficient. This term, which appears nowhere else in the Old Testament, has been given various interpretations. Some regard it as a corporal punishment (perhaps scourging, see *Kerithoth* 10b and kjv), and others as a monetary penalty. Rashi vocalizes the term as *beqōreṯ* and interprets this to mean "during the reading," i.e., the judges were to read Deuteronomy 28:58ff. while the scourging was carried out. This cannot be taken seriously, however. Ibn Ezra maintains that *biqqōreṯ* means "ox whip" and thus conceives of it as a physical punishment, as is also spoken of in the Code of Hammurabi (§202).

Besides the execution of this *biqqōreṯ*, a guilt offering was also required, for the person in question had violated the property of another and had thus become guilty of transgressing God's commandment (Exod. 20:15). According to Leviticus 6:6, the penalty in this offering was a ram without defect.

19:23–25 *"'When you enter the land and plant any kind of fruit tree, regard its fruit as forbidden. For three years you are to consider it forbidden; it must not be eaten. In the fourth year all its fruit will be holy, an offering of praise to the Lord. But in the fifth year you may eat its fruit. In this way your harvest will be increased. I am the Lord your God.'"*

The regulation contained in these verses is once again concerned with a very ancient custom (see discussion on v. 9), but since the idea behind this was no longer acceptable in Israel, its content was transformed. The verses speak of newly planted fruit trees and state that the fruit growing on these was forbidden to their owner for the first three years. The Hebrew here is *'ārēl,* a word derived from the same stem as the noun, *'orlâ(h),* which is usually translated as "foreskin." The trees were therefore to be regarded as "having foreskins" or "uncircumcised" (see kjv, niv margin), this probably being roughly equivalent to the Polynesian notion of *taboo,* i.e., excluded from everyday life and forbidden to common use. The fruits were therefore not to be eaten during this period. Whatever grew in the fourth year was called "holy, an offering of praise to the Lord." The first part of this is clear: the fruit became the Lord's possession and could therefore be eaten exclusively by the priests. The Israelites were therefore to regard this fruit of the fourth year in the same manner as the firstlings of the threshing floor and the wine press, the herd and the flock (Exod. 22:29–30; 23:16; Lev. 23:10). The precise meaning of this "offering of praise to the Lord" is less certain, however. The Hebrew term here, *hillûlîm,* a noun derived from the stem *hālal* ("to praise, jubilate"), appears elsewhere only in

Judges 9:27, which speaks of the "making" or "holding" of *hillûlîm*. Here this is generally translated as holding "festival" (NIV, RSV, NEB; the KJV has "made merry"), but in Leviticus 19:24 the same term is most often interpreted to mean "praise" or "offering of praise" (KJV, RSV, NIV; NAB, "thanksgiving feast"; the NEB has merely "gift"). Whatever the correct translation might be, it is at any rate clear that the ordinary Israelite could not yet eat of the fruit, since this was first permitted to him in the fifth year. Ever since the time of Josephus (*Antiquities* IV 8, 19), attempts have been made to give a more or less rationalistic explanation to the law presented in these verses. Josephus says that fruit trees and vines yield but little fruit during the first years, and what they do produce remains somewhat premature, while Philo observes that these early fruits are not only meager and small, but also have a tart, wild flavor, and can therefore only be considered an uncultivated outgrowth. This explanation is clearly unsatisfactory, however, for it would then have been commanded that the fruit be picked early and destroyed. The words of verse 25, "In this way your harvest will be increased," must likewise not be understood to mean simply that such treatment of the trees would secure a richer yield. This portion of the Lord's law could not be degraded to the mere status of a manual for arboriculture. What is rather at issue here is an ancient custom having a religious background that could no longer be allowed in Israel. The field spirits of earlier times had to make way before the Lord's claim on His own rights. He demanded recognition of His ownership, and Israel could therefore only enjoy the produce of its fruit trees after it had acknowledged this right by making a gift of the required fruits. The directive in Deuteronomy 20:6 pertaining to the produce of vineyards is similarly motivated. Israel had to know that the Lord would grant a rich harvest only if it submitted to Him in obedience.

19:26 *"'Do not eat any meat with blood still in it.*
"'Do not practice divination or sorcery.'"

The first half of this verse for the fourth time (see 3:17; 7:27; 17:10–14) forbids the Israelites from participating in the pagan custom of eating blood, which was motivated by the desire to appropriate the vital force of another creature (17:10–14). The second half is directed against the practice of divination and sorcery. The two verbs used in this connection present continual difficulties in translation, since the train of thought that they involve remains somewhat obscure. It is clear, however, that they give expression to the desire to unveil the future (2 Kings 17:17) and to make use of the knowledge thus gained not only for personal benefit, but also to bring harm on others (Num. 23:23). The motion of the clouds, the flight of birds, and various natural phenomena (e.g., the positions of the stars) played a large role in such attempts at augury, which assumed an important position in pagan cultures. Deuteronomy 18:10–11 presents a list of such occult practices.

19:27 *"'Do not cut the hair at the sides of your head or clip off the edges of your beard.'"*

The commandment given here is directed against a variety of treatments of hair that remain largely obscure to us. It is important to note, however, that offerings of hair were presented both in the Astarte-Tammuz religion of Syria and among various Arabian tribes. The unceasing growth of hair was thought to result from the presence of a mysterious vital force within it, and it was thus considered an effective means for influencing the will of the deity.[24] It is also known that shaving off the hair of the head or beard formed a sign of mourning (Deut. 14:1; Jer. 16:6; Ezek. 44:20; Amos 8:10), while Jeremiah 9:26 (MT 9:25); 25:23; and 49:32 [see RSV of these three verses, also NIV margin]) speaks of inhabitants of the desert (i.e., Arabs) who completely shaved their temples, leaving only a tuft of hair atop the skull. All such customs were excluded from Israel.

19:28 *"'Do not cut your bodies for the dead or put tattoo marks on yourselves. I am the LORD.'"*

This verse is concerned exclusively with customs of mourning (cf. Deut. 14:1). The cutting of one's body was originally connected with the thought that disease and death were caused by demonic powers.[25] The mourners offered their own blood to such beings in order to appease them and thus stop them from further tormenting the dead person. Later, the same rite was performed in order to give expression to one's inner distress through physical pain. The prevalence of this custom even within Israel appears in Jeremiah 16:6 and 41:5, where the prophet mentions such bodily lacerations without any note of disapproval. The custom spoken of had therefore become simply a rite of mourning.[26] The making of bodily incisions also occurred apart from the context of mourning in the attempt to procure the favor of the deity by means of an offering of blood (as was done by the prophets of Baal in 1 Kings 18).

[24]See, William Robertson Smith, *Lectures on the Religion of the Semites,* pp. 323–35, 481f., and also Wellhausen, *Arabisches Heidentum,* pp. 124, 128f.
[25]See Publisher's Note.
[26]See P. Heinisch, *Trauergebräuche,* pp. 57f.

The two Hebrew terms translated as "tattoo marks" occur only here in the Old Testament and seem to mean "burned inscription." The fact that Israel was acquainted with bodily markings appears not only in Exodus 13:16, which speaks of "a sign on your hand and a symbol on your forehead," but also in Isaiah 44:5, where it is stated that, in the Messianic age, the heathen would show themselves as the Lord's possession by making inscriptions on their hands (see also Isa. 49:16). Just as slaves were marked as their master's property by having a sign put on them (see e.g., the Code of Hammurabi §226f.), worshipers of certain gods had the custom of inscribing such a token on some portion of their bodies. According to 3 Maccabees 2:21, an ivy leaf served as the mark for the adherents of the god Dionysus. Bodily markings are spoken of also in Ezekiel 9:4 and Revelation 7:3; 9:4; 13:16; 14:1, 9. The custom was no doubt explicitly forbidden in the present verse because at that time it still retained a strong Canaanite character. Tattooing was common in later Judaism, but its pagan tendencies had by then disappeared.

19:29 " 'Do not degrade your daughter by making her a prostitute, or the land will turn to prostitution and be filled with wickedness.' "

The regulation given here is concerned first of all with "religious immorality," i.e., the constant practice of prostitution in the sanctuary that was motivated sometimes by the desire to enhance the fertility of the land by means of analogical magic, and at other times by the attempt to gain a share in divine power and to ward off demonic forces by engaging in sexual intercourse with "the deity."[27] Throughout the whole of Western Asia, where the sexuality of the gods was universally recognized, such religious prostitution was an element in the worship of the fertility goddess, who in Canaan was named Astarte. The prostitution was most often performed by a *q^edēšâ(h)* or cult prostitute (literally, "consecrated woman"; see discussion on 19:1–2; also Deut. 23:18; Hos. 4:14). For the Israelites, whoever engaged in such activity was not holy *(qādôš)*, but profane *(hōl)*, and the money earned in such a manner could not, as elsewhere, be placed in the sanctuary treasury, since the Lord regarded it as detestable (Deut. 23:18).

The verse is also concerned with prostitution in general, however, for such self-abandonment to the basest passions was common throughout the entire ancient Near Eastern world, and particularly in Canaan.

The texts of Ras Shamra present renewed proof of the important role that the fertility goddess played in the religious fantasy of the Syro-Palestinian

---

[27]It seems that, among the Canaanites, the position of female prostitute was even an inherited right among families of temple servants (see G. Hölscher, ZAW (1919), pp. 54f.

peoples, and this conjunction of religion and sexuality had the most dire consequences for the ancient Near Eastern world. Succumbing to this conjunction could only place Israel on the same path that had led the Canaanites to perdition. The Israelite daughter, who as the seed of Abraham was called to be holy, would then be desecrated, i.e., removed from the sphere of holiness into the profane realm, and the land of the Lord would be filled with *zimmâ(h)* ("wickedness"), a typical term for the sins of prostitution and incest (see discussion on 18:17).

19:30 *"'Observe my Sabbaths and have reverence for my sanctuary. I am the* LORD.'"

Although this is not expressly stated, this verse, which reappears verbatim in Leviticus 26:2, is directed against the importation of pagan practices. The first half, a repetition of verse 3b, insists on the observance of the Lord's Sabbaths, which were in essence completely different from the Babylonian *šabattū*.[28] The second portion of the verse speaks of having reverence for (literally, "fearing") the Lord's sanctuary, which was the dwelling of Israel's God and was therefore reserved exclusively for His worship. The house of the Lord would be defiled if anyone within the circle of Israel failed to stay away from pagan impurity and took part as an Israelite in the Lord's ceremonial service while in such a contaminated state (see also 16:16; 20:3). Israel was always to be mindful of the fact that there was no continuity between the worship of the Lord and that of the other gods, since the two are separated by an abyss.

19:31 *"'Do not turn to mediums or seek out spiritists, for you will be defiled by them. I am the* LORD *your God.'"*

The following regulation forbids the Israelites from making inquiries of "mediums" or "spiritists." The entire ancient Near Eastern world, and the Greeks and Romans as well, believed that the passage of deceased persons into the invisible world gave them access to increased knowledge and that it was possible for the living, especially women (1 Sam. 28:3), to compel them to disclose this knowledge by means of various occult practices. Such a spirit of the dead, *'ôḇ,* could enter into either a man or woman (Lev. 20:27), and the latter thereby became a "medium" who could exercise control over the spirit (1 Sam. 28:3). Because of its increased knowledge, the spirit of the dead could also be called *yid'ōnî,* i.e., "knowing," and like *'ôḇ,* this name was also applied to the man or woman who had

---

[28]See my commentary, *Ezechiël,* p. 223.

command of such a spirit (see e.g., 2 Kings 21:6; 23:24). In 19:31 and elsewhere, *'ôḇ* is translated as "medium," and *yid'ōnî* as "spiritist." The term that is rendered "seek out" here implies a request for advice and assistance, and this is the only place where it is used in relation to spirits of the dead. In all other instances it indicates a turning to the Lord. To seek out such spirits resulted in uncleanness, i.e., exclusion from the Lord's worship with its demand for purity.

19:32 *" 'Rise in the presence of the aged, show respect for the elderly and revere your God. I am the Lord.' "*

The preceding verses which, as we have seen, all have a religious background, are now followed by several regulations which to our mind are more or less socially oriented. The constantly repeated declaration, "I am the Lord," however, indicates that Israel was to learn to also regard the social realm in a religious light, since *every* aspect of its life was subject to the Lord's command.

The first regulation is concerned with having respect for the elderly, for according to Proverbs 16:31 and 20:29, old age is a "crown of splendor" that is given by the grace of God. Because of his greater experience, one who bears this crown stands in the same position with respect to younger persons as parents to their children (Job 12:12). Showing honor to the aged was at the same time an expression of fear for God.

19:33–34 *" 'When an alien lives with you in your land, do not mistreat him. The alien living with you must be treated as one of your native-born. Love him as yourself, for you were aliens in Egypt. I am the Lord your God.' "*

This regulation deals with the *gēr,* a member of another nation who resided among the Israelites and adopted their form of life (see discussion on 16:29). The alien was not to be made a victim of harassment, i.e., nothing was to be done to him that would be disallowed in a relationship with a fellow Israelite (Lev. 25:14, 17; cf. Exod. 22:21; Jer. 22:3; Ezek. 18:7, 16). Such mistreatment—according to the rabbis this also included offending such a person and taking advantage of his ignorance—was to be transformed into love, in accordance with the requirement of verse 18. The Israelites' own past should have driven them to such behavior, for the people had learned from experience what it meant to live in a foreign land. The Old Testament reminded Israel of its obligations toward aliens, widows, and orphans no fewer than thirty-six times (see also 24:22). In comparison to this, it may be noted that the Romans used a single word *(hostis)* for both enemy and alien and that the old Germanic law declared the alien to be legally disqualified.

19:35–36 *"'Do not use dishonest standards when measuring length, weight or quantity. Use honest scales and honest weights, an honest ephah and an honest hin. I am the LORD your God, who brought you out of Egypt.'"*

The next regulation insists that judgment be executed with justice[29] and that absolute honesty prevail in all commercial transactions. The first of these commandments thus forms a repetition of verse 15a, while the second was necessitated by the fact that the primitive measures and scales used at that time were conducive to all manner of deceit (see Deut. 25:13–16; Prov. 11:1; 20:23). The ephah spoken of was a dry measure equal to 36.4 liters, and the hin, a liquid measure equal to 6.07 liters.

19:37 *"'Keep all my decrees and all my laws and follow them. I am the LORD.'"*

This final verse serves as the conclusion to the series of commandments. Several of the regulations from chapters 18 and 19 reappear in chapter 20, but there a statement of the punishment due to the transgressor is added. It is characteristic for the spirit of these regulations that, as had also been the case in chapter 18, the series both begins (v. 2) and ends (v. 37) with a reminder of the close relationship that the Lord had assumed with Israel. The people had to be made aware that they were placed before a new beginning and were henceforth to live as the people of the Lord.

Penal Provisions
(20:1–27)

20:1–2a *The LORD said to Moses, "Say to the Israelites:"*

This chapter, which primarily lists the punishments on the sins spoken of in chapter 18 and only includes a few of the cases from chapter 19, takes strong measures against the desecration of Israel's holiness. The formulation of verse 2 (see KJV) indicates that it was originally preceded by other requirements (see discussion on 17:8).

20:2b–5 *"'Any Israelite or any alien living in Israel who gives any of his children to Molech must be put to death. The people of the community are to stone him. I will set my face against that man and I will cut him off from his people; for by*

---

[29]The author's translation of verse 35 parallels the RSV: "You shall do no wrong in judgment [*mišpaṭ*], in measures of length or weight or quantity." The NIV, in contrast, interprets *mišpaṭ* as "measurement" and has "Do not use dishonest standards when measuring length, weight or quantity."

giving his children to Molech, he has defiled my sanctuary and profaned my holy name. If the people of the community close their eyes when that man gives one of his children to Molech and they fail to put him to death, I will set my face against that man and his family and will cut off from their people both him and all who follow him in prostituting themselves to Molech.' "

The first group of verses prohibits the worship of Molech, which has already been forbidden in 18:21 (see commentary on that verse), and it is here explicitly stated that this applied to both Israelites and aliens *(gēr)*. If either of these would dedicate any children to Molech, they would "surely" (cf. KJV) be put to death. The Hebrew expression used here excludes all possibility of uncertainty concerning the punishment to be carried out. The law knew of only one such punishment, viz., stoning, although the Jewish tradition changed this somewhat. The proceeding usually began with the casting of the guilty person from an elevated place (see Acts 7:57–58, however); stoning took place only if this did not result in death, and in some cases this was then followed by hanging (*Sanhedrin* 45b, 46a). In order to make the punishment more "humane," the person condemned to death was first anaesthetized by being allowed to drink drugged wine (Mark 15:23), i.e., wine in which a small quantity of incense was dissolved.

The stoning was to be performed by the community of Israel, literally, the "people of the land" (see KJV, RSV). Although this phrase was later used to designate the non-Israelite inhabitants of Palestine (Ezra 4:4; 10:2, 11; Neh. 10:31, see KJV, RSV), it is evident from Deuteronomy 13:9; 17:7 that it here rather refers to the people of Israel themselves (cf. also Gen. 23:7, 12). Jewish tradition states that such a death sentence could only be executed on the basis of a clear declaration from two eyewitnesses.

Verses 3 and 4–5 add two further instances to this general rule. In the first verse, the sin of sacrificing to Molech remains undetected, e.g., as could happen if it were carried out in another part of the land. In this case, God Himself—apparently through disease or accident—would cause the transgressor to undergo the punishment resulting from the defilement of the Lord's sanctuary and the profanation of His holy name, which according to 15:31 and 18:21 constituted an attack on the Lord Himself. It should be observed that the lawgiver here assumed that the transgressor continued to take an active part in the worship of the Lord after giving one of his children to Molech and thereby attempted to place Molech on a par with the God of Israel. In so doing, he who had been rendered unclean by communion with Molech not only brought this uncleanness into the Lord's sanctuary, but also desecrated or profaned God's holy nature by removing it from the realm of divine holiness.

Verses 4–5 deal with a far more serious situation, for the sinful deed here involved not only the individual who had directly committed it, but also, in the person of its leaders, the entire Israelite community. Although the deed had been discovered, the people shirked their solemn responsibility to prosecute it and to punish the transgressor by stoning, since the sin of profaning the Lord's holy name was outweighed by, e.g., the social position of the guilty person and his family. If this happened, divine judgment would intervene in all of its terror (17:10–14); the entire family or clan that had thought it could use its influence to enable the transgressor to escape the punishment set by God would be destroyed along with the transgressor, for there could be no place for such persons in Israel. The direct intervention of divine judgment is naturally here related to the fact that the social position of the transgressor and his clan could otherwise lead to eruption of civil war.

20:6 *"'I will set my face against the person who turns to mediums and spiritists to prostitute himself by following them, and I will cut him off from his people.'"*

Verse 6 returns to the sin mentioned in 19:31 of consulting mediums and spiritists in the belief that they possessed powers such as belong to God alone. The actual meaning of such activity appears in the description of it as "prostituting oneself" (see discussion on 17:7), and the punishment is here stated to be a direct intervention of divine judgment in which God defended the holiness of His covenant by destroying the transgressor. The substitution of divine judgment for public punishment could in this context well be related to the difficulty, if not impossibility, of legally establishing the occurrence of the sin. In those cases where the latter could be done, the regulation of verse 27 applied (see comment on that verse).

20:7–8 *"'Consecrate yourselves and be holy, because I am the Lᴏʀᴅ your God. Keep my decrees and follow them. I am the Lᴏʀᴅ, who makes you holy.'"*

These two verses, the first of which forms a repetition of 11:44a, serve as a closing formula for verses 2–6. For verse 7, the reader is referred to what has been observed in connection with 11:44. Israel was to be fully conscious of the absolute antithesis between the service of the Lord and that of other gods and spirits, for it had to make a choice between these two. If the people chose for the holy Yahweh, they were to know that they had to conduct themselves as a holy nation by scrupulously observing His decrees, for these were nothing less than a blueprint for the manner of life that was appropriate to such a holy (i.e., having an exceptional character) people. The Jews today still repeat the liturgical formula, "Blessed art thou, Lord our God, king of the universe, who hast sanctified us by thy commandments,'' in connection with every religious activity, but the content of their life unfortunately no longer corresponds to its form.

20:9–21 *'' 'If anyone curses his father or mother, he must be put to death. He has cursed his father or his mother, and his blood will be on his own head.*

'' 'If a man commits adultery with another man's wife—with the wife of his neighbor—both the adulterer and the adulteress must be put to death.

'' 'If a man sleeps with his father's wife, he has dishonored his father. Both the man and the woman must be put to death; their blood will be on their own heads.

'' 'If a man sleeps with his daughter-in-law, both of them must be put to death. What they have done is a perversion; their blood will be on their own heads.

'' 'If a man lies with a man as one lies with a woman, both of them have done what is detestable. They must be put to death; their blood will be on their own heads.

'' 'If a man marries both a woman and her mother, it is wicked. Both he and they must be burned in the fire, so that no wickedness will be among you.

'' 'If a man has sexual relations with an animal, he must be put to death, and you must kill the animal.

'' 'If a woman approaches an animal to have sexual relations with it, kill both the woman and the animal. They must be put to death; their blood will be on their own heads.

'' 'If a man marries his sister, the daughter of either his father or his mother, and they have sexual relations, it is a disgrace. They must be cut off before the eyes of their people. He has dishonored his sister and will be held responsible.

'' 'If a man lies with a woman during her monthly period and has sexual relations with her, he has exposed the source of her flow, and she has also uncovered it. Both of them must be cut off from their people.

'' 'Do not have sexual relations with the sister of either your mother or your father, for that would dishonor a close relative; both of you would be held responsible.

'' 'If a man sleeps with his aunt, he has dishonored his uncle. They will be held responsible; they will die childless.

'' 'If a man marries his brother's wife, it is an act of impurity; he has dishonored his brother. They will be childless.' ''

With the exception of verse 9, which is related to 19:3, these verses deal exclusively with sexual sins such as have appeared already in chapter 18 and in each case state the punishment due to the transgressor. In most instances there is merely a general statement that the guilty persons "must [surely] be put to death," sometimes with the explanatory addition, "their blood will be on their heads." The death penalty in all likelihood consisted in stoning, the standard ancient Near Eastern punishment. This would then also be what is intended in verse 17, which speaks more generally of being "cut off," and in verse 19, where it is stated that the offenders would "be held responsible." If a man had sexual relations with a mother and her daughter concurrently, all three persons were to be burned (v. 14), but it appears from Joshua 7:25 that this was preceded by stoning. Incineration made the punishment much worse, since the destruction of the body compelled the souls of the dead persons to remain wandering about (see also 21:9; Gen. 38:24). The punishment that verses 20–21 prescribe for having intercourse with the wife of one's uncle or brother was not carried out by human beings, but rather consisted in the fact that the guilty persons would be left childless, an extremely harsh fate to the Israelites (see e.g., Jer. 22:30; Hos. 9:14). Why this punishment applied to only these two particular cases is not clear to me. It should be noted that verse 21, like 18:16, naturally assumes that the brother was still alive, since in certain cases a levirate marriage could be demanded after the death of the latter (Deut. 25:5; Ruth 4:5).

With regard to verse 9, the cursing that is condemned here was the opposite of the "respect" or "honor" commanded in Leviticus 19:3 and Exodus 20:12, respectively. The Hebrew term used here, *qillēl,* indicates nothing less than the denial of the "content" or significance that the Lord had given to one's father and mother. In both word and deed, they were made "light" *(qal)* of, i.e., treated as nonentities, without "weight" or importance (see also Exod. 21:17). Cursing was therefore the opposite of honor, *kibbēd,* the recognition of one's parents' "weight" or significance. As such, it constituted an attack on what God had given, and no one who became guilty of it could retain his place in Israel.

Verses 9, 11–13, 16, and 27, apparently in further explanation of the required punishment, state that "their [his] blood will be on their [his] own heads." It is unclear to me why this was also not included in verses 10 and 14–15. In any case, it is evident from Joshua 2:19; 2 Samuel 1:16; 1 Kings 2:37; and Ezekiel 18:13; 33:4 that this means that those who were guilty had forfeited their lives. Since such a person had caused his own death, revenge could not be taken on others, and the statement thus serves as an indication of how ingrained the practice of blood vengeance was.

20:22–24 *"'Keep all my decrees and laws and follow them, so that the land where I am bringing you to live may not vomit you out. You must not live according to the customs of the nations I am going to drive out before you. Because they did all these things, I abhorred them. But I said to you, "You will possess their land; I will give it to you as an inheritance, a land flowing with milk and honey." I am the LORD your God, who has set you apart from the nations.'"*

There then follows a summary exhortation to the Israelites urging them to observe the Lord's decrees and laws and to beware of adopting pagan customs that were as such incompatible with the service of the Lord, since their own future was at stake in this (''so that the land . . . may not vomit you out''). The verses are reminiscent of 18:24–30, and their theme is continued in verse 26.

20:25 *'' 'You must therefore make a distinction between clean and unclean animals and between unclean and clean birds. Do not defile yourselves by any animal or bird or anything that moves along the ground–those which I have set apart as unclean for you.' ''*

Because of our attachment to logical order, this verse seems out of keeping with chapter 20 as a whole. Whereas the rest of the chapter pertains to human beings, the regulation here suddenly turns to animals and speaks of the distinction between clean and unclean. It is thus incongruous in its present location and would seem rather to belong in chapter 11. Why it has been placed here is unclear to me, but the view that it is a later insertion is in any case incorrect, since verse 26 does not connect well with verse 24. With regard to the content of verse 25, the reader is referred to the comments on chapter 11.

20:26 *'' 'You are to be holy to me because I, the LORD, am holy, and I have set you apart from the nations to be my own.' ''*

The commandment given here reverts to the concern of verses 22–24. Israel is reminded of the distinct position that it was to occupy within its pagan environment (see e.g., Exod. 19:5–6) and is thereby urged to order its life in such a manner that it formed a manifestation of the Lord's holiness (see 19:2).

20:27 *'' 'A man or woman who is a medium or spiritist among you must be put to death. You are to stone them; their blood will be on their own heads.' ''*

This final verse, which would seem to belong immediately after verse 6, is directed against persons who present the occasion for committing the sin spoken of in that verse.

Part Seven

Cultic Regulations
(21:1–25:55)

Rules Pertaining to the Priests
(21:1–24)

1. The Ordinary Priests (21:1–9)

21:1a *The Lord said to Moses, "Speak to the priests, the sons of Aaron, and say to them:"*

As the mediators between the Lord and His people, the priests performed their tasks within the sphere of the holy, and they were therefore in a position to seriously endanger the preservation of the sacred character of the Lord's worship by what they did and by what they left undone. For this reason, their life was subjected to certain requirements that did not apply to lay persons as such. To the Israelite mind, and indeed also for other ancient Near Eastern nations, where the presentation of offerings likewise occupied the central position in religious life, the priest was an exceptional individual. The sons of Aaron therefore had to be more on their guard against profaning what was holy than the other Israelites, since the consequences of this would be so much more serious in their case. It is therefore not surprising that in Israel, as elsewhere, their personal freedom was restricted in more than one respect (see also 10:8–11).

21:1b–3 *" 'A priest must not make himself ceremonially unclean for any of his people who die, except for a close relative, such as his mother or father, his son or*

214

daughter, his brother, or an unmarried sister who is dependent on him since she has no husband—for her he may make himself unclean.'"

The regulations begin by stating what was and was not permitted to ordinary priests—the rules for the high priest were even more stringent (vv. 10–15)—during a time of mourning. It should be observed in this connection that, for the dynamistic mode of thought that Israel shared with the entire ancient world,[1] a corpse was always considered a source of cultic impurity. This notion was so deeply ingrained in the Israelite mind that the law here merely tacitly assumes this, without there being any need to expressly state that contact with a dead body rendered one ritually unclean (see also 22:4; Num. 5:1–4; 19:11). Since this was the case for mere lay persons, it naturally applied even more to the priests, and since cultic uncleanness would bar the latter from exercising their sacred office, they were forbidden what was permitted to the rest of the Israelites. The structure of human society made it impossible to always avoid contact with corpses, however, and for this reason certain exceptions were made to this general rule in behalf of ordinary priests. Such contact was therefore allowed when a close relative had died. The Hebrew for "relative" here literally means "of his flesh," and for the meaning of this expression the reader is referred to the comment on 18:6.

The close relatives listed—mother, father, son, daughter, brother, and unmarried, dependent sister—were all blood members of either the family to which the priest was born or the family of which he was himself head. The same six relatives appear again in Ezekiel 44:25, but, as is also the case in the Septuagint, Peshitta, and Samaritan text of the present verse, the father is there listed first (see discussion on 19:3, however). The wife of the priest is not mentioned among these exceptions. The rabbinic view that this is because she was tacitly included among the "close relatives" cannot be correct, for the meaning of this phrase is explicated in the list of 2b–3a. An appeal to Ezekiel 24:15–18 would also be inappropriate in this connection, since the prophet was there forbidden what everyone would have obviously expected of him. The reason for this omission must lie rather in the fact that, because of the intimate bond between husband and wife, it went without saying that a priest was permitted to defile himself by contact with the dead body of his spouse. The sister was to be unwed, since her marriage would include her within another family group and thus place her outside of the priest's own flesh and blood.

The phrase "any of his people" in verse 1 clearly refers to the unity of

---

[1]See Publisher's Note.

the clan and the consequent obligation of conformity on the part of its members. In the case of death, such conformity was forbidden to the priest. The rabbis' contention that the expression means that a priest was forbidden contact with a corpse if there were others who could take care of the burial *(Siphra)*—and likewise the view that even a high priest could perform the latter if no one else was available—goes beyond the text, for the law is completely clear on this matter.

21:4 *"'He must not make himself unclean for people related to him by marriage, and so defile himself.'"*

The received text of verse 4 requires emendation. The translation, "he shall not defile himself, being a chief man among his people," gives to the Hebrew term *ba'al* a meaning that it has nowhere else, and the King James Version (see also NIV margin on this verse) is therefore here in conflict with both Hebrew idiom and the surrounding context. The verse was likely originally speaking of a woman who had been taken into the priest's immediate family by marriage (see above), i.e., a sister-in-law, and I have thus altered the text in this sense.[2] The priest was therefore here forbidden to mourn the death of a sister-in-law.

21:5–6 *"'Priests must not shave their heads or shave off the edges of their beards or cut their bodies. They must be holy to their God and must not profane the name of their God. Because they present the offerings made to the LORD by fire, the food of their God, they are to be holy.'"*

Although the priest was allowed to participate in mourning in some cases, he could never make use of customs that were pagan in origin and forbidden to every Israelite (19:27–28; Deut. 14:1). The priests could not forget that they were called to be holy, i.e., to conform exclusively to the Lord's will in all that they did and omitted to do, so that they could be at all times in the proper state for performing their priestly task of presenting the "food of their God" (see discussion on 3:11). Failure to live up to this would profane the name of the Lord (see discussion on 18:21).

21:7–8 *"'They must not marry women defiled by prostitution or divorced from their husbands, because priests are holy to their God. Regard them as holy, because they offer up the food of your God. Consider them holy, because I the LORD, who makes you holy, am holy.'"*

---

[2]The NIV here speaks more generally of "people related to him by marriage," whereas the author's translation corresponds to the NEB.

A second limitation of the priest's personal freedom lay in the exclusion of certain women from consideration for marriage, since through his wife a priest could come to share in some defilement that she had acquired from another. Marriage was thus forbidden with a woman who, whether for purely sensual or for "religious" reasons (see discussion on 19:29), freely gave herself to anyone, and likewise with a woman who had not been able to preserve her virginity.[3] The rabbinic contention (*Kiddushin* 78b) that the "dishonored" or "defiled" woman here was the daughter of a forbidden priestly marriage has no basis. A previously married woman who had been divorced by her husband, even if she was not at fault, was also excluded from consideration. The priest was therefore only permitted to marry a virgin, and in most cases this was most likely a daughter of the priesthood (see Luke 1:5). The present context says nothing against marriage to a widow, but all widows except those who had been married to priests are forbidden in Ezekiel 44:22.

The reason for this limitation of the possibilities for marriage is stated most emphatically, with the word *holy* appearing no fewer than four times in verse 8. Since the Lord is holy, He makes His servants holy so they can offer up the "food of their God," and the Israelites were therefore called to regard the priests as holy, i.e., to constantly bear in mind that they were to live within the sphere of the holy, and thus to make no attempt whatsoever to hinder them in this. It is evident from the context that such hindrance lay in the encouragement of a marriage that was known to be forbidden (see also 22:9).

On the basis of verse 8, Jewish tradition claims that a male member of the priestly family—a Kohen, Kahen, Kahn, or Kohn—by right took precedence in the reading of the law in the synagogue (*Horayoth* 12b).

21:9 *"'If a priest's daughter defiles herself by becoming a prostitute, she disgraces her father; she must be burned in the fire.'"*

This holy character of the priest was also to be manifested in the life of his family, and a daughter of the priesthood who lived the life of a prostitute would therefore find no mercy. Such a woman was subjected to a double punishment, since after stoning she must also be burned (see discussion on 20:14). Jewish tradition would limit this to a priestly daughter who was already engaged or married (*Sanhedrin* 50b, 51b), but there is no

---

[3] The author has "dishonored" or "violated" here and interprets this as a separate case, and his translation therefore corresponds more closely to the RSV and NEB than the NIV, which construes the Hebrew term in question together with "prostitution" and translates it as "defiled."

evidence for such a position in verse 9. It may also be noted that the polygamous nature of marriage in Israel meant that only women could be prostitutes, and the verse says nothing concerning the sons of priests.

2. *The High Priest* (21:10–15)

21:10–15 *" 'The high priest, the one among his brothers who has had the anointing oil poured on his head and who has been ordained to wear the priestly garments, must not let his hair become unkempt or tear his clothes. He must not enter a place where there is a dead body. He must not make himself unclean, even for his father or mother, nor leave the sanctuary of his God or desecrate it, because he has been dedicated by the anointing oil of his God. I am the LORD.*

" 'The woman he marries must be a virgin. He must not marry a widow, a divorced woman, or a woman defiled by prostitution, but only a virgin from his own people, so he will not defile his offspring among his people. I am the LORD, who makes him holy.' "

This member of Aaron's family[4] was not only the *primus inter pares* among the priesthood, but was in fact the only person fully qualified to the priestly office. He alone was anointed with the holy oil (16:32; 21:10; Num. 35:25) and bore the Urim and the Thummim (Exod. 28:30; Num. 27:21), and no one but he could wear the sacred garments (Lev. 16:4) and the ephod (1 Sam. 2:28; 14:3; 23:6; 30:7) or enter the Most Holy Place (Lev. 16). In 1 Samuel 21:2, 4, 6 and elsewhere, the high priest is thus referred to simply as *"the* priest." Because he stood above his brothers (v. 10, cf. RSV), the preservation of his holiness was of the greatest importance, and for this reason his freedom was subjected to even greater restrictions than was the case with the ordinary priests.

This applies in the first place to occasions of mourning. The high priest was explicitly forbidden what was apparently allowed to ordinary priests: leaving one's hair loose and unkempt and tearing one's clothing as a sign of mourning, both of which customs arose within ancient Eastern thought as an imitation of the state of death (see discussion of 10:6 and 13:45). This rending of one's clothes was naturally prohibited only when this was a sign of mourning (cf. Matt. 26:65; 1 Macc. 11:71). The exceptions that were permitted to the ordinary priests also did not apply to the high priest, for he could never come near a corpse, even if it was that of his father or mother

---

[4]There is no need to deal with Wellhausen's assertion (Julius Wellhausen, *Prolegomena to the History of Ancient Israel,* tr. J. Sutherland Black and Allan Menzies [New York: Meridian Books, 1957], pp. 148ff.) that the Israelite high priest was an invention dating from the postexilic period, for this is too much in conflict with the facts. Concerning this matter, see Eerdmans, *Das Buch Leviticus,* pp. 34–48.

(see also Num. 6:6–7). In order to guard against all possible defilement, he was not allowed to leave his dwelling in the sanctuary (see 1 Sam. 1:9; 3:2–3) during the period of mourning, and he therefore was barred from participating in the funeral or ceremony of lamentation (*Sanhedrin* 18a). The reason given for the great strictness of these requirements and the demand for separation was that "he has been dedicated by the anointing oil of his God" (v. 12; cf. 10:7; Num. 6:7). This oil is here called the high priest's "dedication" or "consecration" (cf. RSV, NEB; *nēzer*), and not his "crown," the translation chosen in the King James Version following Luther and others (cf. also Num. 6:9, 18).

The second restriction placed on the high priest's freedom concerns the choice of his wife, who could only be a "virgin from his own people." Although it is clear from verses 1 and 4 that the latter phrase embraces all of Israel (see also Ezek. 44:22), Jewish tradition (which appears also in the Septuagint here) would limit it to the high priestly family, and this perhaps did become the custom later. The reason for this restriction—the high priest of Jupiter in Rome had to content himself with a similar limitation—lay in the desire to maintain the purity of the high priestly family. Every high priest had to be the son of a mother who had in no way brought dishonor on the office of her husband.

3. *Physical Defects of the Sons of Priests* (21:16–23)

21:16–23 *The LORD said to Moses, "Say to Aaron: 'For the generations to come none of your descendants who has a defect may come near to offer the food of his God. No man who has any defect may come near: no man who is blind or lame, disfigured or deformed; no man with a crippled foot or hand, or who is hunchbacked or dwarfed, or who has any eye defect, or who has festering or running sores or damaged testicles. No descendant of Aaron the priest who has any defect is to come near to present the offerings made to the LORD by fire. He has a defect; he must not come near to offer the food of his God. He may eat the most holy food of his God, as well as the holy food; yet because of his defect, he must not go near the curtain or approach the altar, and so desecrate my sanctuary. I am the LORD, who makes them holy.'"*

Aaron's descendants were as such entitled in principle to the exercise of the priestly functions, but in order to do so they had to be sound in limb and body. The body of the priest was to give expression to the fullness of life, for he served the living God (Deut. 5:26; 2 Kings 19:4; Ps. 42:2). Anyone who did not satisfy this requirement could not "come near" in order to present offerings (vv. 17, 21) and was also forbidden to "go near the curtain," i.e., to enter the Holy Place (v. 23). A further description of what would bar a person from carrying out the priestly duties was necessary, and twelve defects are thus enumerated here (later Judaism expanded this to 142). Not everything is equally clear in these verses. The word translated as "disfigured" in verse 18[5] seems to refer to a split nose (cf. KJV, "flat nose"), with a corresponding deformation of the palate that would distort the voice, and "deformed" in this same verse[6] would appear to include the defect spoken of in 2 Samuel 21:10. With regard to verse 19, it may be observed that because of the undeveloped state of medicine at that time, a broken arm or leg usually remained crooked. The Hebrew word translated by the NIV as "dwarfed" in verse 20[7] is the same term that is used in Genesis 41 for the "gaunt" or "thin" cows and grain in Pharaoh's dream. The reference in the present verse could be to consumption, but others interpret it as stunted growth (cf. KJV, RSV, NIV). The Hebrew for "eye defect" in this verse[8] is thought by some to mean "running eye" (cf. NEB, "eye discharge"), while Rashi regards it as a reference to misshapen eyebrows or a speck in the eye. The two following terms appear to indicate a skin disease, and the final Hebrew term, *merô(a)ḥ,* seems to refer to an ailment of the testicles. It is possible that the vocalization of this term should be changed to *merwaḥ,* however, and the defect spoken of would then be a hernia (cf. NAB).

A priest's son who was afflicted with one of these defects could eat of the offerings brought by the people, however, and he therefore retained his right to both the holy and the most holy portions of the priestly income. The holy portions included all that was given to the priests, but, with the exception of the fat from the fellowship offerings and the first-born, was not brought on the altar: the fellowship offerings (7:31–34; 10:14–15), the first-born of clean animals (Num. 18:15), the finest of the oil, new wine, and grain (Num. 18:12–13), the tithes (Num. 18:26), and everything that was devoted to the Lord (Num. 18:14). The most holy included whatever was not burned in the sin, guilt, and grain offerings, and also the bread of the Presence (Lev. 24:8–9). It may be recalled that what was most holy could be eaten exclusively in the courtyard of the sanctuary (e.g., Lev. 6:16, 26; 7:6) by the male descendants of Aaron who were ceremonially clean (e.g., 6:18, 29), whereas the holy portions were to be eaten in any clean place and were given also to the ceremonially clean female members of the priestly family (10:14).

---

[5]The author has "disfigured face" here, whereas the NIV has merely "disfigured" (cf. RSV, "mutilated face").

[6]The author has "abnormal limbs" where the NIV has "deformed" (cf. RSV, "limb too long").

[7]The author has "emaciated" here (cf. NAB, "weakly").

[8]The author has "white spot on the eye" (cf. KJV, "blemish in his eye").

A physical defect in a priest evidently had the same significance as the various defects in potential sacrificial animals, for whoever served at the altar and whatever was placed on it had to be completely sound in body. It is possible that Jeremiah, who was of priestly blood but did not serve as a priest, was afflicted with one of the physical defects listed above.

21:24 *So Moses told this to Aaron and his sons and to all the Israelites.*

This verse is a closing formula that has reference at least to chapters 20 and 21 and perhaps embraces the whole of chapters 17–21.

Respect for the Holiness of the Offerings
(22:1–33)

1. The Priest and the Offerings (22:1–16)

Because the priests lived in constant contact with what was holy, and especially insofar as this formed a portion of their daily food, they were exposed to the danger of not always taking sufficient account of the fact that all such things belonged within the special realm of the holy covenant God. In view of this, the following verses cautioned them that the matter of holiness was never to be taken lightly.

22:1–3 *The LORD said to Moses, "Tell Aaron and his sons to treat with respect the sacred offerings the Israelites consecrate to me, so they will not profane my holy name. I am the LORD.*

"Say to them: 'For the generations to come, if any of your descendants is ceremonially unclean and yet comes near the sacred offerings that the Israelites consecrate to the LORD, that person must be cut off from my presence. I am the LORD.'"

The priests are here commanded to "treat with respect" the sacred offerings of Israel, a portion of which formed their daily sustenance, i.e., to exercise proper care and restraint whenever they "come near" in order to eat of them. These "sacred offerings" comprised both what was holy and what was most holy (see discussion on 21:22), and they thus included not only the sacrifices as such, but also the firstlings and tithes and whatever was devoted to the Lord. All of these could be eaten only by one who was clean, i.e., who had nothing that barred him from the exercise of his cultic tasks. If the gifts were most holy, the meal could be partaken of only by male descendants of Aaron in the courtyard of the sanctuary; if they were holy, it could be shared in by any member of the priestly family in a clean place, i.e., the priestly dwelling that had been scrupulously preserved from any uncleanness. Whoever failed in this was to be "cut off" from the

Lord's presence, the site of his ministry (Deut. 10:8; 18:7), i.e., he was to be slain.

22:4–7 *"'If a descendant of Aaron has an infectious skin disease or a bodily discharge, he may not eat the sacred offerings until he is cleansed. He will also be unclean if he touches something defiled by a corpse or by anyone who has an emission of semen, or if he touches any crawling thing that makes him unclean, or any person who makes him unclean, whatever the uncleanness may be. The one who touches any such thing will be unclean till evening. He must not eat any of the sacred offerings unless he has bathed himself with water. When the sun goes down, he will be clean, and after that he may eat the sacred offerings, for they are his food.'"*

These verses give a more detailed statement of what would exclude a priest or a member of his family from eating of the sacred offerings and also describe what such a person was to do in order to recover his right. Anyone who suffered from an infectious skin disease (or leprosy; see NIV margin to verse 4 and the comments on 13:2) or an unhealthy condition of the sexual organs (see comments on 15:2) was unclean and was forbidden contact with what was holy. Such a person was therefore not permitted to eat of the sacred offerings until the prescribed rites of cleansing had been performed (see the comments on chs. 13 and 15). The same applies to whoever had direct or indirect contact with a human corpse (see Num. 19) or had been rendered unclean either by an emission of semen (Lev. 15:16), by intercourse (15:18), or by touching one of the unclean crawling animals listed in 11:29–30. The uncleanness resulting from these things lasted until sundown and required that the affected person wash his body.

22:8 *"'He must not eat anything found dead or torn by wild animals, and so become unclean through it. I am the LORD.'"*

The sacred offerings did not form the sole sustenance of the priest and his family, and verse 8 therefore states what other things could under no condition be eaten by such persons, viz., the meat of animals that had died a natural death or that had been killed by wild animals. The priest was therefore here subjected to a stronger prohibition than was the ordinary Israelite (see 17:15–16), for he possessed a greater degree of holiness in virtue of his office. In Ezekiel 44:31, the regulation is further clarified by the additional specification, "bird or animal."

22:9 *"'The priests are to keep my requirements so that they do not become guilty and die for treating them with contempt. I am the LORD, who makes them holy.'"*

This verse, which in form resembles 8:35 and 18:30, impresses on the priests the fact that they are here confronted with the requirements of the Lord and would imperil their lives if they would transgress these in any respect. The declaration, "I am the LORD, who makes them holy," i.e., who sanctifies the priests by taking them into His service and placing them within the sphere of the holy, simultaneously calls them to preserve this holiness and to respect its presence in their environment (see also 21:8).

22:10–13 *"'No one outside a priest's family may eat the sacred offering, nor may the guest of a priest or his hired worker eat it. But if a priest buys a slave with money, or if a slave is born in his household, that slave may eat his food. If a priest's daughter marries anyone other than a priest, she may not eat any of the sacred contributions. But if a priest's daughter becomes a widow or is divorced, yet has no children, and she returns to live in her father's house as in her youth, she may eat of her father's food. No unauthorized person, however, may eat any of it.'"*

The following paragraph presents a further clarification of who could be regarded as belonging to the family of a priest and who was thereby entitled to eat of the sacred offerings. Verse 10 begins by excluding certain individuals. The Hebrew term *(zār)*, translated as "outside a priest's family,"[9] literally means just "strange" or "different" and only acquires its particular meaning from the context in which it occurs. Also explicitly excluded are the guest—a person who was to be distinguished from the alien *(gēr)*, although both were non-Israelite in origin—and the hired worker, both of whom resided with the priestly family only temporarily and therefore could not be considered as its members. The situation was different with a slave, whether purchased with money or born to a slave woman within the household, and such persons were therefore regarded as members of the priestly family (v. 11).

In contrast to her brothers, the daughter of a priest was placed outside of the family by her marriage (see discussion on 21:3). If a daughter married an "outsider" *(zār)*, i.e., a non-priest, she was no longer permitted to eat of the sacred gifts (v. 12). If the marriage in some manner came to an end and she permanently returned to her father's house, she could once again partake, but this only applied if she had no sons, since the eldest son would otherwise assume his father's position (v. 13). The pericope formed by verses 10–13 then closes as it began by stating that no *zār* ("unauthorized person")[10] could eat of the sacred offerings.

---

[9]The author translates the term as "unauthorized" (cf. NAB, JB, "lay person").

[10]The NIV translates *zār* differently in verses 10 and 13, while the author has "unauthorized" in both cases.

22:14–16 *" 'If anyone eats a sacred offering by mistake, he must make restitution to the priest for the offering and add a fifth of the value to it. The priests must not desecrate the sacred offerings the Israelites present to the L*ORD *by allowing them to eat the sacred offerings and so bring upon them guilt requiring payment. I am the* L*ORD, who makes them holy.' "*

The lawgiver here turns to what was to be done if the commandment of verses 10–13 was violated. Such an act could naturally only take place inadvertently (4:2), for the death penalty inexorably followed on transgressions committed deliberately (see discussion on 4:2). The situation dealt with here is not the same as that of 5:14–16, for whereas that passage was concerned with the unintentional appropriation of something that belonged to the Lord by a lay Israelite, these verses apply rather to members of the priestly family who unconsciously ate something that was holy while they were in a state that forbade them to do so. In this case, a guilt offering did not have to be presented, and all that was required was the restitution of what had been inadvertently eaten with the addition of one-fifth more as a penalty (this was most likely done according to its appraised value; see also 27:13, 15).

The translation of verses 15–16 presents some difficulty in that the verbs used here all appear without further qualification in the third person plural even though the same persons are not intended in each case. The meaning seems to me to be that the priests are forbidden to desecrate the sacred contributions that the Israelites dedicated to the Lord, since they would otherwise bring guilt on the people if any unauthorized persons would eat of the offerings. It may be noted that a certain nonchalance is here presupposed on the part of the priest in question, for he was obligated to warn any unauthorized person who had received something from the sacred offerings. The regulation of verse 14 should therefore be regarded in this light. It is striking in this connection that the unauthorized person was punished, while nothing was done to the priest who formed the occasion for his error. Apparently, some awareness of his own responsibility was presupposed on the part of the latter.

2. *The People and Their Offerings* (22:17–25)

22:17–25 *The L*ORD *said to Moses, "Speak to Aaron and his sons and to all the Israelites and say to them: 'If any of you—either an Israelite or an alien living in Israel—presents a gift for a burnt offering to the L*ORD*, either to fulfill a vow or as a freewill offering, you must present a male without defect from the cattle, sheep or goats in order that it may be accepted on your behalf. Do not bring anything with a* *defect, because it will not be accepted on your behalf. When anyone brings from the herd or flock a fellowship offering to the LORD to fulfill a special vow or as a freewill offering, it must be without defect or blemish to be acceptable. Do not offer to the LORD the blind, the injured or the maimed, or anything with warts or festering or running sores. Do not place any of these on the altar as an offering made to the LORD by fire. You may, however, present as a freewill offering a cow or a sheep that is deformed or stunted, but it will not be accepted in fulfillment of a vow. You must not offer to the LORD an animal whose testicles are bruised, crushed, torn or cut. You must not do this in your own land, and you must not accept such animals from the hand of a foreigner and offer them as the food of your God. They will not be accepted on your behalf, because they are deformed and have defects.'"*

A formula that is identical to that in 17:1–2 here introduces a discussion of the rules that the Israelites had to observe in the selection of animals for their offerings. This naturally applied only to those offerings, e.g., the sin and guilt offerings, in which the choice of the animals was not subjected to definite requirements (4:1–6:7). The verses in this passage are therefore concerned exclusively with freewill and votive gifts that were presented by the people as burnt offerings (vv. 18–20) or fellowship offerings (vv. 21–26).

It is here commanded that the sacrificial animals were to be "without defect" (vv. 19–21; see also 1:3, 10; 3:1, 6; 4:3, 23, 28; etc.), a requirement that was all too often neglected during the time of Nehemiah (Mal. 1:8, 13). To be sure, those who lived outside of Israel were also aware that only the best animals were acceptable as offerings, for religious respect demanded nothing less. The animal was also to be male (see 1:3), since the vital powers of a male were greater than that of a female. Further, it could be taken only from the cattle, sheep, or goats (v. 19), since animals living in the wild belonged to no one (see discussion of 1:3). These rules applied to both burnt offerings and fellowship offerings that were presented in fulfillment of a vow or pledge. Jewish tradition extended the commandment of verse 20 to everything involved in the offering—oil, flour, wine, even the firewood—so that whatever was placed on the altar had to be of the highest quality.

Verses 22–24 enumerate certain defects that rendered an animal unfit for the fellowship offering, but the translation of a few of the Hebrew words used here is uncertain. This is the case with "warts or festering or running sores" in verse 22, and the details of the conditions spoken of in verse 24[11] are naturally also impossible to ascertain. The rabbis contend that the latter

---

[11]The author's translation in verse 24 reads "whatever has been castrated by rubbing, pounding, tearing, or cutting. . . ."

commandment disallows all castrating or gelding of animals, but it should be noted that the verse in no way prohibits the use of such animals for purposes of agriculture. In addition, the formulation of verse 24 says nothing concerning the question of whether castration was performed within or outside of Israel. The rules given here must have applied also to the burnt offerings spoken of in verses 19–20. Only in the case of an animal for the freewill offering were the demands relaxed to some extent, for certain defects were here permitted (v. 23). The two Hebrew terms used in this verse are usually understood to mean that the animals could have limbs too long or too short (cf. RSV).

Since verse 18 has presented the possibility that an alien *(gēr)* might wish to bring an offering to the Lord in fulfillment of a pledge (see also Num. 15:14–16), verse 25 makes clear that the rules given in the preceding verses applied also to the animals offered by such a non-Israelite. The priests therefore had to reject any animal presented by an alien that did not satisfy the stated demands. The nationalism of later Judaism led it to require that the burnt offerings and fellowship offerings presented by aliens be burned in their entirety *(Zebahim* 116a, *Hullin* 13b).

Some have interpreted verse 25 to mean that it was forbidden to purchase from foreigners animals with such defects in order to present them as offerings. In my opinion this is incorrect, not only because it would presuppose a rather large degree of naïveté on the part of the Israelites, but also because the first half of this verse would then have to read somewhat differently. The only thing that might seem to support such an interpretation is the verb form of verse 25a.

3. *Particular Requirements* (22:26–30)

22:26–30 *The Lord said to Moses, "When a cow, a sheep or a goat is born, it is to remain with its mother for seven days. From the eighth day on, it will be acceptable as an offering made to the Lord by fire. Do not slaughter a cow or a sheep and its young on the same day.*

"When you sacrifice an offering of thanksgiving to the Lord, sacrifice it in such a way that it will be accepted on your behalf. It must be eaten that same day; leave none of it till morning. I am the Lord."

A few further qualifications for animals are here added that had to be met if they were to be acceptable as offerings. Verse 27 directs that any sacrificial animal was to be older than seven days, a requirement that corresponds with what is prescribed in Exodus 22:30 (MT 22:29) concerning the first-born of clean animals. It is nowhere stated at what age an animal was too old to be used in an offering, but a distinction is constantly made between older and younger animals. First Samuel 7:9 speaks of a "suckling lamb," Genesis 15:9 of three-year-old animals, and Judges 6:25 of a bull of seven years. Later Judaism demanded one-year-old animals in the burnt offering (Josephus, *Ant.* III 9, 1). Verse 28 forbids the sacrificing of a mother animal and her young on the same day. Whether this requirement was guided by the same line of thought as Deuteronomy 22:6–7, or whether, like Exodus 23:19b, it was made in order to counter a pagan custom, can no longer be determined. The final requirement in verses 29–30 repeats the commandment of 7:15 (cf. 19:5–6), and with regard to its content the reader is referred to the comments on that verse.

4. *Concluding Admonition* (22:31–33)

22:31–33 *"Keep my commands and follow them. I am the LORD. Do not profane my holy name. I must be acknowledged as holy by the Israelites. I am the LORD, who makes you holy and who brought you out of Egypt to be your God. I am the LORD."*

Israel is here urged in a few final words to carefully observe the preceding commandments, for to fail in this would be to profane the Lord's holy name. The Hebrew term used here *(hillēl)* expresses a degradation to the level of the profane *(hōl)*. The Israelites at all times had to bear in mind the fact that the holiness that characterized the Lord's form of life was absolutely peculiar to Himself and was to be held in reverence by whoever would serve Him and be admitted to His fellowship. To profane what was holy would bring Israel into conflict with what the Lord had purposed since the time of the deliverance from Egypt, viz., to live as a holy God amidst a holy people.

Holy Times and Yearly Feasts
(23:1–44)

23:1–2 *The LORD said to Moses, "Speak to the Israelites and say to them: 'These are my appointed feasts, the appointed feasts of the LORD, which you are to proclaim as sacred assemblies.'"*

As verses 2, 4, 37, and 44 indicate, this chapter presents in chronological order a list of the Lord's "appointed feasts," which were to be accompanied by a *miqrā' qōḏeš*. I have rendered this phrase as "sacred day of celebration"[12] (vv. 2, 4, 7, 21, 24, 27, 35–37), a translation which, although it is not entirely correct, is in any case better than "festive

---

[12]The NIV has "sacred assembly."

assembly'' (Böhl) or ''consecrated gathering'' (Edelkoort). The Hebrew verb *qārā'* does not mean ''convoke'' or ''call together,'' but merely ''call,'' and this can take on the meaning of ''call out'' or ''proclaim.'' The Septuagint and Vulgate understood the expression in this manner, although the notion had already arisen earlier in Jewish circles that the *miqrā' qōḏeš* was identical to the ''festive assembly'' (*'ašārâ* [*h*]) spoken of in Isaiah 1:13; Joel 1:14; Amos 5:21; etc. In order to rightly understand this matter, it must be remembered that Israel's reckoning of time was based on the moon. A new month (*hōḏeš*) began whenever the new moon (*hōḏeš*) became visible in the sky, and when the latter was reported by trustworthy witnesses it became the signal for the New Moon festival (1 Sam. 20:5; Amos 8:5; etc.). In order that everyone might know the correct time of the Lord's ''appointed feasts'' and thus observe the requirements that were prescribed for each of these, the precise day was made known by a *miqrā' qōḏeš,* i.e., by sending forth a call *(miqrā').* The qualification of the latter as holy *(qōḏeš)* marks the day as having an exceptional character, since the Lord had set it apart from other days as the time of His appointed feast (see v. 21). The New Moon festival did not belong among these appointed feasts, although the presentation of a burnt offering adopted this ancient feast that the Israelites never tired of celebrating into the ceremonial service of the Lord (Num. 28:11–15; Ezek. 46:6–7). It later became customary to make this a day of rest (Amos 8:5) and a time for paying a visit to the sanctuary (Isa. 1:13–14) or to a prophet (2 Kings 4:22–23), and because of this latter, many prophetic addresses are dated on the first day of the month (Ezek. 26:1; 29:17; 31:1; 32:1; Hag. 1:1). Because the New Moon festival was not an appointed feast proper, it is not mentioned in the present chapter. The Hebrew term translated as ''appointed feast,'' *mô'ēḏ,* is derived from a verb that means to ''designate'' or ''assign,'' and on the basis of Genesis 1:14 this is to be understood as having originally taken place in terms of the constellations.

1. *Sabbath* (23:3)

23:3 *'''There are six days when you may work, but the seventh day is a Sabbath of rest, a day of sacred assembly. You are not to do any work; wherever you live, it is a Sabbath to the* Lord.*'''*

Although the occurrence of the Sabbath had no connection with the course of the stars and verses 4 and 38 indicate that it did not belong among the appointed feasts proper, the list that follows begins with this day. The Sabbath was the only one of Israel's ''days of celebration'' that is spoken of in the Decalogue (Exod. 20:8–11), and since it formed an everlasting sign of the covenant (Exod. 31:13, 17), the importance of observing it was continually impressed on the people (e.g., Exod. 23:12; 35:2; Lev. 19:3, 30; 26:3; Num. 15:32–36; 28:9–10). Some have incorrectly maintained that the celebration of the Sabbath was possible only in a nation of farmers[13] or they have without ground regarded it as a day of the full moon,[14] while Budde[15] claims to have established that it was originally nothing other than the Kenites' "day of Saturn." In spite of the view of Friedrich Delitzsch,[16] this day of the Israelites was also completely different in character from the Babylonian *šabattū,* although the two names are etymologically related. The *šabattū* was the fifteenth day of the month and, as the calendars indicate, was not necessarily a day of rest, whereas the Sabbath always referred to the seventh day and was characterized by the cessation of all work. The Sabbath was also unrelated to the Babylonian celebration of the seventh, fourteenth, nineteenth, twenty-first, and twenty-eighth days of the month, these being cultic days that were primarily a concern of the king, soothsayer, and sorcerer, since the special dangers created on them by the activity of demons made it necessary that the latter refrain from performing their official tasks. Each of these days was called an *ūmu limnu,* "evil day," or *ūmu nuḫ libbi,* "day of quieting of the heart," although this designation applied only to the gods, and the days were not, like Israel's Sabbath, considered holy, transferred from normal life to the sphere of the divine, and marked in their special character by the prohibition of all daily work. Israel's Sabbath was also determinative for the structure of its year, for this came to be framed in terms of weeks rather than months. The Passover, the feast that signaled a new beginning both in the course of the year and in the life of the people, formed the holy week in this year, and it was followed seven weeks later by the celebration of the harvest in the Feast of Weeks (Exod. 23:16; 34:22; Num. 28:26–31; Deut. 16:9–12) or Pentecost (Gr. *pentēkostē,* "fiftieth [day]"). The Sabbath furthermore controlled the progression of years, for the "week year" or sabbatical year and the "seven weeks year" or Year of Jubilee each had a unique character (Lev. 25). Although the name "Sabbath" may therefore not have originated in Israel, the content that it took on derived from the self-revelation of the God of the covenant, who filled it with spiritual treasures and made it the key for understanding His creation. As such, this

---

[13] E.g., B. Stade, *Biblische Theologie,* p. 177.

[14] E.g., W. Meinhold, *Sabbath und Woche im Alten Testament* (1905), and S. Mowinckel, *Le décalogue,* pp. 75f.

[15] *The Journal of Theological Studies* (1928), pp. 1f.

[16] *Die grosse Täuschung* I (1920), pp. 99f.

day was an occasion, not for fear, but for rejoicing in the Lord's consecrated rest (Exod. 23:12; Deut. 5:12–15; Isa. 58:13; Hos. 2:11). The rhythmic character that the Sabbath gave to the Israelites' life, which is met with nowhere else in the ancient Near Eastern world, contributed to distinguishing them as a peculiar people, and it at the same time exerted an extremely favorable influence both on their capacity for work and on their manner of life in general.

The prohibition of all work on the Sabbath applied even during the seasons of plowing and harvest (Exod. 34:21), and buying and selling were likewise forbidden (Amos 8:5). Like the Day of Atonement (Lev. 16:31; 23:32), it is called a *šabbaṯ šabbāṯôn,* a "Sabbath of rest" or day of complete rest (see also Exod. 31:14; 35:2). The fact that the sabbath year is also designated a *šabbaṯ šabbāṯôn* (Lev. 25:4) is evidence that the prohibition of all work was not to be understood absolutely, although the painstaking and forced abstinence of Judaism, which turned the permission to rest into an imperative, did tend in this direction (see the Mishnah tractate, *Shabbath*) and transformed the intended benefits of the Sabbath into a difficult accomplishment. The work spoken of here is apparently not the same as the "regular work" forbidden in verses 7, 25, and 35, i.e., normal daily occupations such as farming and manual labor, but the difference between these is unclear, especially since the Sabbath prohibition in Numbers 28:25 does not apply to "work," but to "regular work." In the Pentateuch, the activities forbidden on the Sabbath day include plowing and harvesting (Exod. 34:21), the gathering of manna (Exod. 16:16–30), baking and boiling (Exod. 16:23), lighting a fire (Exod. 35:3), and the gathering of wood (Num. 15:32–36); elsewhere, the carrying of loads (Jer. 17:21) and conducting of business (Neh. 13:15–21; Amos 8:5) are also declared to be impermissible. Breaking the Sabbath demanded the death penalty (Exod. 31:12–17; 35:2), but the prophet Ezekiel nevertheless decried the fact that the Sabbath rest was not always observed (Ezek. 20:13).

2. *Passover* (23:4–8)

23:4–8 " '*These are the LORD's appointed feasts, the sacred assemblies you are to proclaim at their appointed times: The LORD's Passover begins at twilight on the fourteenth day of the first month. On the fifteenth day of that month the LORD's Feast of Unleavened Bread begins; for seven days you must eat bread made without yeast. On the first day hold a sacred assembly and do no regular work. For seven days present an offering made to the LORD by fire. And on the seventh day hold a sacred assembly and do no regular work.*' "

This, the first of Israel's annual feasts, is with full justice designated by J. Pedersen[17] the "foundation feast of the nation." The ceremony was originally strictly domestic in character (Exod. 12), but its connection with the Feast of Unleavened Bread *(maṣṣôt)* transformed it into a temple feast in which the paschal lamb took on the additional character of an offering.[18] The feast began on the fourteenth day of the first month (Exod. 12:2; it appears in Exod. 13:4 that this was the month of Abib), this indicating that the Israelite year began in the spring rather than the autumn (the latter is implied in Exod. 23:16; 34:22). In addition, this date places the celebration of the feast during the time of the full moon, since Israel's months always commenced with the new moon. The Passover thus began when the first full moon after the spring equinox ascended to its culmination. The precise moment of beginning is literally stated to be "between the two evenings" (cf. RSV margin on v. 5), an expression that also occurs in Exodus 16:12; 29:39; 30:8; Numbers 9:3, 5; 28:4, 8. Some think that this means "by the light of the full moon," while others interpret it as "between the two settings," viz., that of the sun and that of the moon. The most likely meaning, however, is "between the beginning and the end of evening's fall," or more precisely, "at twilight," before total darkness has come. This would therefore be directly before the beginning of the fifteenth day of the month (cf. 2 Chron. 30:15; 35:1), for Israel's days began in the evening.[19] The first day of the feast is called the Passover Feast (Exod. 34:25) or simply Passover (Lev. 23:5; Num. 28:16; 33:3; 2 Kings 23:22; Ezek. 45:21), a name that translates the Hebrew term *pesaḥ* or its Aramaic form *pashā'* (cf. the adjective *paschal*). Although the word *pesaḥ* (from the verb *pāsaḥ,* "to pass by") was originally related to the passage of the moon through its culmination and this ancient Near Eastern feast at first had an astronomical significance, there is no longer any trace of this in the Old Testament. The Passover of Israel was not a nature feast, for from the outset it was here given a historical content. Under the influence of divine revelation, the original character of this day was completely altered—the Christian church did the same in its celebration of Easter and Christmas, the dates of which are likewise connected with the sun and the moon—and *pesaḥ* came to express the "passing over" *(pāsaḥ,* Exod. 12:13, 27) of the

---

[17]In "Passahfest und Passahlegende," ZAW (1934), p. 169.

[18]See my commentary, *II Kronieken,* pp. 378f.

[19]The practice in later Judaism was to begin the feast roughly after three o'clock in the afternoon (see the Mishnah tractate, *Pesahim* 58a, and also Josephus, *Antiquities* VI 9, 3). Because of this, Jewish exegetes generally understood "between the two evenings" to embrace the entire afternoon and early evening, but this is surely incorrect (see, e.g., Hoffmann, *Das Buch Leviticus,* pp. 140f.).

angel of death as he spared the Israelite first-born at the commencement of the deliverance from Egypt. The manner in which the Passover lamb was to be eaten under the light of the full moon (Exod. 12:6) also calls to mind this event. The one-year-old lamb, which originally symbolized nothing more than the burgeoning life of nature, thus acquired a deeper meaning and in its death formed an expression of substitutionary and expiatory suffering, while the feast itself testified both to the Lord's grace as this became manifest in Israel's deliverance, and to His avenging judgment that provoked the bitter lamentation of the Egyptians.

Verses 4–8 make no mention of the manner in which the lamb was to be eaten, for this had been definitively established at the time of the Exodus from Egypt (Exod. 12:1–11). Only the time when this was to be done is indicated here (v. 5). For the rest, the present context follows Exodus 12:14–16 in speaking of the eating of the round, yellow cakes or "matzos" (Jewish Passover bread), of the presenting of offerings by fire, and of the special character of the first and last days of the Feast of Unleavened Bread. This feast took place at the beginning of the harvest and involved the eating of bread made from the fresh meal without yeast, and was so closely bound up with the Passover that Ezekiel speaks of a Passover feast lasting seven days (Ezek. 45:21; cf. Deut. 16:1–8), while the mention of the Feast of Unleavened Bread in 2 Chronicles 30:13, 21 and Ezra 6:22 tacitly implies the Passover as well.

Although the round, yellow cakes that were eaten must have in form and color originally brought to mind the lunar disk,[20] in Israel they symbolized the current barley harvest. Moreover, together with the fire offerings that were to be brought each day (a further description of these appears in Num. 28:16–25), they also directed the people's attention to the Giver of blessings, for the first and seventh days of the eating of these *maṣṣôṯ* were set apart as days of complete rest that were holy to the Lord.

3. *Firstfruits* (23:9–14)

23:9–14 *The Lord said to Moses, "Speak to the Israelites and say to them: 'When you enter the land I am going to give you and you reap its harvest, bring to the priest a sheaf of the first grain you harvest. He is to wave the sheaf before the Lord so it will be accepted on your behalf; the priest is to wave it on the day after the Sabbath. On the day you wave the sheaf, you must sacrifice as a burnt offering to*

---

[20]Abraham Shalom Yahuda, *The Language of the Pentateuch in its Relation to Egyptian* [London: Oxford University Press: Humphrey Milford, 1933], p. 96. Yahuda points out that such thin, round cakes are still today baked in the sun from unleavened dough and, as a rule, sold only to poor persons, thus forming a true "bread of affliction" (Deut. 16:3).

the LORD a lamb a year old without defect, together with its grain offering of two-tenths of an ephah of fine flour mixed with oil—an offering made to the LORD by fire, a pleasing aroma—and its drink offering of a fourth of a hin of wine. You must not eat any bread, or roasted or new grain, until the very day you bring this offering to your God. This is to be a lasting ordinance for the generations to come, wherever you live.''*

The Israelites were always to bear in mind that the land of Canaan was the Lord's possession and that they had only the rights of tenants (25:23). They were also to be aware that the fertility of Canaan's soil was not due to one of the Baals but rather the Lord's gift of grace, since the granting of the harvest formed His blessing on His people. Israel was therefore called to acknowledge both of these facts each year by bringing to the divine Owner the tribute that was due Him (see also discussion on 19:23–25). Just as the full strength of life was thought to come to expression in the first-born of human beings (cf. Gen. 49:3), that portion of the crop that first became ripe was considered the best of the harvest, and this therefore had to be surrendered to the Lord as a sign of the dedication of the harvest. Only after this had been done could a person eat of the produce of the land without bringing sin on himself, and thus rejoice in the fact that God's blessing rested on his household (Ezek. 44:30). Whereas Exodus 22:29; 23:19; 34:26; Leviticus 2:12; and Numbers 18:12–13 merely presuppose or command the bringing of firstfruits, the verses of our text give a fuller description of the ceremony that this involved. It is evident from the detailed liturgy contained in Deuteronomy 26:1–11—like Numbers 18:12–13, however, this passage is concerned with the presentation of firstfruits by the individual, and not, as in the present context, by the people as a national unity[21]—that the firstfruits originally formed an offering (see also Lev. 2:12), but in Israel they became a portion of the income of the priests (Num. 18:13). The notion that the Lord had a claim on the firstfruits was still expressed by the presentation of them at the sanctuary, however. It appears in Nehemiah 10:36–38 that, at the time this was written, the firstfruits were brought to the temple in solemn procession and deposited in one of the storerooms. The rabbis maintain in the tractate *Bikkurim* (I 3, 10), where a sharp distinction is made between firstfruits, tithes, and the *terûmâ(h)* (''contribution''), that firstfruits were demanded exclusively of the seven products listed in Deuteronomy 8:8. The presentation of these occurred in the manner of the *tenûpâ(h),* i.e., they were waved back and forth in the direction of the altar (see discussion on 7:30).

---

[21] With regard to the liturgy of Deuteronomy 26:1–11, see e.g., A. R. Hulst, *Het karakter van de cultus in Deuteronomy* (1938), pp. 91–101.

The firstfruits spoken of in verses 9–14 are those of the produce of the field, the barley being reaped in April/May and the wheat harvest following two and three weeks later. It is commanded that an *'ōmer* of these be presented to the priest as a wave offering. This Hebrew term is usually translated as "sheaf" here (as in NIV), but both the rabbinic exegesis and the Jewish tradition (*Menahoth* 66a, 68b) contradict this. It is in any case clear that in Numbers 15:20 the *'ōmer* of firstfruits had the form of a cake made from barley meal mixed with water. Both the Septuagint and the Mishnah, which devotes a separate tractate, *Hallah,* to these cakes, speak of dough in this connection—the image that Paul uses in Romans 11:16 is based on this conception—but the reference is actually to a type of groats that was ground in large quantities once a year. I have chosen to leave the word *'ōmer,* which in Exodus 16:36 indicates one-tenth of an ephah and in Deuteronomy 24:19; Ruth 2:7, 15; and Job 24:10 means "sheaf," untranslated in the present context.[22]

The waving of this *'ōmer* was to take place "on the day after the Sabbath" (v. 11). There is a problem as to which Sabbath is meant here, for this could be either the Sabbath of the week-long feast, or the first day of Passover, i.e., the 15th of Nisan, which, like the Day of Atonement (v. 32), is called a "sabbath" because it was a day of rest. The Pharisees and Sadducees were never able to agree on this, and the matter still remains in dispute.[23] Jewish tradition, which is represented in the Septuagint translation here, sides with the Pharisees and places the day of the waving of the *'ōmer* on the 16th of Nisan, i.e., the second day of Passover, and this is naturally of decisive importance for the dating of the Feast of Weeks (see v. 15). On these terms, the Sabbath of verse 11 would be the day of rest spoken of in verse 7. This position strikes me as at least the most probable, and it is further supported by the consideration that, in a land like Canaan, where the great differences in climate caused the time of harvest to vary somewhat, a precise determination of the date for the presentation of the *'ōmer* was necessary. As in Exodus 12, the Passover and the Feast of Unleavened Bread are therefore here bound into a single whole that speaks of divine blessing as well as a new beginning for the people.

The *'ōmer,* which was merely waved and was therefore not placed on the altar, was accompanied by an offering (vv. 12–13) composed of a one-year-old lamb as a burnt offering, two-tenths of an ephah (i.e., 7.28 liters) of raw meal as a grain offering (the amount is otherwise always one-tenth ephah, Exod. 29:40; Num. 28:9, 13–14; 29:4), and a fourth of a

---

[22]The KJV, RSV, and NIV all translate it as "sheaf."

[23]See Hoffmann, *Das Buch Leviticus,* pp. 159–215.

hin (i.e., about 1.5 liters) of wine as a drink offering. Just as has been stated in Leviticus 19:23–25 with respect to fruit trees, verse 14 directs that nothing gathered in the new harvest could be eaten in any form whatsoever before the *'ōmer* had been brought to the Lord and the prescribed offerings made (cf. Josh. 5:11). It may be observed in closing that numerous nations, the Egyptians included, had the custom of presenting to the deity its due portion of the new harvest before the people were allowed to eat of it.

4. *The Feast of Weeks* (23:15–22)

23:15–22 *"'From the day after the Sabbath, the day you brought the sheaf of the wave offering, count off seven full weeks. Count off fifty days up to the day after the seventh Sabbath, and then present an offering of new grain to the LORD. From wherever you live, bring two loaves made of two-tenths of an ephah of fine flour, baked with yeast, as a wave offering of firstfruits to the LORD. Present with this bread seven male lambs, each a year old and without defect, one young bull and two rams. They will be a burnt offering to the LORD, together with their grain offerings and drink offerings–an offering made by fire, an aroma pleasing to the LORD. Then sacrifice one male goat for a sin offering and two lambs, each a year old, for a fellowship offering. The priest is to wave the two lambs before the LORD as a wave offering, together with the bread of the firstfruits. They are a sacred offering to the LORD for the priest. On that same day you are to proclaim a sacred assembly and do no regular work. This is to be a lasting ordinance for the generations to come, wherever you live.*

"'When you reap the harvest of your land, do not reap to the very edges of your field or gather the gleanings of your harvest. Leave them for the poor and the alien. I am the LORD your God.'"

Although no name is given to this feast in this passage, it is called the "Feast of Weeks" in Exodus 34:22 and Deuteronomy 16:10, the "Feast of Harvest" in Exodus 23:16, the "day of firstfruits" in Numbers 28:26, and in view of the fact that it was to be celebrated on the fiftieth (Gr. *pentēkostē*) day after the day the *'ōmer* was presented, it has also been designated "Pentecost." The Feast of Weeks marked the official end of the harvest, and it was therefore in nature and essence a time of thanksgiving for the produce of the land. Since Exodus 19:1 states that the giving of the Law at Mount Sinai began in the third month after Passover, later Jewish tradition related this feast to the events at Sinai. The Feast of Weeks was thus referred to in the main synagogal prayer as the "time of the giving of our law,"[24] and the connection between Passover and Pentecost was regarded as indicating that deliverance (Passover) without law (Sinai) comes

---

[24]Hoffmann, *Das Buch Leviticus*, pp. 224–40.

235

to nothing. Unfortunately, however, Judaism transformed this law into a new "house of bondage." The Jews designate that the time between Passover and Pentecost *sᵉp̄îrâ(h),* "the counting" (viz., of the *'ōmer* days), for "seven full weeks" (literally, "sabbaths") had to be counted off from the day on which the *'ōmer* was brought (v. 15), and an offering of new grain was then to be presented on the day after the seventh Sabbath (i.e., week; v. 16). After the destruction of the city and temple of Jerusalem in A.D. 70 made it impossible to maintain the original harvest character of the Feast of Weeks, the latter was transformed into a feast of the Law in which the customary decoration of the synagogue with flowers was the only thing that formed a reminder of the earlier celebration.

The "offering of new grain" (v. 16), i.e., grain from the new harvest (cf. 26:10; Num. 28:26), was to consist of a wave offering of two loaves of bread,[25] and it appears from Exodus 34:22 that these were made of wheat meal, each loaf containing one-tenth of an ephah (3.64 liters). Both of these were to be made with yeast, like the Israelites' normal fare, and they thus formed an expression of thanksgiving for daily bread. Because the loaves were leavened, they could not be placed on the altar (cf. 2:11), but were rather waved before the Lord. Like the *'ōmer* presented in the feast of firstfruits, they were therefore given to the priest.

There is a problem here with regard to the question of what was to be sacrificed on the altar. Verse 18 speaks of a burnt offering consisting of seven one-year-old lambs without defect, one young bull, and two rams, along with the accompanying grain and drink offerings. Verse 19 then requires, in addition, a sin offering consisting of a male goat and a fellowship offering of two one-year-old lambs, and verse 20 directs that these be waved before the Lord together with the bread of the firstfruits (the two loaves of v. 17) and thus be given to the priest. A comparison with verse 12 reveals that the burnt offering here was particularly large. In view of the fact that Numbers 28:26–31, which likewise deals with the Pentecost offering, prescribes almost the same burnt offering, the suspicion arises that verses 18 and 19a have incorrectly been transposed from Numbers 28:27–31 to the present context and that Leviticus 23 therefore originally spoke of nothing more than the two loaves and the fellowship offering of two lambs. A burnt offering would then have been presented at the beginning of the harvest (v. 12), and a fellowship offering at its conclusion. Since this fellowship offering was brought by the people as a whole and not by an individual, the standard practice of giving it to the offerer (see ch. 3)

---

[25]The author's translation here is literally "wave loaves" (cf. KJV; the RSV has "loaves of bread to be waved").

did not apply, and it rather formed a wave offering, which thus became the portion of the priest. In later sacrificial procedure, the offerings of Numbers 28 were considered the official offerings, while those of Leviticus 23 were regarded as *mûsāp,* additional offerings that accompanied the Pentecost loaves.

The Israelites could never give thanks without at the same time showing love to their less fortunate neighbors, and verse 22 therefore explicitly repeats the commandment of Leviticus 19:9–10.

5. *The First Day of the Seventh Month* (23:23–25)

23:23–25 *The* LORD *said to Moses, "Say to the Israelites: 'On the first day of the seventh month you are to have a day of rest, a sacred assembly commemorated with trumpet blasts. Do no regular work, but present an offering made to the* LORD *by fire.'"*

Like the seventh day, the seventh year, and the Year of Jubilee which was celebrated after seven weeks of years, the seventh month was holy to the Lord, and the first day of this had to thus be observed as a sacred day of rest. Numbers 28:11–15 directs that a burnt offering with its accompanying grain and drink offerings be presented at each new moon, and the appearance of the year's seventh new moon was celebrated with particular solemnity. Verse 24 calls the latter a "memorial day with resounding" (*tᵉrû'â[h]*; 29:1 has "day of *tᵉrûâ[h]*"), i.e., the sounding of the ram's horn *(šôpār),* not to be confused with the trumpet *(hᵃṣōṣᵉrâ[h])* blown during the presentation of festal offerings (Num. 10:10), which had a less deep and awesome sound.[26]

In any case, since the time of the Seleucids the Jews have celebrated this day as New Year's Day *(rō'š haššānâ[h]),* and they later devoted an entire tractate to its discussion. It is not entirely clear that this was done already in ancient Israel, however, and it seems to me that this position is given to the first day of the seventh month only in 25:20–22 (see the comments on those verses).[27] The seventh month was the sacred month in Israel, and both the Day of Atonement and the Feast of Tabernacles were celebrated during this time of the year. The blowing of the ram's horn—elsewhere this was done in order to drive off evil spirits, since New Year's Day was the time when the gods determined human fortunes for the coming year (cf. the ringing of bells and sounding of guns and other noisemakers on New

---

[26]The KJV, RSV, and NIV all interpret *tᵉrû'â(h)* as indicating the trumpet sound. The NIV reading in verse 24 is "sacred assembly with trumpet blasts."

[27]On this issue, see also L. J. Pap, *Das Israelitische Neujahrsfest,* p. 19.

Year's Day)—was not intended to bring Israel to the Lord's remembrance. This *šôpār yôḇēl* (cf. Josh. 6:4, "trumpets of rams' horns") spoke rather of divine judgment (see also Matt. 24:31; 1 Cor. 15:52; 1 Thess. 4:16; Rev. 8–11) and thus drew attention to heavenly concerns. A detailed description of the offering by fire that was to be presented on this day is given in Numbers 29:2–6 (see also Ezek. 45:18).

6. *The Day of Atonement* (23:26–32)

23:26–32 *The LORD said to Moses, "The tenth day of this seventh month is the Day of Atonement. Hold a sacred assembly and deny yourselves, and present an offering made to the LORD by fire. Do no work on that day, because it is the Day of Atonement, when atonement is made for you before the LORD your God. Anyone who does not deny himself on that day must be cut off from his people. I will destroy from among his people anyone who does any work on that day. You shall do no work at all. This is to be a lasting ordinance for the generations to come, wherever you live. It is a sabbath of rest for you, and you must deny yourselves. From the evening of the ninth day of the month until the following evening you are to observe your sabbath."*

According to Jewish tradition, this day was the last of the "ten days of penance" that began on the first day of the seventh month. Since the Day of Atonement has already been discussed at length in Leviticus 16, it is here only said that this was the "day of *kippurîm*," i.e., of complete atonement (this designation appears elsewhere only in Lev. 25:9). In explanation of the plural form used in the Hebrew, the *Zohar* states that there arose here two streams of love, one being the longing for atonement that flowed from the hearts of sinners, and the other the grace of God that descended from on high. Such an interpretation may have its appeal, but nothing of this is indicated in the Hebrew text.

The Day of Atonement was the Israelites' only prescribed fast day,[28] although others were later added to this (Zech. 7:2–5; 8:19).[29] Whoever neglected to celebrate this day as a time of complete rest or failed to strictly observe the fast was subject to the Lord's punishment. Verse 32 specifies that the rest was to be observed "from evening to evening" (see RSV; the NIV has "from the evening . . . until the following evening"), since the day did not begin with the evening. The opening and close of the evening (*Kol Nidrē* and *Ne'ilah*) still today retain a particularly solemn character in synagogal worship.

---

[28]The author translates "humble yourselves (by fasting)" where the NIV has merely "deny yourselves." See NIV margin on verses 27, 29, 32.

[29]See van Nes, *Jodendom,* pp. 279f.

7. The Feast of Tabernacles (23:33–36)

23:33–36 *The LORD said to Moses, "Say to the Israelites: 'On the fifteenth day of the seventh month the LORD's Feast of Tabernacles begins, and it lasts for seven days. The first day is a sacred assembly; do no regular work. For seven days present offerings made to the LORD by fire, and on the eighth day hold a sacred assembly and present an offering made to the LORD by fire. It is the closing assembly; do no regular work.'"*

In Exodus 23:16 and 34:22, which belong to the oldest portion of the Mosaic law, this feast is referred to simply as the "Feast of Ingathering," and nothing more is said concerning its date than that it was to take place "at the end of the year" (23:16) or "at the turn of the year" (34:22). These verses also fail to specify the length of the feast and say nothing about dwelling in booths, for they refer to it merely as a festival of thanksgiving that took place at the close of the agricultural year but was indefinite as to both its date and its duration. In Leviticus 23; Deuteronomy 16:13–15; and 31:9–13, however, the ceremony is referred to as the "Feast of Tabernacles," and Leviticus 23:34 states that it was to begin on the fifteenth day of the seventh month and last for seven days. These same seven days appear also in Numbers 29:12–34 and Deuteronomy 16:13–15, although the former passage, which presents a complete list of the daily offerings, gives no name to the celebration, and neither passage speaks of dwelling in booths. Ezekiel 45:25 likewise speaks of the seven days without mentioning either the name of the feast or the custom of dwelling in booths, but the latter practice is spoken of in Nehemiah 8:14–17. Leviticus 23 alone directs that the seven-day feast conclude with a *ʿaṣereṯ* on the eighth day, which was to be a "sacred day of celebration"[30] on which no regular work could be performed. The Hebrew term *ʿaṣereṯ*, which is translated in the NIV as "closing assembly," literally means "festive assembly." Second Chronicles 7:9 and Nehemiah 8:18 also speak of this assembly, but 1 Kings 8:65,[31] Deuteronomy 16:13, and Ezekiel 45:25 fail to mention it, and it therefore apparently did not form a part of the Feast of Tabernacles proper. The *ʿaṣereṯ* later developed into a "day of rejoicing of the law," i.e., the day on which the annual public reading of the Torah came to an end and could therefore begin anew.

The above makes clear beyond any reasonable doubt that the Feast of Tabernacles, like the other annual feasts of Israel, was not a purely Mosaic

---

[30]The NIV has "sacred assembly."
[31]Concerning the text of 2 Chronicles 7:9 and 1 Kings 8:65, see my commentary, *II Kronieken*, p. 122.

institution that had never been celebrated previously. The ceremony was derived from ancient agricultural practices, and Wensinck[32] has shown it to be at least highly probable that the custom of living in booths was originally related to primitive ideas concerning dangerous times in which it seemed undesirable to remain in one's former abode. There was naturally no longer any place for such a ''harvest feast'' in Israel, however, and like Passover and Pentecost, the celebration therefore had to be given a new content. Through the presentation of the prescribed offerings, the agricultural festival was dedicated to the Lord, and the custom of living in booths henceforth formed an expression of the Israelites' life in the desert and the Lord's saving power.[33]

Like the Passover, the Feast of Tabernacles began at the time of the full moon. It began on the fifteenth day of the month of Ethanim (i.e., Tishri, September/October) and lasted for seven/eight days, with the closing assembly falling on the twenty-second day of the month. It was originally a festival of thanksgiving for the fruit harvest, and as such it was the most joyous of Israel's feasts (Judg. 21:19–21; 1 Sam. 1:3–5) and was therefore often referred to simply as ''the festival'' or ''feast''' (1 Kings 8:2, 65; 12:32; 2 Chron. 7:8–9; Neh. 8:14; John 7:37; also in the rabbinic literature). In Leviticus 23:39 and Judges 21:19 it is called the ''festival to the LORD,'' for it both began and ended with a sacred assembly and involved the presentation of more offerings to the Lord than did any other feast (see Num. 29:12–39). Concerning the Jews' celebration of the Feast of Tabernacles, see my commentary on *Ezra and Nehemiah,* 1939, p. 214.

8. *Closing Formula* (23:37–38)

23:37–38 *('' 'These are the LORD's appointed feasts, which you are to proclaim as sacred assemblies for bringing offerings made to the LORD by fire–the burnt offerings and grain offerings, sacrifices and drink offerings required for each day. These offerings are in addition to those for the LORD's Sabbaths and in addition to your gifts and whatever you have vowed and all the freewill offerings you give to the LORD.' ''*)

The law pertaining to the annual feasts, which began in verse 4, ends with a closing formula in which it is once again made clear that Israel could have no other festive celebrations than the six that are enumerated in this chapter, and that these were to be consecrated to the Lord by presenting the prescribed offerings. These concluding verses also go beyond the opening

---

[32]*Verhandelingen der Koninklijke Akademie* (1925), XXV no. 2.

[33]See L. J. Pap, *Das Israelitische Neujahrsfest,* pp. 33f.

formula of verse 4, for emphasis is here placed on the fact that these feasts, in their yearly recurrence, could in no way infringe on Israel's regular observance of the Sabbath. The Israelites shared their festivals, or at least their original form, with the surrounding nations, and since the Sabbath was the exclusive possession of Israel, it took precedence over the feasts. The celebration of a feast did not alter the Sabbath, but the Sabbath rather augmented the ceremonial requirements of the feast. In addition, the Israelites had to bear in mind that the offerings required during the feasts could never interfere with their presentation of votive and freewill offerings, for the Lord continued to expect these of the people as a token of their love for His worship.

9. Further Instructions Concerning the Feast of Tabernacles (23:39-43)

23:39-43 *" 'So beginning with the fifteenth day of the seventh month, after you have gathered the crops of the land, celebrate the festival to the Lord for seven days; the first day is a day of rest, and the eighth day also is a day of rest. On the first day you are to take choice fruit from the trees, and palm fronds, leafy branches and poplars, and rejoice before the Lord your God for seven days. Celebrate this as a festival to the Lord for seven days each year. This is to be a lasting ordinance for the generations to come; celebrate it in the seventh month. Live in booths for seven days: All native-born Israelites are to live in booths so your descendants will know that I had the Israelites live in booths when I brought them out of Egypt. I am the Lord your God.' "*

After the closing formula of the preceding verses, the discussion once again turns back to the Feast of Tabernacles. The compiler of this chapter of Leviticus has included this material taken from another source at this point, since, in distinction from verses 33–36, further rules are here given pertaining to the construction of the booths (v. 40) and to the length of time that the people were to live in them (v. 42). In addition, verse 39 maintains the ancient connection of this celebration with the ingathering of the crops of the land—Deuteronomy 16:13 speaks more precisely of the "produce of your threshing floor and your winepress" (the fruit harvest and vintage came in October)—and verse 43 establishes a new connection between this feast and the Exodus from Egypt. Lastly, verse 42 restricts the habitation in booths to persons born in Israel, and the Feast of Tabernacles was thus made into a uniquely Israelite celebration.

23:44 *So Moses announced to the Israelites the appointed feasts of the Lord.*

In a concluding statement, this portion of the law is expressly ascribed to

Moses (cf. 21:24). The Israelites were therefore made aware that the customs that distinguished their festive celebrations from those of the surrounding nations derived from the man who, under the direction of God, set forth Israel's form of life once and for all.

The Lampstand and the Bread of the Presence
(24:1–9)

Chapter 24 brings together a variety of concerns, some of which pertain to two articles within the sanctuary (the lampstand, vv. 1–4; the bread of the Presence, vv. 5–9), and some of which deal with the matter of penal justice (blasphemy, vv. 10–16; retribution, vv. 17–23). It is unclear to me what considerations could have induced the compiler to insert this material between the regulations for the annual feasts (cf. 23) and those for the sabbatical year and Year of Jubilee (ch. 25).

1. *The Golden Lampstand* (24:1–4)

24:1–4 *The Lord said to Moses, "Command the Israelites to bring you clear oil of pressed olives for the light so that the lamps may be kept burning continually. Outside the curtain of the Testimony in the Tent of Meeting, Aaron is to tend the lamps before the Lord from evening till morning, continually. This is to be a lasting ordinance for the generations to come. The lamps on the pure gold lampstand before the Lord must be tended continually."*

Whereas Exodus 25:31–40 and 37:17–24 describe at length the structure of the golden lampstand[34] and Numbers 8:1–4 tells how it was set up within the tabernacle, the verses of our passage (vv. 2–3 are almost a literal repetition of Exod. 27:20–21) are concerned with the provision of the oil required for the lampstand. This oil was to be of the best quality, and it was to be brought by the people and prepared for use by the priests. Particular care had to be taken in this matter, for under no condition could the lamp be allowed to go out during the night. Light was to be continually present within the tabernacle (1 Sam. 3:3), and the altar fire had to be kept burning before it at all times, for the sanctuary formed the Lord's dwelling and the place where He partook of the "food" of His offerings.[35] As the relief on the triumphal arch of Emperor Titus in Rome indicates, the lampstand with its seven arms gave the impression of a stylized almond tree with seven branches, and it has now become a symbol of Judaism. It is noteworthy that this article of the sanctuary is referred to in verse 2 as a

---

[34]See my commentary, *II Kronieken*, pp. 88f.
[35]See my book, *Gods Woord*², p. 25.

mā'ôr (''light-bearer'') and in verse 4 as a *mᵉnōrâ(h)* (''lampstand''), and also that verse 2 emphasizes the unity (the Hebrew term here, *nēr*, is singular; cf. RSV), and verse 4 the multiplicity (*nērôṯ* is plural; cf. RSV), of the lamps. Since the second part of verse 3 is clearly a closing formula, verse 4 strikes me as a later insertion that was added in order to make clear that the lampstand was to be made of pure gold and consist of more than one lamp.

2. *The Bread of the Presence* (24:5–9)

24:5–9 *''Take fine flour and bake twelve loaves of bread, using two-tenths of an ephah for each loaf. Set them in two rows, six in each row, on the table of pure gold before the LORD. Along each row put some pure incense as a memorial portion to represent the bread and to be an offering made to the LORD by fire. This bread is to be set out before the LORD regularly, Sabbath after Sabbath, on behalf of the Israelites, as a lasting covenant. It belongs to Aaron and his sons, who are to eat it in a holy place, because it is a most holy part of their regular share of the offerings made to the LORD by fire.''*

Whereas the golden table for the bread of the Presence is described in Exodus 25:23–30 (see also Exod. 37:10–16), the present passage deals with the bread itself. The Hebrew expression for this bread literally means ''bread of the face'' (viz. of the Lord). The Chronicler refers to this as ''layer-bread'' (*ma'ᵃreḵeṯ*, NIV, ''bread set out on the table,'' 1 Chron. 9:32; 23:29; Neh. 10:33 [MT 10:34]), Numbers 4:7 designates it *''tāmîḏ* bread''* (cf. KJV, RSV; NIV, ''bread that is continually there''), and in 1 Samuel 21:6 it is called ''consecrated bread.'' Corresponding to the tribes of Israel, there were twelve loaves of bread, and these were set in two rows of six on the ''ceremonially clean'' (i.e., made of pure gold) table before the Lord, near the Most Holy Place. Each of the flat loaves consisted of two-tenths of an ephah (i.e., 4.5 liters) of raw meal, and although it is not stated that they were to be made without yeast, this seems likely to me in view of the later tradition (Josephus, *Antiquities* III 6, 6 and 10, 7; *Menahoth* 5, 1). Pure incense was added to each row of loaves so that they could serve as an *'azkārâ(h),* a term that is usually translated as ''memorial portion'' (see discussion on 2:2). Tradition maintains that the incense was placed next to the bread in two golden cups and subsequently burned on the altar, but the original intention could well have been that the incense was to be sprinkled on the bread. The Septuagint states that salt was also to be added, and this most likely became the custom in later Judaism, which therefore regarded the bread of the Presence as a grain offering (see 2:13). The bread was to be replaced after it had stood ''before the LORD'' for a week, and since the old bread remained most holy, it could be eaten exclusively within the sanctuary by the male members of the priesthood (cf. 1 Sam. 21:6; Mark 2:26).

Bread of a similar nature was also found in other parts of the ancient world such as Babylon, North Syria (Ras Shamra), and Rome. There it was presented as a meal to the deity in the belief that the deity partook of it. For the Israelites, the presentation of the bread of the Presence, like the observance of the Sabbath (Exod. 31:16), was a lasting convenantal obligation (v. 8), and this grain offering therefore served as a weekly renewal of the covenant.

The Blasphemer
(24:10–23)

24:10–14 *Now the son of an Israelite mother and an Egyptian father went out among the Israelites, and a fight broke out in the camp between him and an Israelite. The son of the Israelite woman blasphemed the name of the LORD with a curse; so they brought him to Moses. (His mother's name was Shelomith, the daughter of Dibri the Danite.) They put him in custody until the will of the LORD should be made clear to them.*

Then the LORD said to Moses: "Take the blasphemer outside the camp. All those who heard him are to lay their hands on his head, and the entire assembly is to stone him."

The incident related here took place shortly after the Exodus from Egypt, for it appears that Moses did not know how to deal with the man who had cursed the Lord's name and he first had to ascertain what the will of God was in this matter. This would not have been necessary, however, if he had already known the punishment for cursing one's parents (Exod. 21:17) and the prohibition against blaspheming God (Exod. 22:28), or even the third commandment (Exod. 20:7). The parentage of the individual under concern indicates that he belonged to the assemblage of people who accompanied the Israelites on their journey (Exod. 12:38), and it is noteworthy in this connection that the author continually emphasizes the fact that, although the guilty person had followed Israel, he was of mixed blood and therefore was not a true member of the nation (vv. 10–11).

The sequence of events here is clear. The man had had a quarrel with a person of pure Israelite descent, and the Hebrew verb used in verse 10 makes clear that this erupted in physical violence. In order to weaken his opponent, he then blasphemed the name of the latter's God, i.e., the name of the Lord. Actually, the word *blaspheme* does not accurately represent the meaning of the Hebrew text. The author here uses two verbs, the first *(nāqaḇ),* which the NIV translates as "blaspheme," literally meaning "to pierce," with the intent of debilitating a person. The second term, rendered as "curse" (cf. KJV, RSV; NIV has "with a curse"), actually means to declare someone to be "contentless" or without significance, and thus to deny that he has any power. In this connection, it is necessary to remember that, for the ancient Near Eastern mind, there existed a close connection between a nation (and each of its members) and its god. The strength of a nation derived from its god, and the attempt to weaken the god by the pronouncement of specific magical formulas resulted in the simultaneous weakening of the people (cf. Balaam's oracles concerning Israel). The transgressor spoken of in these verses attempts to take such action against his adversary. He "pierces" the Lord's name and declares Him to be without content or significance, thereby intending to render the Israelite man powerless. It should be noted here that to the ancient Near Eastern mind (this same idea also appears elsewhere), the spoken word, and to an even greater degree the magical formula, were effective in and of themselves provided they were uttered in the correct manner. The guilty person here therefore did not pronounce a curse in our sense of the word, but rather attacked the Lord's holy nature and declared this to be without content or significance.

Word of this was brought to Moses, and because of the gravity of the matter, he immediately placed the man in custody in order to prevent him from escaping his due punishment. Since Moses did not know exactly what punishment was appropriate, however, he inquired of the Lord as to how he was to deal with the situation. The answer that he then received could not be more clear: such an assault on the Lord's holy nature demanded nothing less than the death penalty. The transgressor was subject to death by stoning, and this was to take place outside the camp which, since it was ceremonially clean, would be defiled by the execution of the death penalty, and the entire community of Israel would then be excluded from any cultic communion with the Lord. All who had heard the blasphemous utterance were first to place their hands on the head of the condemned man (v. 13), and in accordance with the instruction given in Deuteronomy 17:7, these witnesses were then to begin the stoning. The laying on of hands here is usually regarded as a pronouncement of guilt, but this view seems to me incorrect. Through their hearing of the curse, the witnesses had been infected by the potent magical words, and they had thus in a certain sense come to share the guilt. The imposition of hands then served to transfer their guilt to the blasphemer, just as the sinner transferred his guilt to the sacrificial animal by means of the *sᵉmîḵâ(h)* (see discussion of 1:4) and Aaron transferred the sins of the people to the goat for Azazel (16:21–22).

24:15–16 *"Say to the Israelites: 'If anyone curses his God, he will be held responsible; anyone who blasphemes the name of the Lord must be put to death. The entire assembly must stone him. Whether an alien or native-born, when he blasphemes the Name, he must be put to death.'"*

Besides the execution of divine judgment, it was also necessary that measures be taken against the recurrence of such an incident. In so doing, verses 15–16 make a distinction between the sin of a person who "curses his god"[36] and that of one who "blasphemes the name of the Lord." In the first case, it merely stated that the offender "will be held responsible," and the punishment is thus left unspecified. In the second case, the guilty person, whether this was an alien *(gēr)* or a native-born Israelite, always had to be put to death. Some[37] have interpreted this distinction to mean that the *'elōhîm* of verse 15 is the "God of heaven and earth" and that it is less serious to treat Him with contempt than to adopt a similar attitude toward the God of the covenant. Verse 15 would thus be referring to the "universal God," and verse 16 to God in His particular relationship to Israel. Such a view, however, loses sight of the fact that Israel resolutely applied the title "God of heaven and earth" to its own covenantal God (Gen. 14:22; 24:3) and could therefore never have regarded an insult to the former as less significant than one to the latter. If this interpretation was correct, verse 15 would have to refer to *'elōhîm* (God) in an unqualified sense, like Exodus 22:28, for the specification that it was *his ''elōhîm"* implies that there also had to be another *'elōhîm.* Furthermore, this position ignores the fact that Israel also understood the word *'elōhîm* in the sense of "rulers of the invisible world," i.e., the world of the spirits, and that it could thus embrace both good and evil gods (or, gods and demons). The entire story of Balaam is based on this understanding, for when the latter sought Yahweh, he twice met *'elōhîm,* although he failed to acknowledge this to the messengers from Balak (Num. 22:8–13, 19–20; see also Deut. 10:17).

Such considerations make the meaning of the present verses completely clear. Since the Israelites were accompanied by many people of diverse origin during their journey through the desert (Exod. 12:38), it was necessary that two cases be distinguished in the matter of blasphemy. On the one hand, a person could curse *(qillēl)* "his god," declaring the latter to be without content or significance, and thus deny that he had any power at his disposal. In this instance, the blasphemer could only wait to see how his

---

[36]The NIV capitalizes "God" here, whereas the author's interpretation of these verses takes it to be a common noun.

[37]E.g., de Wilde, *Leviticus,* p. 140.

"god" would react to such contemptuous treatment and whether he would be struck by divine judgment. On the other hand, one could "pierce" *(nāqaḇ)* the Lord's name and thus attack Him in His holy nature. In this case, the death penalty had to be carried out without the least hesitation. Over against this emphasis on the deadly seriousness of this "piercing," the harmlessness of the "cursing" was thus regarded with scarcely disguised mockery. The Lord Himself looked after the honor of His name, but if a person would dare to declare his own god to be without significance or power, it was up to the latter to do the same—if he was indeed able. Verse 16 adds that the Lord was zealous to preserve the honor of His name not only among His own people, but also among aliens *(gēr),* since although a foreign resident in Israel could perhaps worship his own god, this did not give him the right to attack the holiest possession of the nation in which he lived (Exod. 20:7).

As a final observation, it may be noted that this pericope provoked a peculiar reaction on the part of the Jews. On the one hand, this incident induced them to forbid the utterance of the name of the Lord (Yahweh) and to declare it taboo, and they thus replaced it with "Lord" or "God" when Scripture was read in the synagogue (see discussion on 1:1).

On the other hand, they interpreted verses 15–16 to mean *(Sanhedrin* 56) that although it was in general forbidden to pronounce one of the Lord's names (e.g., "Lord" or "God") in a curse, the death penalty was to be enacted only when a person used the name "Yahweh" in this manner. The rabbis punished the maledictory utterance of such descriptive names with scourging or banishment, but similar use of the name "Yahweh" was subject to the death sentence. For Judaism, "Yahweh" was nothing less than *the Name (haššēm,* or in its Aramaic form, *šema'),* and because of this, the original reading in verse 11, *šēm yhwh* ("the name of the LORD"), was altered to *haššēm* ("the Name") in transcription, while in verse 16b the proper name *yhwh* was merely dropped after *šēm.* It would seem proper to me to restore the original text in both instances.[38]

24:17–23 *"'If anyone takes the life of a human being, he must be put to death. Anyone who takes the life of someone's animal must make restitution—life for life. If anyone injures his neighbor, whatever he has done must be done to him: fracture for fracture, eye for eye, tooth for tooth. As he has injured the other, so he is to be injured. Whoever kills an animal must make restitution, but whoever kills a man must be put to death. You are to have the same law for the alien and the native-born. I am the LORD your God.'"*

---

[38]The NIV does this in verse 11, but not in 16b.

Then Moses spoke to the Israelites, and they took the blasphemer outside the camp and stoned him. The Israelites did as the Lord *commanded Moses.*

After it has been made clear how the maledictory utterance of the Lord's name was to be dealt with, a few other punishments are also specified, these applying to murder and the inflicting of injury. It is evident from verse 23 that this material was inserted into the narrative concerning the blasphemer by another writer.

Verse 17 states that a murderer was to be put to death. It may be observed in this connection that the Book of the Covenant, the oldest collection of laws that was given a place in the Pentateuch, has already distinguished between murder and manslaughter and permitted a person guilty of the latter to flee to a place of refuge (Exod. 21:12–14). Unlike the Code of Hammurabi (§207f.), these verses make no distinction between the murder of a free person and that of a slave, for the social position of the victim was completely irrelevant in this matter. Life as such, regardless of to whom it belonged, was something inviolable. The situation was naturally somewhat different in the case of animals, however, for whoever took the life of another person's animal (e.g., out of hatred for the owner) was merely to make proper restitution (v. 18). The conclusion of verse 18 therefore does not have the same meaning as Exodus 21:23 and Deuteronomy 19:21, where the same words, "life for life," appear, since these verses give expression to the rigid, ancient law of retribution *(jus talionis)*. If this were indeed the point of this expression, it would have been placed at the end of verse 17. To indicate this difference in meaning, I have chosen to translate the Hebrew here as "one living being for another."[39]

The law of retribution came to expression in the following verses (vv. 19–22), however, where the formula "an eye for an eye and a tooth for a tooth" becomes the general rule (cf. Exod. 21:23–25). Whoever inflicted injury on another person was to be punished by having the same done to himself. Two observations may be made with respect to this. First of all, the lawgiver did not allow the prescribed punishment to be influenced by the social position of the aggrieved party. This situation was completely different in other ancient legal codes. In the law of Hammurabi, the principle of retribution applied only when a free person had been victimized, with a fine being sufficient in other cases (§196f), while in the Hittite law (I §7a, 8b) fines were the only form of punishment. Secondly, the principle of retribution was not to be confused with the law of blood vengeance. The

---

[39]The NIV does have merely "life for life."

latter unleashed an ever increasing spread of violence, whereas the former was an attempt, however primitive, to restrain the lust for vengeance and to subject the reactions of individuals to the will of the community.[40] Verse 22 furthermore directed that the alien *(gēr,* see under 16:29) was governed by this same law. In the land of the Lord there could be only one law, viz., that which He had given. This juridical equivalence between alien and native-born (see also Exod. 12:19, 49; Num. 15:29–30; also other verses in Leviticus) was an exception in the ancient world, and in this respect divine revelation was far ahead of the norms of civilization. It took centuries before aliens were humanely treated, and there are often failures in this regard today.

The Sabbatical Year and the Year of Jubilee
(25:1–55)

1. *The Sabbatical Year* (25:1–7)

25:1–7 *The LORD said to Moses on Mount Sinai, "Speak to the Israelites and say to them: 'When you enter the land I am going to give you, the land itself must observe a sabbath to the LORD. For six years sow your fields, and for six years prune your vineyards and gather their crops. But in the seventh year the land is to have a sabbath of rest, a sabbath to the LORD. Do not sow your fields or prune your vineyards. Do not reap what grows of itself or harvest the grapes of your untended vines. The land is to have a year of rest. Whatever the land yields during the sabbath year will be food for you—for yourself, your manservant and maidservant, and the hired worker and temporary resident who live among you, as well as for your livestock and the wild animals in your land. Whatever the land produces may be eaten.'"*

As has been observed earlier, the idea of the Sabbath governed all of Israel's appointed feasts: the Sabbath (seventh day), Pentecost (after the seventh week following the Passover), the seventh month, the sabbatical year (seventh year), and the Year of Jubilee (the seven times seventh year; see discussion on 23:3). The ordinances pertaining to the sabbath year and the Year of Jubilee were controlled by the principle that, although the Lord had indeed given the land of Canaan to the Israelites, it had not thereby ceased to be His own possession. Israel had only usufructuary rights to Canaan, and in its use of the land it was to observe the Lord's requirements.

There was more than one side to the sabbatical year. In Exodus

---

[40]See my book, *Gods Woord²*, p. 336; also J. Hempel, *Das Ethos des Alten Testaments* (1938), pp. 46f.

23:10-11 it is regarded from a social and humanitarian perspective, since the sabbath rest of the land here formed the occasion for poor persons, and also animals, to freely partake of its produce.[41] Leviticus 25:1-7, in contrast, although it does not disregard social and humanitarian concerns (vv. 6-7), draws attention primarily to the land's right to have a "sabbath of rest" (v. 4) every seventh year, a rest which, like that of the Sabbath day (23:3, 38), was dedicated to the Lord. The land is therefore in a certain sense personified here; it had been granted its own rights by its divine owner, and the Israelites were required to respect these. The previously held view that it was economic considerations that induced the lawgiver to direct that the land be left fallow every seventh year is therefore incorrect. Unlike elsewhere in the ancient Near Eastern world,[42] the primary concern here is not the simple fact that the land was left fallow, but rather the inclusion of this agricultural practice within the overall framework of the sabbath idea. This notion of a sabbath rest for everyone and everything is a religious conception that is met with only in Israel.[43] The verses under discussion therefore expressly direct that, although a person could farm his land for six successive years in order to satisfy his needs, he was to grant it a "sabbath of rest" (or "time of complete rest," v. 6; the same expression, *šabbaṯ šabbāṯôn*, is used in 23:3, 32) in the seventh year and content himself with whatever grew of itself in his fields and vineyards. The produce of that year is referred to literally as the "sabbath of the land" (v. 6; see KJV and RSV), and everyone, from the owner to the animals, was allowed to partake of this freely. No one could make any special claim to what grew during this sabbath year. For this reason, there is also no mention of harvest, it being merely stated that the produce of the land could be eaten (v. 7). The fact that Exodus 23:10-11 explicitly mentions the rights of the needy, while Leviticus 25:6-7 does not, may not be taken to indicate any essential difference between these two passages, for if the latter takes note even of the needs of animals, it could not deny those of the poor.

Some have considered this conception of the sabbath year utopian, unjustly implying that Israel's lawgiver must have been unacquainted with the realities of life. Since Nehemiah's contemporaries pledged themselves to

---

[41]The law of Deuteronomy 15:1-6 does not pertain to the sabbatical year itself, but rather commands the creditor not to press his debtor (who was without income) for payment after the end of the seventh year, i.e., after the passing of the sabbatical year. Debts could at this time no longer be collected, at least not from fellow Israelites. See also Eerdmans, *Alttestamentliche Studien,* IV, p. 125.

[42]See O. Opitz, *Zeitschrift für Assyriologie* (1927), pp. 104f.

[43]See my book, *Gods Woord*[2], pp. 119f.

obey this law (Neh. 10:31), even though their social structure was much more complicated than that of the Mosaic period, and the Jews of Greek and Roman times also observed the sabbath year (see Flavius Josephus, *Antiquities* XI 8, 6; XIII 8, 1; XIV 10, 6; 1 Macc. 6:49, 53), there is no basis for maintaining that the law concerning the sabbath year was utopian in a primitive society such as ancient Israel. Although the Israelites failed miserably in their observance of this during preexilic times (Lev. 26:34–35, 43; 2 Chron. 36:21), this was far from the only law that was disregarded (see the complaint of Hosea in Hos. 8:12; also Jer. 34:24). It is evident from 2 Kings 19:29 that the yield of a fallow field in Palestine was greater than might be expected, and it may also be noted that, even today, the spring harvest provides the greater part of the fellahs' grain.[44]

2. *The Year of Jubilee* (25:8–55)

The school of Wellhausen has incorrectly regarded this year as a priestly invention dating from the time of the Exile and, in spite of the fact that the agricultural regulations of many other ancient peoples correspond to this law at many points, considered it to be an even greater utopian fantasy than the sabbatical year. The name "Year of Jubilee" derives from the fact that it began on the tenth day of the seventh month, i.e., the Day of Atonement, with the sounding of the ram's horn.[45] Although this instrument is referred to as the *šôpār* in verse 9, it is elsewhere called the *yôḇēl,* and in verses 10–13 the year that it announced was thus designated the "year of the *yôḇēl."* It is generally thought that this is the year *following* the seventh sabbath year, i.e., the fiftieth year by our figures. This would mean, however, that at the end of every seventh sabbath of years, Israel would have two successive years of a special character—the sabbatical year, and then the Year of Jubilee—and it is highly unlikely that this could have been the case. Such a position overlooks the fact that verse 8, unlike 23:15, does not state that the counting was to begin *after* a particular date. In 23:15, the counting began "from the day after the Sabbath," whereas 25:8 only commanded Israel to "count off seven sabbaths of years." This therefore means that the sabbatical year on which the counting began was the first of the fifty years spoken of (vv. 10–11), and the seventh sabbatical year would then be the fiftieth year counted. In conformity to this, verses 11–12 clearly describe the Year of Jubilee as a sabbath year.

---

[44]The laws of Exodus 21:2–6 and Deuteronomy 15:12–18 have no connection with the sabbatical year, and the emancipation reported in Jeremiah 34:8–22 was a special measure taken in a time of dire need as a futile attempt to appease the Lord.

[45]Cf. NEB of verse 9. The author regards the translation "trumpet," which appears in the KJV, RSV, and NIV, as "less than correct."

In the regulations pertaining to the Year of Jubilee, which is undoubtedly equivalent to the "year of freedom" spoken of in Ezekiel 46:17, we are presented with the further unfolding of the thought that was fundamental to Israel's perspective: Canaan was the Lord's possession, and the people were only tenants (v. 23). This means that, in Israel, there could be no sale of immovable property in the modern Western sense. Purchase of such property was actually tantamount to assuming a lease for a maximum of forty-nine years, and the seller always retained the right to cancel the purchase by settling with the buyer on the amount of money that was still payable (this was naturally done in accordance with the original purchase price), taking into account in this the number of years that the buyer had made use of the property. If the seller was either incapable or undesirous of making use of this right of redemption, the property nevertheless returned to his possession automatically in the next Year of Jubilee. The sale of a field was therefore actually nothing more than the sale of a certain number of its harvests (vv. 13–18, 23–28). Similarly, the sale of a house was equivalent to renting it for a specified period of time (vv. 29–34). It was inevitable that this arrangement would have an effect on the purchase price of such property. More importantly, however, it was thereby made impossible to "add house to house and join field to field" (Isa. 5:8; Mic. 2:2), and both large landownership and pauperism were therefore prevented to some degree. The character and structure of the life of the Lord's people had to be distinct from that of the other nations not only religiously, but also socially.

Some have unjustly argued that the regulations for the Year of Jubilee were motivated by a communistic line of thought, or at least that they were an attempt to create a system somewhere between communism and private property ownership.[46] The law here was based on religious rather than socio-economic concerns (see above), however, and its consequence was not merely the unhindered preservation of private property, but also the eradication of all social decay. The Israelites were repeatedly given the opportunity to begin anew, and the impoverished were enabled to maintain themselves in society.

Besides the selling of immovable property, the Israelites had previously also, like the entire ancient world, taken part in the selling of human beings in situations of debt (2 Kings 4:1; Neh. 5:5; Isa. 50:1; Amos 2:6; 8:6; Matt. 18:25). This was henceforth made unlawful, however, since every Israelite was a servant (*'ebed,* literally, "slave") of the Lord (v. 42) and could therefore never become the possession of another (vv. 35–55).

---

[46]Eerdmans, *Alttestamentliche Studien* IV, p. 126.

25:8–13 *" 'Count off seven sabbaths of years—seven times seven years—so that the seven sabbaths of years amount to a period of forty-nine years. Then have the trumpet sounded everywhere on the tenth day of the seventh month; on the Day of Atonement sound the trumpet throughout your land. Consecrate the fiftieth year and proclaim liberty throughout the land to all its inhabitants. It shall be a jubilee for you; each one of you is to return to his family property and each to his own clan. The fiftieth year shall be a jubilee for you; do not sow and do not reap what grows of itself or harvest the untended vines. For it is a jubilee and is to be holy for you; eat only what is taken directly from the fields.*

" 'In this Year of Jubilee everyone is to return to his own property.' "

A. General requirements (25:8–13)

The law concerning the Year of Jubilee, which appears here only in the Pentateuch (Num. 36:4 assumes that it is in force), begins by giving a precise specification of the date when this most important year in the social and economic life of Israel was to begin. The year always coincided with the seventh sabbatical year, and it was inaugurated by the sounding of the ram's horn (see above; also see the comment on 23:23–25) on the Day of Atonement, i.e., the tenth day of the seventh month (Tishri). Just as the Day of Atonement, the final day of the period that opened the new year, signified the renewal of Israel's spiritual and ethical life, the Year of Jubilee marked the renewal of its social relationships. At this time, the Lord "makes all things new": the land was given back to its original owners, houses were reclaimed by their former occupants, and persons sold as slaves returned to their families. Previous inequities were set right and previous adversities were overcome. The requirement of verse 10 that "each of you is to return to his family property" is repeated in verse 13, and the fact that the latter verse serves as a superscription for the following series of regulations indicates how important the lawgiver considered this requirement. Both farmland and vineyard also experienced this renewal, for since this was their sabbath year, they were left fallow and their food could be eaten not only by their owner, but also by other persons and animals (v. 11). In the Year of Jubilee, the Israelites were once again taught that they were to live in faith that the Lord would satisfy their needs (cf. Exod. 16:17–30).

25:14–19 *" 'If you sell land to one of your countrymen or buy any from him, do not take advantage of each other. You are to buy from your countryman on the basis of the number of years since the Jubilee. And he is to sell to you on the basis of the number of years left for harvesting crops. When the years are many, you are to increase the price, and when the years are few, you are to decrease the price,* *because what he is really selling you is the number of crops. Do not take advantage of each other, but fear your God. I am the Lord your God.*

"'Follow my decrees and be careful to obey my laws, and you will live safely in the land. Then the land will yield its fruit, and you will eat your fill and live there in safety.'"

B. *Purchase and sale of land* (25:14–19)

The regulations concerning land transactions open by stating that fellow Israelites were to make no attempt to "take advantage of each other" (i.e., to charge too much or offer too little), the same requirement that was made in 19:33 with respect to aliens.[47] The people had to refrain from any endeavor to exploit the Year of Jubilee for their own profit. Verse 17 therefore repeats this fundamental principle together with a warning that the Lord, who hears and sees everything, would not allow such procedures to go unpunished (cf. 19:13–14). The land was given to the Israelites for the satisfaction of their needs and as a safe place of residence, but they would only be able to look forward to these gifts of divine grace if they lived in unconditional obedience to the Lord's requirements (vv. 18–19). The possibility that land could be sold to a member of another nation is not even presented in these verses, this forming an indication of the lack of complexity in the social relationships of that time. The price of land was to be settled by mutual agreement, and since what was actually being sold was not the land itself, but a number of crops, the decisive factor in this was to be the number of years, and thus harvests, remaining until the next Year of Jubilee (v. 16). In such a transaction, the fear of God was to compel both buyer and seller to respect one another's legitimate interests (v. 17).

25:20–22 *"'You may ask, "What will we eat in the seventh year if we do not plant or harvest our crops?" I will send you such a blessing in the sixth year that the land will yield enough for three years. While you plant during the eighth year, you will eat from the old crop and will continue to eat from it until the harvest of the ninth year comes in.'"*

C. *A reflection on the sabbatical year* (25:20–22)

These verses are included in response to an objection against the institution of the sabbatical year that might have been made by those who trusted solely in worldly calculation. Because of this, we should have expected

---

[47]Unlike the NIV, the author translates 19:33 and 25:14 similarly. Cf. RSV.

them to appear following verse 7, but it is impossible that they could have been transposed to their present position accidentally. Following Rashi, many have pointed out that verses 20–22 presuppose a different chronological system than verses 1–7. The latter verses assume that the year began in the autumn, for sowing (November/December) and reaping (April/May) fall in the same year (vv. 4–5), while the harvest would come at the opening of the following year if the year were to begin in the spring. In contrast to this, verses 20–22 presuppose a year that began in the spring. Since neither sowing nor harvesting could take place in the seventh year, fear could arise that there would be insufficient food (v. 20). In answer to this, it is stated that the harvest of the sixth year would be so abundant that it would last for three years. Since planting could only be resumed in the eighth year (November/December) and the next harvest would therefore not come until the ninth year (April/May), the harvest of the sixth year would have to be sufficient until this time.

This change in chronology indicates that verses 20–22 must date from a later time than 1–7, for the shifting of New Year's Day from autumn to spring—the latter system also influenced the festival calendar in chapter 23—took place some time in the future (perhaps under Solomon).[48] These verses must therefore have been inserted at a time when this transfer of the beginning of the year to the spring created great difficulties with respect to the sabbatical year. Rather than being shown any human response to these difficulties, the Israelites were called to place their faith and trust in the Creator's power to make a single harvest so abundant that it would furnish more than enough food for the intervening years. One who was anxious thought exclusively of the seventh year, forgetting that land that had not been farmed for an entire year became rock hard and would likely produce only a small crop, even if it was plowed over more than once. The Lord's fatherly care sees further than such anxiety, however, and He would make the crop of the sixth year last until the resumption of normal harvesting in the ninth year.

25:23–28 *"'The land must not be sold permanently, because the land is mine and you are but aliens and my tenants. Throughout the country that you hold as a possession, you must provide for the redemption of the land.*

"'If one of your countrymen becomes poor and sells some of his property, his nearest relative is to come and redeem what his countryman has sold. If, however, a man has no one to redeem it for him but he himself prospers and acquires sufficient means to redeem it, he is to determine the value for the years since he sold it and refund the balance to the man to whom he sold it; he can then go back to his

---

[48]See Heinisch, *Das Buch Leviticus,* pp. 8–10.

255

own property. But if he does not acquire the means to repay him, what he sold will remain in the possession of the buyer until the Year of Jubilee. It will be returned in the Jubilee, and he can then go back to his property.'"

D. *Redemption of land* (25:23–28)

Whereas verses 13–19 dealt with the selling of landed property, verses 23–28 are concerned with the manner in which land could be returned to the possession of the seller. In connection with this, the reason is first given why there could properly speaking be no actual sale of land. The Lord declared that "the land is mine," and the people therefore had only the rights of tenants (v. 23). Because of this, only the crops, and not the land itself, could become an object of trade. Unless two parties preferred to allow the transaction to come to an end automatically with the arrival of the next Year of Jubilee, the seller always retained the right to cancel the sale by redemption of the property, either through his own means or with the help of a close relative (cf. Jer. 32:8–12). When this was done, the price that was paid to redeem the land was determined in the same manner as the original purchase price (v. 16), i.e., the harvests that the buyer had obtained from it were considered as money already returned by the seller. If the seller elected to make use of the right of redemption, the buyer could not refuse to accept a modest offer, for harvest always remained an uncertain affair, and the coming of the next Year of Jubilee erased the need for any redemption money at all. It is likely that the right of redemption was used more often than not. The story of Naboth (1 Kings 21) illustrates how attached the Israelites were to their land, and Ruth's experience reveals that relatives did not easily evade their moral duty to redeem property. Because of this, verse 25 assumes that a person could be induced to sell his land only if he became poor. Numbers 36 also bears clear witness to the degree of attachment that the people felt toward their land.

25:29–34 *"'If a man sells a house in a walled city, he retains the right of redemption a full year after its sale. During that time he may redeem it. If it is not redeemed before a full year has passed, the house in the walled city shall belong permanently to the buyer and his descendants. It is not to be returned in the Jubilee. But houses in villages without walls around them are to be considered as open country. They can be redeemed, and they are to be returned in the Jubilee.*

"'The Levites always have the right to redeem their houses in the Levitical towns, which they possess. So the property of the Levites is redeemable—that is, a house sold in any town they hold—and is to be returned in the Jubilee, because the houses in the towns of the Levites are their property among the Israelites. But the pastureland belonging to their towns must not be sold; it is their permanent possession.'"

E. *Redemption of houses* (25:29–34)

A distinction is here made between houses in walled cities and houses in unwalled villages. The former could be sold and were thus permitted to change ownership, and the only restriction was that for twelve months the seller retained the right to buy the house back. It is not stated whether, in this situation, the number of months that the buyer had resided in the house was given a monetary value and thus subtracted from the redemption price, but on the basis of the preceding verses this is quite probable. In any case, the sale of a house in a walled city was not canceled in the Year of Jubilee (vv. 29–30). Houses in villages, however, were considered to belong with the land, since they were indispensable for the purposes of agriculture. These therefore were treated in the same manner as landed property; the right of redemption was always available to the seller, and if this right was not made use of, such a house was nevertheless given back in the next Year of Jubilee (v. 31). A further distinction must be made with regard to houses that were the property of Levites. These could never be sold in perpetuity, even if they were located in walled cities, for they were at all times redeemable and returned to the seller automatically in the next Year of Jubilee (vv. 32–33). Such houses, at least if they were located in the Levitical towns (the present verses thus assume the existence of these, and no other type of Levitical property is spoken of), therefore constituted an exceptional category. The same was the case with the landed property of a Levitical town. Since this belonged, not to an individual, but to the community of Levites that resided there, it could at no time become an object of sale (v. 34).

25:35–38 *"'If one of your countrymen becomes poor and is unable to support himself among you, help him as you would an alien or a temporary resident, so he can continue to live among you. Do not take interest of any kind from him, but fear your God, so that your countryman may continue to live among you. You must not lend him money at interest or sell him food at a profit. I am the* Lord *your God, who brought you out of Egypt to give you the land of Canaan and to be your God.'"*

F. *Communal obligations* (25:35–38)

Israel was never to regard its national unity as a matter of chance. Its members constituted an extended family, and therefore they were always to be ready to come to each other's assistance. If someone began to fall into poverty and became "unable to support himself" (the Hebrew literally means "his hand wavers"), this process was to be thwarted by his neighbors (among whom he lived, v. 35), who were to offer their help in order to make life possible for such a person. The Israelites had to give the same assistance to one of their countrymen as they would to ''an alien or a temporary resident'' (the emended reading in v. 35). Rashi and Ibn Ezra interpret this to mean that an impoverished person was to be helped even if he was an alien or a temporary resident, but this cannot be correct, since such a person was not a ''countryman'' (the Hebrew term here literally means ''brother''; cf. Deut. 24:14). The meaning is rather that an impoverished Israelite was to become the object of no less love than was shown to an alien *(gēr,* see discussion on 16:29)—a person who, although he was of foreign extraction, had a claim to certain rights (Exod. 22:21; 23:9; Deut. 10:18–19; 14:29; 16:11–12; 24:14, 19–22)—or to a temporary resident who enjoyed the kind hospitality of an Israelite (Lev. 22:10; 25:40). Israel's responsibilities here were thus similar to those of the diaconal ministry of the church. A brother Israelite could not be allowed to live the life of a pauper (see 2 Kings 4:1, however), but was to be provided with support and employment. Another form of aid could be the loaning of money or of food, but in this case no interest could be charged (elsewhere in the Near East this could be thirty percent or higher[49]), nor could a greater amount be demanded in return. Under no condition was a person to profit from the poverty of one of his countrymen. The Lord had no desire to remain the God of anyone who acted in such a manner, for this would be in total conflict with what He had purposed in delivering Israel from Egypt.

25:39–46 *''If one of your countrymen becomes poor among you and sells himself to you, do not make him work as a slave. He is to be treated as a hired worker or a temporary resident among you; he is to work for you until the Year of Jubilee. Then he and his children are to be released, and he will go back to his own clan and to the property of his forefathers. Because the Israelites are my servants, whom I brought out of Egypt, they must not be sold as slaves. Do not rule over them ruthlessly, but fear your God.*

''Your male and female slaves are to come from the nations around you; from them you may buy slaves. You may also buy some of the temporary residents living among you and members of their clans born in your country, and they will become your property. You can will them to your children as inherited property and can make them slaves for life, but you must not rule over your fellow Israelites ruthlessly.' ''

G. *Prohibition of Israelite enslavement* (25:39–46)

It has already been observed (p. 252) that in Israel, as throughout the entire ancient world, a person would sometimes sell himself to his creditor

---

[49] See my commentary, *Ezra en Nehemiah,* p. 190.

in order to relieve his indebtedness. Whereas in all other nations such a "sale" reduced the person to the status of a slave, this was never to be the case in Israel. Exodus 21:1–4 established rules that ensured the personal freedom of a "Hebrew," i.e., an Israelite and his nearest kin, for it is there directed that, with a few exceptions, the servitude that resulted from a transaction of this nature could last no longer than six years. After this length of time, the person was to be allowed to depart in freedom, with no payment being demanded of him (see also Deut. 15:12–18).

The lawgiver now returns to this matter. Although verse 39 speaks of an Israelite who "becomes poor . . . and sells himself," it is equally possible to translate this as "is sold" (cf. KJV) and regard it as a reference to the compulsory sale of an indebted person (2 Kings 4:1; Neh. 5:5; Isa. 50:1; Amos 2:6; 8:6; Matt. 18:25). It is not likely that this is the meaning, however, for it is evident from the preceding verses that the lawgiver would not have permitted the Israelites such a right with respect to their countrymen.

The law of Leviticus narrows the reference of this prohibition to a certain degree, for whereas Exodus 21:1–4 speaks of a "Hebrew servant," these regulations applied only to Israelites.[50] The Israelite had a higher status than the Hebrew and could under no condition be subjected to slavery. If he sold himself, he could descend only to the rank of a hired worker or temporary resident, and such persons were naturally assigned other work than a slave. In other words, an Israelite could sell only his capacity for work, but not his body. If he did this, the integrity of his family had to be preserved; an unmarried man therefore became a hired worker, and a married man, a temporary resident. In all cases, the arrival of the next Year of Jubilee automatically put an end to the Israelite's servitude, and he then resumed his position within his clan as a free man and had his family property restored to him (vv. 39–41). Verse 42 states the reason for these requirements with unmistakable clarity. Every Israelite was the Lord's *'ebed* and could therefore never become the *'ebed* of a fellow Israelite, since the latter was himself an *'ebed* of the Lord. In this verse, the first occurrence of *'ebed* is translated as "servant" and the second as "slave" (but cf. NEB), but this is done only because the notion of being the Lord's "slave" is somewhat offensive to our way of thinking. For us, God is "our Father," whereas for Israel He was "the Lord" *('ādôn)*. Since the Israelite was a slave only in name, he could not be treated as a slave and ruled over "ruthlessly"(vv. 43, 46), as the Egyptians had done (Exod. 1:13–14). The fear of God at all times had to restrain a master from dealing with his Israelite servant in this fashion (v. 43).

---

[50]See my book, *Gods Woord*², p. 314.

Like the other nations of the ancient world, however, Israel could not do without slaves altogether. These could be bought only from the surrounding nations or from temporary residents of foreign origin and their clans (see Exod. 12:49), whether they were born within or outside of Canaan. The regulations of Leviticus 25 did not apply to such persons; they had permanently lost their freedom and become the property of someone else, and they therefore could be inherited like other possessions. Verse 46 allows the Israelites to "make them slaves for life." Nevertheless, it is evident from Exodus 21:20–26 and Deuteronomy 23:15–16 that Israel's law offered protection even to the slave, and the Israelites were thus far beyond the other nations of antiquity also in this respect.

25:47–55 *"'If an alien or a temporary resident among you becomes rich and one of your countrymen becomes poor and sells himself to the alien living among you or to a member of the alien's clan, he retains the right of redemption after he has sold himself. One of his relatives may redeem him: An uncle or a cousin or any blood relative in his clan may redeem him. Or if he prospers, he may redeem himself. He and his buyer are to count the time from the year he sold himself up to the Year of Jubilee. The price for his release is to be based on the rate paid to a hired man for that number of years. If many years remain, he must pay for his redemption a larger share of the price paid for him. If only a few years remain until the Year of Jubilee, he is to compute that and pay for his redemption accordingly. He is to be treated as a man hired from year to year; you must see to it that his owner does not rule over him ruthlessly.*

"'Even if he is not redeemed in any of these ways, he and his children are to be released in the Year of Jubilee, for the Israelites belong to me as servants. They are my servants, whom I brought out of Egypt. I am the LORD your God.'"

H. *Prohibition of enslavement to foreigners* (25:47–55)

An Israelite who had sold himself to one of his countrymen remained in bondage until his release in the next Year of Jubilee, but if a person was compelled to sell himself to an alien or a temporary resident in Canaan, all possible action had to be taken in order to secure his redemption and make his time of servitude as brief as possible, even though what he had actually sold was not himself, but only his capacity for work. Because of this, the Israelite was to be regarded as a hired worker for the duration of his servitude, and he could therefore not be treated "ruthlessly." In addition, the negotiations concerning his redemption had to carefully take into account the monetary equivalent of the work he had performed as a servant, and this sum then had to be deducted from the price for which he sold himself into bondage. The possibility was naturally left open that the servant's own work would enable him to purchase his release (v. 49), and this indicates that such an Israelite occupied a relatively independent position. Verse 53 furthermore makes evident that close observation of the treatment that he received during his time of servitude was assumed on the part of his fellow Israelites, a telling example of the communal awareness that was to prevail within Israel. If it had not been possible to redeem the Israelite, the arrival of the next Year of Jubilee nevertheless brought the release of both him and his family (among whom he had been able to remain living, v. 54).

The law of Leviticus 25 ends with a reminder that Israel as a whole, and each individual Israelite in particular, was the Lord's servant and, as such, His inalienable possession (v. 55). This was the fundamental religious concept that determined the social regulations of this chapter, just as Israel's cultic laws had social implications.

Part Eight

Blessings and Punishments
(26:1–46)

Leviticus 26 is one of the most moving chapters, not only in the Book of Leviticus and the Pentateuch as a whole, but in the entire Old Testament revelation. In looking toward the future, the Lord laments the fact that He soon might be compelled to chastise His people. If they, in utter ungratefulness, should sinfully reject the love that He had shown to them, He would have no choice but to cause them to feel the destructive weight of His divine indignation, even as this love continued to reach out to them. As a single, poignant lament of divine love, the chapter also contains a warning and a prayer that the Israelites would not have to undergo such punishment.

The Great Commandment
(26:1–2)

26:1–2 *"'Do not make idols or set up an image or a sacred stone for yourselves, and do not place a carved stone in your land to bow down before it. I am the Lord your God.*

"'Observe my Sabbaths and have reverence for my sanctuary. I am the Lord.'"

The opening verses state the central thought that was to guide Israel's life if it desired to be worthy of the Lord's blessing and to fully enjoy the riches that were offered to it in the covenant. The Israelites were never to waver in their conviction that the Lord alone had the right to be called God. Not even the least notice could therefore be given to any other gods or idols beside Him, the latter being referred to here (as in 19:4) as "nonentities" in order to indicate that they were nothing more than a product of the darkened human understanding. There was then also no place for anything related to the worship of such nonentities: "images," a fruit of the notion that God belonged to this world (cf. Deut. 4:15–19), and "sacred stones" *(maṣṣēḇâ[h])* or standing pillars (cf. RSV, NEB; Exod. 23:24; 34:13; Deut. 7:5), a customary object in Baal worship that implied that God was tied to a specific location, with His divine power, as it were, enclosed in a stone. The worship of stones with emblems[1] is also forbidden, but the meaning of the Hebrew expression used here *('eḇen maśkît)* is not entirely clear. The word *maśkît* appears also in Numbers 33:52 (NIV, "carved images"), where it is mentioned along with idols and high places in connection with the religions of the Canaanites.[2] "Sculpted stone" has been proposed as a translation,[3] but this seems to me to be in error. I am rather inclined to regard *'eḇen maśkît* as a reference to boundary stones (these have been discovered also in the plain of the Tigris and Euphrates) on which various emblems of gods and demons had been engraved. The protection of landed property was entrusted to such deities, and the owner therefore conferred on them a variety of divine honors. Israel's worship could be directed to no one other than the Lord, however. Another manner in which this was made completely clear was through Israel's commitment to keep the Lord's Sabbaths from week to week in accordance with the prescribed regulations. As the only religious holiday that was the exclusive possession of Israel, the Sabbath was set apart from normal daily pursuits and sanctified by its own special offerings. Regular observance of the Sabbath was thus an essential part of the Israelites' covenant life (cf. Exod. 31:12–17).

Israel's Obedience and the Lord's Blessing (26:3–13)

26:3–13 *"'If you follow my decrees and are careful to obey my commands, I will send you rain in its season, and the ground will yield its crops and the trees of the field their fruit. Your threshing will continue until grape harvest and the grape harvest will continue until planting, and you will eat all the food you want and live in safety in your land.*

"'I will grant peace in the land, and you will lie down and no one will make you

---

[1]The author's translation in 26:1, where the NIV has "carved stones." RSV and NEB, "figured stones."

[2]Siphra, remarkably enough, interprets this as a prohibition against covering an area outside the central sanctuary with stones in order to serve as a place where one could prostrate himself in worship of the Lord.

[3]E.G., Edelkoort in Numbers 33:52. Cf. NIV, "carved stone."

afraid. I will remove savage beasts from the land, and the sword will not pass through your country. You will pursue your enemies, and they will fall by the sword before you. Five of you will chase a hundred, and a hundred of you will chase ten thousand, and your enemies will fall by the sword before you.

" 'I will look on you with favor and make you fruitful and increase your numbers, and I will keep my covenant with you. You will still be eating last year's harvest when you will have to move it out to make room for the new. I will put my dwelling place among you, and I will not abhor you. I will walk among you and be your God, and you will be my people. I am the LORD your God, who brought you out of Egypt so that you would no longer be slaves to the Egyptians; I broke the bars of your yoke and enabled you to walk with heads held high.' "

After this brief outline of what the Lord asked of Israel in the covenant, a description is given of the rich blessings that the people would share if they lived a life of complete obedience to the Lord's commandments. The first blessing spoken of is rain (vv. 3–4), this being the *sine qua non* for life in Canaan. Because of the presence of the Nile, rain was not essential in Egypt, but without rain, Canaan would become a dead land with rock hard ground (1 Kings 17:1). The Lord thus promised to send "rain in its season," and the writer here uses a word *(gešem)* that indicates an abundance of rain. The Lord therefore would not be stingy in His blessing, and the rain would be given at the appropriate time. Gentle early rains would fall in October and November and make the land ready for plowing and sowing; strong winter storms would come from mid-December to mid-March in order to saturate the ground, filling the wells and making the springs overflow; and the later rains of April would cause the ears of grain and the fruit to swell and enable the fields to endure the heat of summer. The granting of the necessary rain at the proper time would allow the land to produce to its fullest capacity and yield an abundant harvest (Deut. 11:14; Jer. 5:24; Hos. 6:3), whereas a failure of the rains meant famine and misery. If Israel obeyed the Lord's commands, the grain would be so plentiful (cf. Amos 9:13) that the threshing and harvest of April and May, the proverbial time of rejoicing (e.g., Ps. 4:7; Isa. 9:3), would continue until the grape harvest in August and September, when the joyful Feast of Tabernacles was celebrated (Deut. 16:13–14; Judg. 21:19–21; 1 Kings 8:2; 12:32); and the grape harvest would likewise continue until the time of planting that began after the early rains. The people would then also live in the land "in safety"[4] (literally, "in confidence," cf. 25:19), without anxiety about the satisfaction of their daily needs.

Besides abundant harvests, there would also be no one to plunder or

---

[4]The author translates this as "without concern."

destroy what the Israelites possessed (v. 6). Although Canaan was constantly coveted by the inhabitants of the desert, since its rich agricultural land provided what they could not obtain in the steppe (e.g., Judges 6), and it sometimes became the battlefield of nations—the armies of Egypt and Mesopotamia met there more than once—the promise is given that there would be no enemies in the land. Canaan would also remain free of the savage animals that constituted a second source of disaster in times of war (Exod. 23:29; 2 Kings 17:15; Isa. 35:9). Such a time of abundance, peace, and safety, in which no one had any reason to be afraid (v. 6), would provide the ideal setting for the coming King of Israel (Isa. 17:2; Mic. 4:4). If war nevertheless arose, the Israelites would have only to pursue their enemies, for the latter would inexplicably be weakened and the sword would accomplish its destructive purposes almost on its own (vv. 7–8, cf. Deut. 32:30; Josh. 23:10; Isa. 30:17; also Judg. 7:22).

A further feature in this vision of the future is the manifestation of God's favor in the prolific growth of Israel into a great nation, as had been foretold in the covenant promise of Genesis 12:2. In a series of historical blessings, the Lord "keeps" (literally, "causes to stand" or "take shape") His covenant with Israel, so that everyone could see and be assured that He makes good on His promises (v. 9). In spite of this growth in population, there would always be a plentiful supply of food; the old harvest would not yet have been consumed when room had to be made for the abundance of the new (v. 10). This prosperity, moreover, would not be something transitory, for the Lord would make His "dwelling place" (or "tabernacle," cf. NIV margin; John 1:14) with the Israelites and, as He had done before in the garden of Eden, would walk among them, a sign of perfect harmony and order (vv. 11–12). The goal that had been set during the time of Moses would thus become reality: the Lord would be Israel's God, and Israel, the Lord's people (v. 12; Exod. 6:7; 25:8; 29:45–46), and the Lord would then have no reason to "abhor" the people of Israel (literally, "treat as something objectionable"; see also vv. 15, 30, 43–44; Jer. 14:19).

In order that Israel might know that this picture of the future, however all-surpassing it may seem, could indeed become reality, the description closes with a reminder that the Lord, the author of this vision, is the same God who performed unbelievable feats during the time of bondage in Egypt. He transformed the Israelites from an enslaved into a free nation and enabled them to walk "with heads held high" by breaking the "bars of [the] yoke" that had been placed on their necks as if they were beasts of burden (cf. Isa. 9:4; 10:27; 14:25). If Israel did not subject itself to another yoke by worshiping the "nonentities" spoken of in verse 1, it could therefore enjoy the freedom that belonged to the children of God.

Israel's Disobedience and the Lord's Punishment
(26:14–39)

26:14–15 *" 'But if you will not listen to me and carry out all these commands, and if you reject my decrees and abhor my laws and fail to carry out all my commands and so violate my covenant.' "*

After this vision of the Lord's blessing, a picture is drawn of the divine wrath that could also meet Israel in the future. Blessing and curse were both intimately bound up with the actions of the people. The Lord took the first step of addressing the Israelites in order to make known His will and to disclose the wealth of blessings that would be theirs if they obeyed His law. Israel was then left to decide in complete freedom whether or not it would listen and comply with the Lord's commandments. There was no choice other than this either/or. Failure to listen would be a disdainful rejection of the law as something not worthy of notice, an aloofness that signified abhorrence, and it was therefore tantamount to a violation of the covenant (v. 15). The Lord called the latter "my covenant" because He, and not Israel, was its initiator, He, and not Israel, its owner. The Israelites were therefore neither permitted nor able to deal with this covenant as they pleased, for they had no choice but to either conform to its demands or "violate" it (literally, "invalidate" it, deprive it of its meaning).

If Israel would decide to respond in such a manner, it would have only to await its fate. A description of the distress and misery that would ensue is then given which, in distinction from the more general depiction of the blessings of obedience, goes into great detail. In this description it becomes evident that, on the one hand, the Lord would unleash such a degree of misery only with reluctance (as appears from the repetition of the pronoun *I* in the Hebrew text of vv. 16, 24, 28, 32),[5] and on the other hand, that He nevertheless has firmly resolved not to remain passive in the face of such disdain for the covenant (see vv. 14, 18, 21, 23, 27). It is also made clear that if the people persisted in their obstinacy, the situation would only go from bad to worse, and exile would finally become inevitable. Nevertheless, in all of these punishments the Lord holds fast to His saving purposes. His punishments are not an end, but only a means, for through them the Lord continues to speak (vv. 18, 21, 23, 27) and to summon Israel to repentance: "Return, faithless people; I will cure you of backsliding" (Jer. 3:22).

---

[5]The author translates "I, yes I" in these verses, whereas the NIV renders this as "I myself" in verses 24 and 32. Cf. KJV in verse 28, "I, even I."

26:16–17 *"'Then I will do this to you: I will bring upon you sudden terror, wasting diseases and fever that will destroy your sight and drain away your life. You will plant seed in vain, because your enemies will eat it. I will set my face against you so that you will be defeated by your enemies; those who hate you will rule over you, and you will flee even when no one is pursuing you.'"*

The list of punishments begins with sickness: "wasting diseases" and "fever" (see also Matt. 8:14–15; John 4:52). These still remain the greatest plagues in the lands of Syria and Palestine, and although the Lord had already protected the Israelites against them (Exod. 15:26; 23:25), they would now cause their life to waste away (cf. Deut. 28:22, 59–61). These diseases would be made all the worse by the fact that the food that the people planted would be stolen by their enemies. The latter would attack from all sides, since Israel's army, having lost courage because the Lord had turned against them (cf. 17:10; 20:3, 5–6), could offer no resistance and would take flight even when there was no reason to do so (see Judg. 6:2).

26:18–20 *"'If after all this you will not listen to me, I will punish you for your sins seven times over. I will break down your stubborn pride and make the sky above you like iron and the ground beneath you like bronze. Your strength will be spent in vain, because your soil will not yield its crops, nor will the trees of the land yield their fruit.'"*

Continued failure to listen would result in punishment seven times more severe. This "seven" is not to be understood in an arithmetic sense, for as the Semitic number of totality (cf. Deut. 28:7, 25; Ps. 79:12), it rather indicates punishment in full measure. Israel's self-assurance, based on the fertility of the land and the prosperity that it provided (cf. Deut. 8:11–18), would be undermined by the withholding of the rain and all of the following fatal consequences (Deut. 11:17; 28:23–24; 1 Kings 18). Human effort would then be of no avail; the land would remain parched and smitten by dust storms, and the fruit trees barren (Jer. 14:2–6; Joel 1:16–20; Amos 4:7), and the hunger and thirst that ensued would bring all types of disease in their wake.

26:21–22 *"'If you remain hostile toward me and refuse to listen to me, I will multiply your afflictions seven times over, as your sins deserve. I will send wild animals against you, and they will rob you of your children, destroy your cattle and make you so few in number that your roads will be deserted.'"*

Conditions would grow worse if the people still persisted in their hostility. Finding no more food in the fields, savage animals would roam about,

267

preying on livestock, children, and even adults, and they would eventually become so dominant that no one would dare to leave his dwelling (2 Kings 17:25–26; Ezek. 14:15; Zeph. 3:6).

26:23–26 *"'If in spite of these things you do not accept my correction but continue to be hostile toward me, I myself will be hostile toward you and will afflict you for your sins seven times over. And I will bring the sword upon you to avenge the breaking of the covenant. When you withdraw into your cities, I will send a plague among you, and you will be given into enemy hands. When I cut off your supply of bread, ten women will be able to bake your bread in one oven, and they will dole out the bread by weight. You will eat, but you will not be satisfied.'"*

If this still did not lead to repentance, the Israelites would be afflicted by war and plague, captivity and enslavement, and also famine. A sword would be sent "to avenge the breaking of the covenant," i.e., the covenant that Israel had sought to back out of would rise against it by way of the sword wielded by its enemies. When the people took flight to the cities in an attempt to find safety behind their walls (Jer. 4:5; 35:11), the crowding together would make them victim to an outbreak of pestilence that would kill both human beings and animals (Exod. 9:3; Jer. 24:10; Amos 4:10) and would finally compel them to surrender (Jer. 21:6–7; Ezek. 5:12) and to submit to enslavement, the dishonoring of their women, or even a worse fate (2 Kings 15:16; Isa. 13:16; Hos. 10:14; Amos 1:13). Since everything would then have been laid waste (Deut. 20:19–20; Judg. 6:4; 9:45; 2 Kings 3:19, 25), a famine of such severity would break out that, whereas every family had formerly needed its own oven, a single oven would now be more than sufficient for ten families. Bread, which as the "staff of life" was essential to survival, would be so scarce (Ps. 105:16; Isa. 3:1; Ezek. 4:16–17; 5:16; 14:13) that each individual would receive only a very small, carefully weighed out portion that would leave his hunger unsatisfied (Hos. 4:10; Mic. 6:14).

26:27–33 *"'If in spite of this you still do not listen to me but continue to be hostile toward me, then in my anger I will be hostile toward you, and I myself will punish you for your sins seven times over. You will eat the flesh of your sons and the flesh of your daughters. I will destroy your high places, cut down your incense altars and pile your dead bodies on the lifeless forms of your idols, and I will abhor you. I will turn your cities into ruins and lay waste your sanctuaries, and I will take no delight in the pleasing aroma of your offerings. I will lay waste the land, so that your enemies who live there will be appalled. I will scatter you among the nations and will draw out my sword and pursue you. Your land will be laid waste, and your cities will lie in ruins.'"*

Israel's hostility toward the Lord continues in spite of all this, and as a result He now opposes them in "anger."[6] The famine would lead to the worst horror imaginable: parents eating the flesh of their children (v. 29; Deut. 28:53–57; 2 Kings 6:28–29; Jer. 19:9; Lam. 2:20; 4:10; Ezek. 5:10; also see Josephus' account of the fall of Jerusalem in A.D. 70, *War* VI 4). In order to break the Israelites' opposition to the covenant once and for all, an end would be made of all the cultic places and objects where they had sought support: the "high places," where Baal and Ashtoreth were worshiped, and the "incense altars" (this was once incorrectly translated as "solar columns"[7]) where divine honor was conferred on them. These places that had been sacred to Israel would now be filled with corpses, both those of the people who came to give expression to their needs but instead met their death, and those of the gods to whom they came.[8] The word applied to the latter in verse 30, *gillûlîm,* which is used no fewer than thirty-nine times by the prophet Ezekiel, draws a parallel between human excrement and the form of the idol images and is the most contemptuous term in the Hebrew language.[9]

It therefore seems that every connection between the Lord and Israel has been severed. The general devastation would level all of the sanctuaries and cities, and the people would therefore be prevented from either presenting their offerings (note that, in contrast to the qualification *"my* sanctuary" in v. 2, v. 31 has *"your* sanctuaries") or preserving their lives. In performing this destruction Himself, the Lord demonstrates once again that He is utterly different from the other "gods." They could not exist without temples, worshipers, and offerings, but He would always remain God regardless of all such things. The desolation would be so total that, even Israel's enemies, although they had been the means by which God had executed His vengeance, would be appalled (v. 32). The Lord would therefore finally put an end to the national existence of Israel. The people would be scattered *(zārâ[h])* like grain at threshing time (Jer. 31:10; 49:32, 36; Ezek. 12:14–15; 20:23) and would leave behind them a completely wasted land, precisely the opposite of what it had been when they took possession of it (Deut. 8:7). Even along the way to captivity the Lord's anger would not leave the Israelites in peace, for He would pursue them with the sword in order to prevent anyone from returning (v. 33; Ezek. 5:2, 12; 12:14; 21:8–12).

---

[6]The author translates this as "fury"; cf. KJV, RSV.

[7]See my commentary, *Ezechiël,* p. 83.

[8]In verse 30 of the NIV, "dead bodies" and "lifeless forms" are translations of the same Hebrew term, which literally means "corpse" (cf. KJV and RSV).

[9]See my commentary, *Ezechiël,* p. 84.

26:34–39 *" 'Then the land will enjoy its sabbath years all the time that it lies desolate and you are in the country of your enemies; then the land will rest and enjoy its sabbaths. All the time that it lies desolate, the land will have the rest it did not have during the sabbaths you lived in it.*

" 'As for those of you who are left, I will make their hearts so fearful in the lands of their enemies that the sound of a wind-blown leaf will put them to flight. They will run as though fleeing from the sword, and they will fall, even though no one is pursuing them. They will stumble over one another as though fleeing from the sword, even though no one is pursuing them. So you will not be able to stand before your enemies. You will perish among the nations; the land of your enemies will devour you. Those of you who are left will waste away in the lands of their enemies because of their sins; also because of their fathers' sins they will waste away.' "

The condition in which the land and the people would then be left is described in the following verses with a measure of divine irony. During the time of its residence in Canaan, Israel has deprived the land of its rightful periods of rest in the regularly recurring sabbatical years (Lev. 25). Now it is able to enjoy this rest, for it lies completely barren; but the people, no longer present, are performing the work of slaves for their enemies (vv. 34–35). On the basis of this, Rashi has computed that the seventy years of exile served as compensation for the seventy sabbath years that Israel withheld from the land between the time of Joshua and their captivity. Unfortunately for this view, however, the seventy years mentioned in Jeremiah 25:11 and 29:10 (also 2 Chron. 36:21) were the time allotted to Babylon, not the length of the exile.

As for the exiles themselves, those who have once lived in "stubborn pride" (v. 19) and fancied themselves capable of challenging the Lord (vv. 21, 23, 27) have now become spineless cowards, fearful as helpless children (*mōrek̠*, "fearful," in v. 36 is derived from *rāk̠ak̠*, "to be soft, tender"). So timid would they be that they would become frightened at the sound of a falling leaf and stumble over one another in their senseless flight from apparitions. Their numbers would thus steadily diminish and death would draw near to all (Ezek. 4:17; 24:23; 33:10), for their sins and those of their fathers would be like malignant germs that threaten their lives (v. 39).

26:40–46 *" 'But if they will confess their sins and the sins of their fathers–their treachery against me and their hostility toward me, which made me hostile toward them so that I sent them into the land of their enemies–then when their uncircumcised hearts are humbled and they pay for their sin, I will remember my covenant with Jacob and my covenant with Isaac and my covenant with Abraham, and I will remember the land. For the land will be deserted by them and will enjoy its sabbaths while it lies desolate without them. They will pay for their sins because* *they rejected my laws and abhorred my decrees. Yet in spite of this, when they are in the land of their enemies, I will not reject them or abhor them so as to destroy them completely, breaking my covenant with them. I am the LORD their God. But for their sake I will remember the covenant with their ancestors whom I brought out of Egypt in the sight of the nations to be their God. I am the LORD.''*

These are the decrees, the laws and the regulations that the LORD established on Mount Sinai between himself and the Israelites through Moses.

After Israel has suffered all of this—the sword (vv. 16–17), famine (vv. 19–20), wild animals (v. 22), and plague (v. 25), all of which are mentioned together also in Ezekiel 14:21—they would be led to search their hearts, mend their ways, and turn back to the Lord. This could take place only if they confessed "their sins" (v. 40; literally, cast their sins on themselves) and sought the cause of their misery within themselves. At the same time, they would have to acknowledge their solidarity with the sins of their fathers and, in contrast to the contemporaries of Jeremiah and Ezekiel (Jer. 31:29; Ezek. 18:2), come to regard the spiritual and moral corruption of Israel as a single historical process. Their sin is here designated "treachery" *(ma'al)*—an attack on what belonged to the Lord (see discussion on 5:15), in this case, His covenant—and "hostility" (literally, provocation of an encounter), an attitude that is taken in spite of the Lord's undiminished faithfulness to His covenant. Repentance would lead the Israelites to humble (v. 41; literally, "bow deeply") their "uncircumcised hearts," i.e., hearts that had formerly been utterly foreign to the covenant in motivation and outlook (cf. Deut. 10:16; 30:5; Jer. 4:4; 9:25–26). Just as it is necessary that the land lie desolate and thus receive its sabbaths, so the people would have to "pay for their sin" and endure what they have until now willfully evaded, since they refused to look for the cause of their misery within themselves and sought to disown responsibility for their sins (v. 41). When Israel then turns back to the Lord, bearing its guilt and acknowledging His right to punish them, the Lord would remember both the covenant and the land, i.e., He would grant what each of these required (cf. Gen. 8:1; Exod. 2:24) by restoring the covenant that Israel had spurned and the land that it had brought to ruin (v. 42). It is evident in this verse that the two of these, the land and the covenant made with the people, belonged together (cf. 18:28). The Lord's mercies therefore triumph over judgment (James 2:13), for "where sin increased, grace increased all the more" (Rom. 5:20). Israel's turning back to the Lord is not immediately followed by its return to the land, however, since the Lord's grace does not compromise His justice; the land first has to receive the rest that is due to it, and the people must bear their guilt as an intolerable burden (v. 43). Nevertheless, this grace would protect them from being completely destroyed in the land of their exile, for in spite of Zion's complaint in Isaiah 49:14, the Lord would never forsake her, and in spite of Israel's abhorrence, He would never break the covenant He had made with Jacob, Isaac, and Abraham (note the retrospective order). The Lord, who declares that "I am God, and not man" (Hos. 11:9), thus preserves intact the goal that had been set at the time when the Israelites' ancestors were delivered from Egypt, viz., that He is to be Israel's God, and Israel is to be His people (v. 45; cf. Exod. 6:6–8).

Two final observations may yet be made in connection with Leviticus 26. First, it has become almost commonplace to argue on the basis of verse 34 that this chapter was written either during or after the Exile, a view that inevitably leads to its division into a large number of short fragments.[10] Others would date it during the time after the fall of Samaria when captivity seemed imminent, preferably the time of Hezekiah.[11] With regard to this question, it is clear that Leviticus 26 speaks of the occupation of Canaan as an accomplished fact rather than a future event. Against this background, the Israelites were presented with the choices that would either enable them to retain possession of the land or cause them to lose it. To maintain that the possibility of exile could have been conceived only after Assyria and Babylonia had already become world powers and the spiritual and moral corruption of the Israelites had reached previously unknown portions, however, would be a fundamental misunderstanding of the gift of prophecy as this developed in Israel through the inspiration of divine revelation. Anyone who simultaneously took into account the Lord's holiness and the general Semitic influences on Israelite life would soon have come to the conclusion that the history of Israel would have very dramatic consequences. Leviticus 26 (also Deuteronomy 28) thus bears witness to this and earnestly admonishes the people that the word of the Lord, which in all times and circumstances remains the sole truth, must be the only guide for their conduct.

As a second observation, it is fully consistent with the "immanent" character of Old Testament revelation that the description of the blessings and punishments that the Lord would respectively bring on Israel for its obedience or disobedience to the covenant pertain exclusively to life in this world. There is no mention of either the bliss of heaven or the torments of hell. Nevertheless, the message is clear in Leviticus 26 that the manner of life that a person chooses on this earth is of decisive importance.

---

[10]See the commentary of Bertholet.

[11]See Heinisch, *Das Buch Leviticus.*

Part Nine

The Redemption of Persons, Animals, and Land
(27:1–34)

Like sacrifice and prayer, the making of vows was common throughout the ancient world. Vows were made out of the desire to lend force to one's prayer by promising to present a gift to the deity if certain conditions were met. This desire also appeared among the Israelites, for vows were made by Jacob at Bethel (Gen. 28:20–22), by Jephthah as he went to battle (Judg. 11:30–31), by Hannah in Shiloh (1 Sam. 1:11), and by Absalom at Geshur (2 Sam. 15:8; see also Pss. 22:25; 61:5, 8; 65:1; 66:13–14; 76:11; 116:14; Isa. 19:21; Jonah 1:16; Nah 1:15 [MT 2:1]; Mal. 1:14). In making a vow, a person demonstrated his love for the Lord's worship or his thankfulness for an answer to prayer by earnestly resolving to dedicate something or someone as a gift to the Lord (e.g., Hannah and her child), to deny himself certain pleasures (e.g., the Nazirite, Num. 6:2–8), or to present a certain offering (Lev. 6:6).

It was elsewhere not uncommon, however, that a vow could be misused as a means for inducing the deity to satisfy some personal desire, with the payment of what had been promised then being forgotten, and this indeed sometimes happened in Israel as well. The Israelites were as little innocent of the thoughtless making of vows as members of the church of Christ have been, for fallen human nature remains everywhere the same. Only with the help of a rich measure of grace can a person overcome his continual mistrust of the Lord's intentions and live in the assurance that there is really no need to exercise "caution" in relation to the Lord. In this respect, the attitude of Hannah in making her vow is far superior to that of Jacob. The misuse of vows stands behind the requirements of Leviticus 22:21–23 and Numbers 30:2–15, and likewise the statement in Deuteronomy 23:21–23 that, although it is no sin to refrain from making a vow, a vow that had once been made was always to be kept (see also Prov. 20:25; Eccl. 5:4–7; Mal. 1:14). The law of the present chapter is motivated by this same concern, and the various regulations given here provide an insight into the manner in which the Israelites sometimes attempted to escape the consequences of vows that had been made without due consideration. The same matter is also dealt with in unambiguous fashion in the tractate *Arakhin*, which reveals that vows gradually degenerated into meaningless formulas that were increasingly opposed by the rabbis.

The Votive Dedication of Persons
(27:1–8)

27:1–8 *The Lord said to Moses, "Speak to the Israelites and say to them: 'If anyone makes a special vow to dedicate persons to the Lord by giving equivalent values, set the value of a male between the ages of twenty and sixty at fifty shekels of silver, according to the sanctuary shekel; and if it is a female, set her value at thirty shekels. If it is a person between the ages of five and twenty, set the value of a male at twenty shekels and of a female at ten shekels. If it is a person between one month and five years, set the value of a male at five shekels of silver and tnat of a female at three shekels of silver. If it is a person sixty years old or more, set the value of a male at fifteen shekels and of a female at ten shekels. If anyone making the vow is too poor to pay the specified amount, he is to present the person to the priest, who will set the value for him according to what the man making the vow can afford.'"*

Two ways in which persons were dedicated to the deity elsewhere in the ancient Near Eastern world could naturally not be allowed in Israel: the dedication of persons by means of death (human sacrifice), and the dedication of sons and daughters by means of cultic prostitution. Israel did, however, have the Nazirite vow of dedication (Num. 6) and the dedication of persons to the sanctuary (the *nᵉtînîm* or temple servants, Ezra 2:58; 8:20; Neh. 7:60; 11:3). The present verses merely state the rules in accordance with which a person dedicated by vow could be redeemed. This involved a special tariff similar to that paid for the redemption of the firstborn offspring of animals and human beings (Exod. 13:13; 34:20; Num. 18:16), and it appears in 2 Kings 12:4 that the money that was collected in this manner was given to the sanctuary. The lawgiver did not regard the votive dedication of persons as the normal form for a vow, for in verse 2 he expressly called this a "special vow" (see also Lev. 22:21; Num. 15:3, 8). If such a vow was nevertheless made, it was to consist of an equivalent value in money. A male between the ages of twenty and sixty was valued at fifty shekels of silver, and a female of this age at thirty shekels, and in order to eliminate the possibility of fraud, the weight of the shekel was fixed in accordance with the sanctuary shekel (see discussion on v. 25).[1] The value of males from five to twenty years old was set at twenty shekels, and of females of the same age at ten shekels, and male and female children between one month and five years were valued at five and three shekels, respectively. The latter are spoken of also in Numbers 18:16, but no price is specified for females in this verse, since only firstborn male offspring had to be redeemed. Children younger than one month were not given a value, and because of this the Jews held no ceremony of mourning for an infant who died within a month of birth. For persons above sixty years of age, the respective valuations were fifteen shekels for a man and ten shekels for a woman. The difference between the values of male and female was thus smaller here, and in connection with this *Arakhin* 19a states: "an old man is a misfortune in the house, but an old woman in the house is a treasure and a token of good." It is in any case clear that the specified monetary values were related to the amount of work that the respective persons could be expected to perform. Verse 8 presents the possibility that someone might wish to dedicate a person to the Lord without having taken sufficient account of the financial consequences of this. In this case, the priest was to make the valuation in accordance with what the person making the vow could afford (cf. 5:11; 14:21–22).

The Votive Dedication of Animals
(27:9–13)

27:9–13 *"'If what he vowed is an animal that is acceptable as an offering to the Lord, such an animal given to the Lord becomes holy. He must not exchange it or substitute a good one for a bad one, or a bad one for a good one; if he should substitute one animal for another, both it and the substitute become holy. If what he vowed is a ceremonially unclean animal—one that is not acceptable as an offering to the Lord—the animal must be presented to the priest, who will judge its quality as good or bad. Whatever value the priest then sets, that is what it will be. If the owner wishes to redeem the animal, he must add a fifth to its value.'"*

A distinction is made here between clean and unclean animals, i.e., animals that were and were not acceptable as offerings to the Lord. If a vow was made of the former, it was in all cases to be given to the sanctuary for use in the offerings presented there, for through the vow it had become

---

[1]The average price of a male or female slave was thirty shekels of silver (Exod. 21:32).

holy (v. 9). Such an animal could therefore never be exchanged for another, whether the substitute be greater or lesser in value. If a person nevertheless attempted to do this—this must have most often involved the substitution of an inferior animal (see Mal. 1:8)—both animals were to be given to the sanctuary (v. 10). The situation was different in the dedication of an unclean animal. Since such an animal could never be brought within the sanctuary (22:19–20), it was sold for the price set by the priest, with the money then being given to the sanctuary (vv. 11–12). Bargaining was not permitted here, for "whatever value the priest then sets, that is what it will be." Verse 13 presents the possibility that the person who had dedicated an animal later desired to reclaim it and had thus perhaps come to regret his vow. Since the vow had already been made, the animal was to be redeemed, this being done by paying into the temple coffers, as a penalty of sorts, one-fifth more than the value set by the priest (cf. 6:5).

The Votive Dedication of Houses
(27:14–15)

27:14–15 "'If a man dedicates his house as something holy to the Lord, the priest will judge its quality as good or bad. Whatever value the priest then sets, so it will remain. If the man who dedicates his house redeems it, he must add a fifth to its value, and the house will again become his.'"

The rule here is the same as with an unclean animal: a house was to be sold at the price determined by the priest and the proceeds then given to the sanctuary. Here also there could be no bargaining, for the value set by the priest "will remain" (v. 14; literally, "will stand"). If the owner came to regret his vow, he could buy the house back by adding a fifth to its appraised value as a penalty.

The Votive Dedication of Land
(27:16–25)

27:16–25 "'If a man dedicates to the Lord part of his family land, its value is to be set according to the amount of seed required for it—fifty shekels of silver to a homer of barley seed. If he dedicates his field during the Year of Jubilee, the value that has been set remains. But if he dedicates his field after the Jubilee, the priest will determine the value according to the number of years that remain until the next Year of Jubilee, and its set value will be reduced. If the man who dedicates the field wishes to redeem it, he must add a fifth to its value, and the field will again become his. If, however, he does not redeem the field, or if he has sold it to someone else, it can never be redeemed. When the field is released in the Jubilee, it will become holy, like a field devoted to the Lord; it will become the property of the priests.

> *" 'If a man dedicates to the Lᴏʀᴅ a field he has bought, which is not part of his family land, the priest will determine its value up to the Year of Jubilee, and the man must pay its value on that day as something holy to the Lᴏʀᴅ. In the Year of Jubilee the field will revert to the person from whom he bought it, the one whose land it was. Every value is to be set according to the sanctuary shekel, twenty gerahs to the shekel.' "*

The rules given here leave the basic idea that governed the laws pertaining to land in Israel untouched. Landed property was inalienable and was to be returned to its owner at the proper time, and the making of a vow did nothing to change this. The implications of this were far-reaching, for the possibility of an Israelite sanctuary, and thus also the priesthood connected with it, ever becoming involved in large landownership was thereby eliminated. The priesthood did possess such power in other nations, and even the church of Christ has far too often forgotten this Old Testament principle and therefore become responsible for many abuses. The right to possess land in mortmain has indeed not always been a source of blessing.

The rules governing the dedication of land were therefore similar to those pertaining to its sale (25:23–28). Not the land itself was dedicated, but merely its crops, and these only until the coming of the next Year of Jubilee. In his valuation of land, the priest was to take two things into account. First of all, he was to allow for the value of the seed it required, this being determined in accordance with the expected yield. A homer, or ten ephahs (i.e., 364 liters, 19:36), of barley seed is said to be worth fifty shekels of silver (v. 16). Secondly, he was to take into consideration the number of years that remained until the next Year of Jubilee. There were two possibilities in this regard: the dedication extended from one Year of Jubilee until the next (v. 17), or it pertained to only a portion of this period (v. 18). In either case, the value set by the priest became absolute law. If the man who had made the vow should choose to withdraw from it—he could of course do so only if the land had not yet been sold by the sanctuary—he was permitted to recover his land by paying a penalty of one-fifth more than the set value into the sanctuary treasury (v. 19). If, however, he had attempted to escape the consequences of his ill-considered deed by selling the land to someone else, the provision of 25:23–24 with respect to the right of redemption no longer applied. The land remained in the possession of the buyer until the next Year of Jubilee, and at its release it irrevocably became the property of the priesthood (cf. Num. 18:14). The reasons for this requirement were humanitarian, since it was assumed that the buyer was unaware that the land was dedicated to the Lord when he purchased it. The seller was not allowed to profit by such an arrangement, since the dedication of his land was made permanent. The buyer could

277

enjoy its produce until further notice, but the land itself was inalienable (vv. 20–21)—it was therefore equivalent to what had been devoted to the Lord (v. 28)—and the rights of the Lord that had been actualized in the vow were maintained without restriction.

Verses 22–24 deal with the votive dedication of land that had been bought (see 25:23) and therefore did not belong to one's family inheritance. Since the possibility existed here that the owner could at some time choose to make use of his right of redemption and this would be detrimental to the sanctuary, the man who had made the vow was immediately to pay the set value of the land for the period until the next Year of Jubilee into the temple treasury. This requirement was of course based on the consideration that, if the land was redeemed, a similar amount was to be paid back to the buyer.

Verse 25 once again (see v. 3) explicitly states that the sanctuary shekel, which weighed approximately 14.5 grams (Exod. 30:13), was to form the standard in all valuations.

Exceptions
(27:26–29)

27:26–29 " 'No one, however, may dedicate the firstborn of an animal, since the firstborn already belongs to the LORD; whether a cow or sheep, it is the LORD's. If it is one of the unclean animals, he may buy it back at its set value, adding a fifth of the value to it. If he does not redeem it, it is to be sold at its set value.

" 'But nothing that a man owns and devotes to the LORD—whether man or animal or family land—may be sold or redeemed; everything so devoted is most holy to the LORD.

" 'No person devoted to destruction may be ransomed; he must be put to death.' "

These verses discuss two restrictions that were placed on the right of making a votive dedication of one's possessions to the Lord. The first of these (vv. 26–27) applies to the firstborn of animals, which, since they already belonged to the Lord (Exod. 13:2, 12, 15; 34:19), could not be given to Him a second time. If the animal was unclean and, as such, excluded from use by the sanctuary (e.g., a donkey, Exod. 13:13; 34:20), the person who made the vow could redeem it by paying its set value plus a penalty of one-fifth more (cf. 5:16). If he declined to do this, the animal was to be sold and the proceeds given to the temple treasury.

The second restriction concerned things that had been devoted to the Lord. There were three types of such devotion in Israel: devotion in warfare, which was equivalent to total destruction (e.g., Num. 21:2; Josh.

6:17; 1 Sam. 15:3, see NIV margin on these verses); judicial devotion, which was enacted if certain of the Lord's commandments were violated (Exod. 22:20; Lev. 20:2; Deut. 13:13–16, see NIV margin); and the "priestly devotion" spoken of here (except in v. 29), so named because objects devoted in this manner became part of the priests' income (Num. 18:14). A person, animal, or portion of one's inherited land (not purchased land, see v. 22) could therefore be devoted to the Lord, given to Him unconditionally, and it was thereby made most holy and became an inalienable possession of the sanctuary. Whatever was devoted in this manner could neither be redeemed, nor sold for the benefit of the temple treasury, for it belonged irrevocably to the priesthood (Num. 18:14; Ezek. 44:29). In the case of a human being, however, devotion was tantamount to the death sentence (v. 29). The devotion spoken of in this verse was judicial (see above) rather than priestly, since every Israelite would have otherwise been enabled to rid himself of a fellow human being (e.g., a child or a slave) by devoting him to the Lord, something that obviously could never have been allowed.

The Redemption of Tithes
(27:30–33)

27:30–33 *"'A tithe of everything from the land, whether grain from the soil or fruit from the trees, belongs to the LORD; it is holy to the LORD. If a man redeems any of his tithe, he must add a fifth of the value to it. The entire tithe of the herd and flock—every tenth animal that passes under the shepherd's rod—will be holy to the LORD. He must not pick out the good from the bad or make any substitution. If he does make a substitution, both the animal and its substitute become holy and cannot be redeemed.'"*

Although this is not clear in the presentation, these verses actually discuss a third exception to the rules governing votive dedication. Tithes could of course also not be subject to dedication, for as a form of rent that the Israelite tenants owed to the divine Owner of the land, they already belonged to the Lord.

As in Israel, the presentation of tithes was a very ancient custom in other nations of antiquity, where they were given not only as a sign of respect to one's superiors (Gen. 14:20), but also as a gift to the deity (Gen. 28:22). The tithe took on a different character in post-Mosaic Israel, however, since it then became subject to the thought that the people were no more than tenants and that the bounty of their crops and cattle formed an expression of the Lord's goodness. Verse 30 therefore begins by taking note of this.[2] Whereas the law applying to tithes is developed at greater length in Deuteronomy 14:22–29, this law provided excellent matter for the excesses of the Pharisees, who demanded tithes even of dill and cummin, the so-called "garden herbs" (Matt. 23:23; Luke 11:42). This speaks of the sacrificial meal that was held when these were presented and the priests had received their share (see also Deut. 12:17–18), these verses merely mention the possibility of redemption (v. 31) and forbid any substitution (v. 33). The latter was apparently attempted in the tithes of animals, which are spoken of also in 2 Chronicles 31:6. Verse 32 states that "every tenth animal that passes under the shepherd's rod" must be surrendered to the Lord (cf. Jer. 33:13; Ezek. 20:37). According to the tractate *Bekhoroth* 58b, the animals were driven into a type of pen having a narrow exit that compelled them to pass through in single file. Every tenth animal was then marked by being tapped with a piece of wood coated with red dye. There was naturally a great temptation here to arrange things so that the best animals were not marked, and it is this that the lawgiver opposes. If such an "exchange" was detected, both animals became the property of the sanctuary in accordance with the rule of verse 10. Although the substitution of animals was therefore prohibited, redemption was allowed both with grain and fruit and with animals, but this again required the addition of twenty percent to the set value (v. 31; cf. vv. 13, 19, 27). Both the Mishnah and Philo assert that the animal tithe was required only of the yearly increase of the herd. There is no basis for this in the text, however, since the tithing of the entire herd is clearly indicated.

27:34 *These are the commands the Lᴏʀᴅ gave Moses on Mount Sinai for the Israelites.*

The Book of Leviticus ends with a closing formula that bears much resemblance to 26:46. This does not mark the conclusion merely of chapter 27, however, but rather applies to the whole of the so-called Sinai laws.

---

[2]After the Exile, tithes acquired more the character of a tax taken for those who served in the temple (Neh. 10:38–39; 13:5, 10; Mal. 3:8–10).